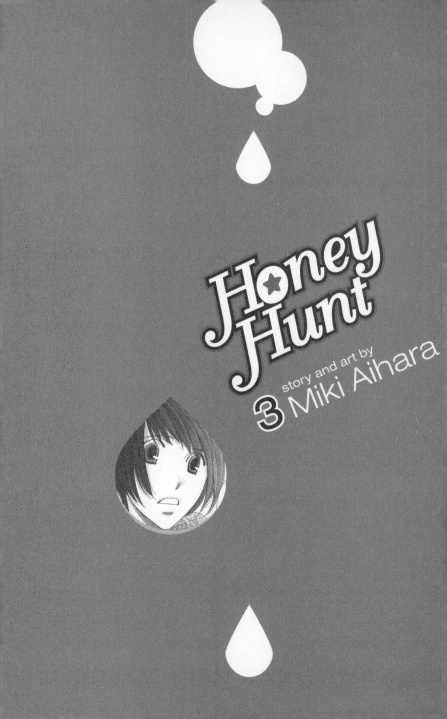

Honey Hunt

story and art by

3 Miki Aihara

CHARACTERS

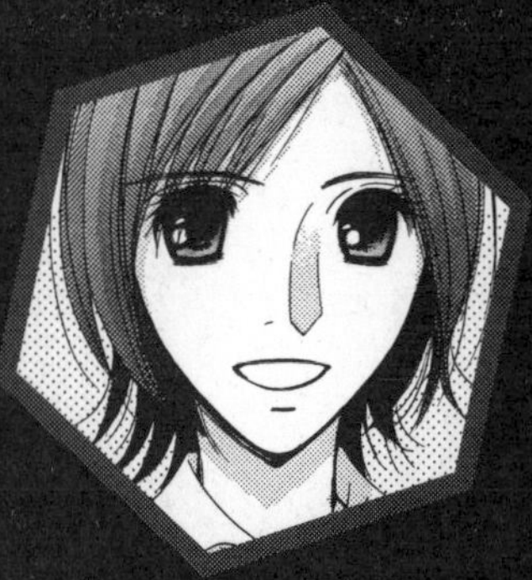

YURA ONOZUKA ★

The only child of celebrity parents. She is a surprisingly average, ordinary girl, considering her father is a world-famous musician and her mother is an award-winning actress.

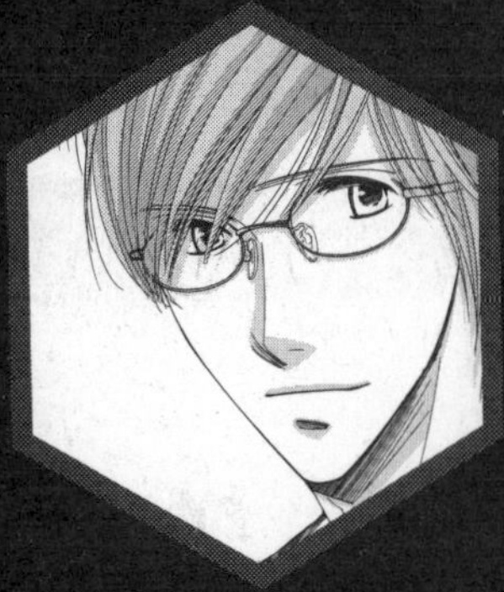

KEIICHI MIZOROGI ★

President of the entertainment company Meteorite Productions. He scouted Yura and became her manager.

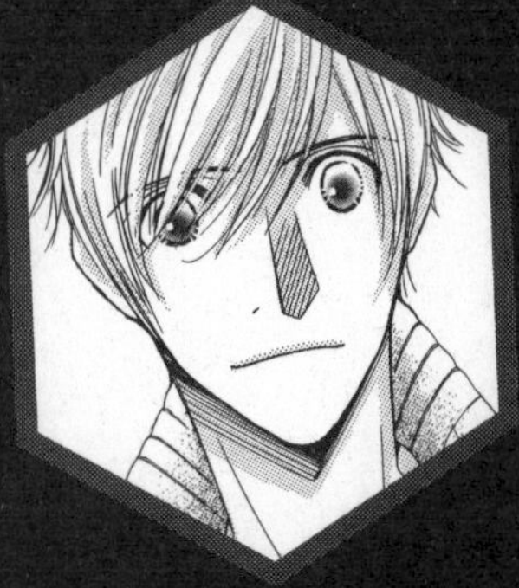

Q-TA MINAMITANI ★

The singer of popular music group Assha (also known as "h.a."). He likes Yura.

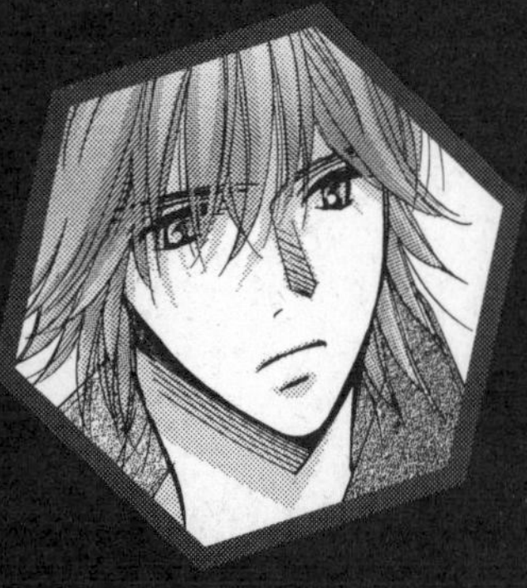

HARUKA ★

A member of the pop idol group KNIGHTS. Q-ta's twin brother and rival.

Honey Hunt 3

STORY

★ After her parents' divorce, Yura decides to get back at her mother by competing with her to become a better actress. Yura moves into Keiichi's house and starts her new life.

★ Keiichi encourages her to try out for the "Noodle Girl" project, for which she lands the lead role. But what Keiichi didn't tell her was that the project is more than a commercial—it also includes a tie-in TV drama. At her first meeting with other cast members, she receives congratulatory kisses from Q-ta and Haruka, who were also cast for the project.

★ Yura starts to develop a crush on Q-ta, who is kind and cute and patiently listens to her. At the same time, Haruka finds himself drawn to Yura by her mysterious charm.

★ At the press conference for the project, one reporter reveals Yura's secret—that she is the daughter of a celebrity couple. When Yura finds out that Keiichi was the one who leaked the information, she runs away and decides to leave the agency. However, because she wants the role of Natsuki, she decides to stay with Meteorite through the "Noodle Girl" project.

★ Yura's nervousness gets the better of her again at the script reading, and she can't make it through her lines. Rinko Koizumi, a veteran actress cast as Natsuki's mother, gives her a hard time throughout the session. After some encouraging words from Keiichi, Yura decides to trust him again and give it one more try...

Honey Hunt 3

CONTENTS

CHAPTER 11 ... 7

CHAPTER 12 ... 42

CHAPTER 13 ... 79

CHAPTER 14 ... 113

CHAPTER 15 ... 149

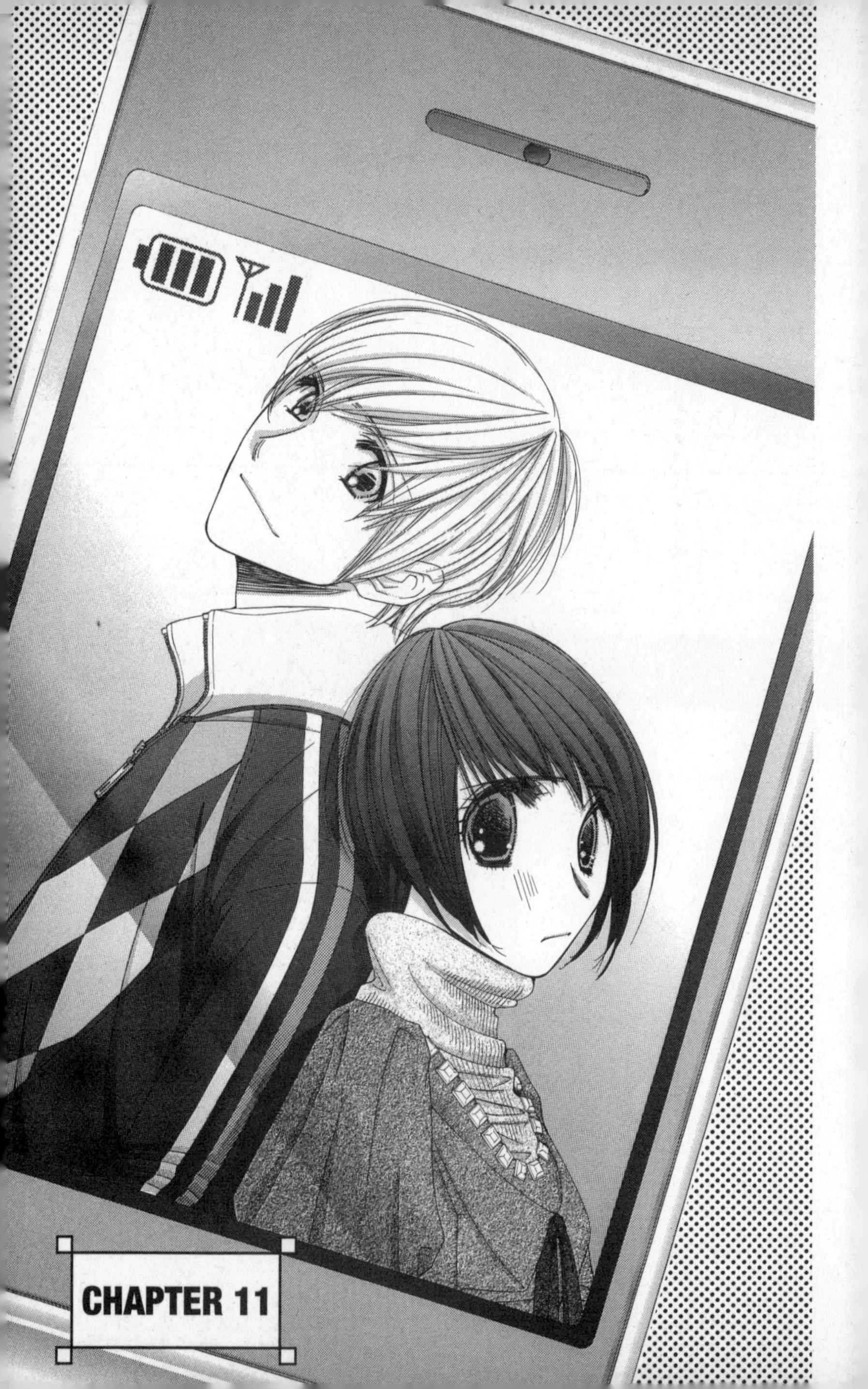
CHAPTER 11

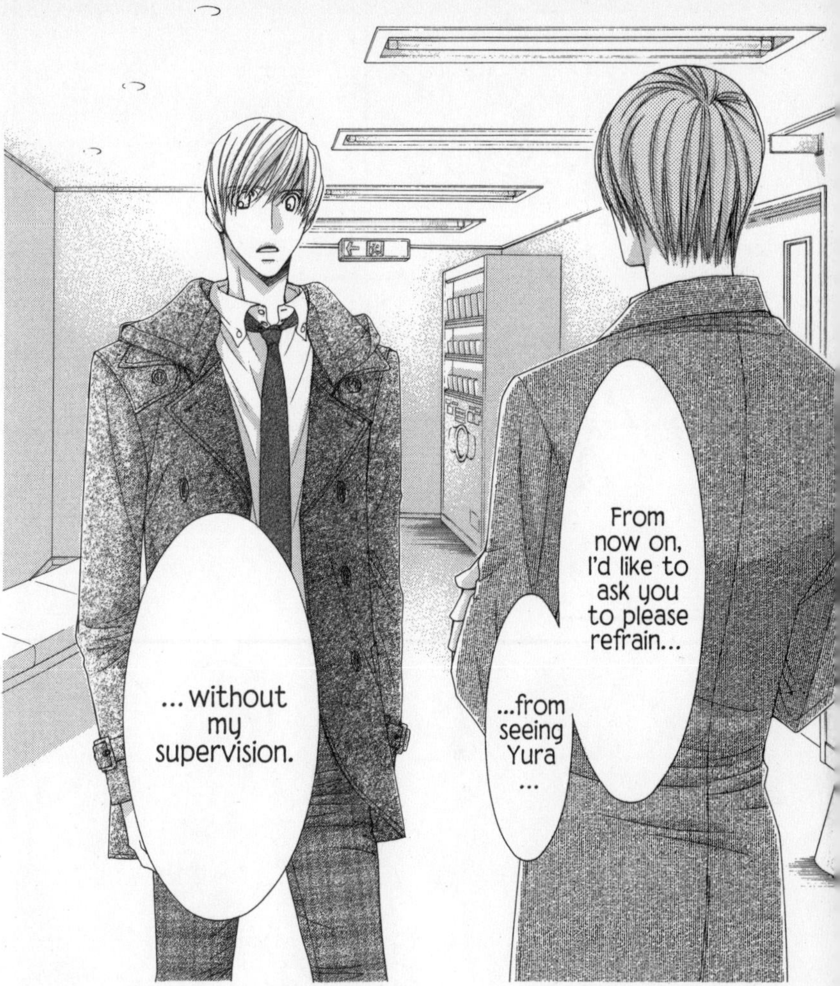
From now on, I'd like to ask you to please refrain...
...from seeing Yura ...
... without my supervision.

Honey Hunt

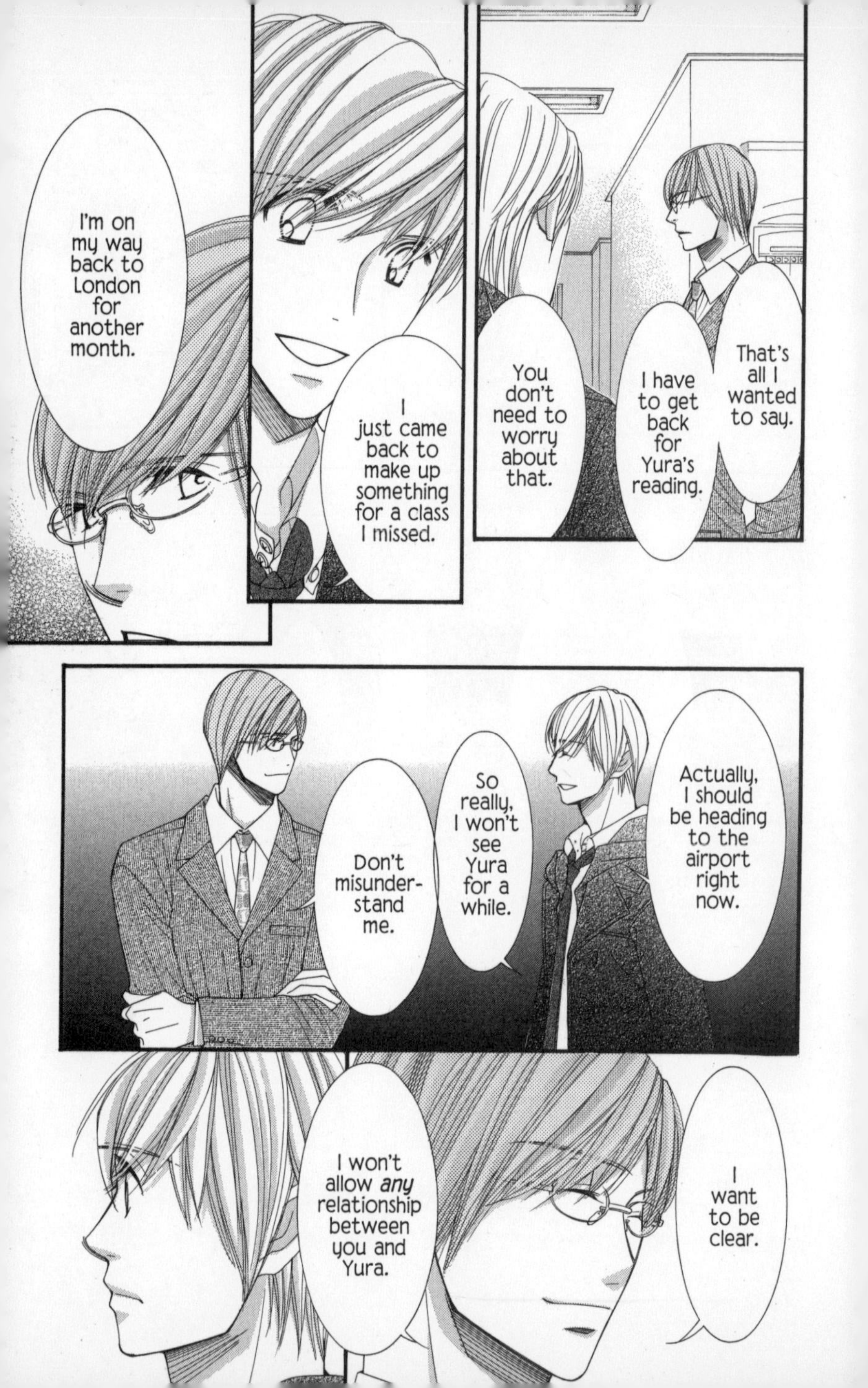
That's all I wanted to say.
I have to get back for Yura's reading.
You don't need to worry about that.
I just came back to make up something for a class I missed.
I'm on my way back to London for another month.
Actually, I should be heading to the airport right now.
So really, I won't see Yura for a while.
Don't misunderstand me.
I want to be clear.
I won't allow *any* relationship between you and Yura.

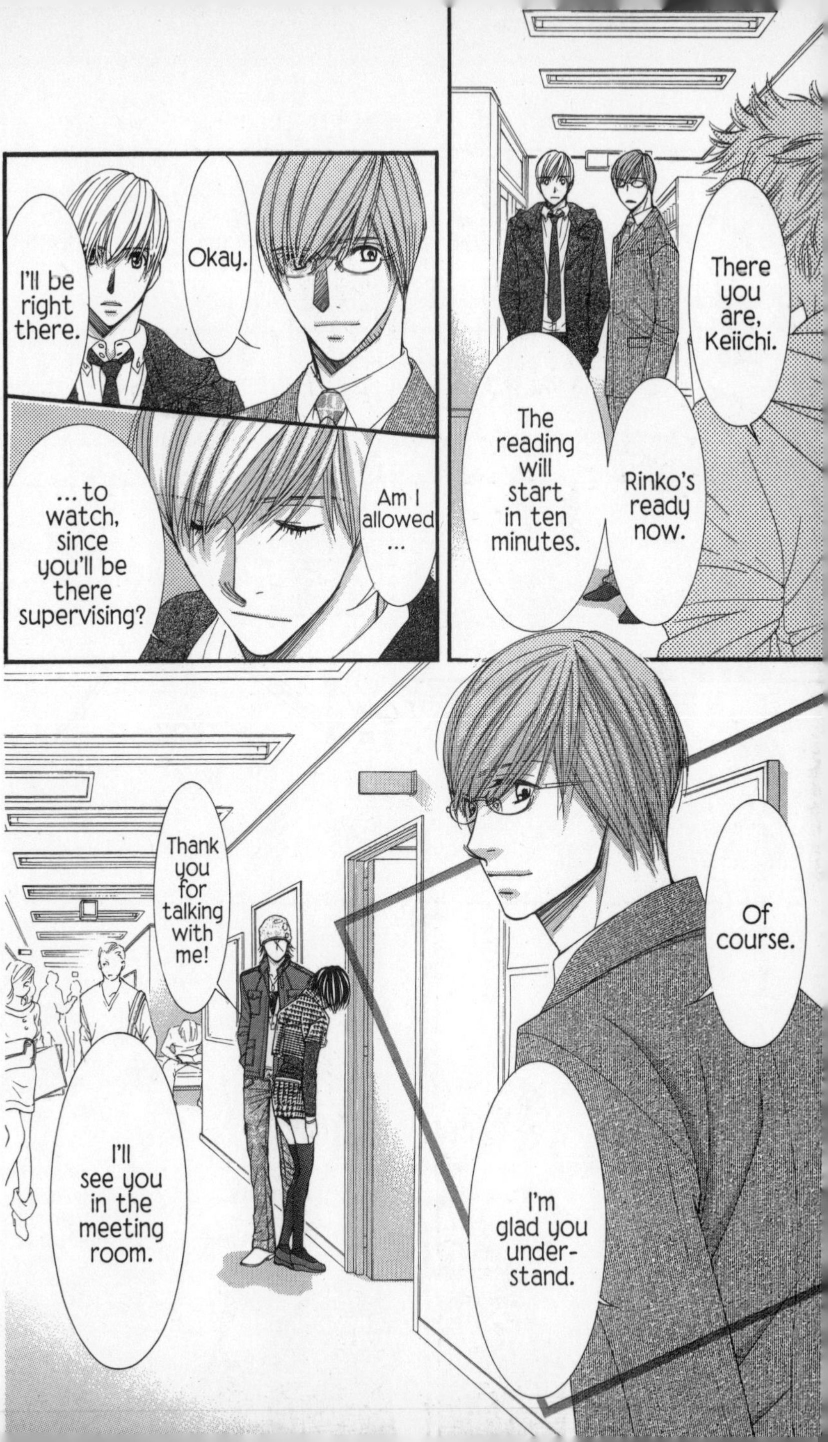
There you are, Keiichi.
Rinko's ready now.
The reading will start in ten minutes.
Okay.
I'll be right there.
Am I allowed...
...to watch, since you'll be there supervising?
Of course.
I'm glad you understand.
Thank you for talking with me!
I'll see you in the meeting room.

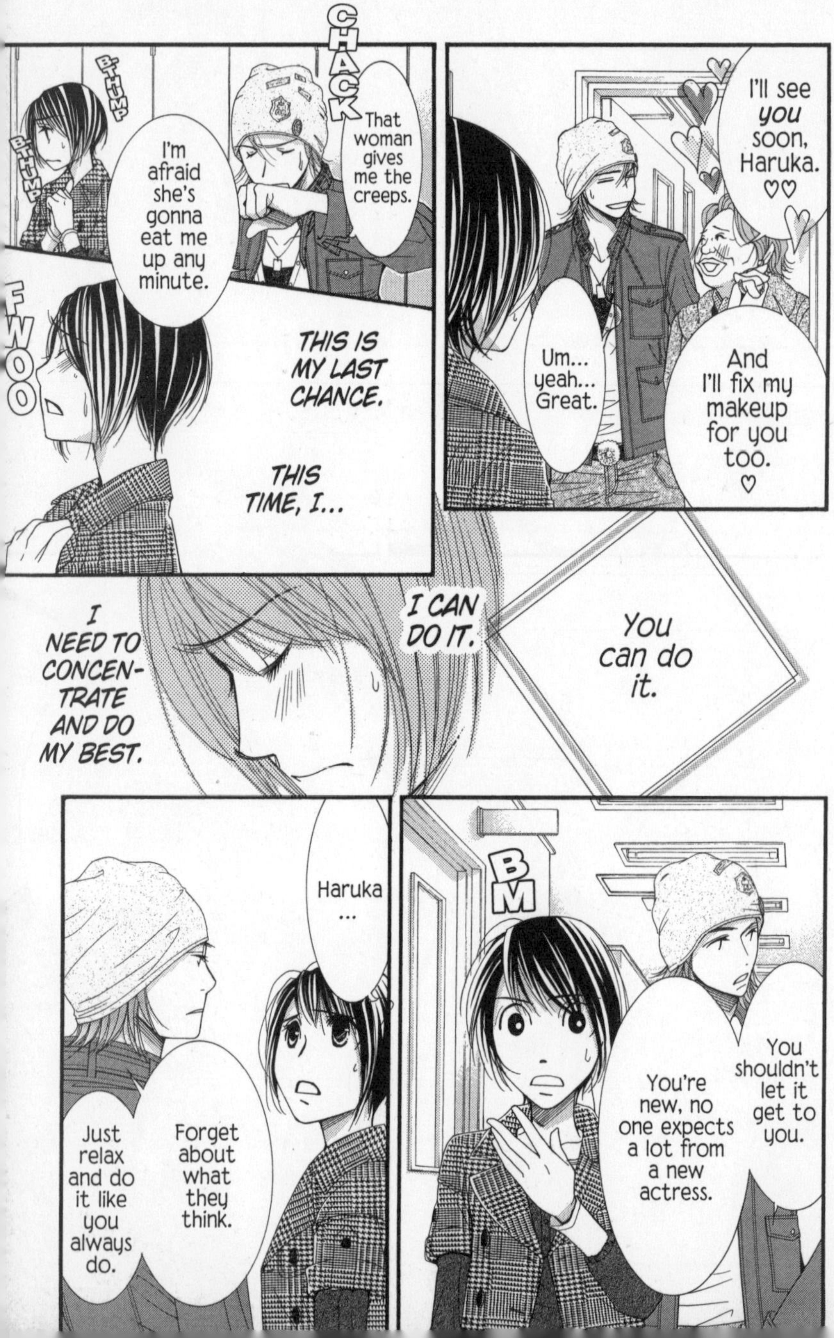
I'll see *you* soon, Haruka. ♡♡
And I'll fix my makeup for you too. ♡
Um... yeah... Great.
CHACK
That woman gives me the creeps.
B-THUMP B-THUMP
I'm afraid she's gonna eat me up any minute.
FWOO
THIS IS MY LAST CHANCE.
THIS TIME, I...
You can do it.
I CAN DO IT.
I NEED TO CONCEN-TRATE AND DO MY BEST.
BM
You shouldn't let it get to you.
You're new, no one expects a lot from a new actress.
Haruka...
Forget about what they think.
Just relax and do it like you always do.

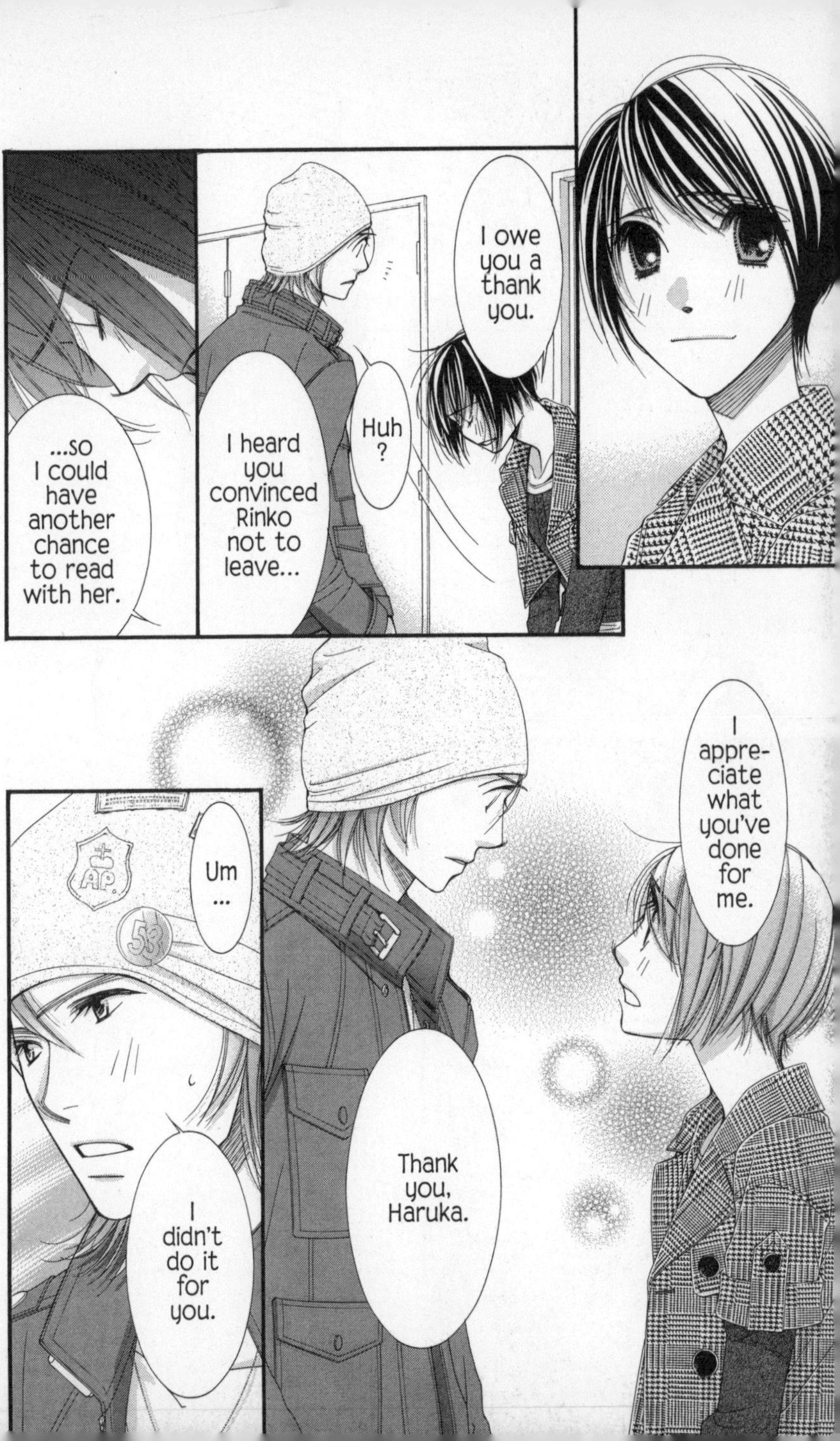
I owe you a thank you.
Huh?
I heard you convinced Rinko not to leave...
...so I could have another chance to read with her.
I appreciate what you've done for me.
Thank you, Haruka.
Um ...
I didn't do it for you.

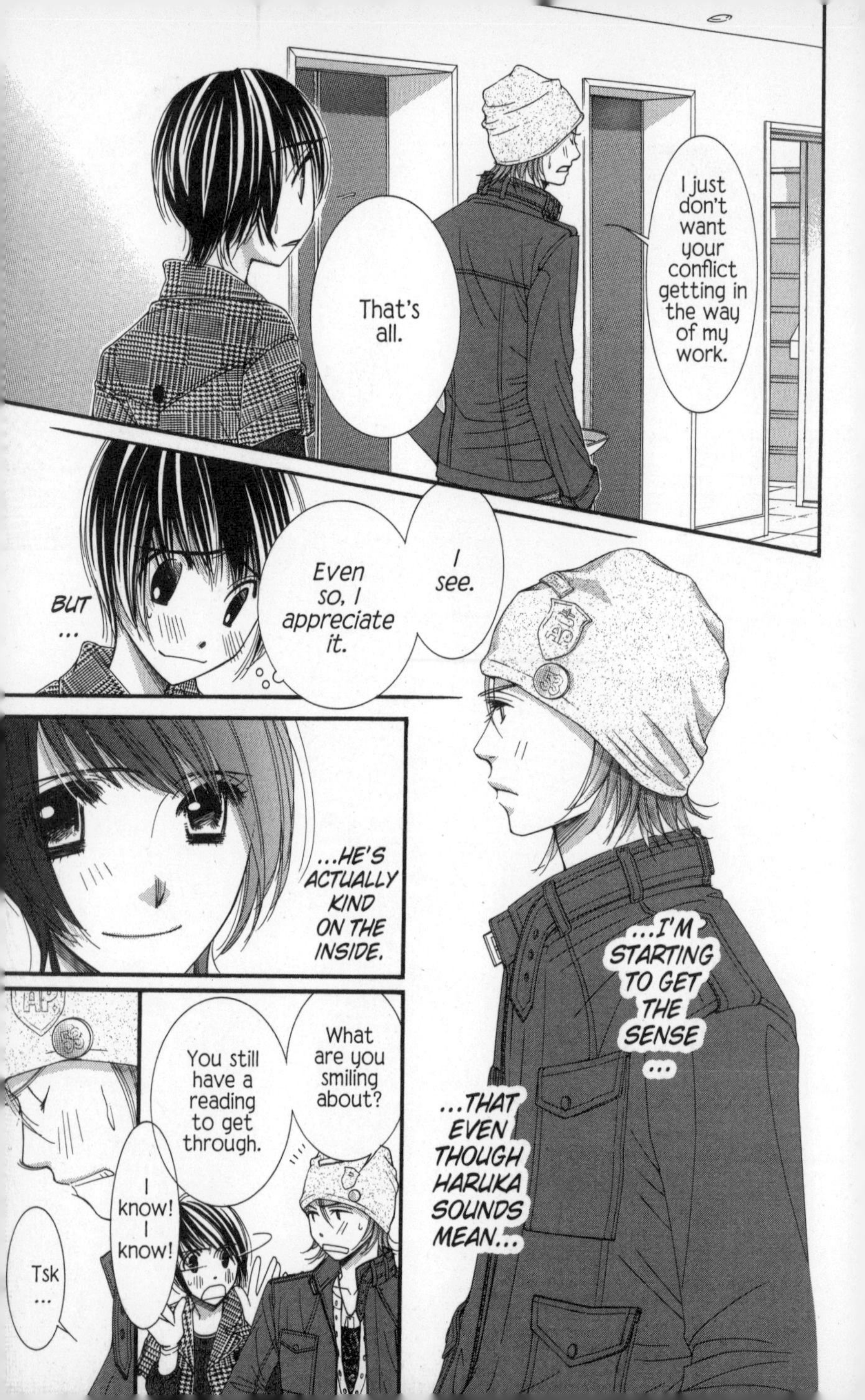
I just don't want your conflict getting in the way of my work.
That's all.
I see.
Even so, I appreciate it.
BUT ...
...I'M STARTING TO GET THE SENSE ...
...THAT EVEN THOUGH HARUKA SOUNDS MEAN...
...HE'S ACTUALLY KIND ON THE INSIDE.
What are you smiling about?
You still have a reading to get through.
I know! I know!
Tsk ...

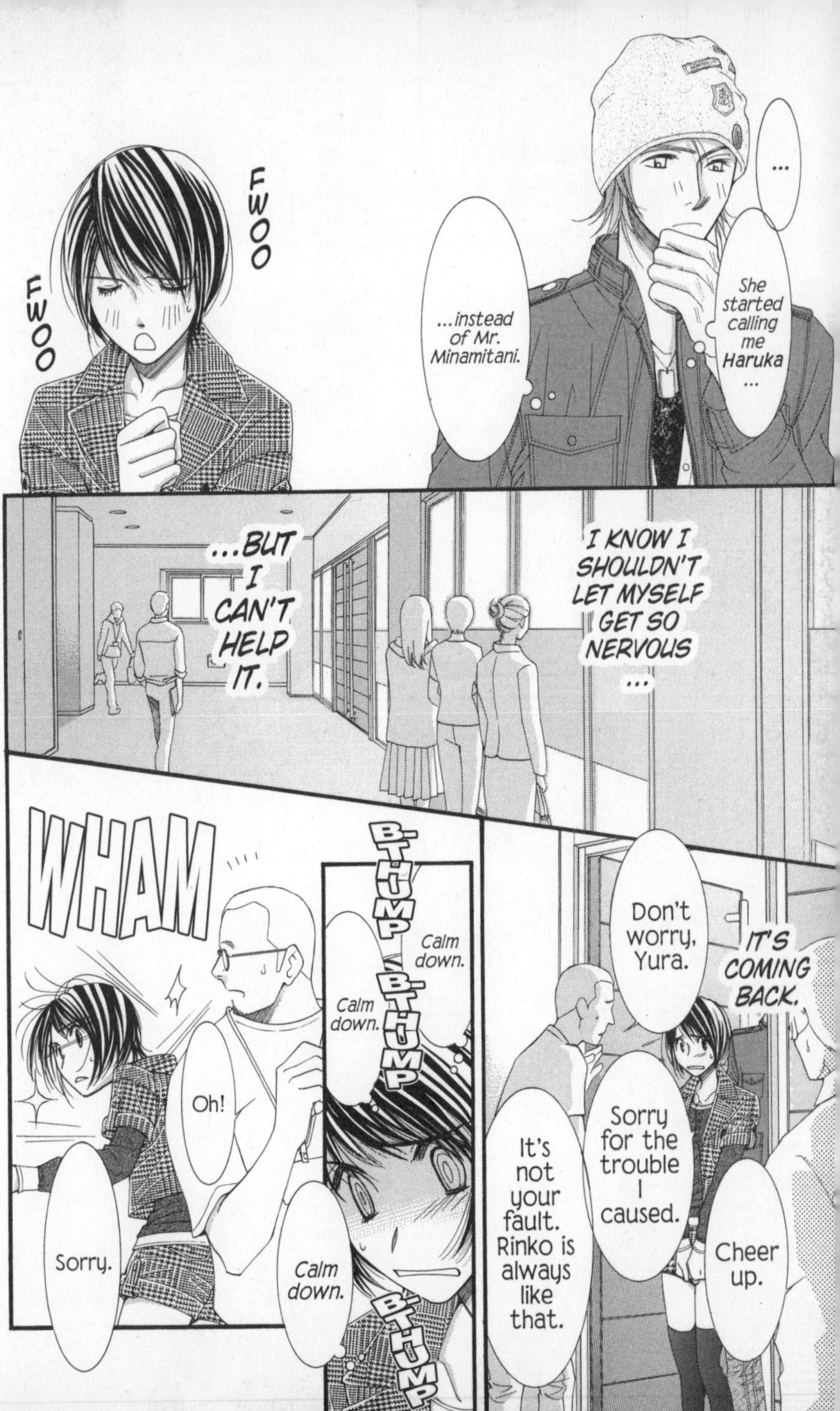
...
She started calling me Haruka ...
...instead of Mr. Minamitani.
FWOO
FWOO
I KNOW I SHOULDN'T LET MYSELF GET SO NERVOUS ...
...BUT I CAN'T HELP IT.
IT'S COMING BACK.
Don't worry, Yura.
Cheer up.
Sorry for the trouble I caused.
It's not your fault. Rinko is always like that.
B-THUMP
Calm down.
B-THUMP
Calm down.
Calm down.
B-THUMP
WHAM
Oh!
Sorry.

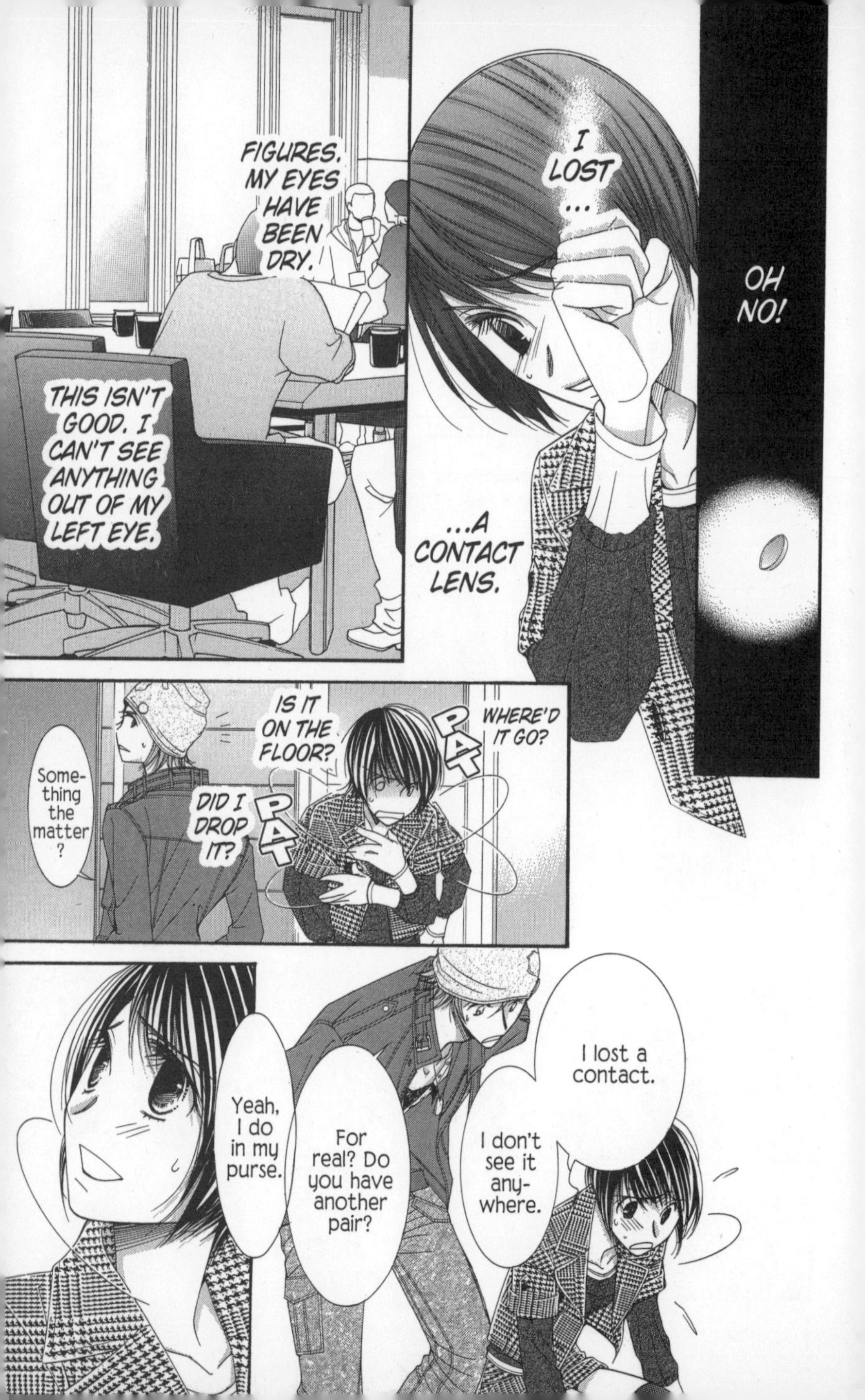
OH NO!
I LOST ...
...A CONTACT LENS.
FIGURES. MY EYES HAVE BEEN DRY.
THIS ISN'T GOOD. I CAN'T SEE ANYTHING OUT OF MY LEFT EYE.
WHERE'D IT GO?
PAT
IS IT ON THE FLOOR?
PAT
DID I DROP IT?
Something the matter?
I lost a contact.
I don't see it anywhere.
For real? Do you have another pair?
Yeah, I do in my purse.

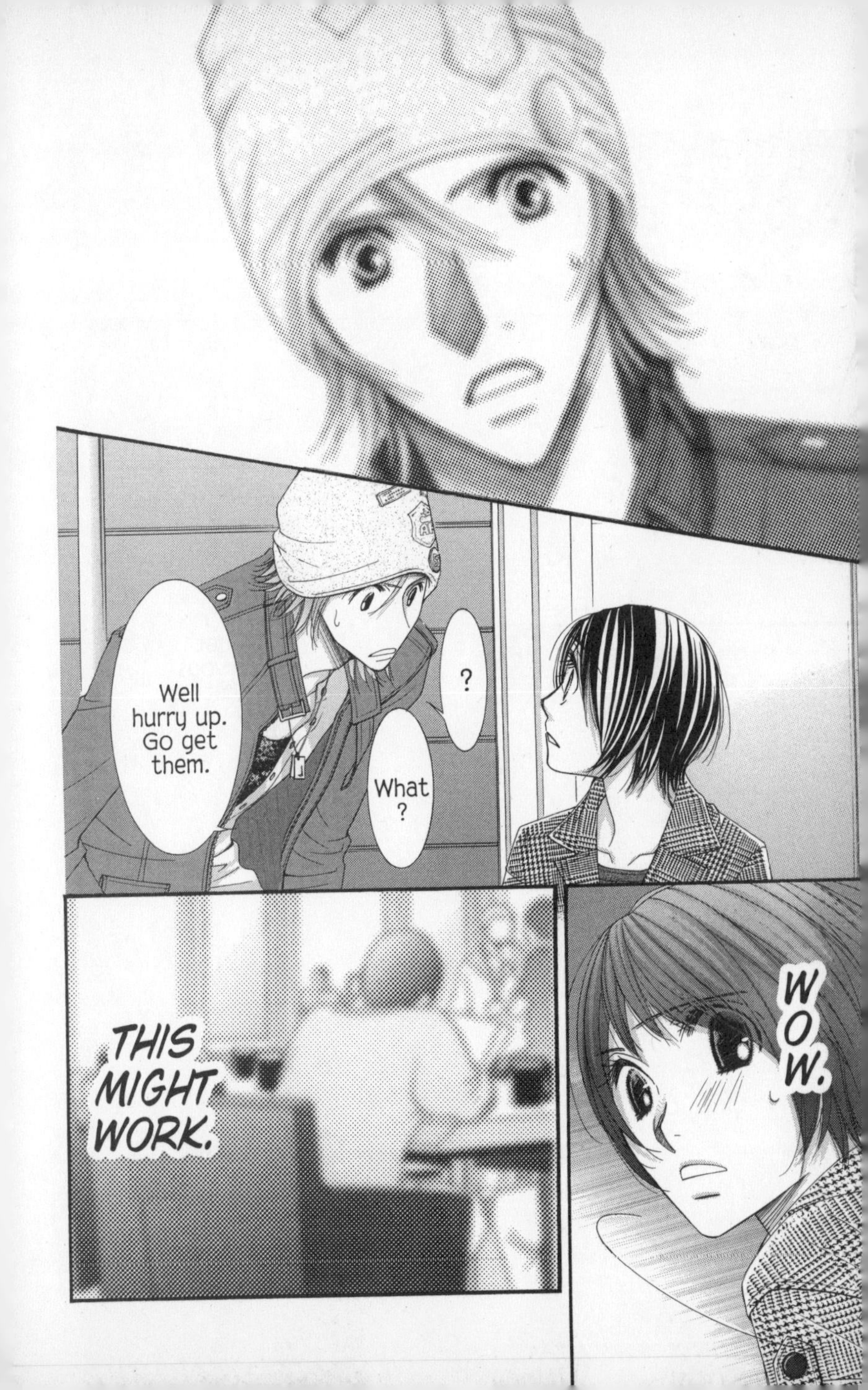
?
What?
Well hurry up. Go get them.
WOW.
THIS MIGHT WORK.

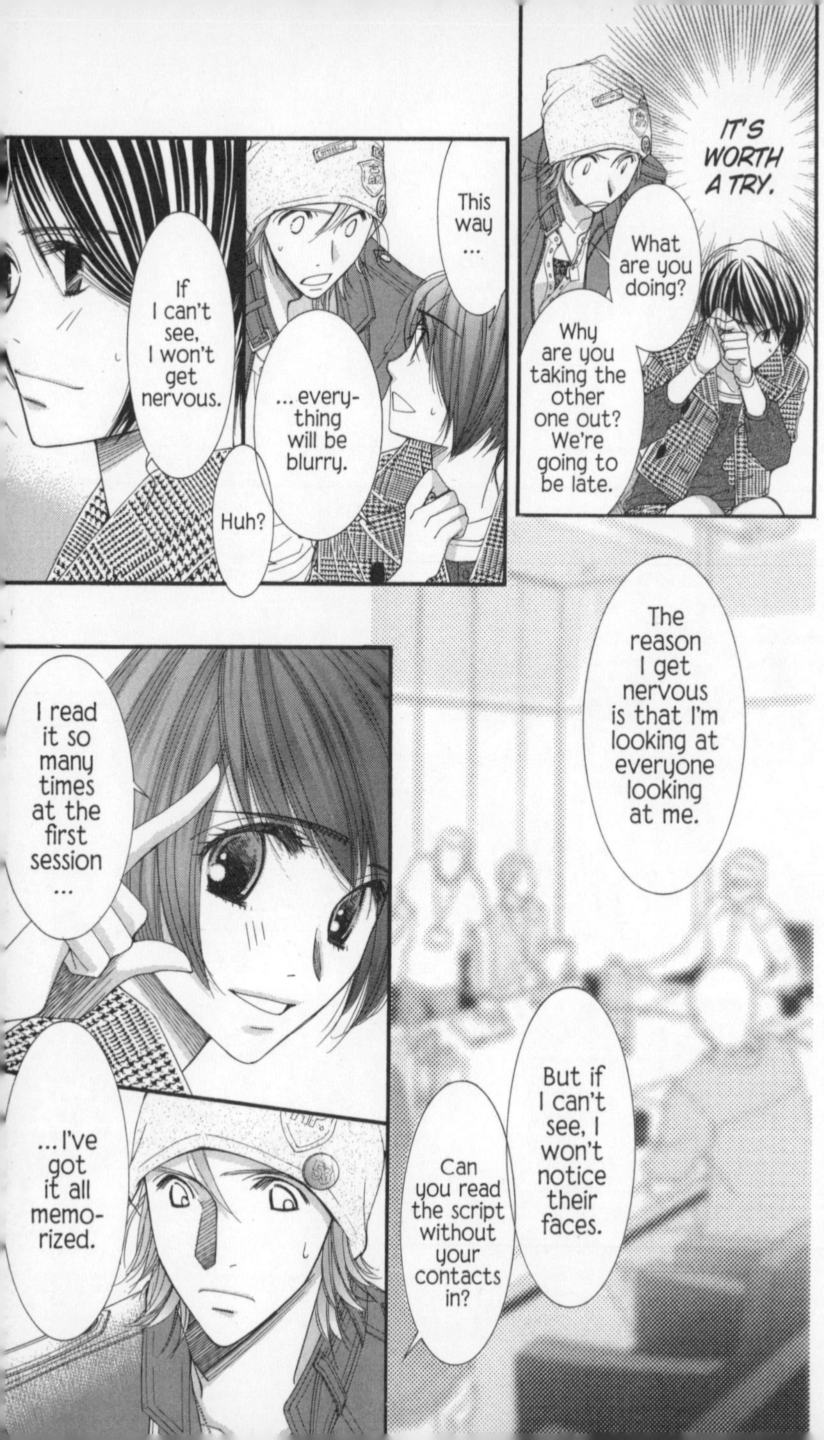
IT'S WORTH A TRY.
What are you doing?
Why are you taking the other one out? We're going to be late.
This way...
...everything will be blurry.
Huh?
If I can't see, I won't get nervous.
The reason I get nervous is that I'm looking at everyone looking at me.
But if I can't see, I won't notice their faces.
Can you read the script without your contacts in?
I read it so many times at the first session...
...I've got it all memorized.

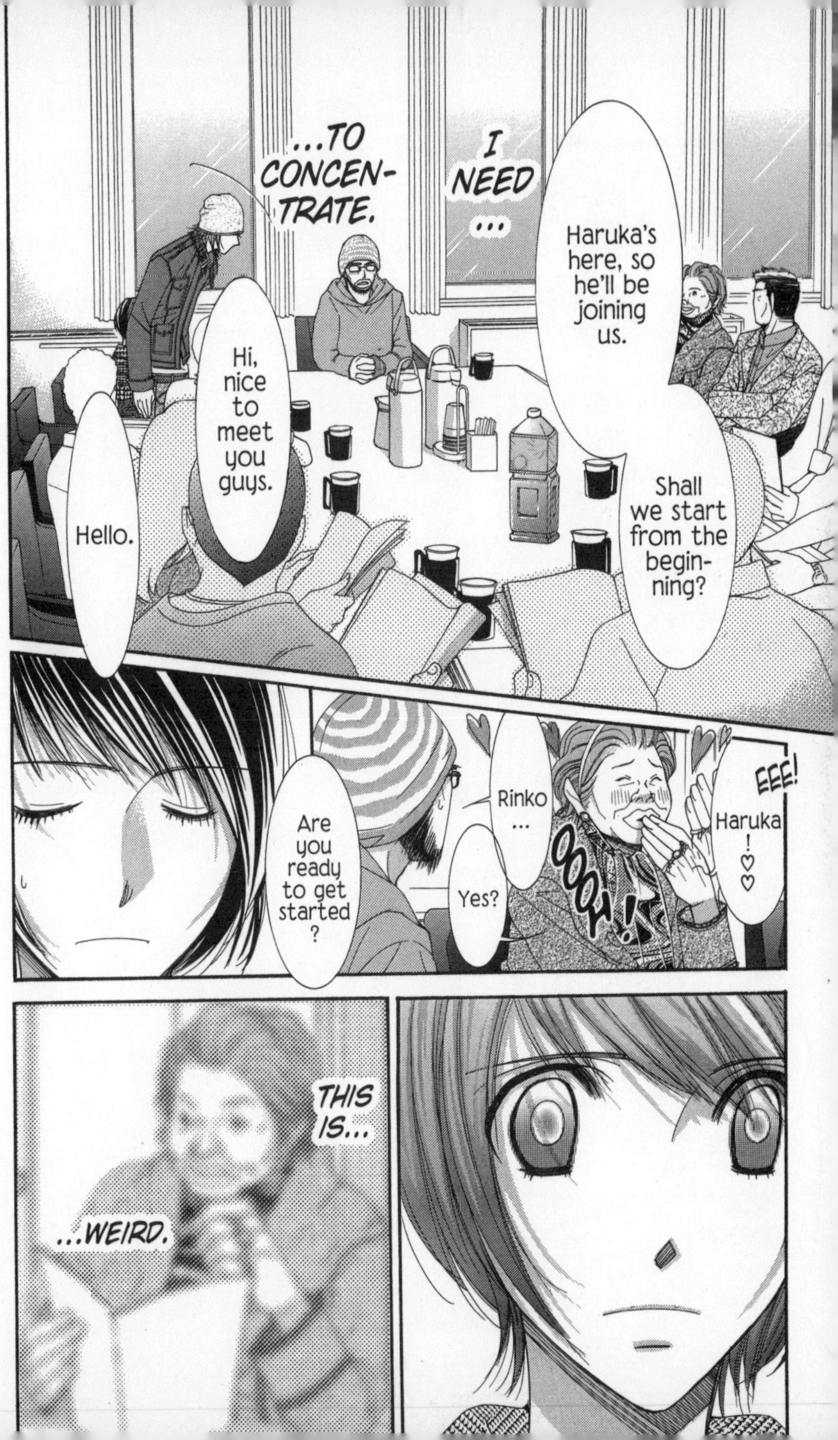
Haruka's here, so he'll be joining us.
I NEED...
...TO CONCEN-TRATE.
Shall we start from the begin-ning?
Hi, nice to meet you guys.
Hello.
EEE!
Haruka! ♡ ♡
OOOH!
Rinko...
Yes?
Are you ready to get started?
THIS IS...
...WEIRD.

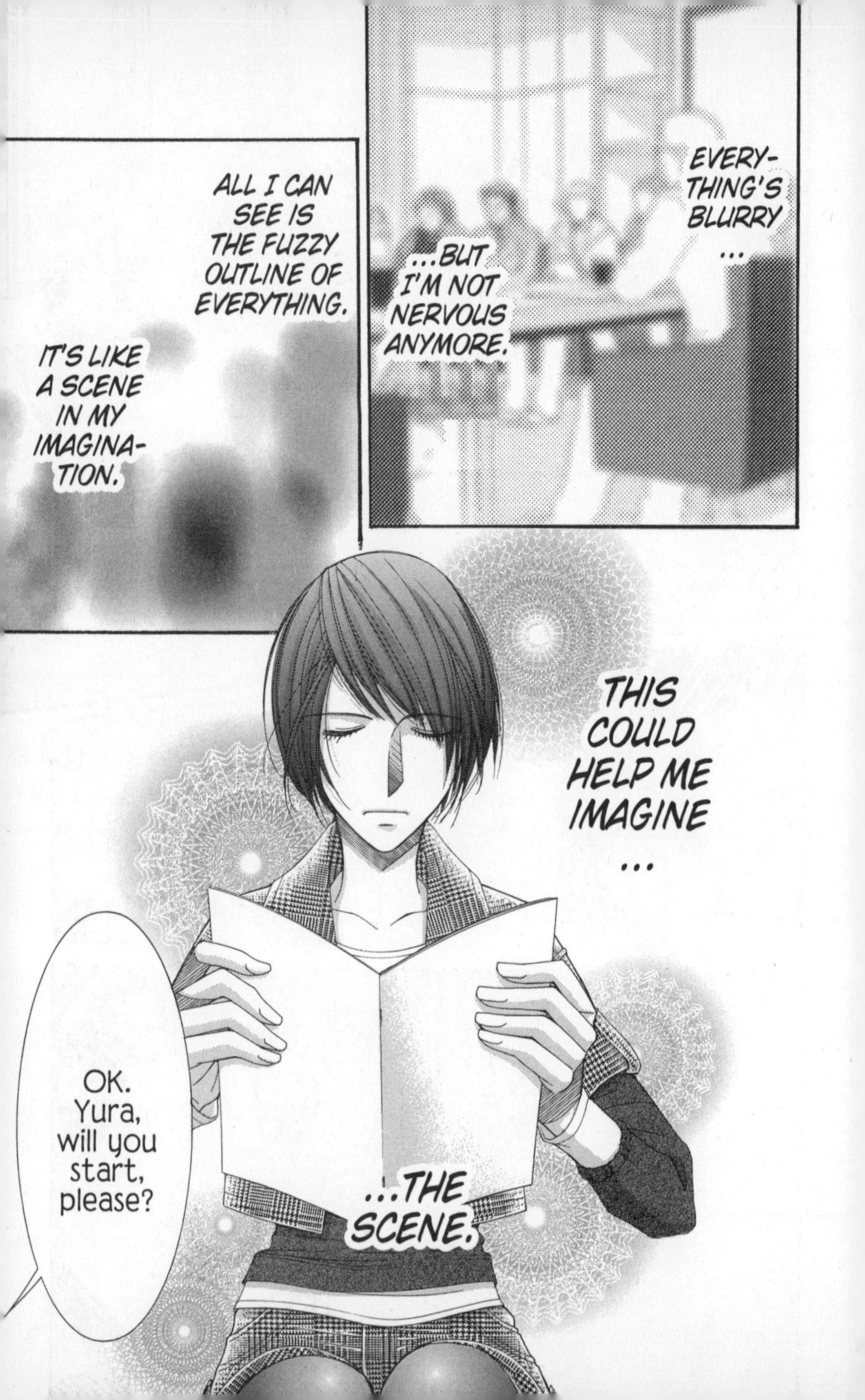
EVERYTHING'S BLURRY...
...BUT I'M NOT NERVOUS ANYMORE.
ALL I CAN SEE IS THE FUZZY OUTLINE OF EVERYTHING.
IT'S LIKE A SCENE IN MY IMAGINATION.
THIS COULD HELP ME IMAGINE...
...THE SCENE.
OK. Yura, will you start, please?

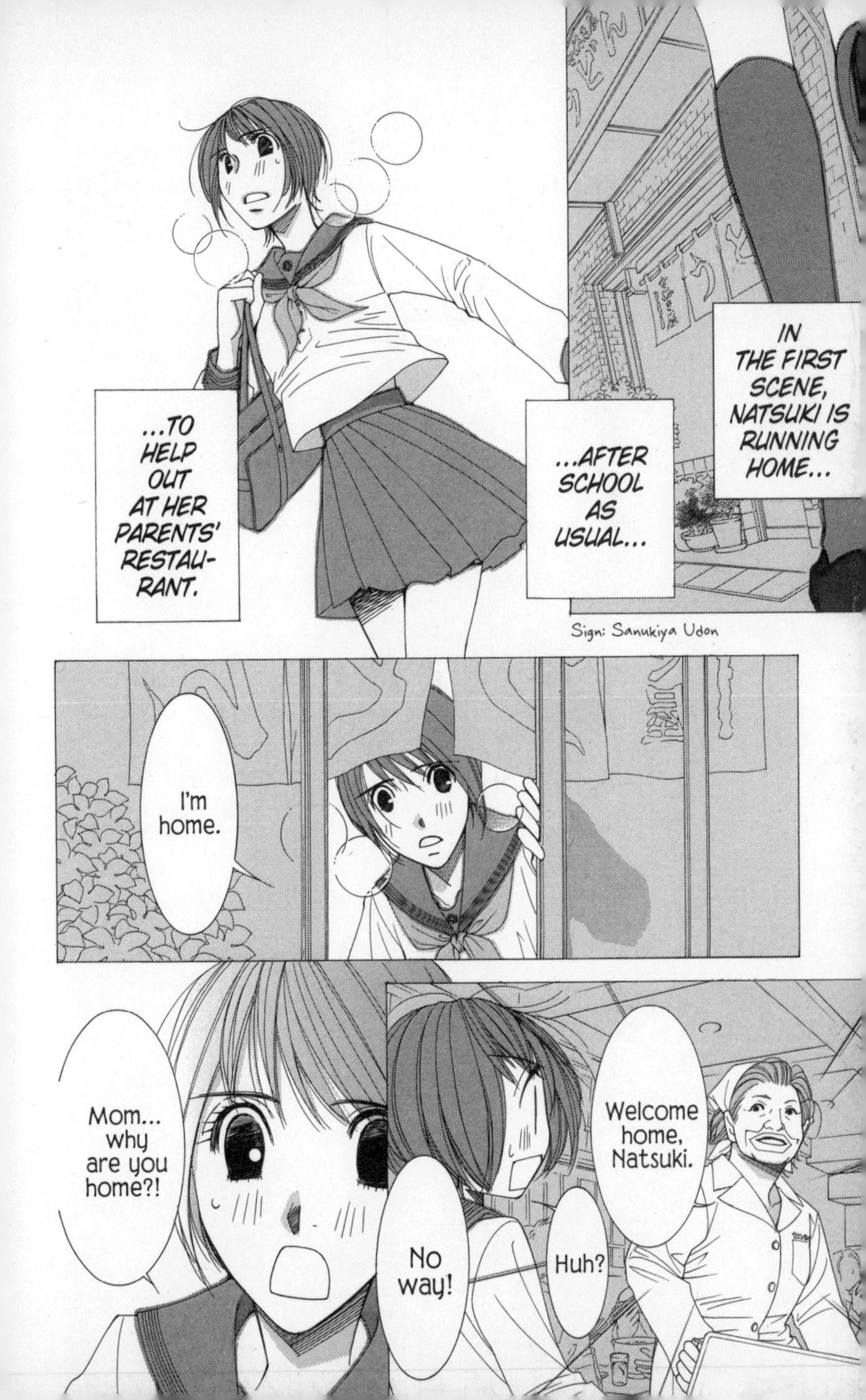
IN THE FIRST SCENE, NATSUKI IS RUNNING HOME...
Sign: Sanukiya Udon
...AFTER SCHOOL AS USUAL...
...TO HELP OUT AT HER PARENTS' RESTAU-RANT.
I'm home.
Welcome home, Natsuki.
Huh?
No way!
Mom... why are you home?!

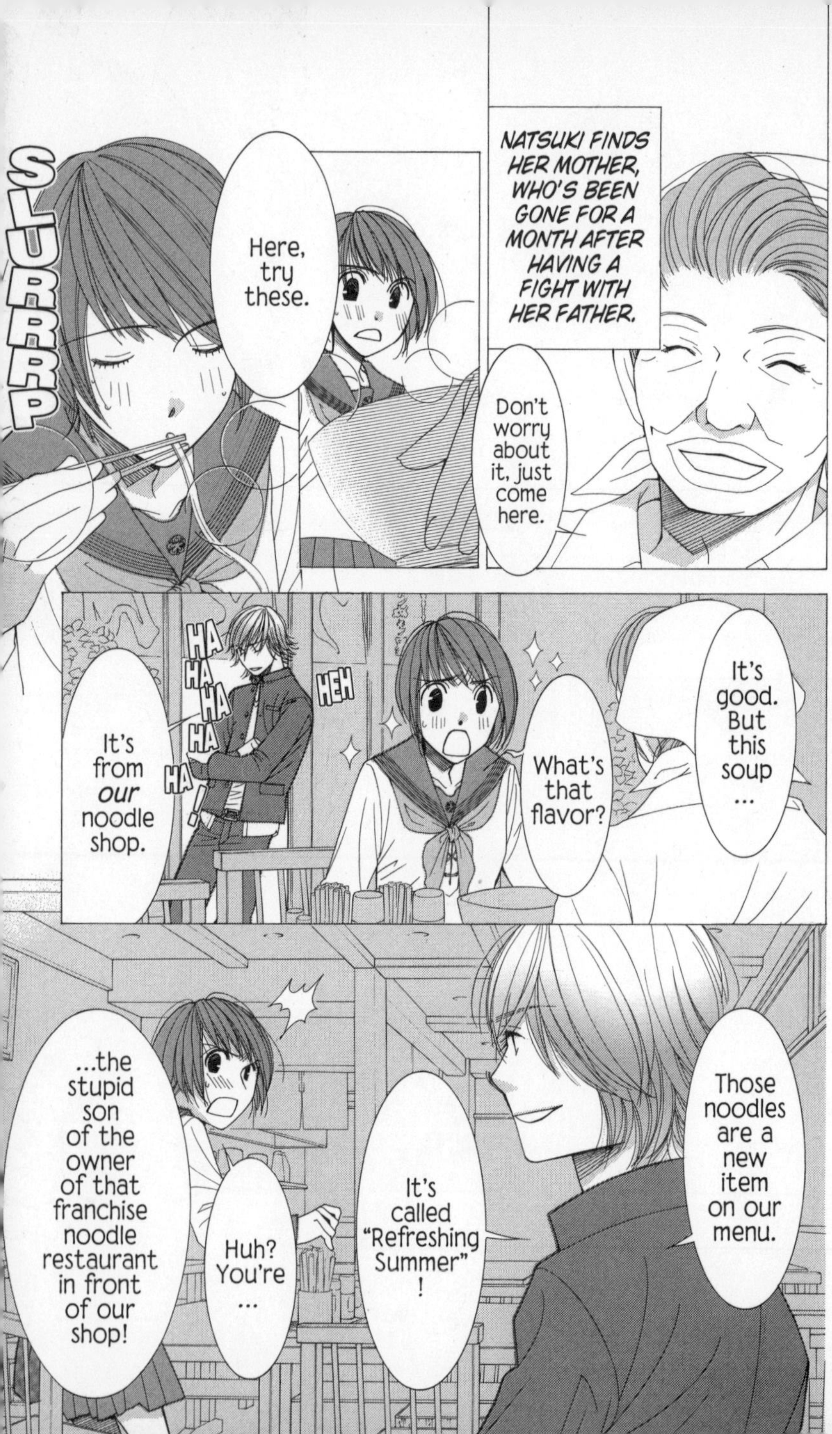
NATSUKI FINDS HER MOTHER, WHO'S BEEN GONE FOR A MONTH AFTER HAVING A FIGHT WITH HER FATHER.
Don't worry about it, just come here.
Here, try these.
SLURRRP
It's good. But this soup ...
What's that flavor?
HEH
HA HA HA HA HA !
It's from *our* noodle shop.
Those noodles are a new item on our menu.
It's called "Refreshing Summer" !
Huh? You're ...
...the stupid son of the owner of that franchise noodle restaurant in front of our shop!

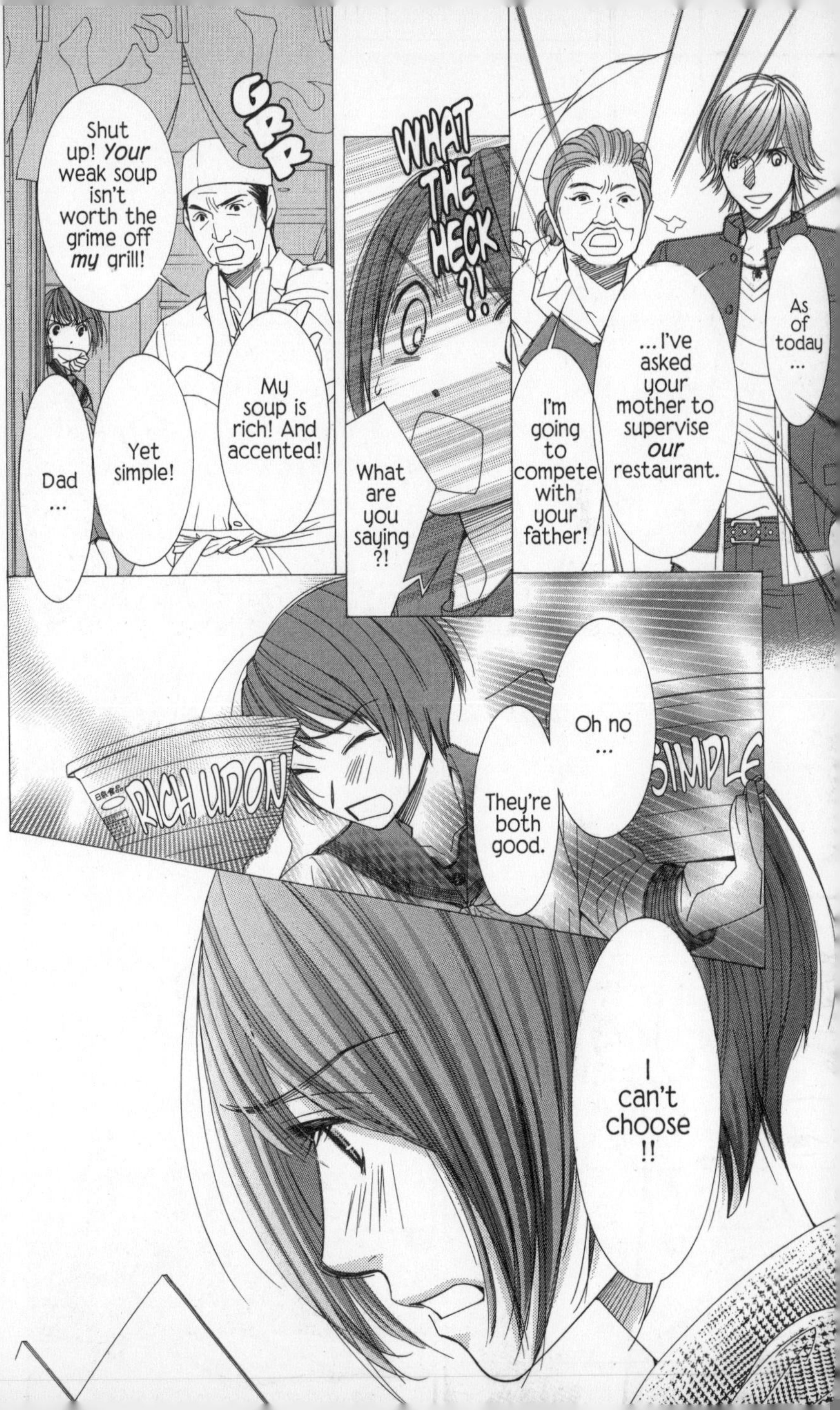
As of today ...
... I've asked your mother to supervise *our* restaurant.
I'm going to compete with your father!
WHAT THE HECK ?!
What are you saying ?!
GRR
Shut up! *Your* weak soup isn't worth the grime off *my* grill!
My soup is rich! And accented!
Yet simple!
Dad ...
SIMPLE
Oh no ...
They're both good.
RICH UDON
I can't choose !!

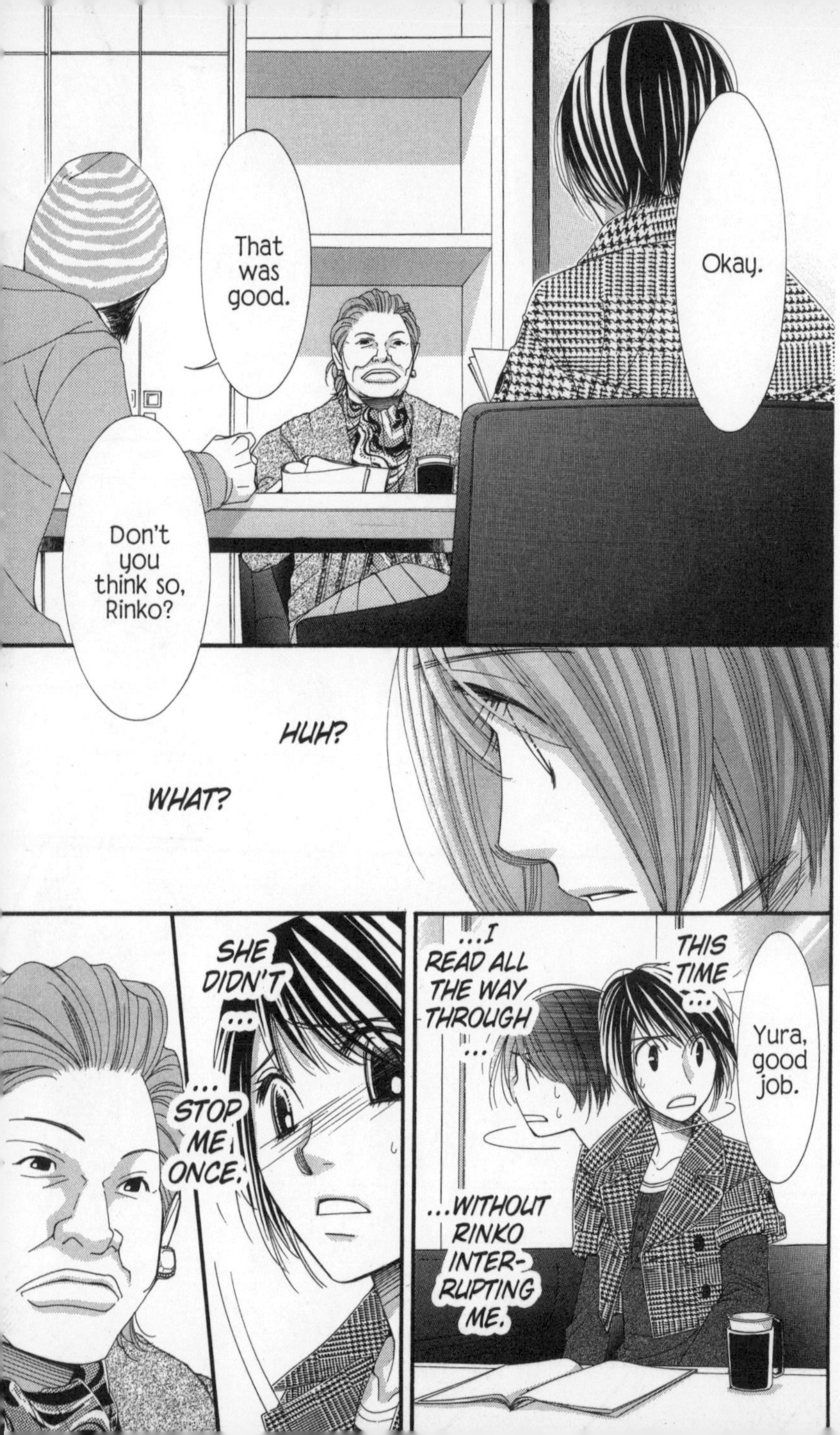
Okay.
That was good.
Don't you think so, Rinko?
HUH?
WHAT?
Yura, good job.
THIS TIME...
...I READ ALL THE WAY THROUGH...
...WITHOUT RINKO INTERRUPTING ME.
SHE DIDN'T...
...STOP ME ONCE.

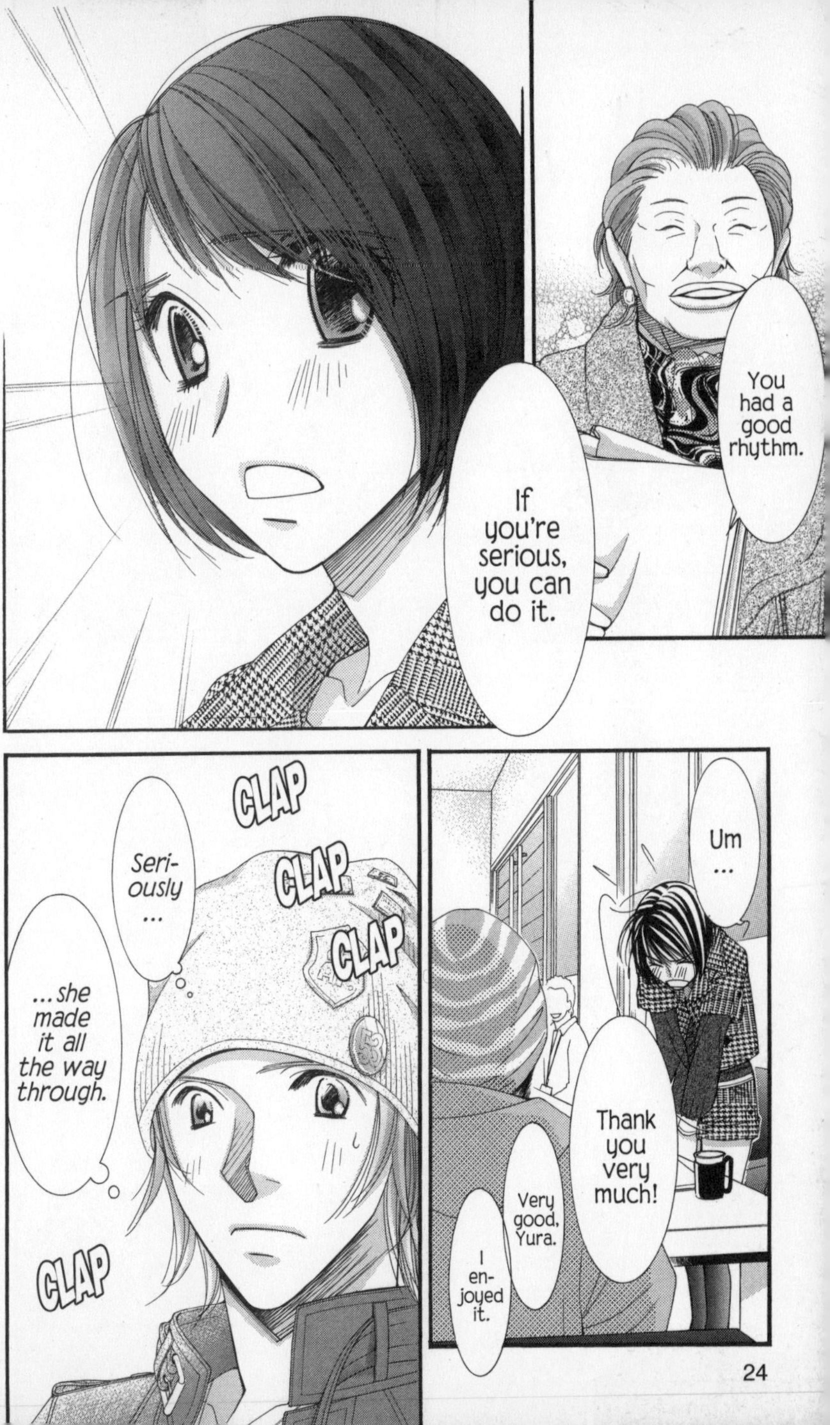

You had a good rhythm.
If you're serious, you can do it.
Um ...
Thank you very much!
Very good, Yura.
I enjoyed it.
CLAP
Seri-ously ...
CLAP
CLAP
...she made it all the way through.
CLAP

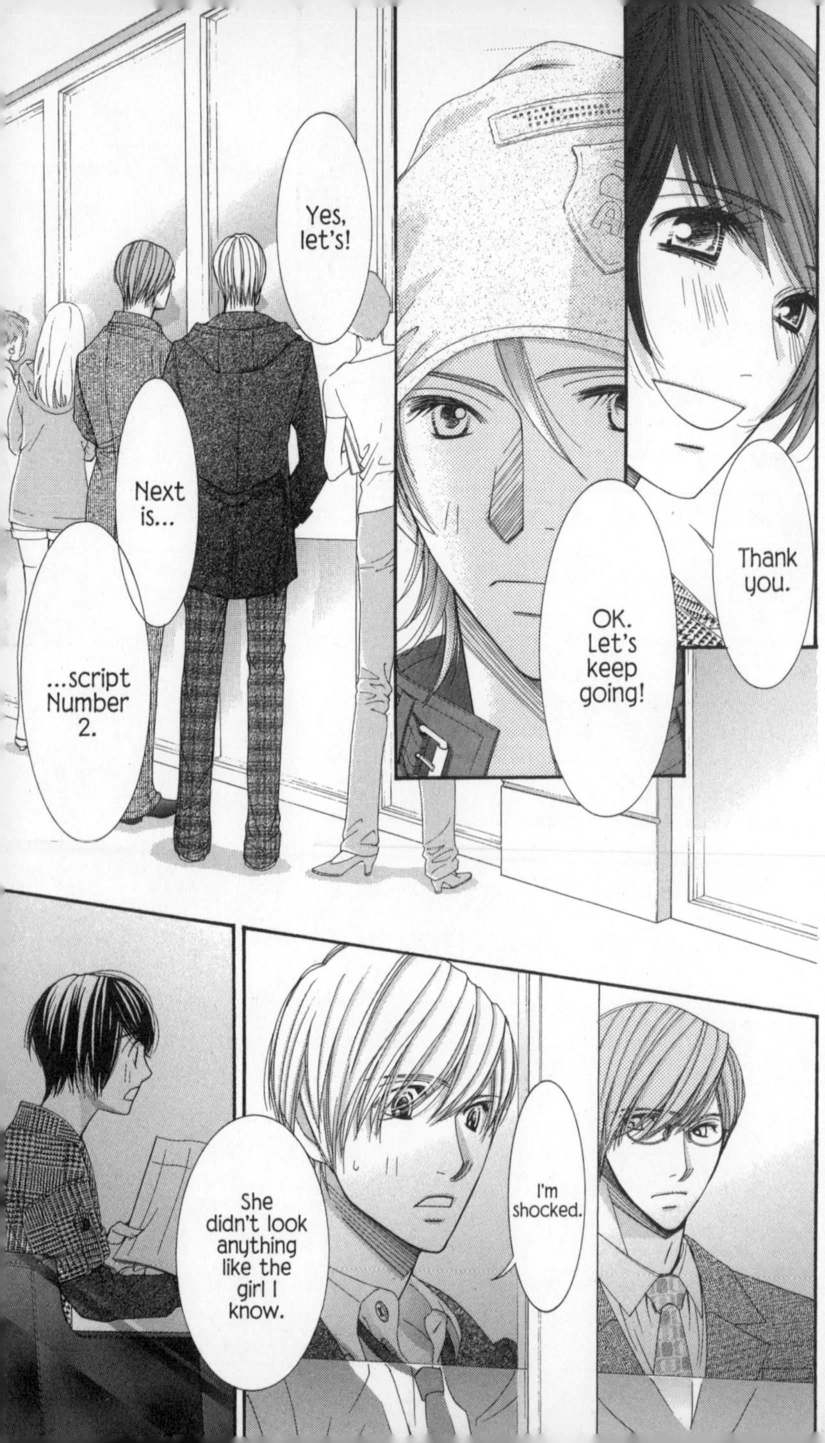
Thank you.
OK. Let's keep going!
Yes, let's!
Next is...
...script Number 2.
I'm shocked.
She didn't look anything like the girl I know.

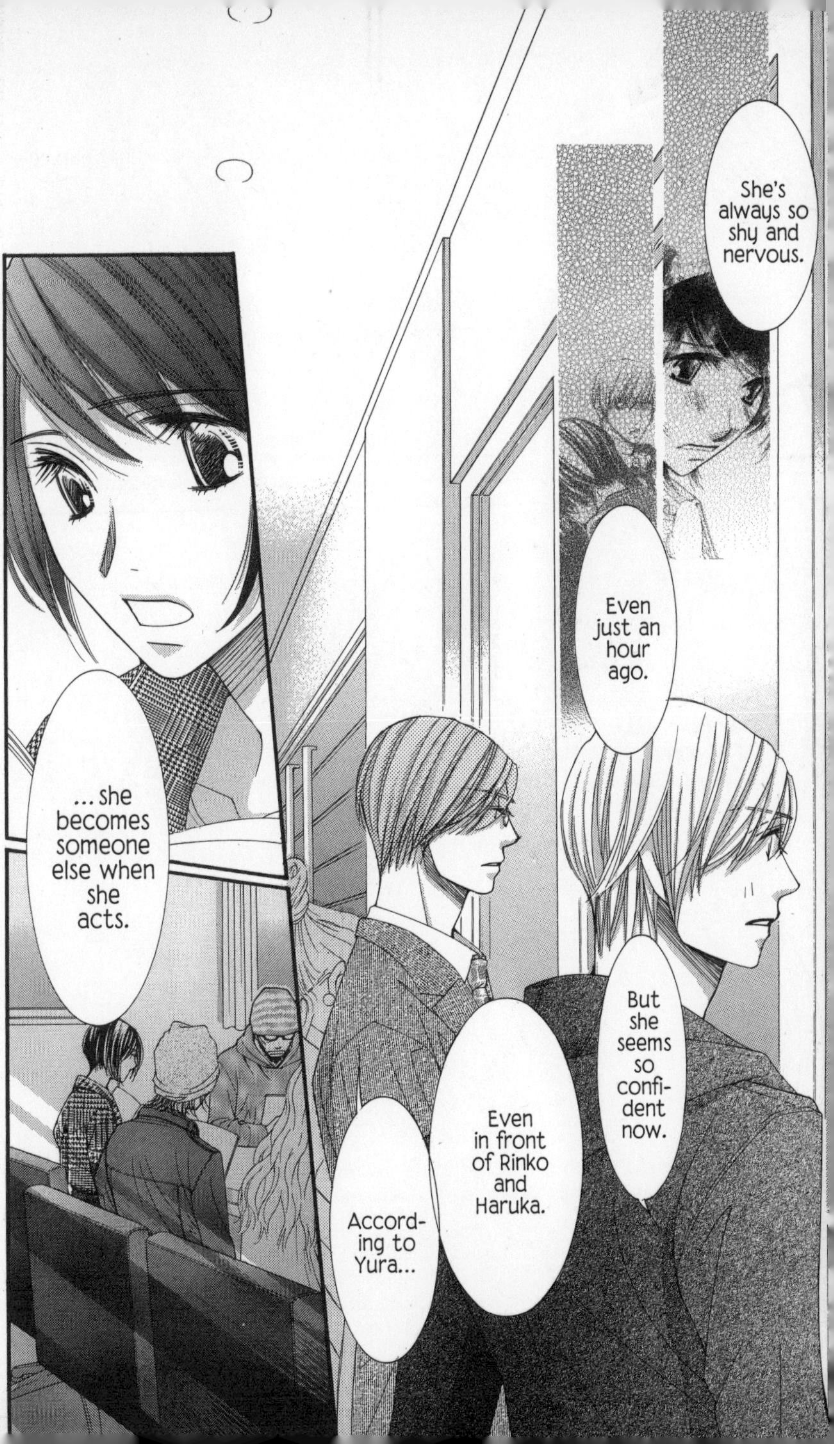
She's always so shy and nervous.
Even just an hour ago.
But she seems so confident now.
Even in front of Rinko and Haruka.
According to Yura...
...she becomes someone else when she acts.

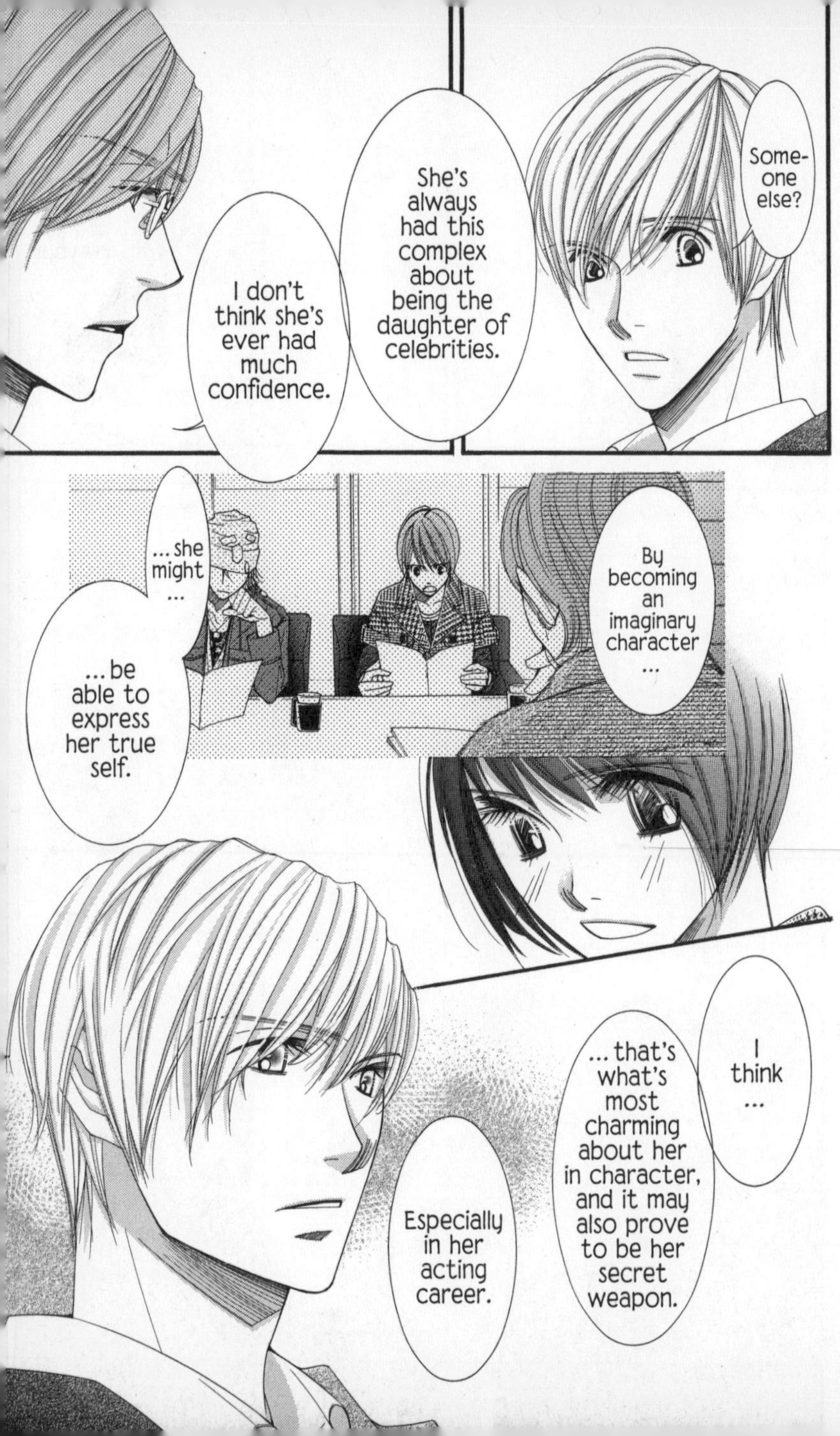
Some-one else?
She's always had this complex about being the daughter of celebrities.
I don't think she's ever had much confidence.
By becoming an imaginary character...
...she might...
...be able to express her true self.
I think...
...that's what's most charming about her in character, and it may also prove to be her secret weapon.
Especially in her acting career.

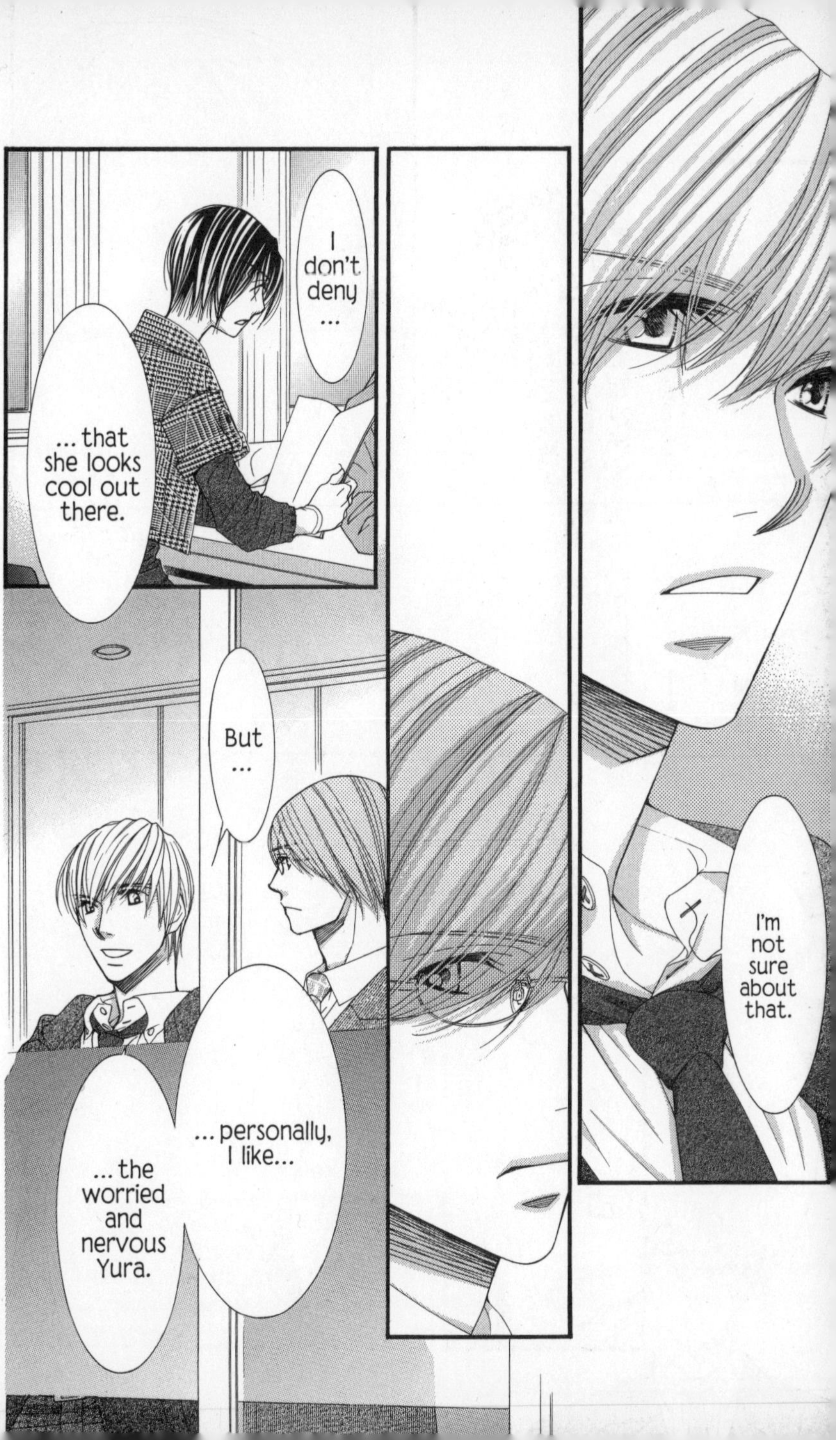
I'm not sure about that.
I don't deny...
...that she looks cool out there.
But...
...personally, I like...
...the worried and nervous Yura.

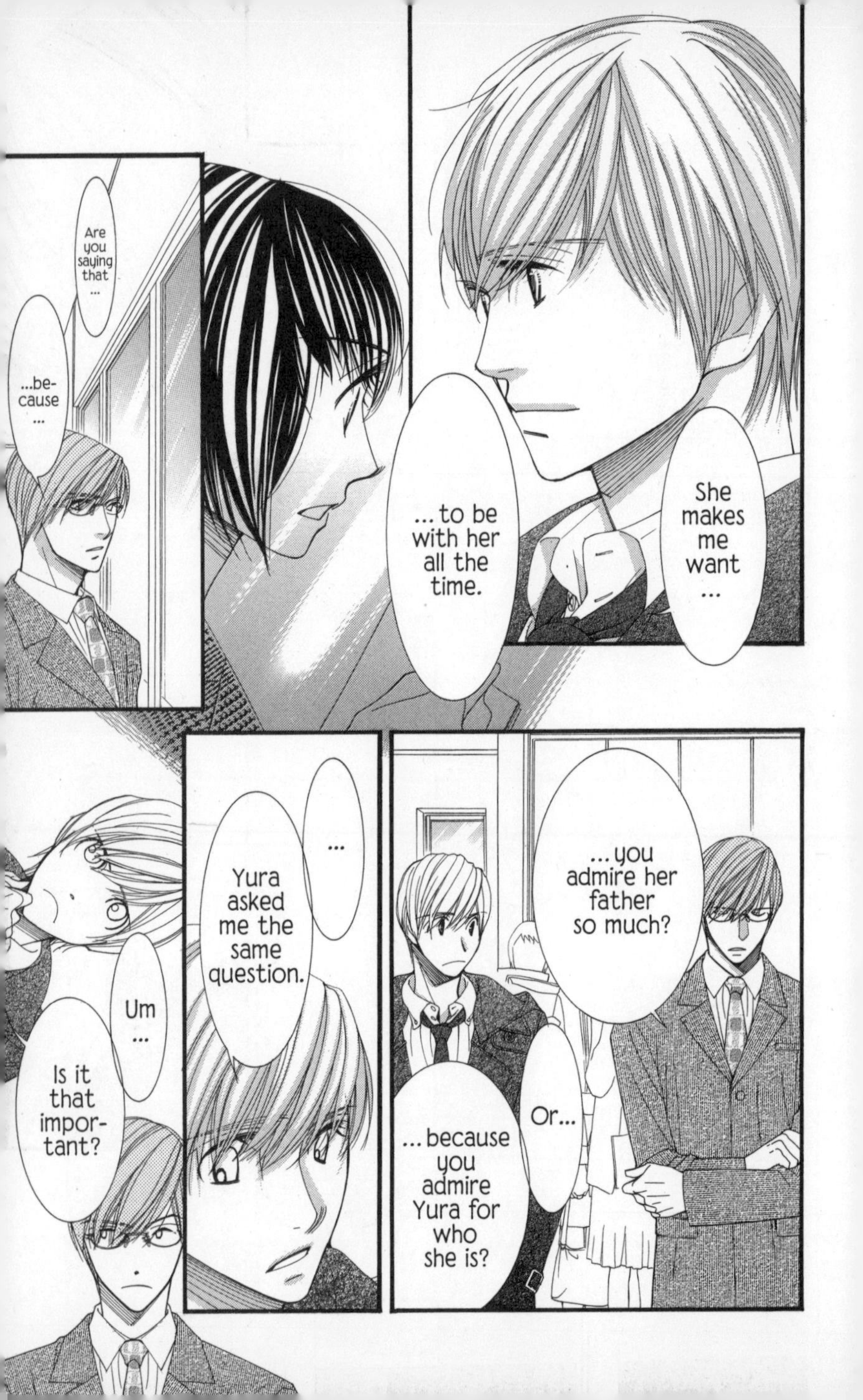
She makes me want ...
... to be with her all the time.
Are you saying that ...
...be- cause ...
... you admire her father so much?
Or...
... because you admire Yura for who she is?
...
Yura asked me the same question.
Um ...
Is it that impor- tant?

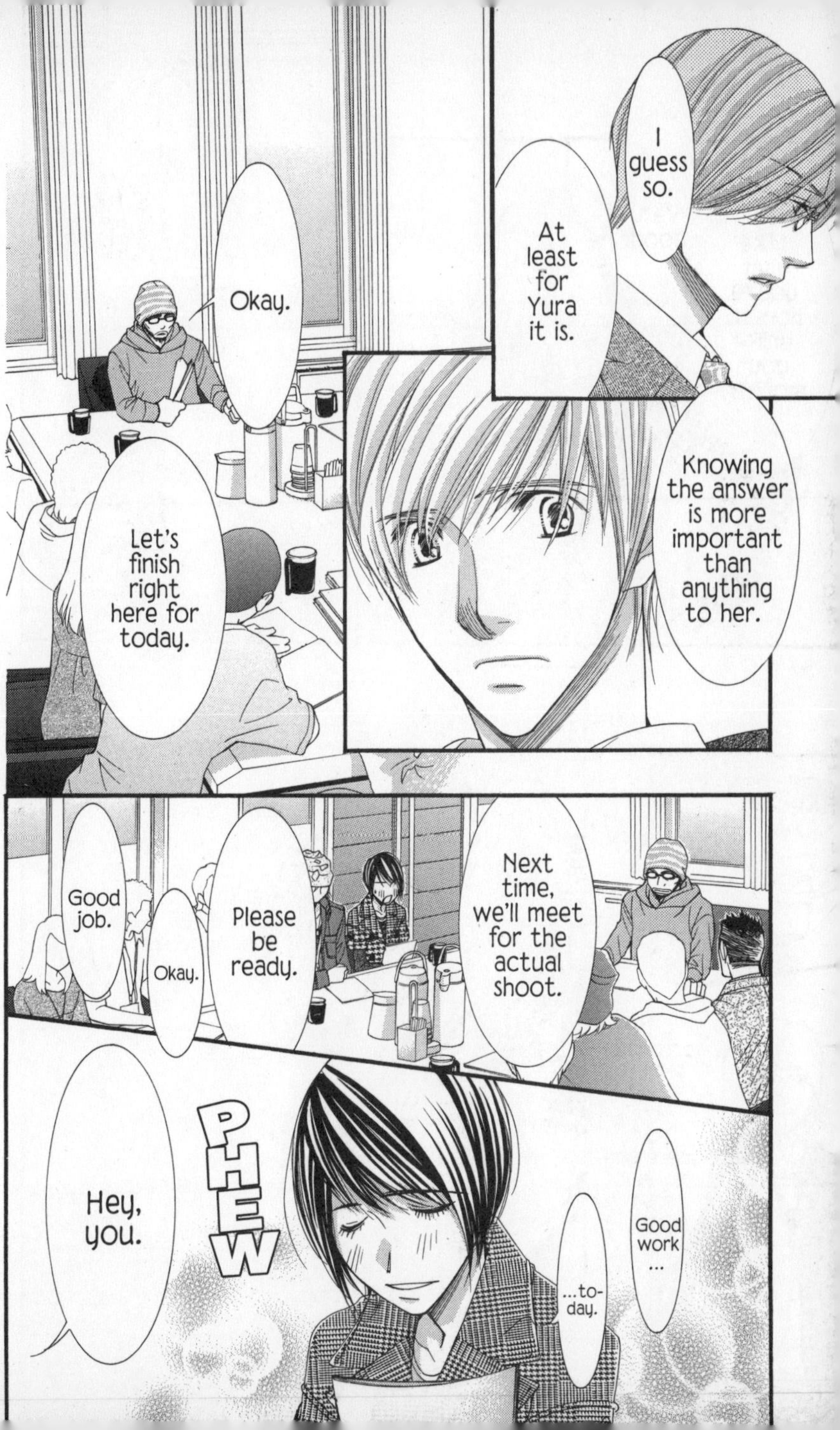
I guess so.
At least for Yura it is.
Knowing the answer is more important than anything to her.
Okay.
Let's finish right here for today.
Next time, we'll meet for the actual shoot.
Please be ready.
Okay.
Good job.
Good work...
...to-day.
PHEW
Hey, you.

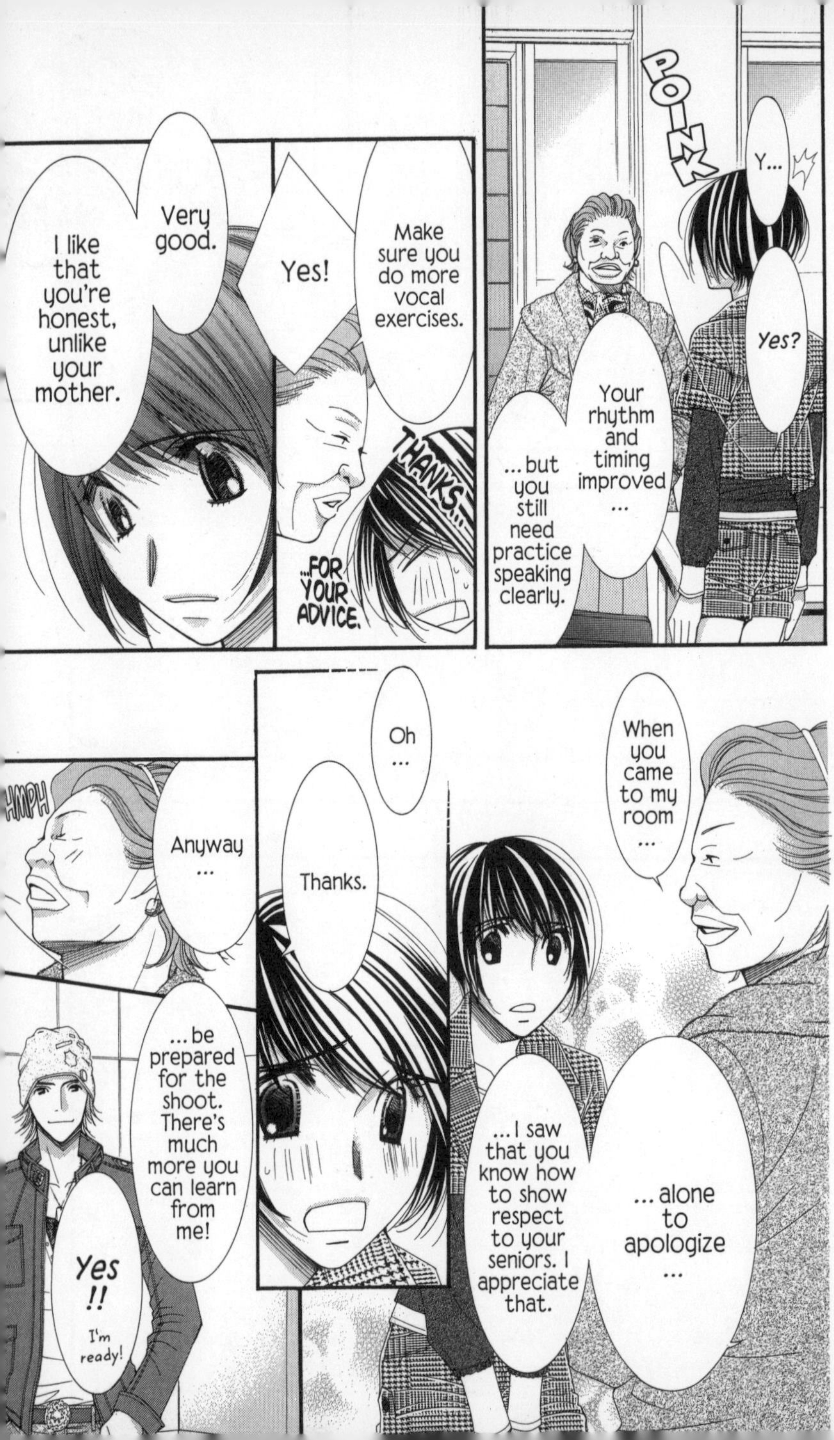
POINK
Y...
Yes?
Your rhythm and timing improved...
...but you still need practice speaking clearly.
Make sure you do more vocal exercises.
Yes!
THANKS...
...FOR YOUR ADVICE.
Very good.
I like that you're honest, unlike your mother.
When you came to my room...
...alone to apologize...
...I saw that you know how to show respect to your seniors. I appreciate that.
Oh...
Thanks.
HMPH
Anyway...
...be prepared for the shoot. There's much more you can learn from me!
Yes!!
I'm ready!

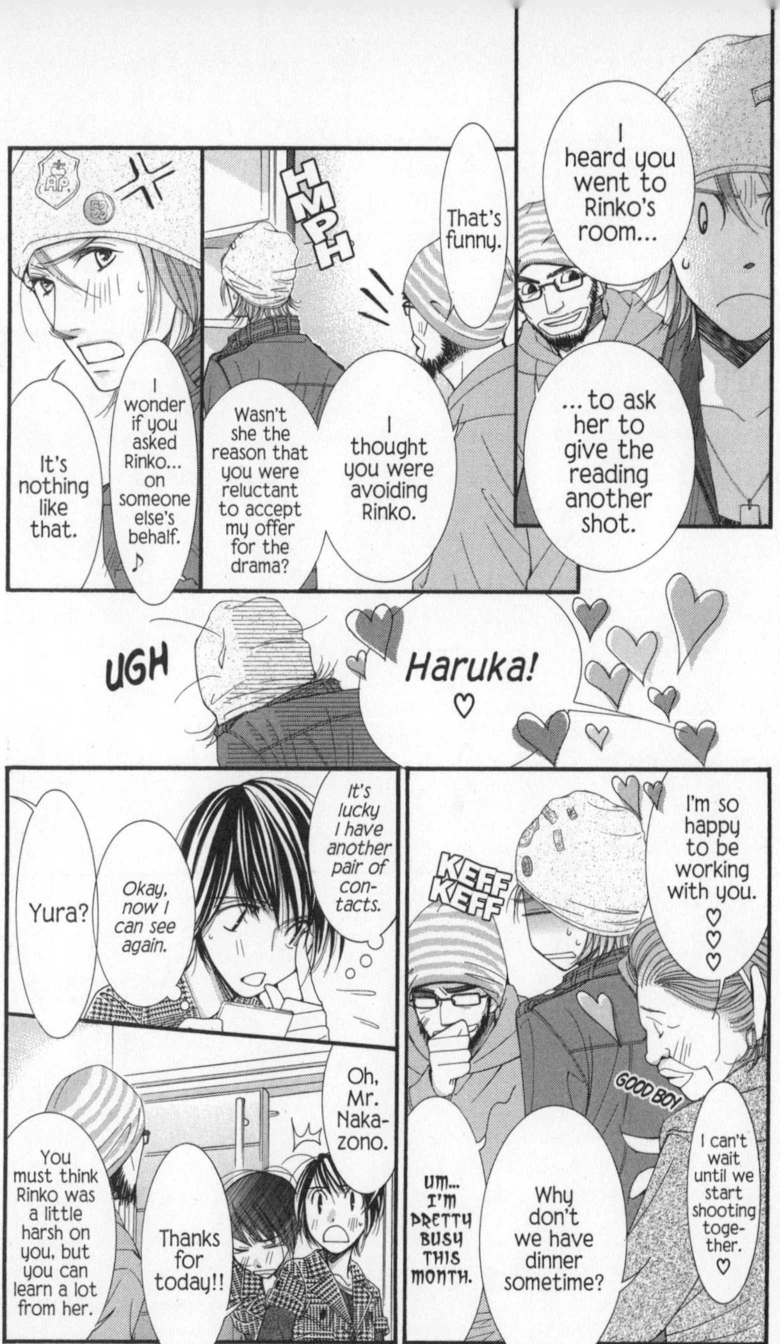
I heard you went to Rinko's room...
...to ask her to give the reading another shot.
That's funny.
HMPH
I thought you were avoiding Rinko.
Wasn't she the reason that you were reluctant to accept my offer for the drama?
I wonder if you asked Rinko... on someone else's behalf. ♪
It's nothing like that.
Haruka! ♡
UGH
I'm so happy to be working with you. ♡♡♡
KEFF KEFF
GOOD BOY
I can't wait until we start shooting together. ♡
Why don't we have dinner sometime?
UM... I'M PRETTY BUSY THIS MONTH.
It's lucky I have another pair of contacts.
Okay, now I can see again.
Yura?
Oh, Mr. Nakazono.
Thanks for today!!
You must think Rinko was a little harsh on you, but you can learn a lot from her.

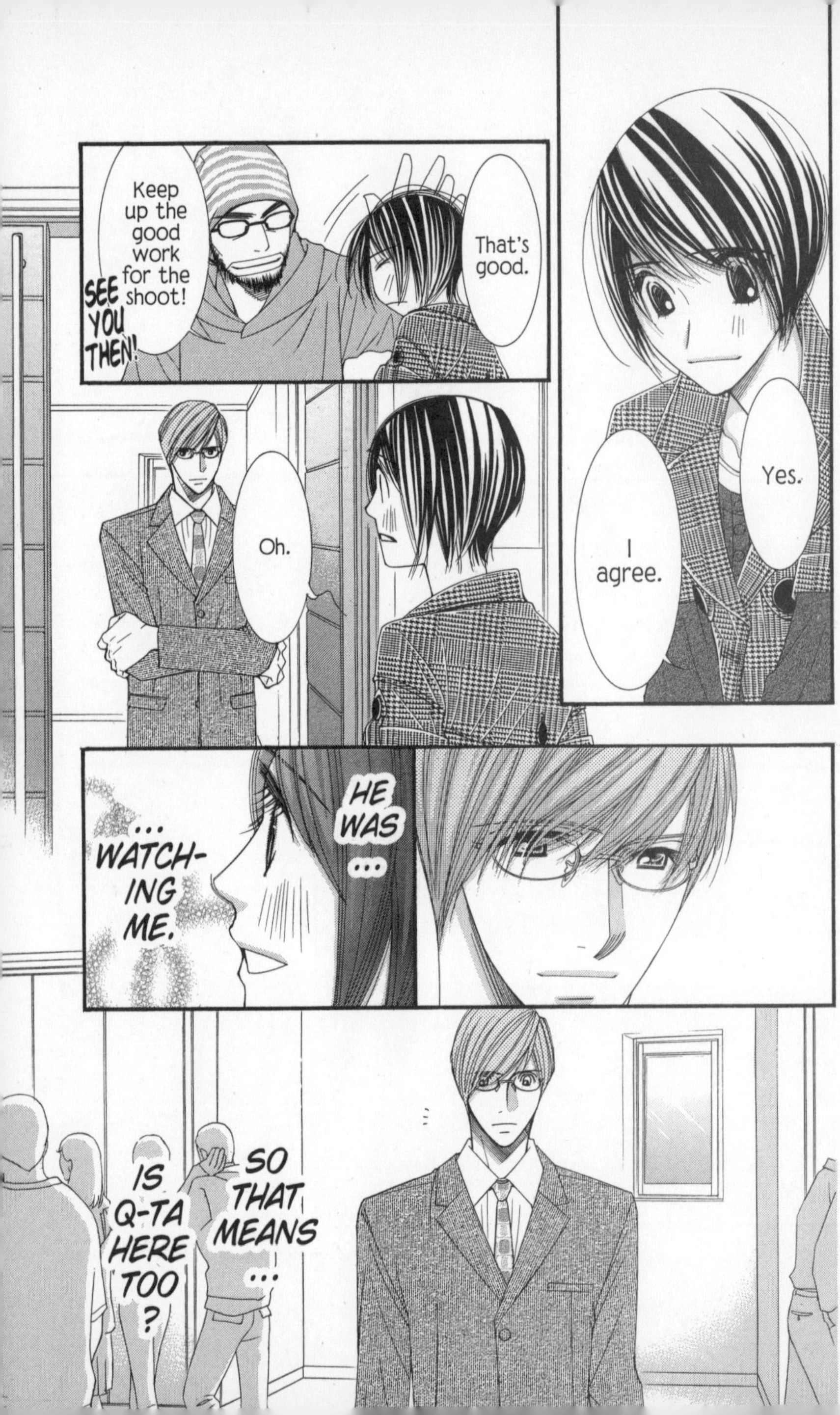
Yes.
I agree.
That's good.
Keep up the good work for the shoot!
SEE YOU THEN!
Oh.
HE WAS...
...WATCHING ME.
SO THAT MEANS...
IS Q-TA HERE TOO?

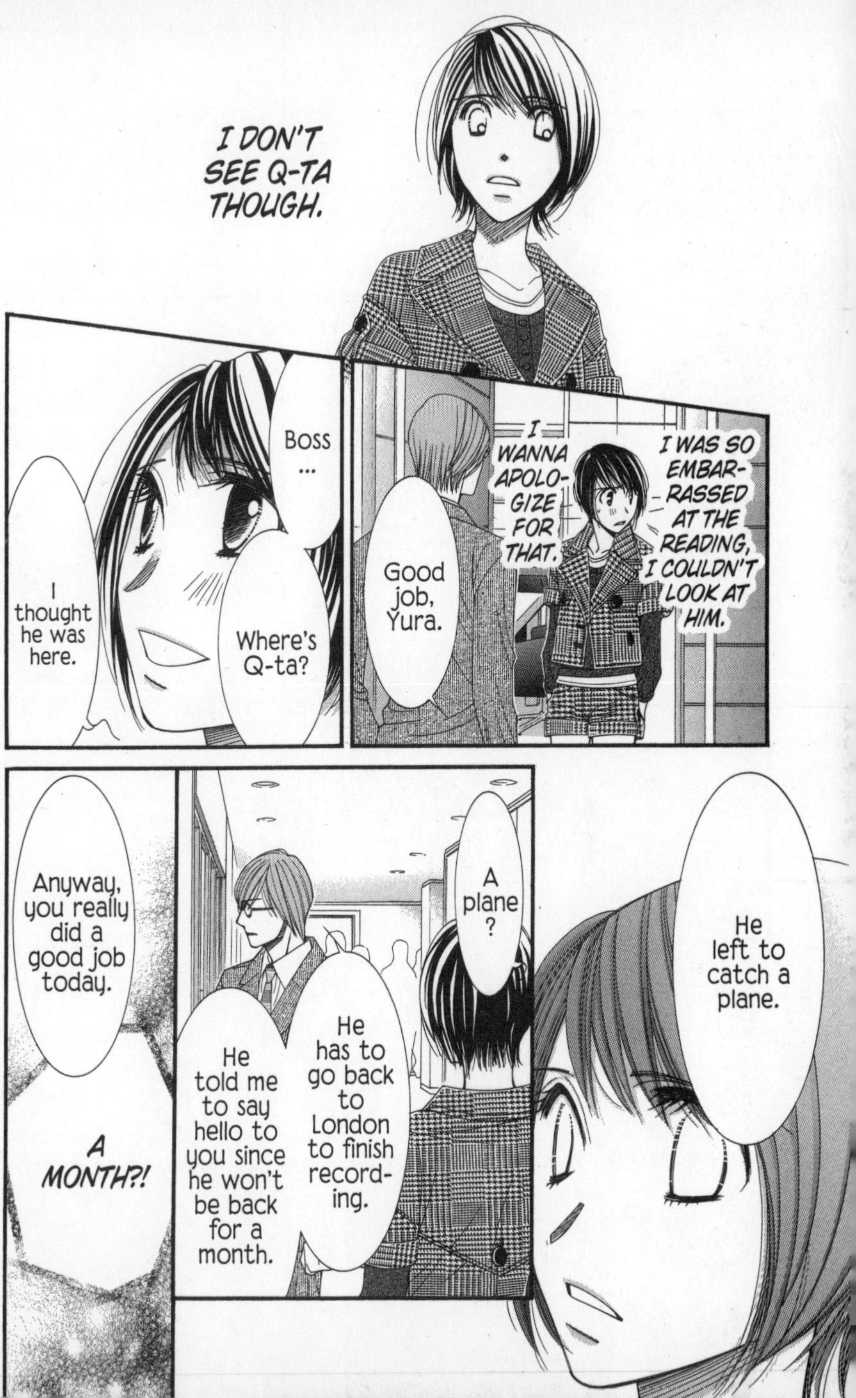
I DON'T SEE Q-TA THOUGH.
I WAS SO EMBARRASSED AT THE READING, I COULDN'T LOOK AT HIM.
I WANNA APOLOGIZE FOR THAT.
Good job, Yura.
Boss ...
Where's Q-ta?
I thought he was here.
He left to catch a plane.
A plane?
He has to go back to London to finish recording.
He told me to say hello to you since he won't be back for a month.
Anyway, you really did a good job today.
A MONTH?!

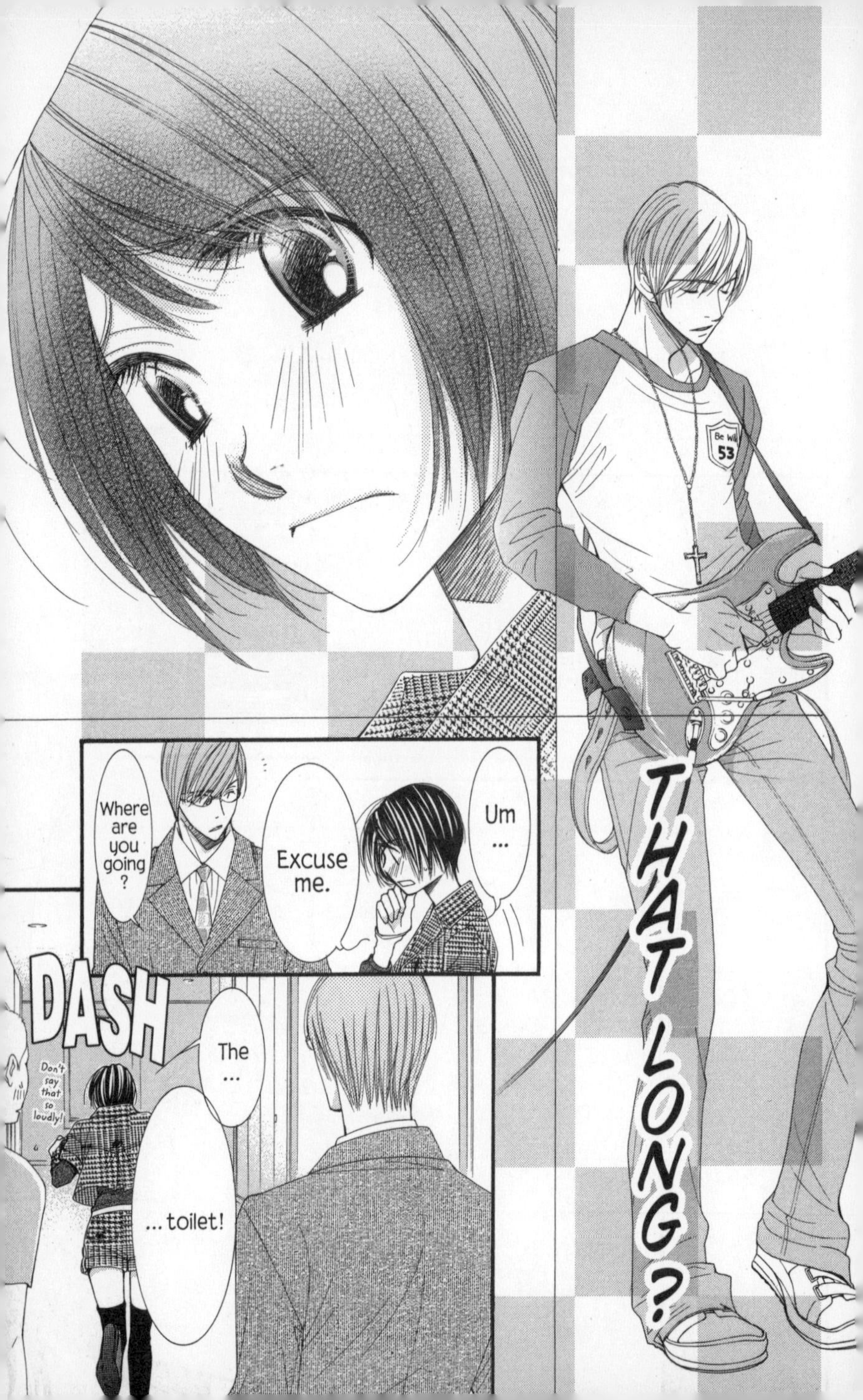
THAT LONG?
Um ...
Excuse me.
Where are you going?
The ...
... toilet!
DASH
Don't say that so loudly!

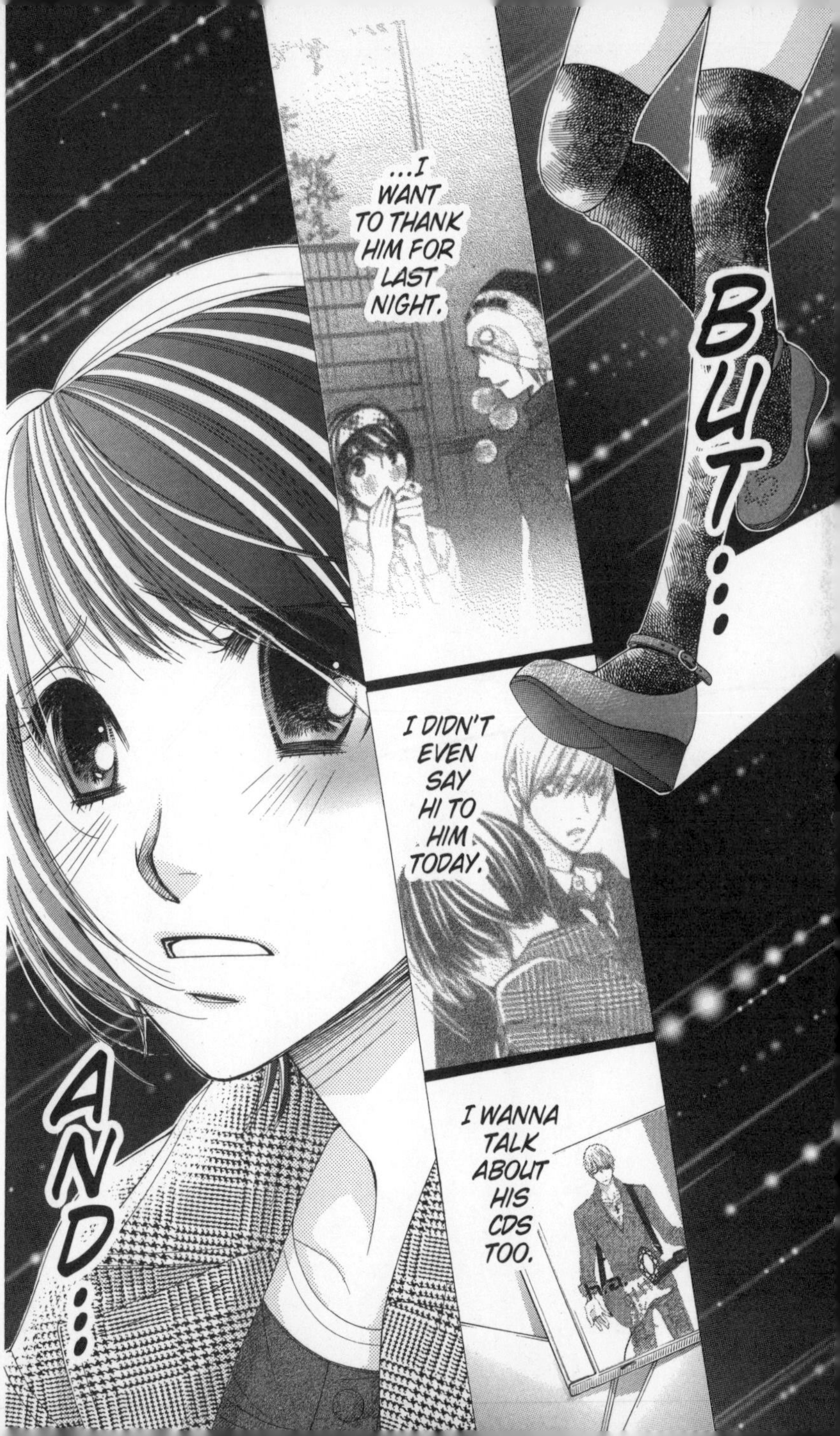
BUT...
...I WANT TO THANK HIM FOR LAST NIGHT.
I DIDN'T EVEN SAY HI TO HIM TODAY.
I WANNA TALK ABOUT HIS CDS TOO.
AND...

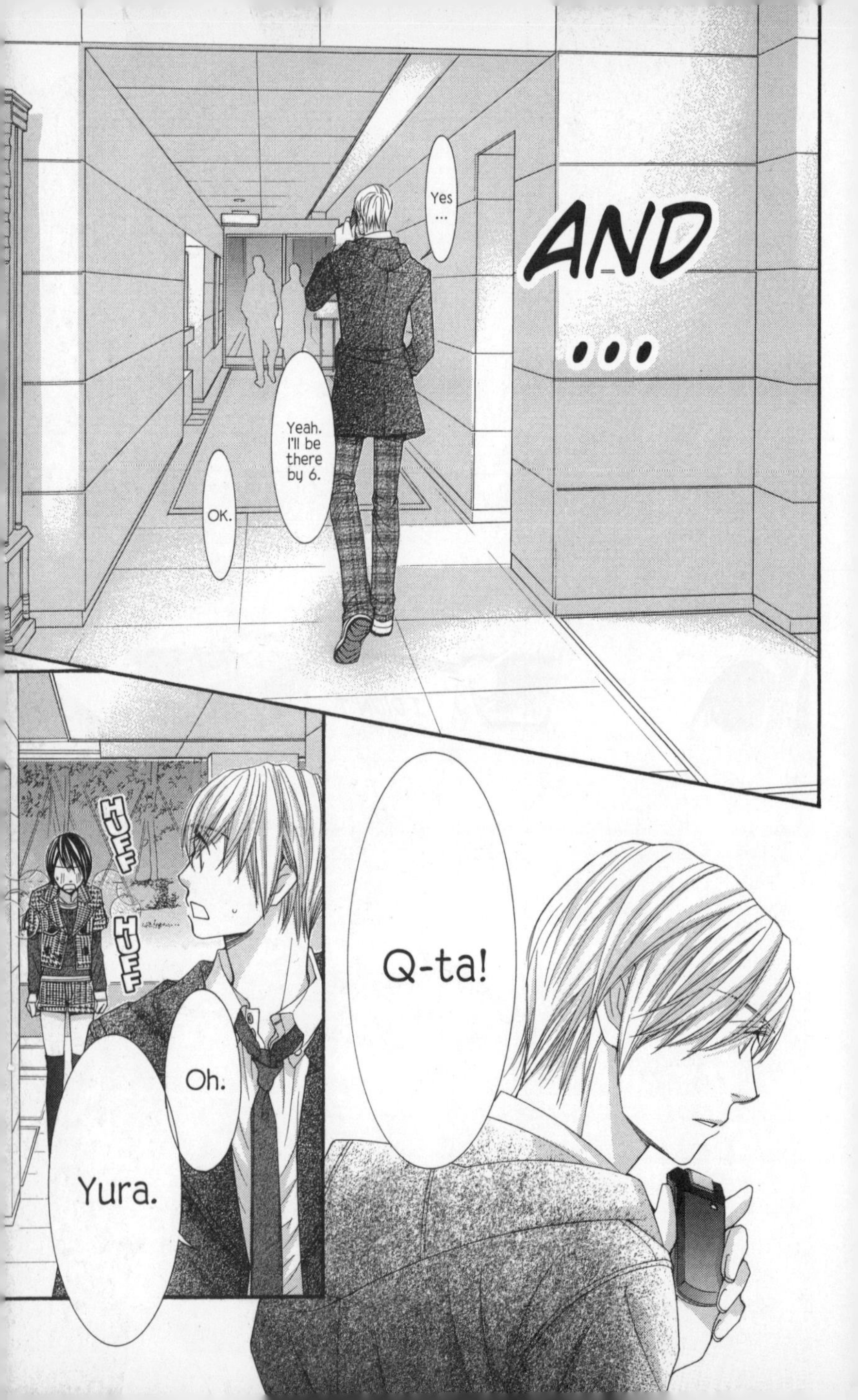
AND ...
Yes ...
Yeah. I'll be there by 6.
OK.
Q-ta!
HUFF HUFF
Oh.
Yura.

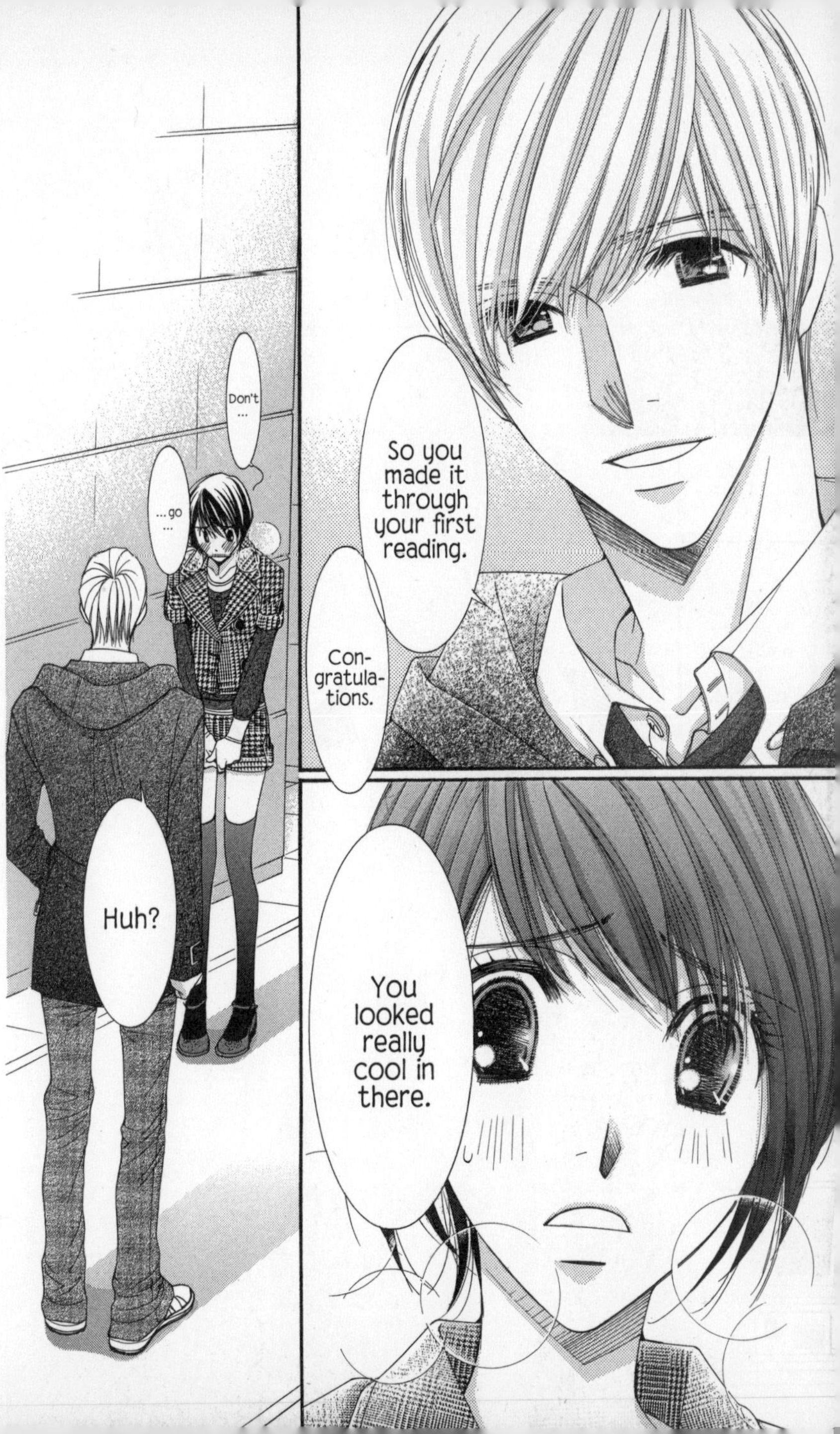
So you made it through your first reading.
Con-gratula-tions.
You looked really cool in there.
Don't ...
...go ...
Huh?

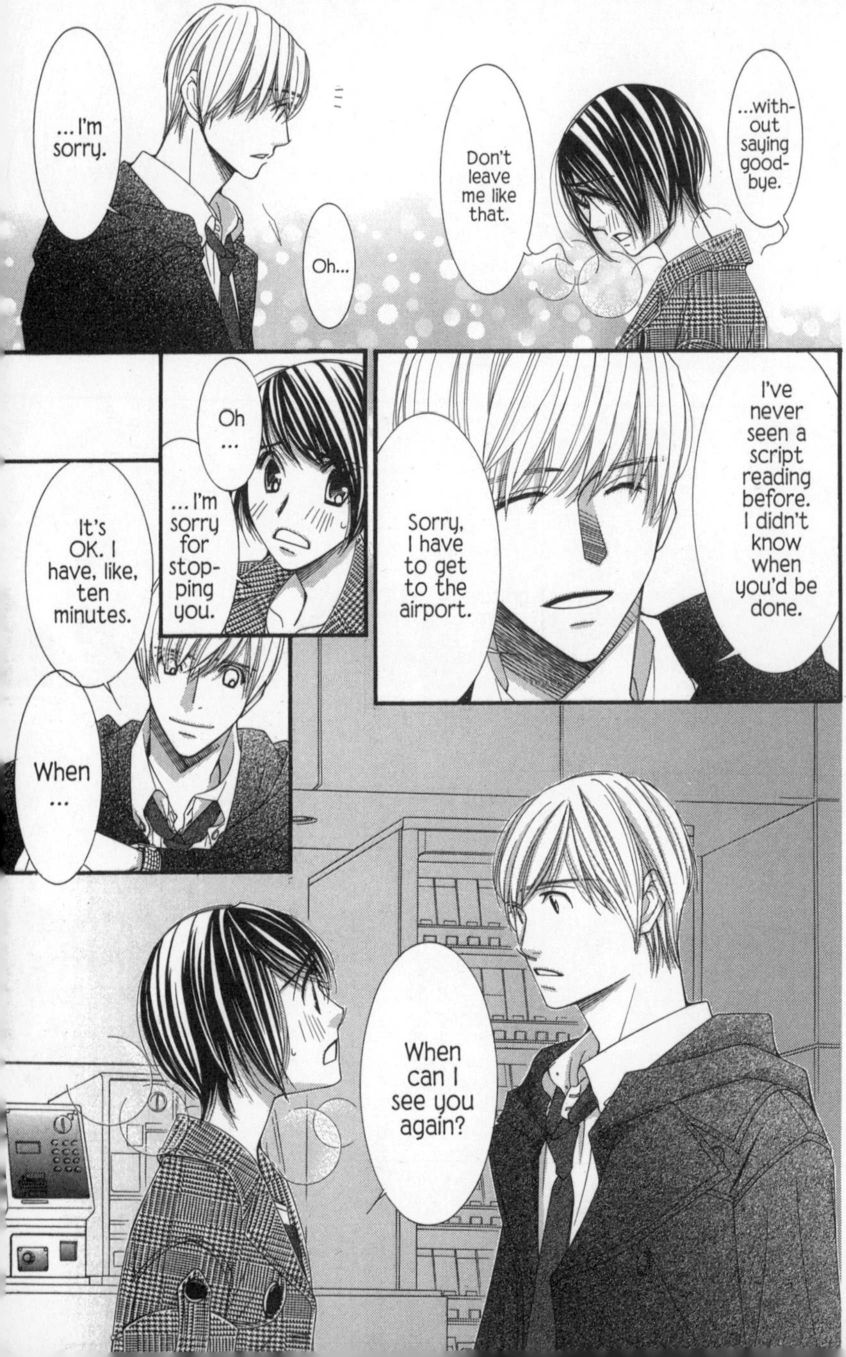
...with-out saying good-bye.
Don't leave me like that.
Oh...
...I'm sorry.
I've never seen a script reading before. I didn't know when you'd be done.
Sorry, I have to get to the airport.
Oh ...
...I'm sorry for stop-ping you.
It's OK. I have, like, ten minutes.
When ...
When can I see you again?

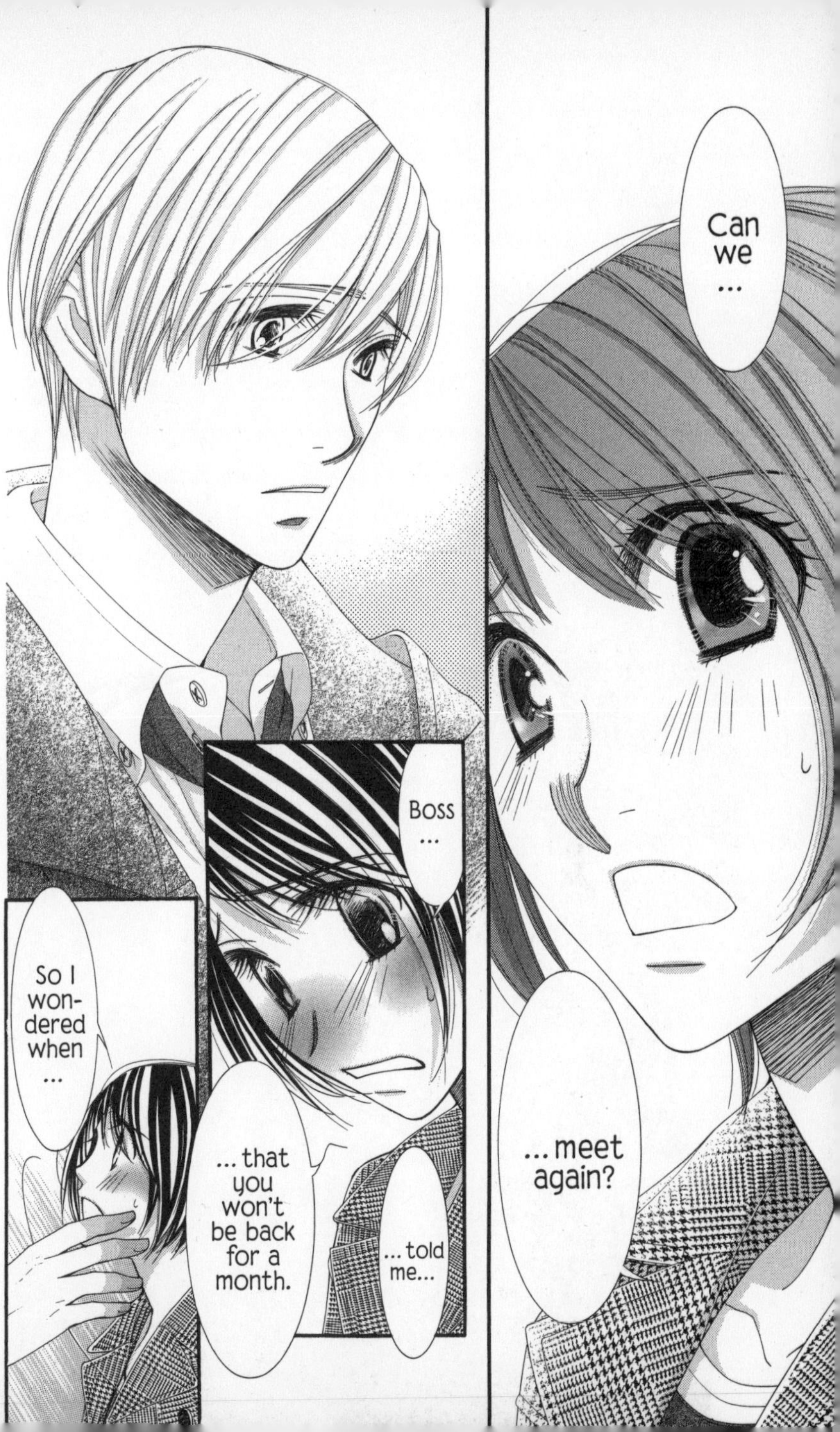
Can we ...
... meet again?
Boss ...
... told me...
... that you won't be back for a month.
So I wondered when ...

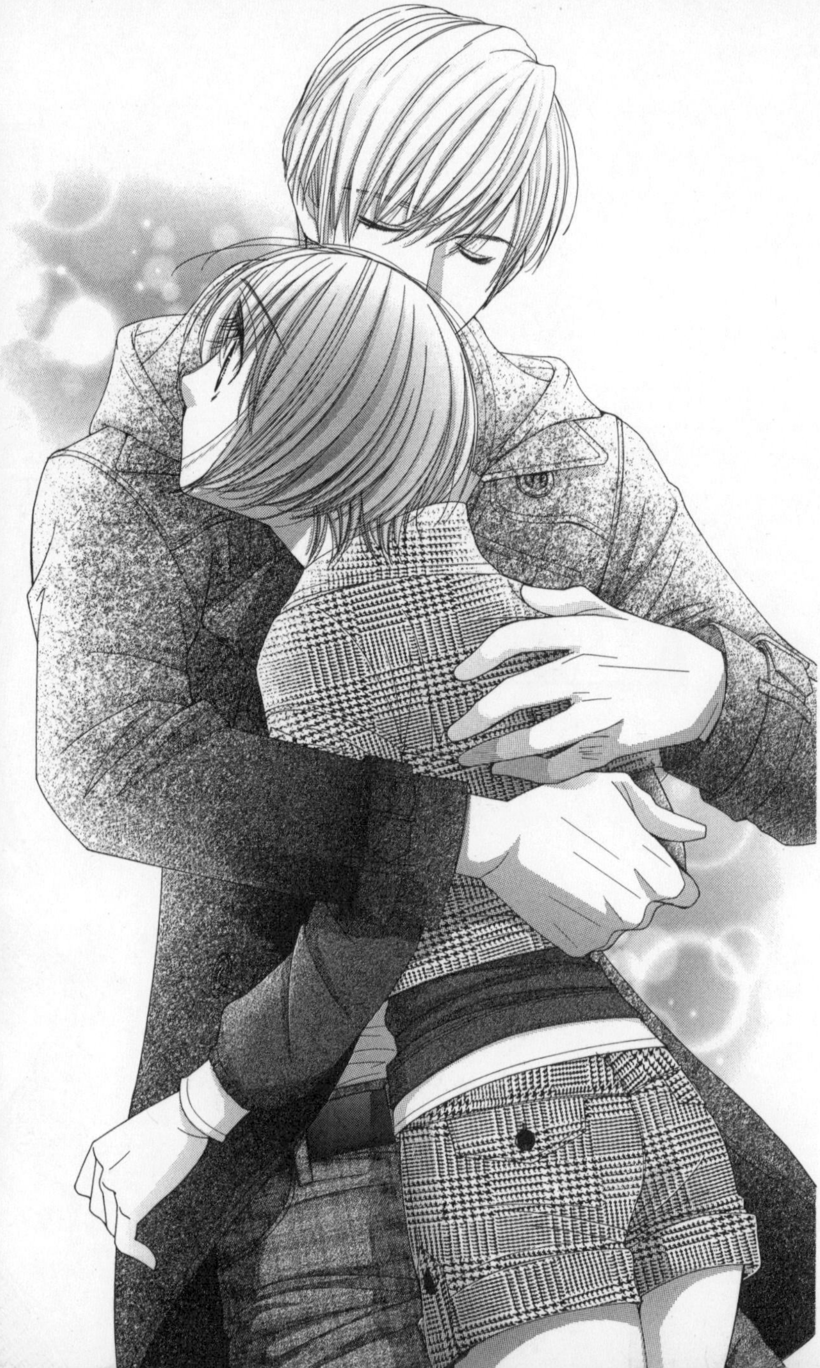

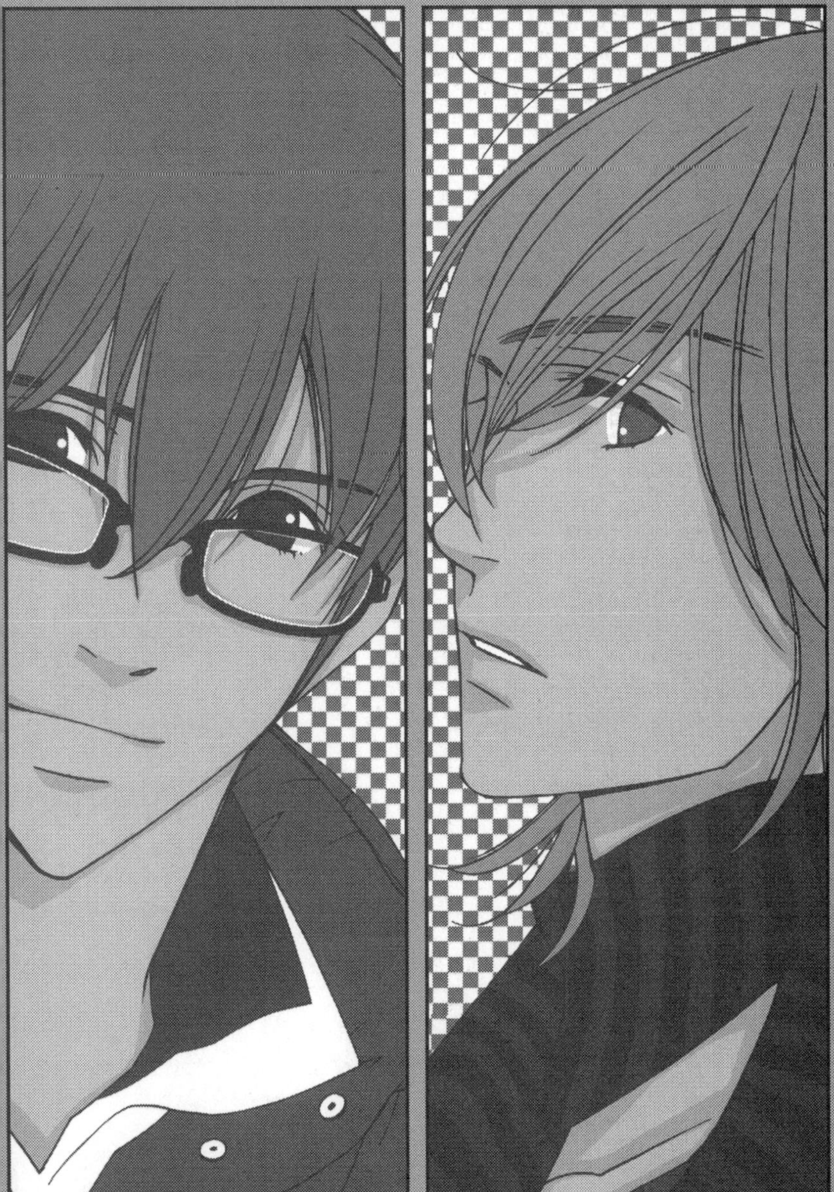

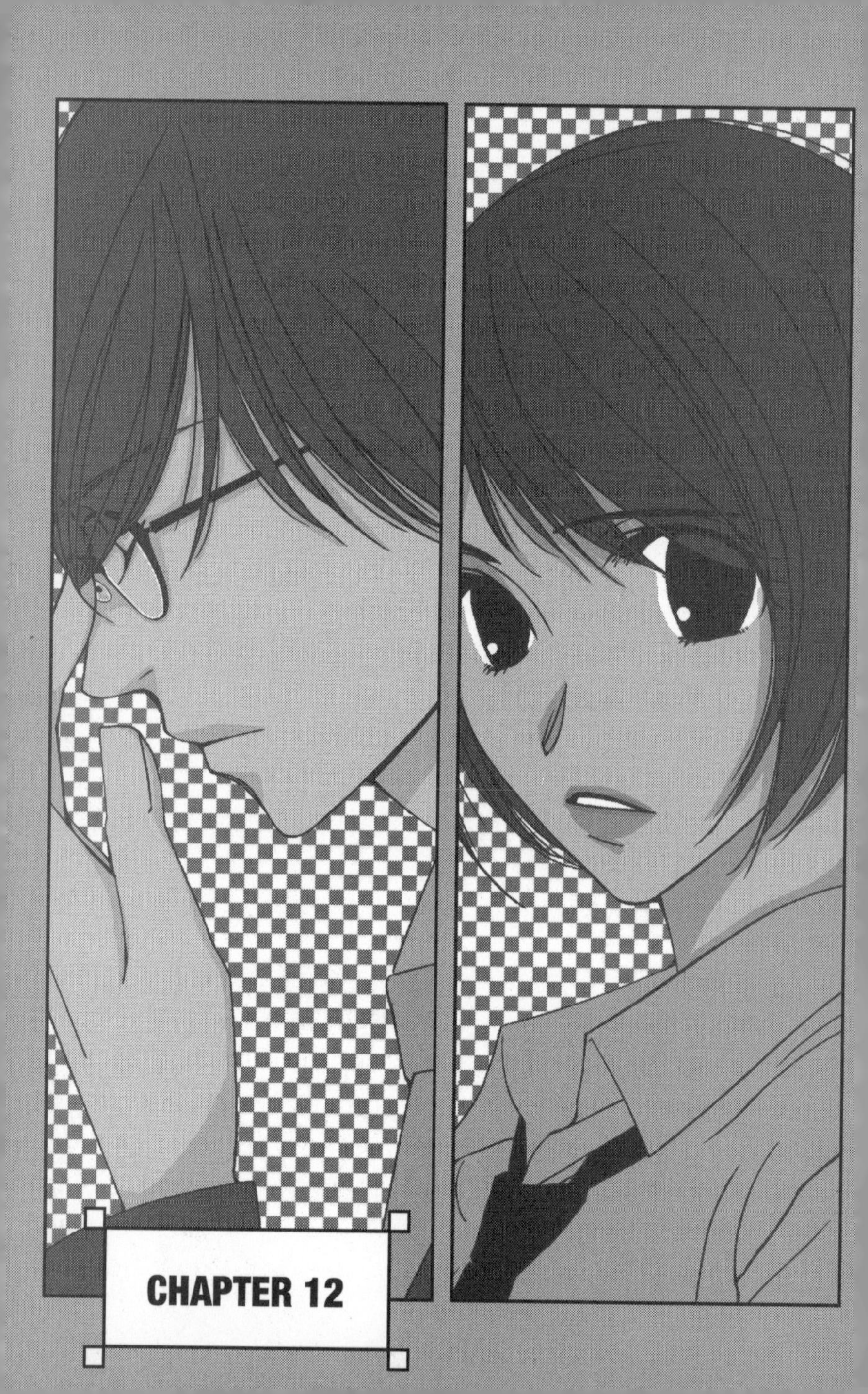

CHAPTER 12

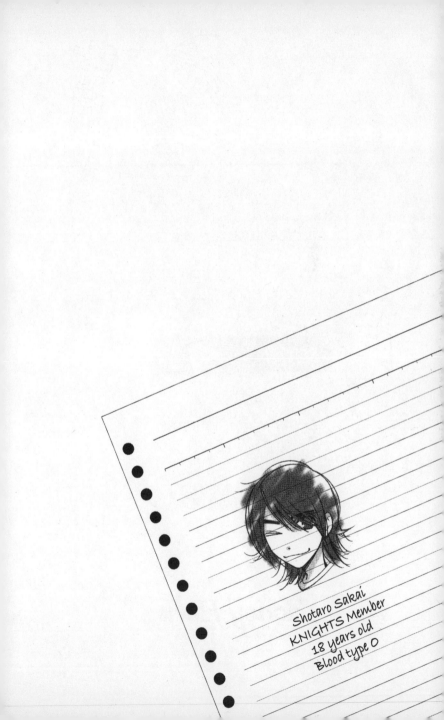

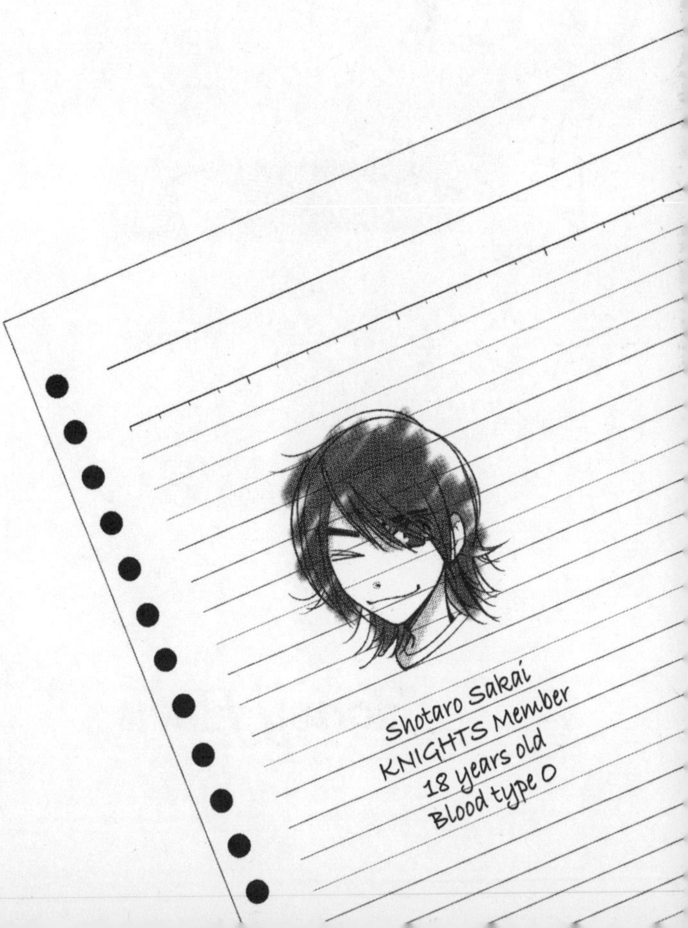
Shotaro Sakai
KNIGHTS Member
18 years old
Blood type O

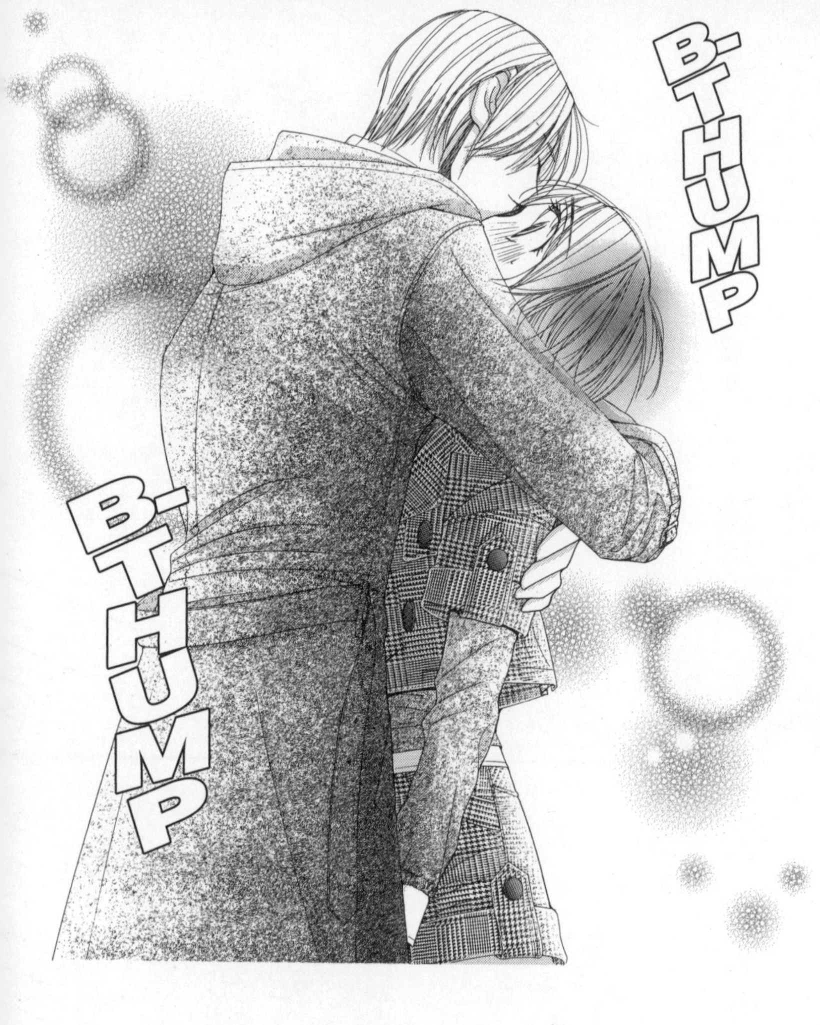
B-THUMP
B-THUMP

Honey Hunt

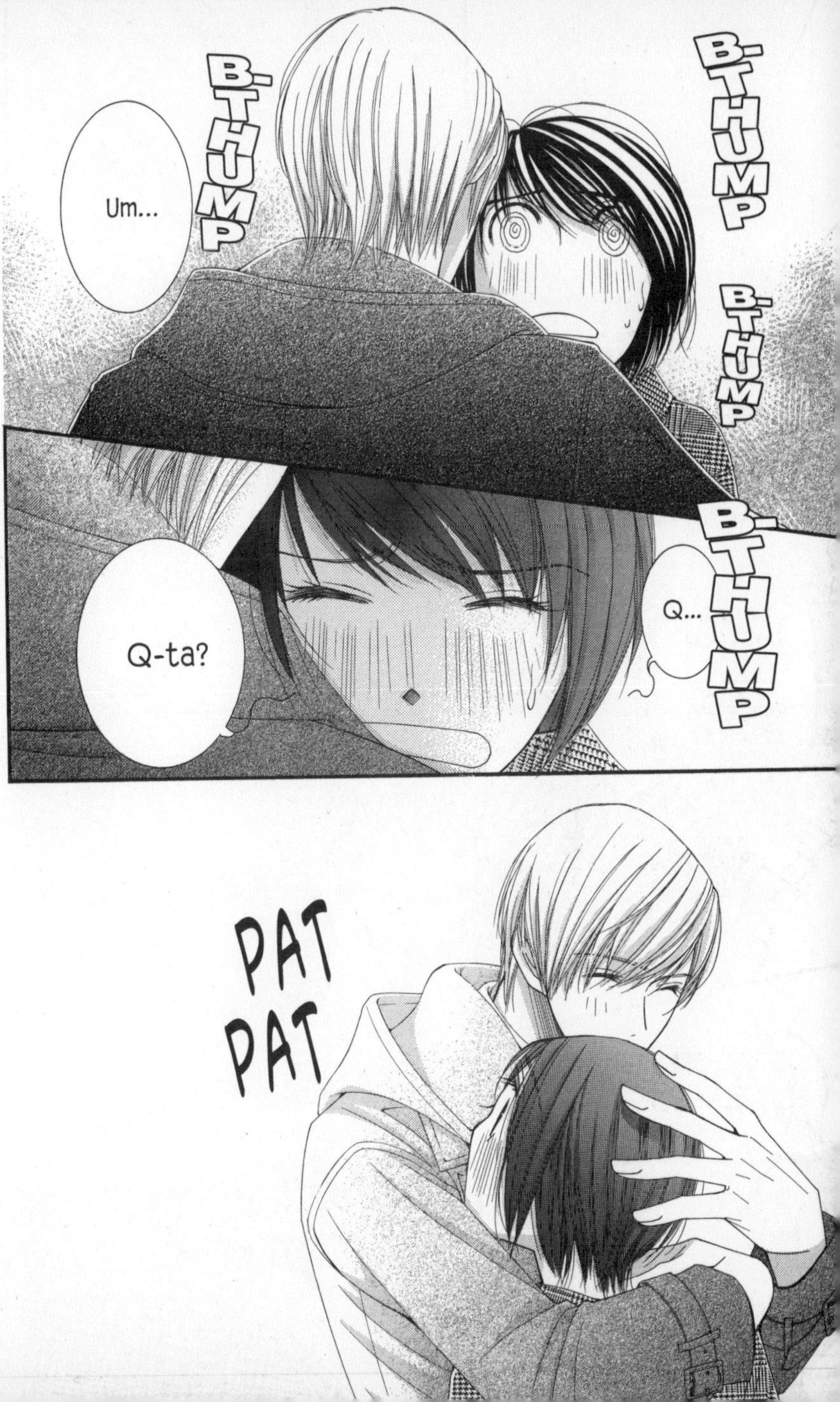
B-THUMP
B-THUMP
Um...
B-THUMP
B-THUMP
Q...
Q-ta?
PAT PAT

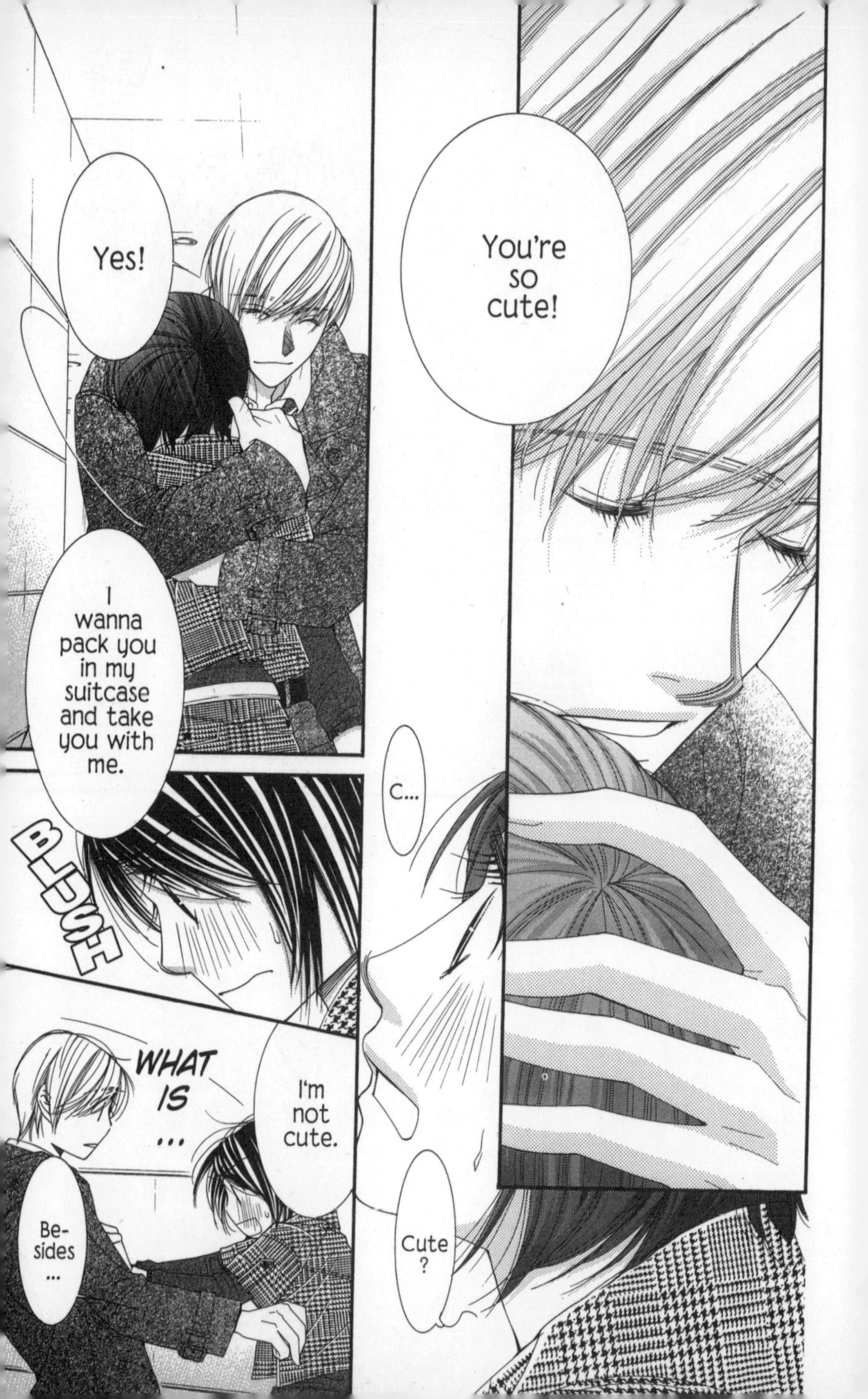
You're so cute!
C...
Cute?
Yes!
I wanna pack you in my suitcase and take you with me.
BLUSH
I'm not cute.
WHAT IS ...
Besides ...

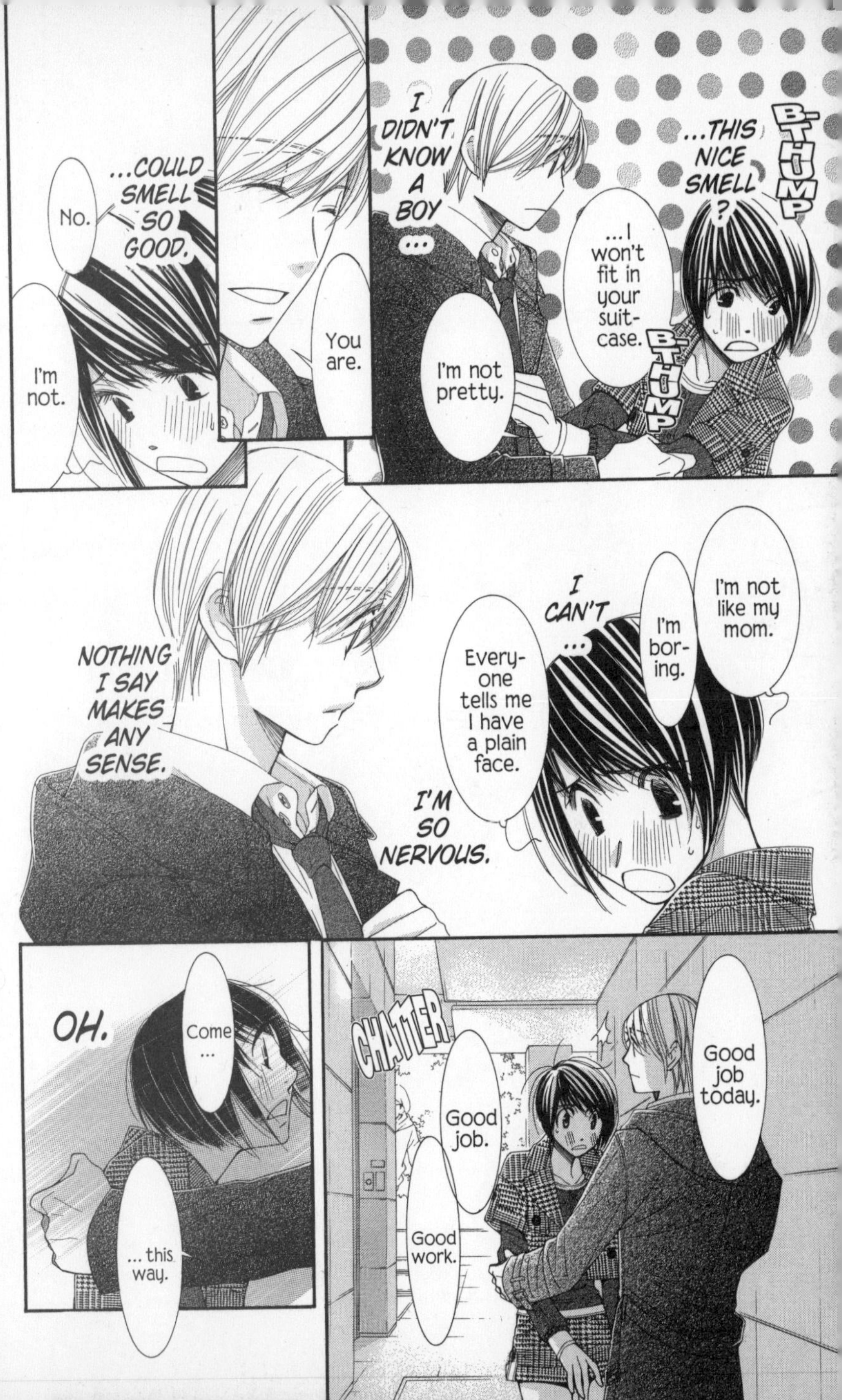
B-THUMP
...THIS NICE SMELL?
...I won't fit in your suitcase.
B-THUMP
I DIDN'T KNOW A BOY...
I'm not pretty.
You are.
...COULD SMELL SO GOOD.
No.
I'm not.
I'm not like my mom.
I'm bor-ing.
I CAN'T...
Every-one tells me I have a plain face.
I'M SO NERVOUS.
NOTHING I SAY MAKES ANY SENSE.
Good job today.
CHATTER
Good job.
Good work.
Come...
OH.
... this way.

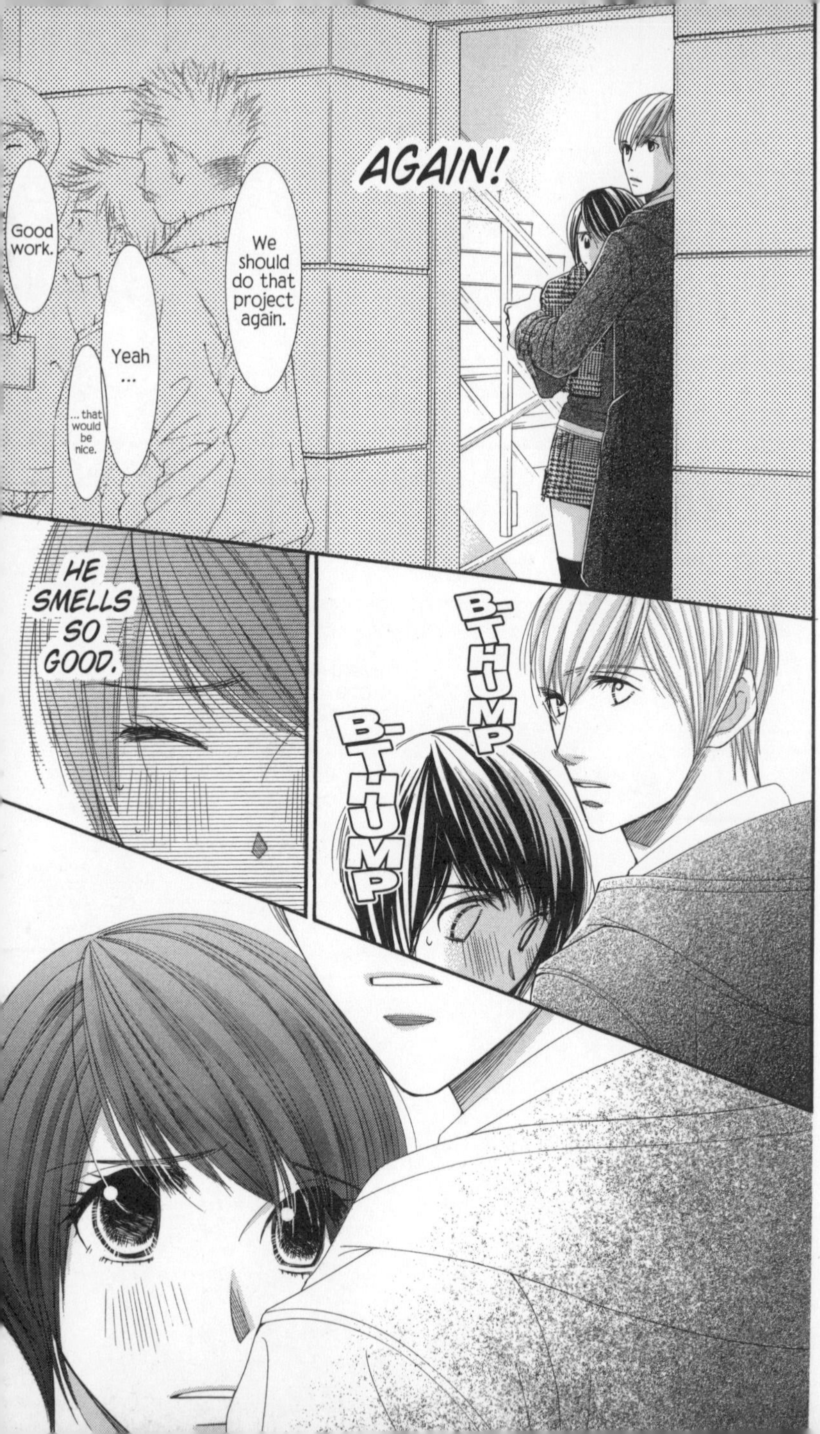

AGAIN!
We should do that project again.
Good work.
Yeah ...
... that would be nice.
B-THUMP
B-THUMP
HE SMELLS SO GOOD.

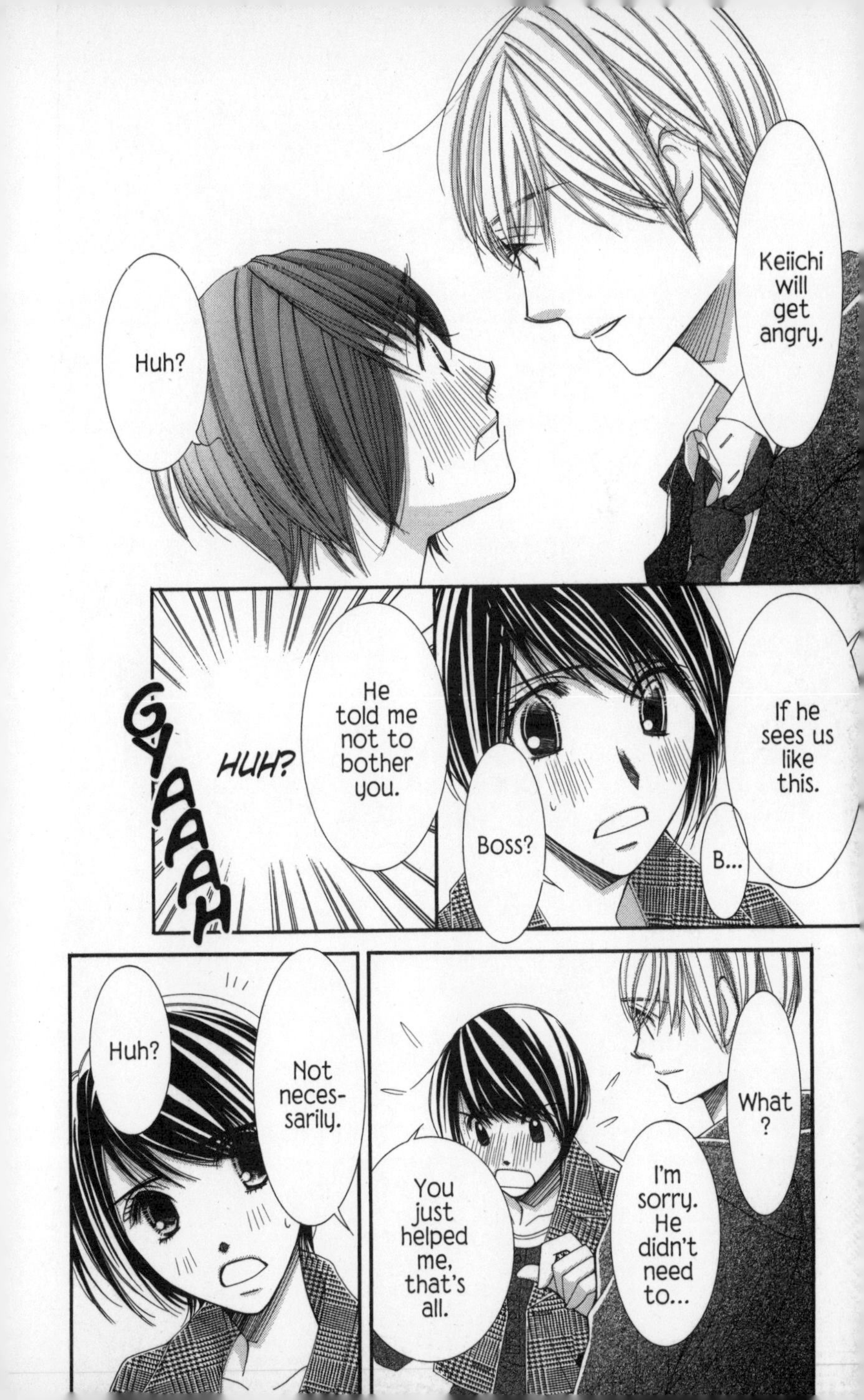
Keiichi will get angry.
Huh?
If he sees us like this.
B...
Boss?
He told me not to bother you.
HUH?
GAAAAH
What?
I'm sorry. He didn't need to...
You just helped me, that's all.
Not neces-sarily.
Huh?

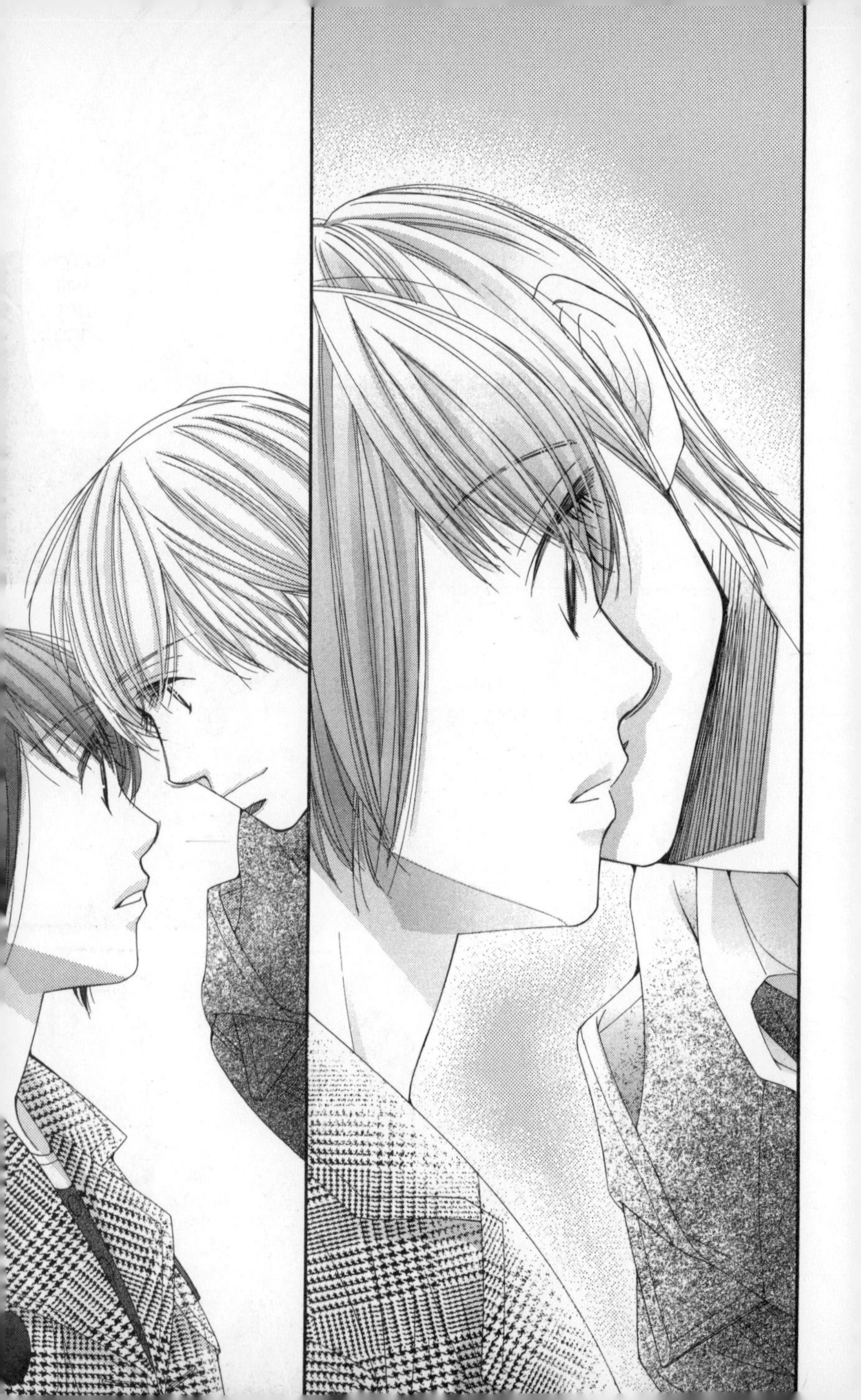

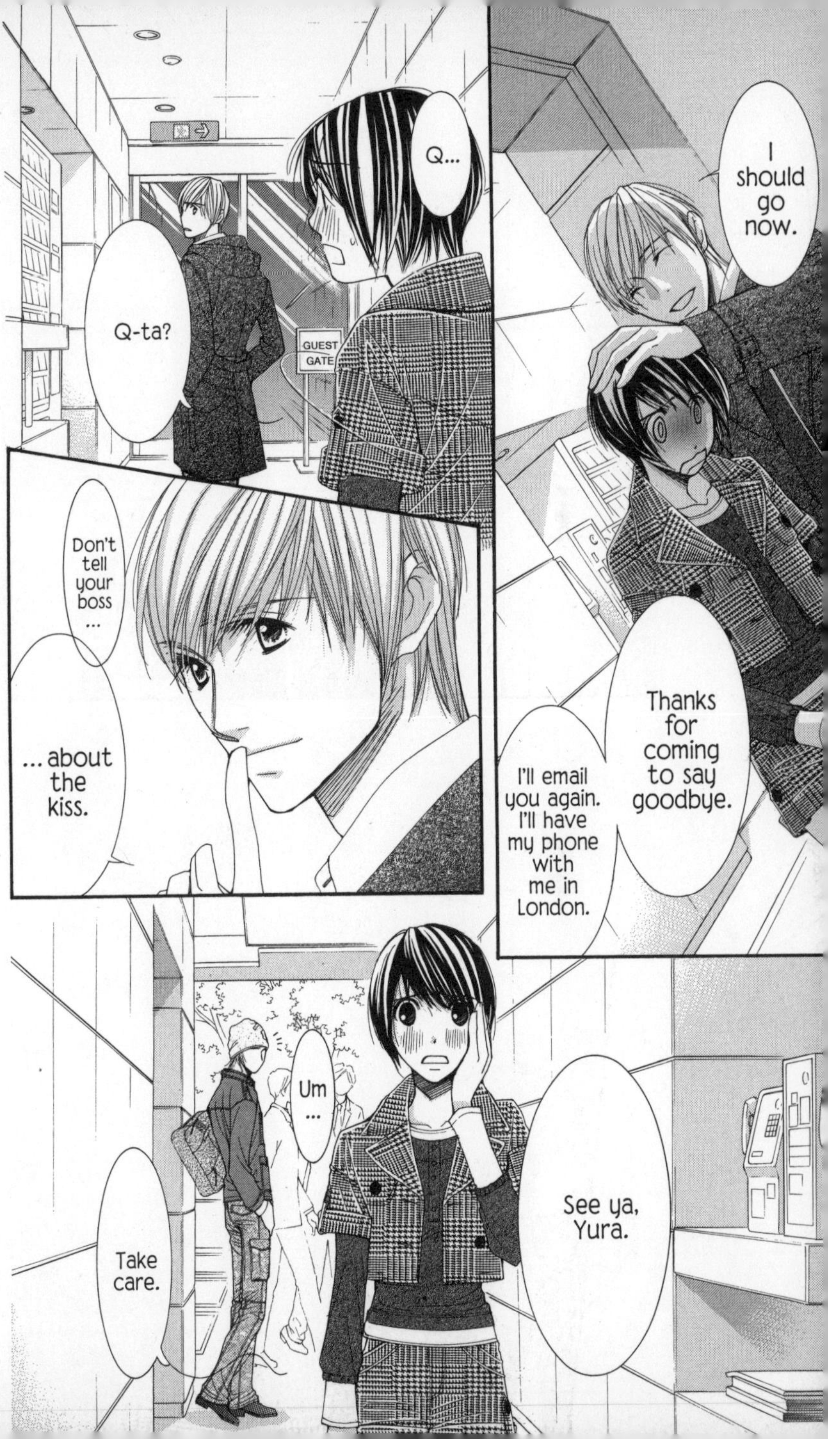
I should go now.
Thanks for coming to say goodbye.
I'll email you again. I'll have my phone with me in London.
Q...
Q-ta?
GUEST GATE
Don't tell your boss ...
... about the kiss.
See ya, Yura.
Um ...
Take care.

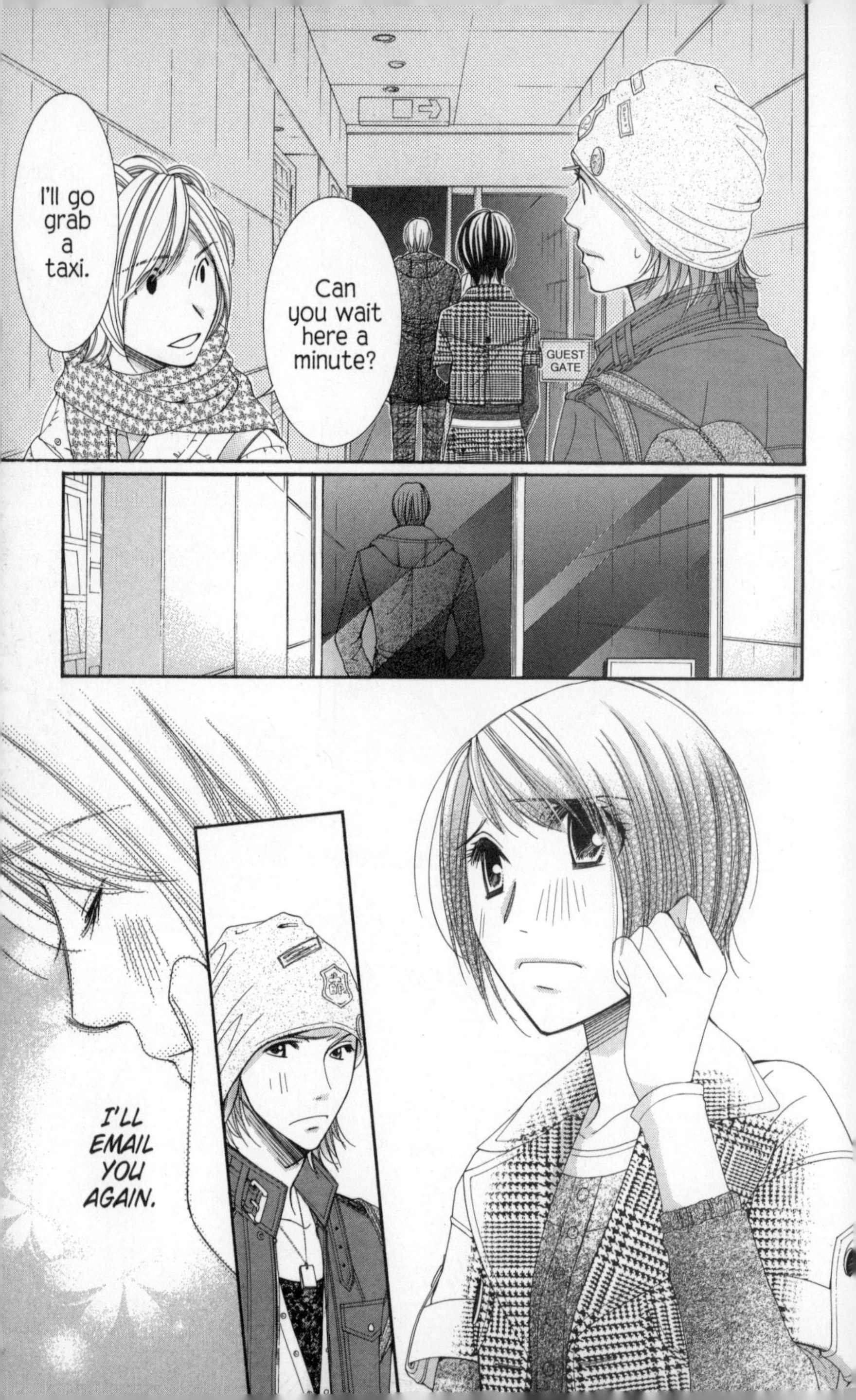
Can you wait here a minute?
I'll go grab a taxi.
GUEST GATE
I'LL EMAIL YOU AGAIN.

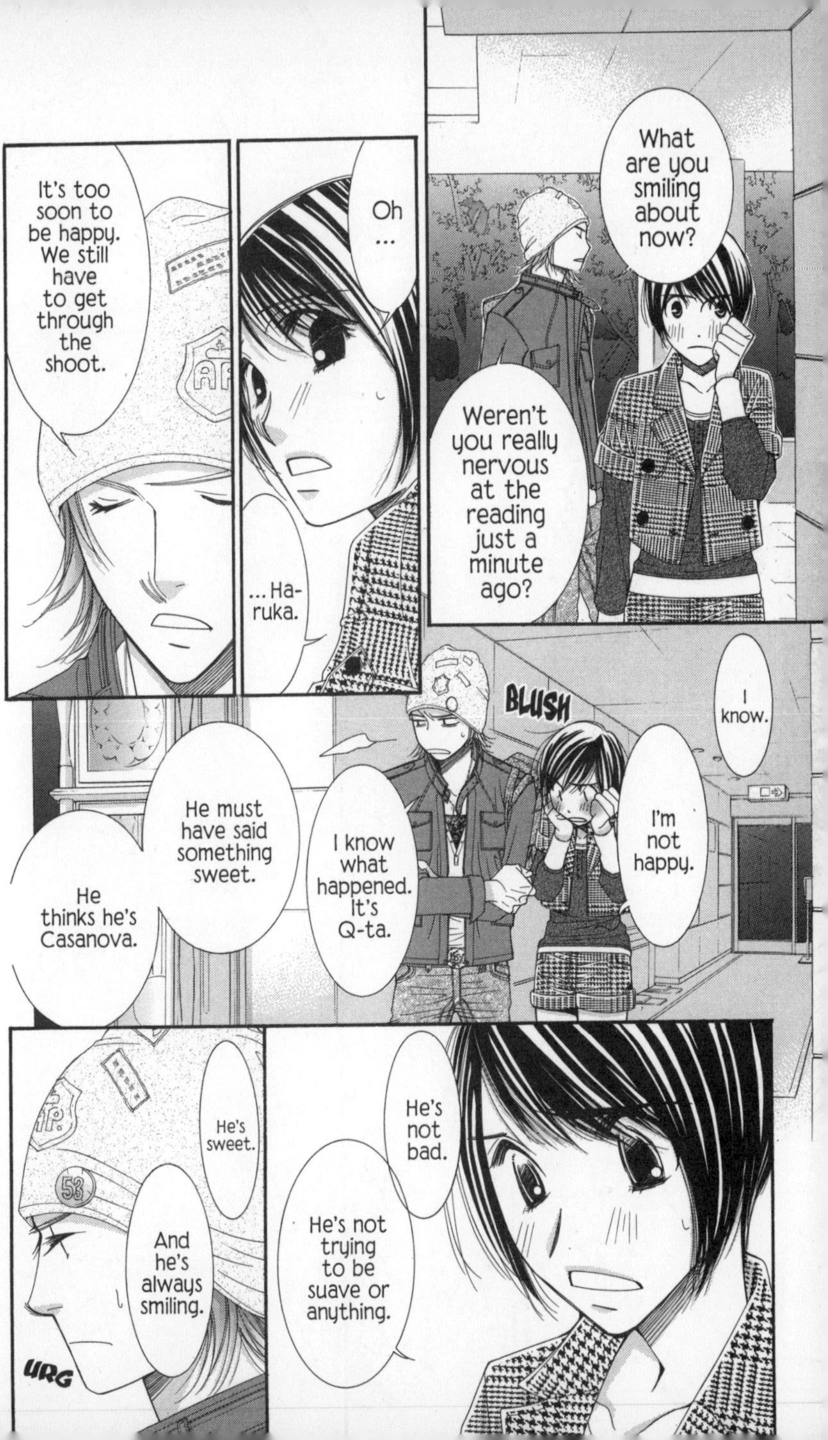
What are you smiling about now?
Weren't you really nervous at the reading just a minute ago?
Oh ...
... Ha-ruka.
It's too soon to be happy. We still have to get through the shoot.
I know.
BLUSH
I'm not happy.
I know what happened. It's Q-ta.
He must have said something sweet.
He thinks he's Casanova.
He's not bad.
He's not trying to be suave or anything.
He's sweet.
And he's always smiling.
URG

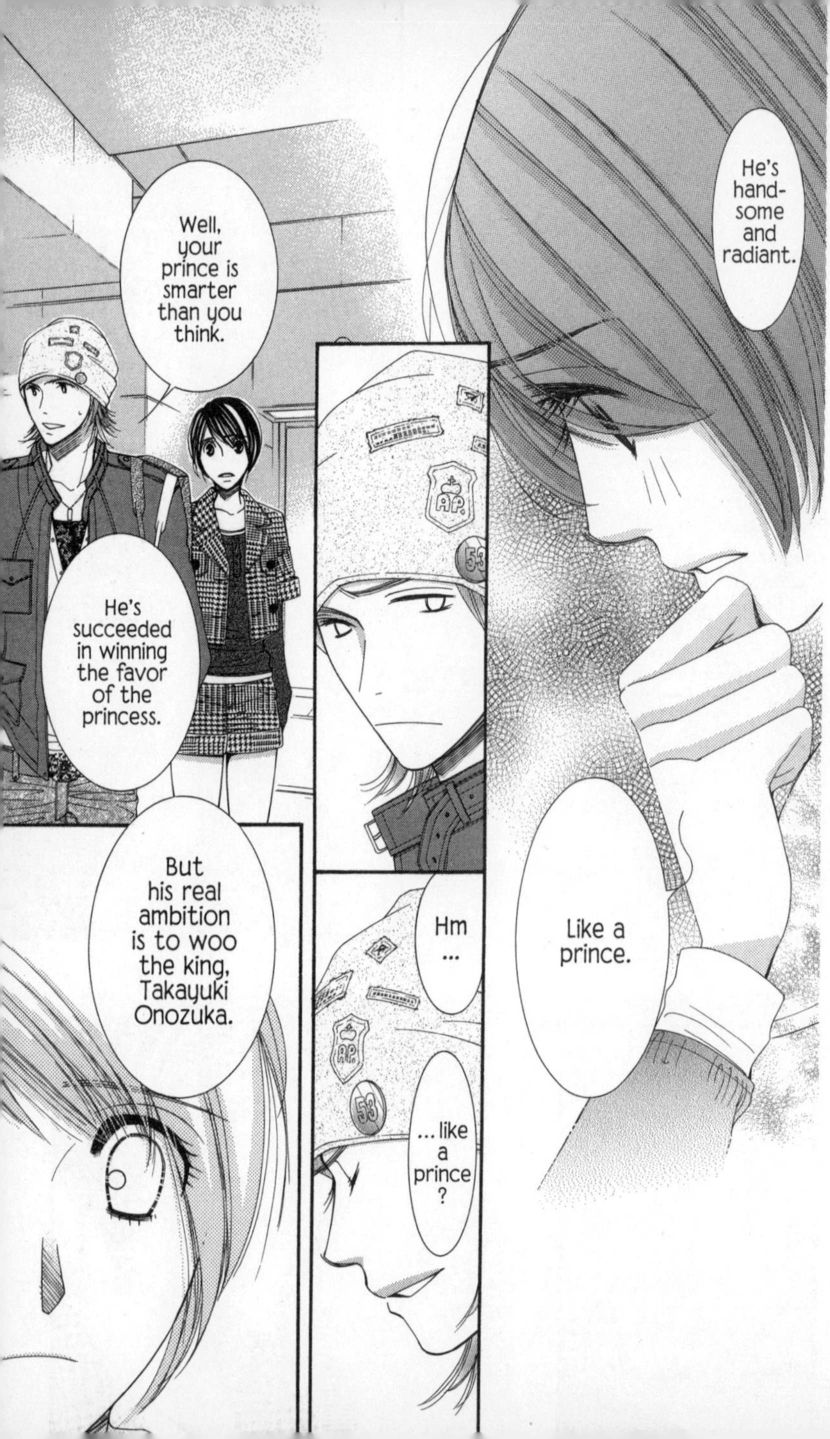
He's hand-some and radiant.
Like a prince.
Well, your prince is smarter than you think.
He's succeeded in winning the favor of the princess.
Hm ...
... like a prince?
But his real ambition is to woo the king, Takayuki Onozuka.

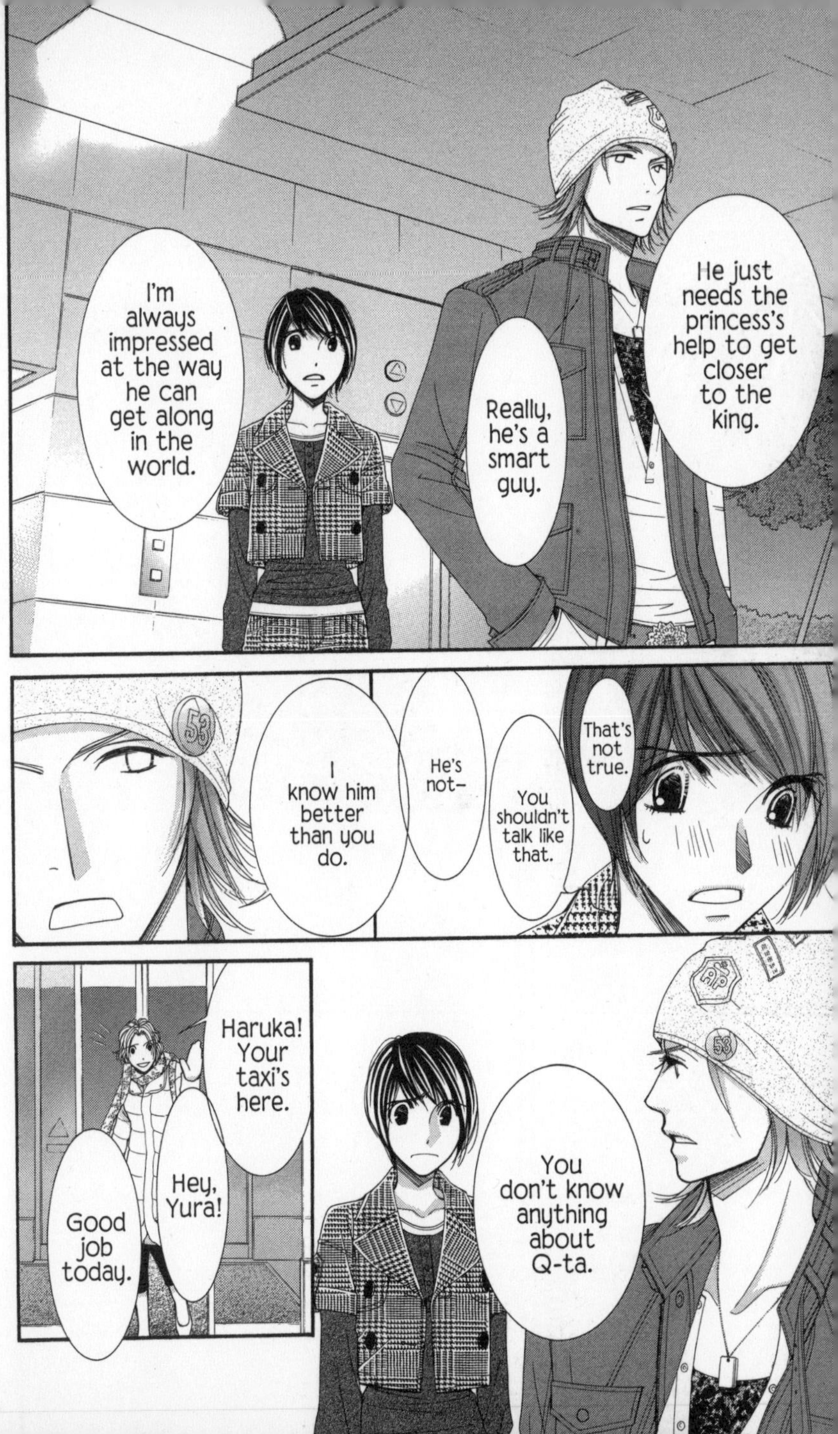
He just needs the princess's help to get closer to the king.
Really, he's a smart guy.
I'm always impressed at the way he can get along in the world.
That's not true.
You shouldn't talk like that.
He's not—
I know him better than you do.
You don't know anything about Q-ta.
Haruka! Your taxi's here.
Hey, Yura!
Good job today.

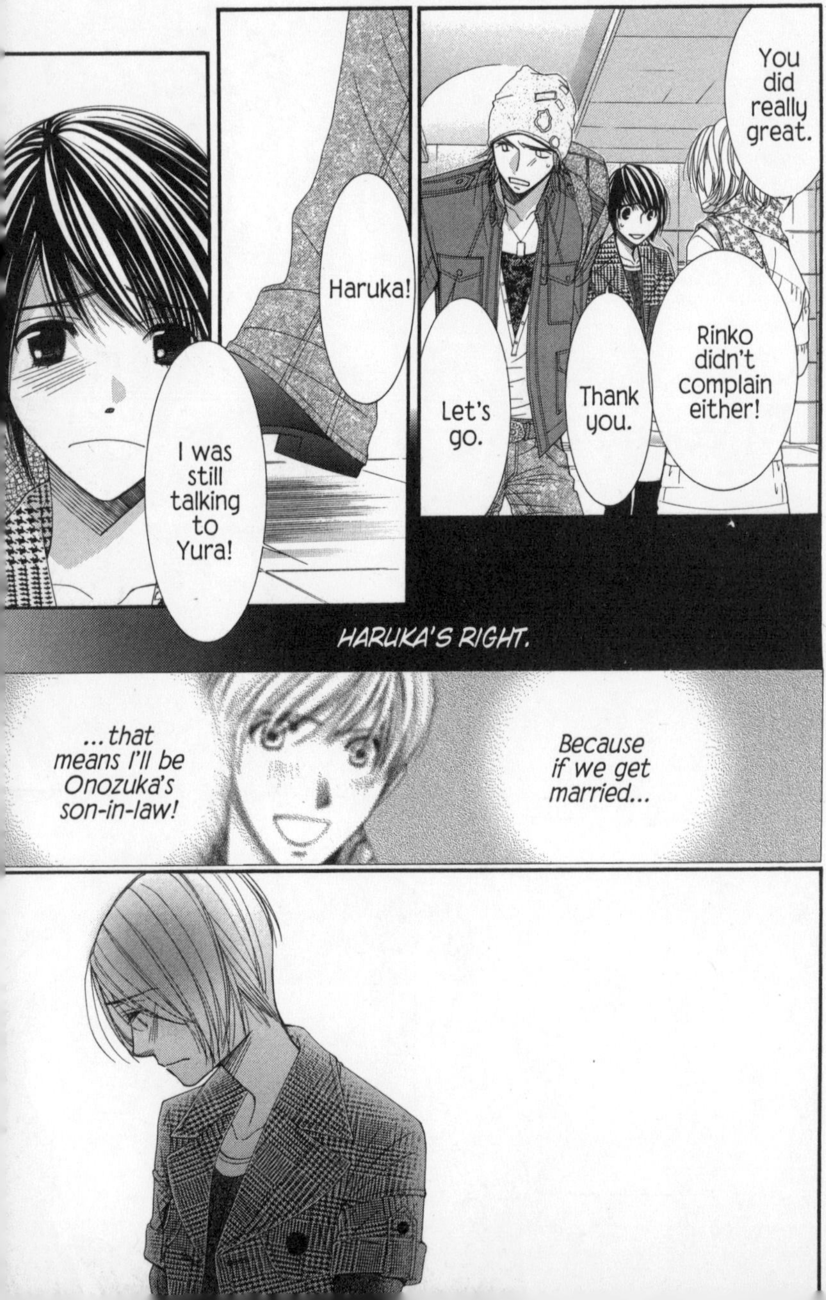
You did really great.
Rinko didn't complain either!
Thank you.
Let's go.
Haruka!
I was still talking to Yura!
HARUKA'S RIGHT.
Because if we get married...
...that means I'll be Onozuka's son-in-law!

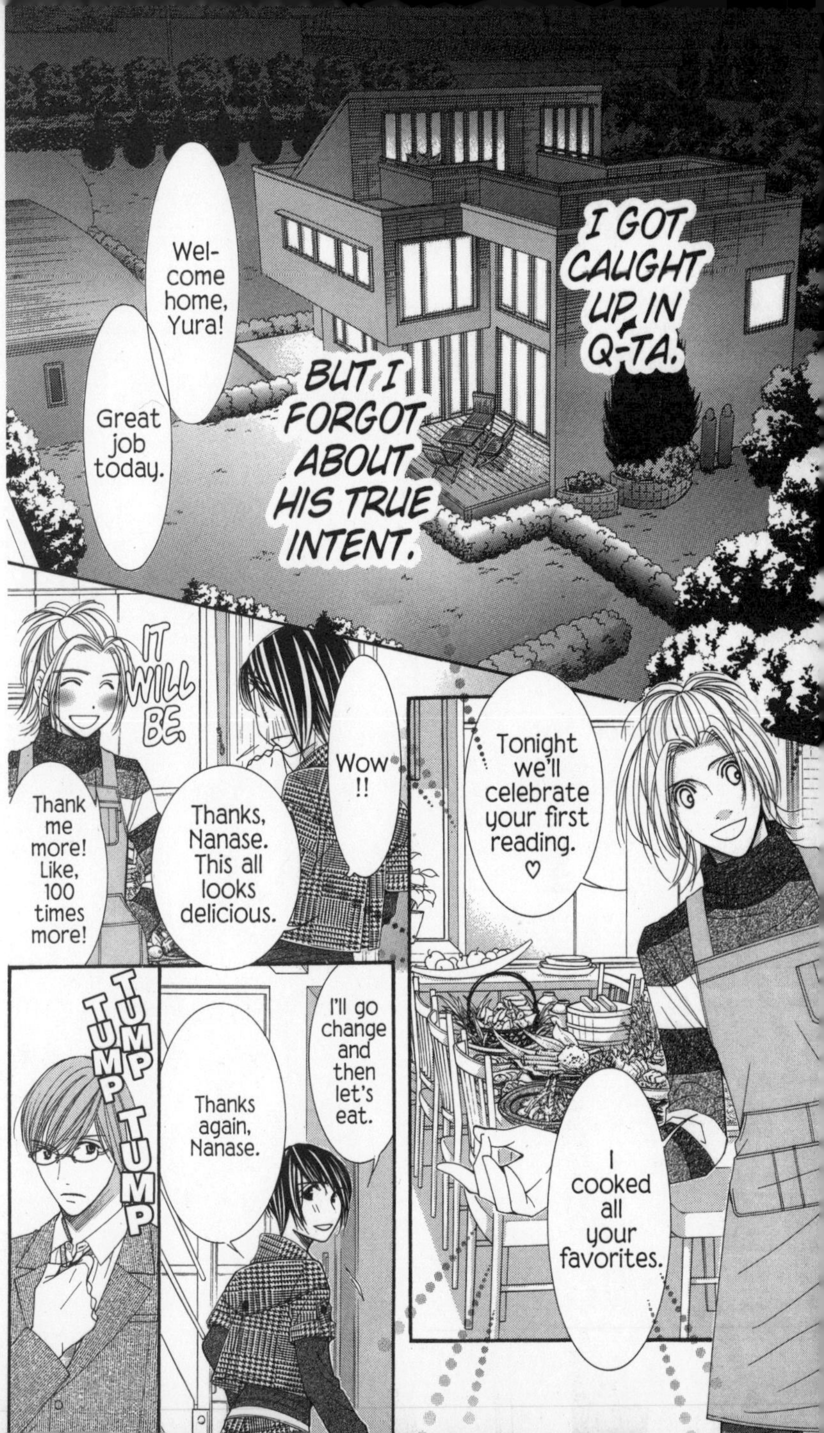
I GOT CAUGHT UP IN Q-TA.
BUT I FORGOT ABOUT HIS TRUE INTENT.
Wel-come home, Yura!
Great job today.
Tonight we'll celebrate your first reading. ♡
I cooked all your favorites.
Wow!!
Thanks, Nanase. This all looks delicious.
IT WILL BE.
Thank me more! Like, 100 times more!
I'll go change and then let's eat.
Thanks again, Nanase.
TUMP TUMP
TUMP TUMP

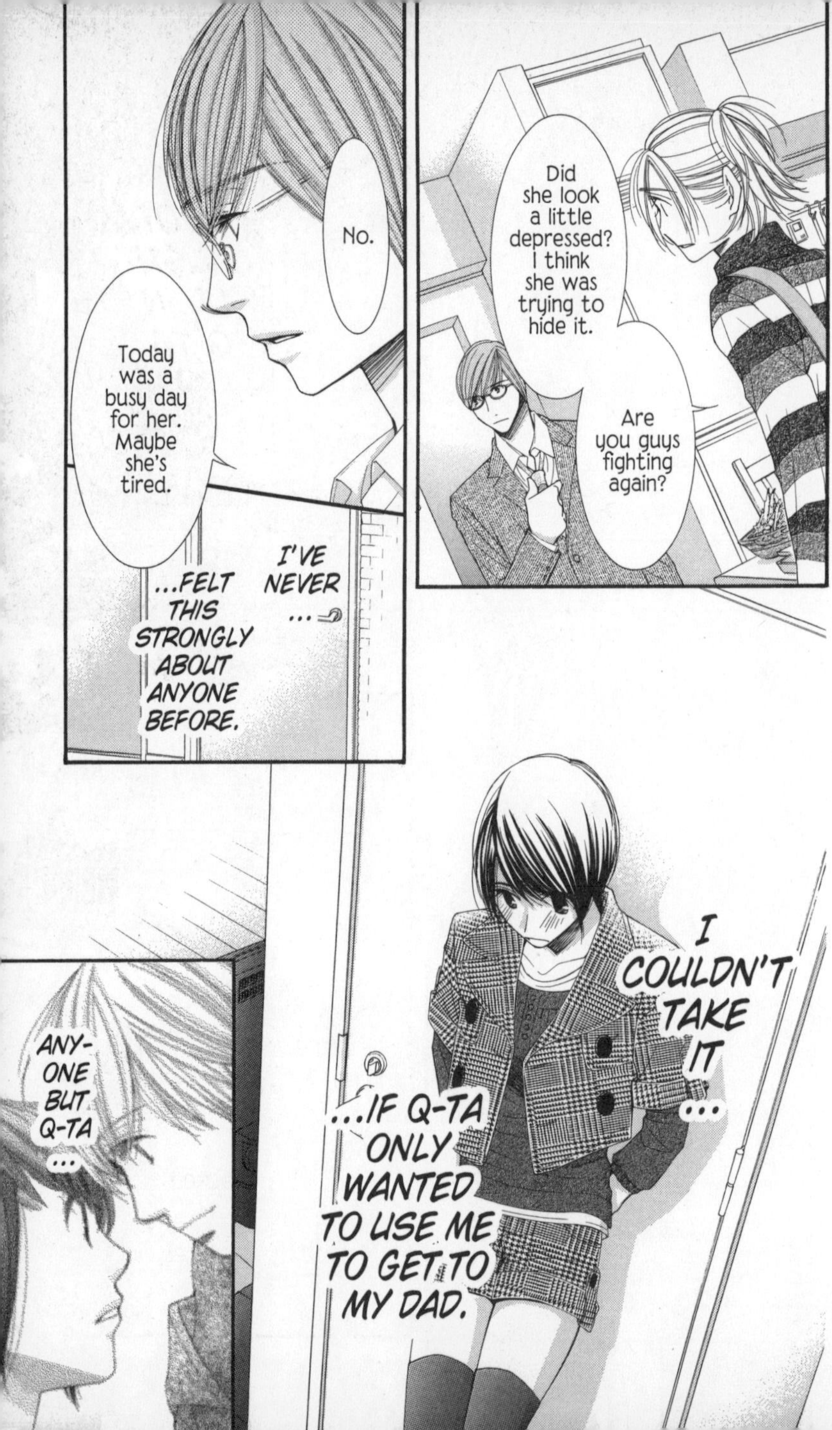
Did she look a little depressed? I think she was trying to hide it.
Are you guys fighting again?
No.
Today was a busy day for her. Maybe she's tired.
I'VE NEVER ...
...FELT THIS STRONGLY ABOUT ANYONE BEFORE.
I COULDN'T TAKE IT ...
...IF Q-TA ONLY WANTED TO USE ME TO GET TO MY DAD.
ANY-ONE BUT Q-TA ...

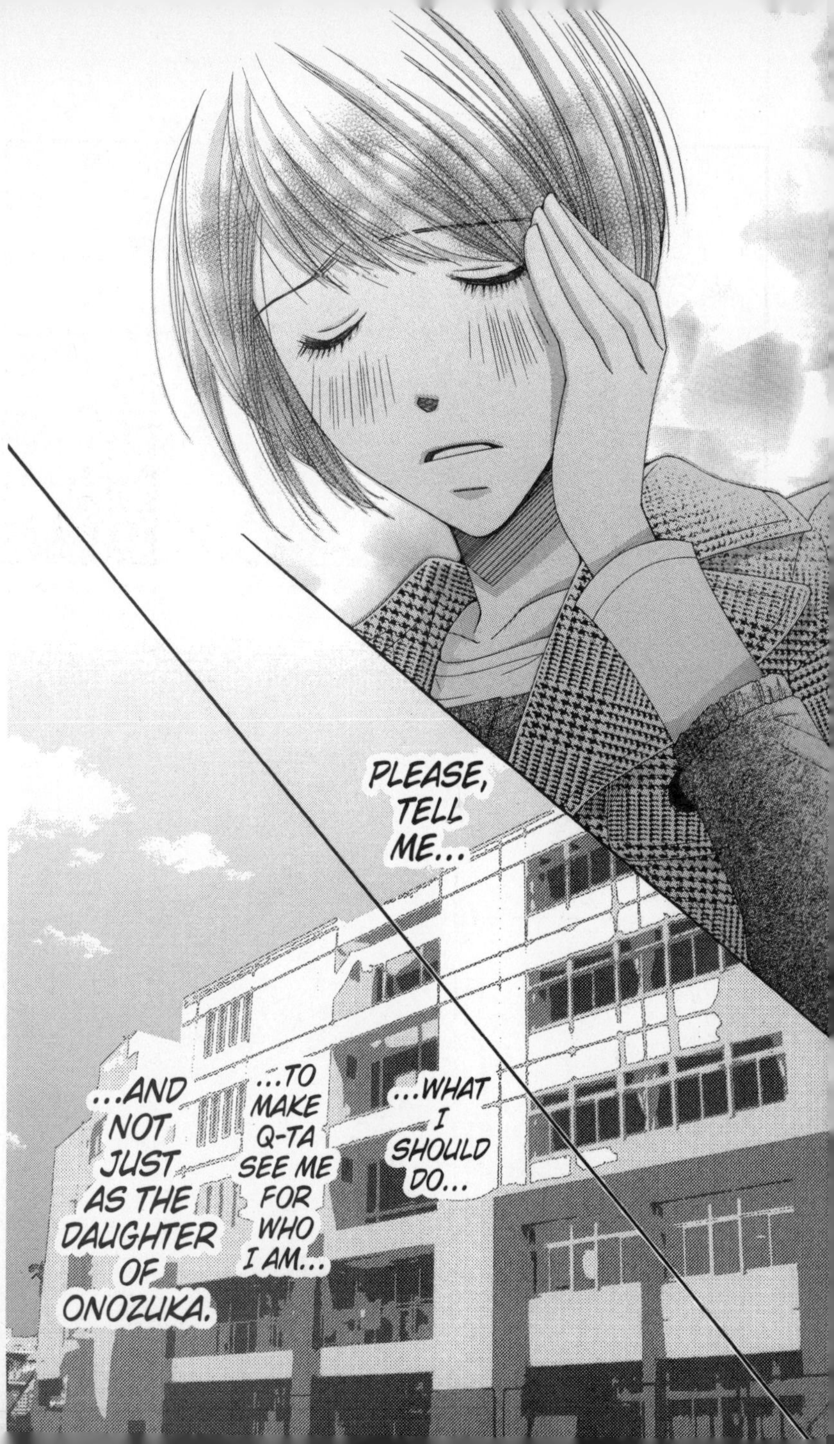
PLEASE, TELL ME...
...WHAT I SHOULD DO...
...TO MAKE Q-TA SEE ME FOR WHO I AM...
...AND NOT JUST AS THE DAUGHTER OF ONOZUKA.

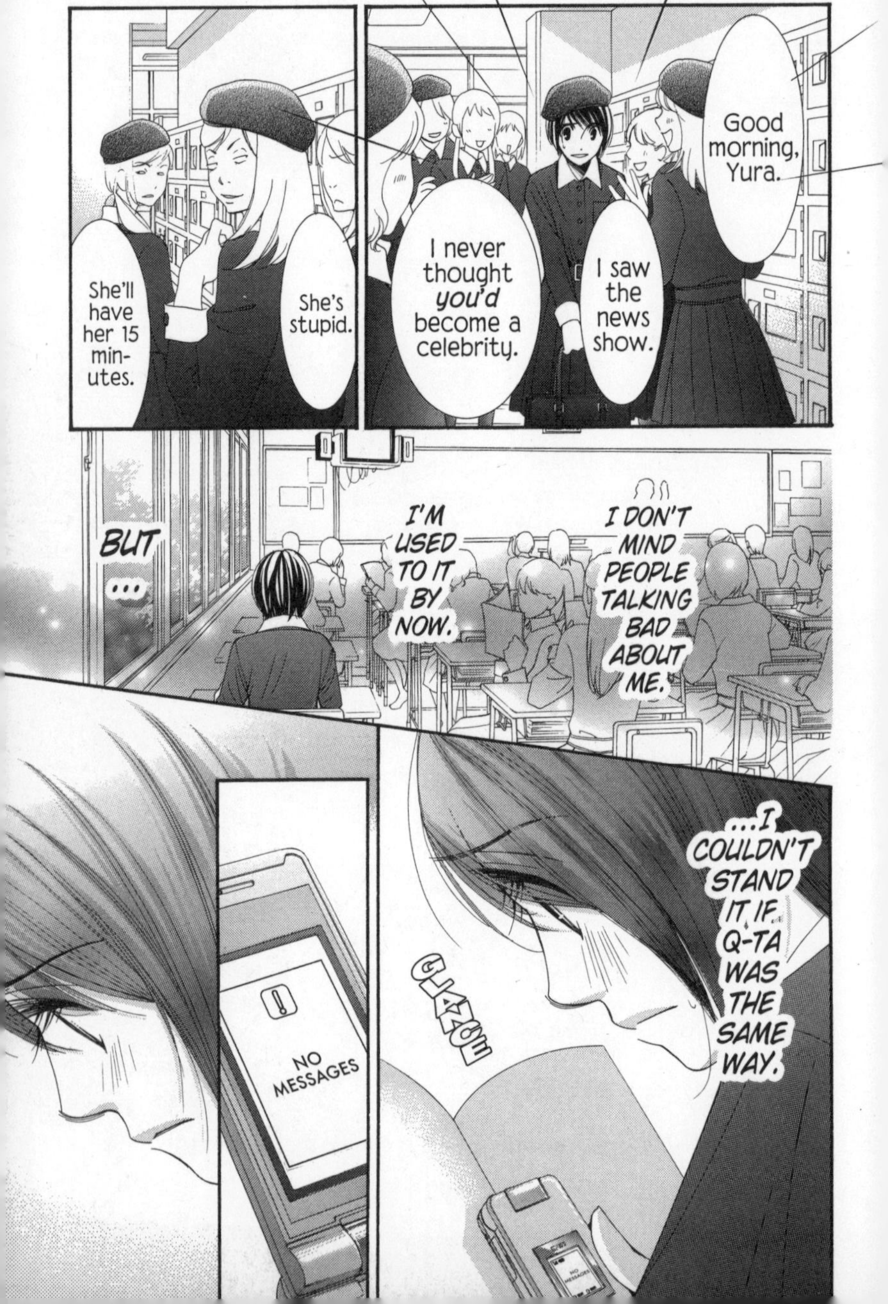
Good morning, Yura.
I saw the news show.
I never thought you'd become a celebrity.
She's stupid.
She'll have her 15 min-utes.
I DON'T MIND PEOPLE TALKING BAD ABOUT ME.
I'M USED TO IT BY NOW.
BUT...
...I COULDN'T STAND IT IF Q-TA WAS THE SAME WAY.
GLANCE
NO MESSAGES

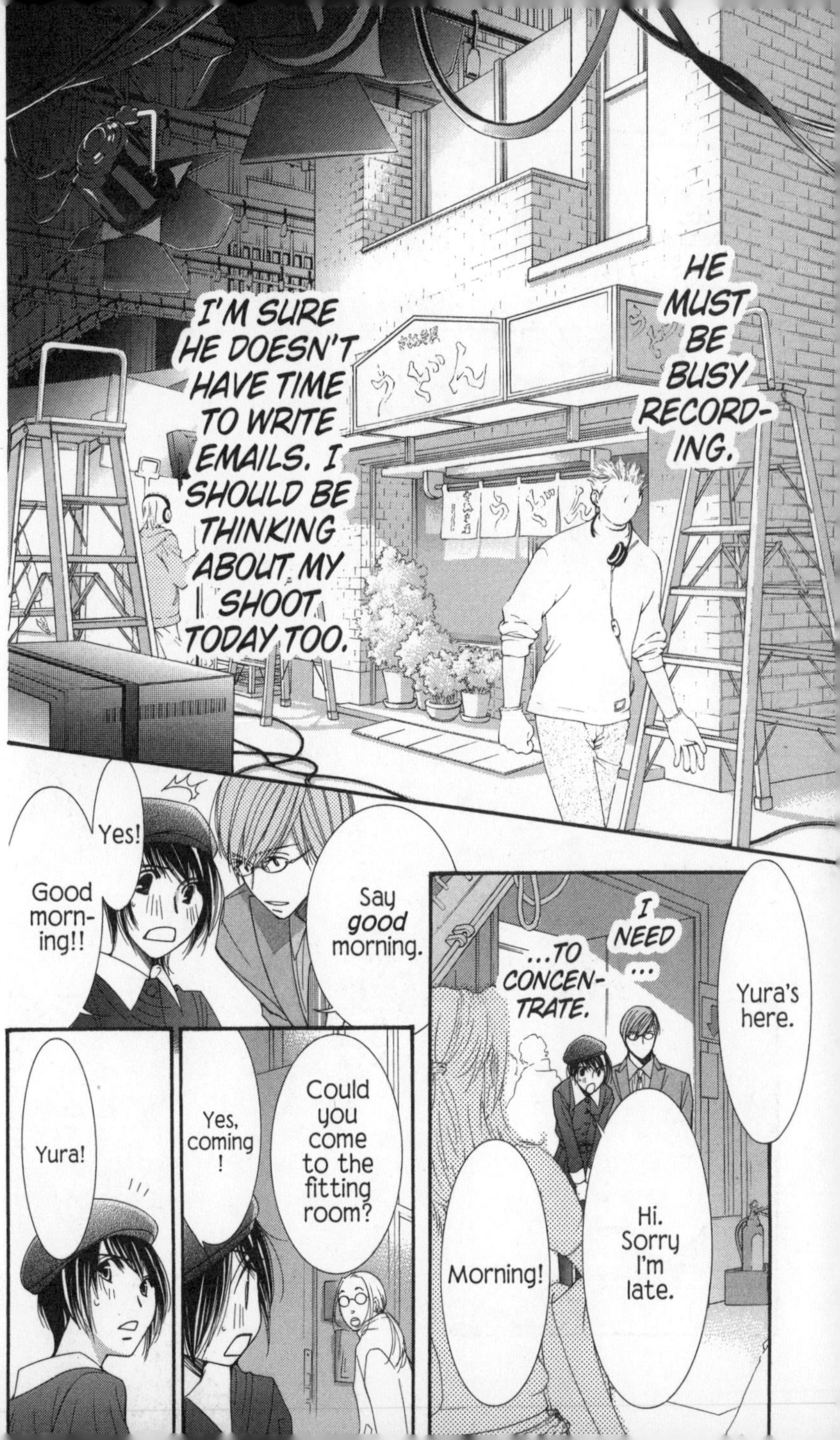
HE MUST BE BUSY RECORDING.
I'M SURE HE DOESN'T HAVE TIME TO WRITE EMAILS. I SHOULD BE THINKING ABOUT MY SHOOT TODAY TOO.
Yura's here.
I NEED ...
...TO CONCENTRATE.
Hi. Sorry I'm late.
Morning!
Say *good* morning.
Yes!
Good morning!!
Could you come to the fitting room?
Yes, coming!
Yura!

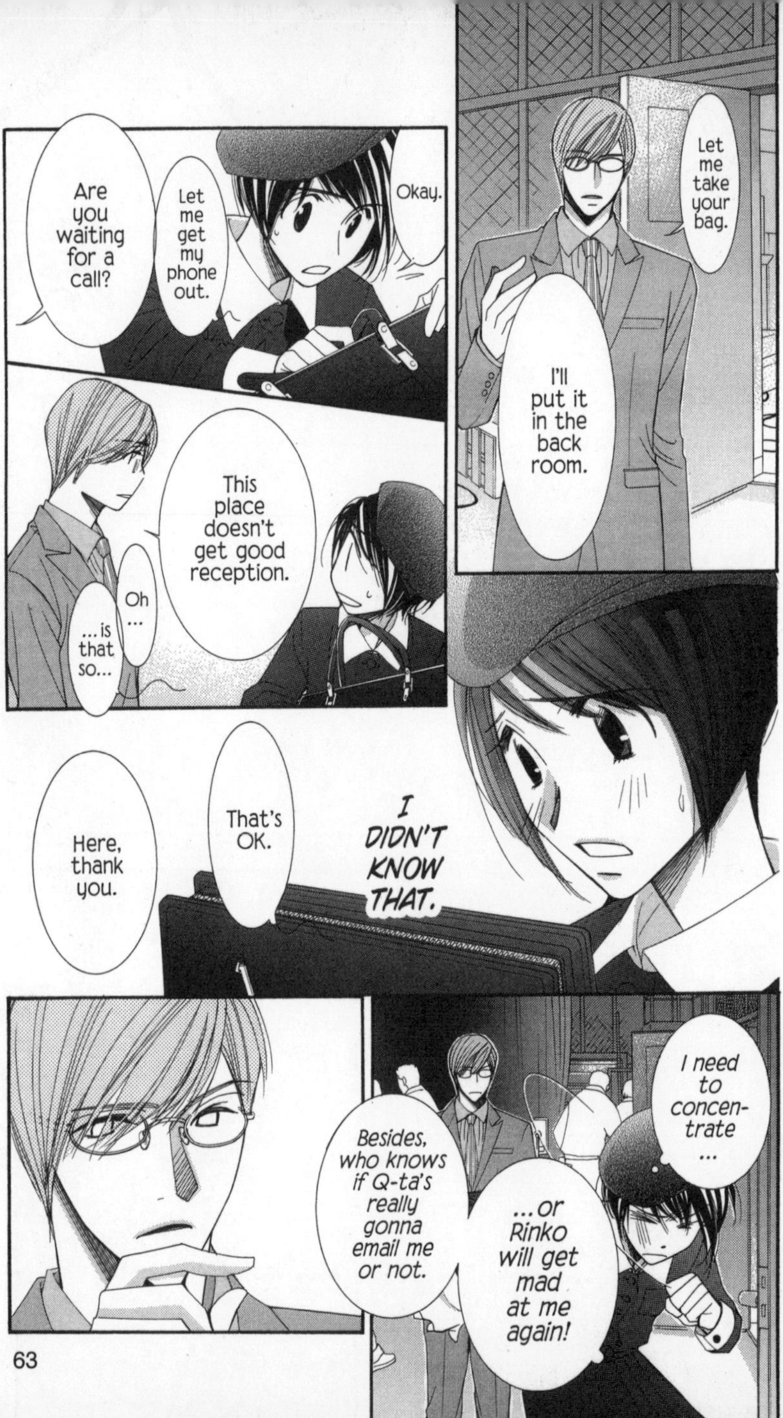
Let me take your bag.
I'll put it in the back room.
Okay.
Let me get my phone out.
Are you waiting for a call?
This place doesn't get good reception.
Oh...
...is that so...
I DIDN'T KNOW THAT.
That's OK.
Here, thank you.
I need to concentrate...
...or Rinko will get mad at me again!
Besides, who knows if Q-ta's really gonna email me or not.

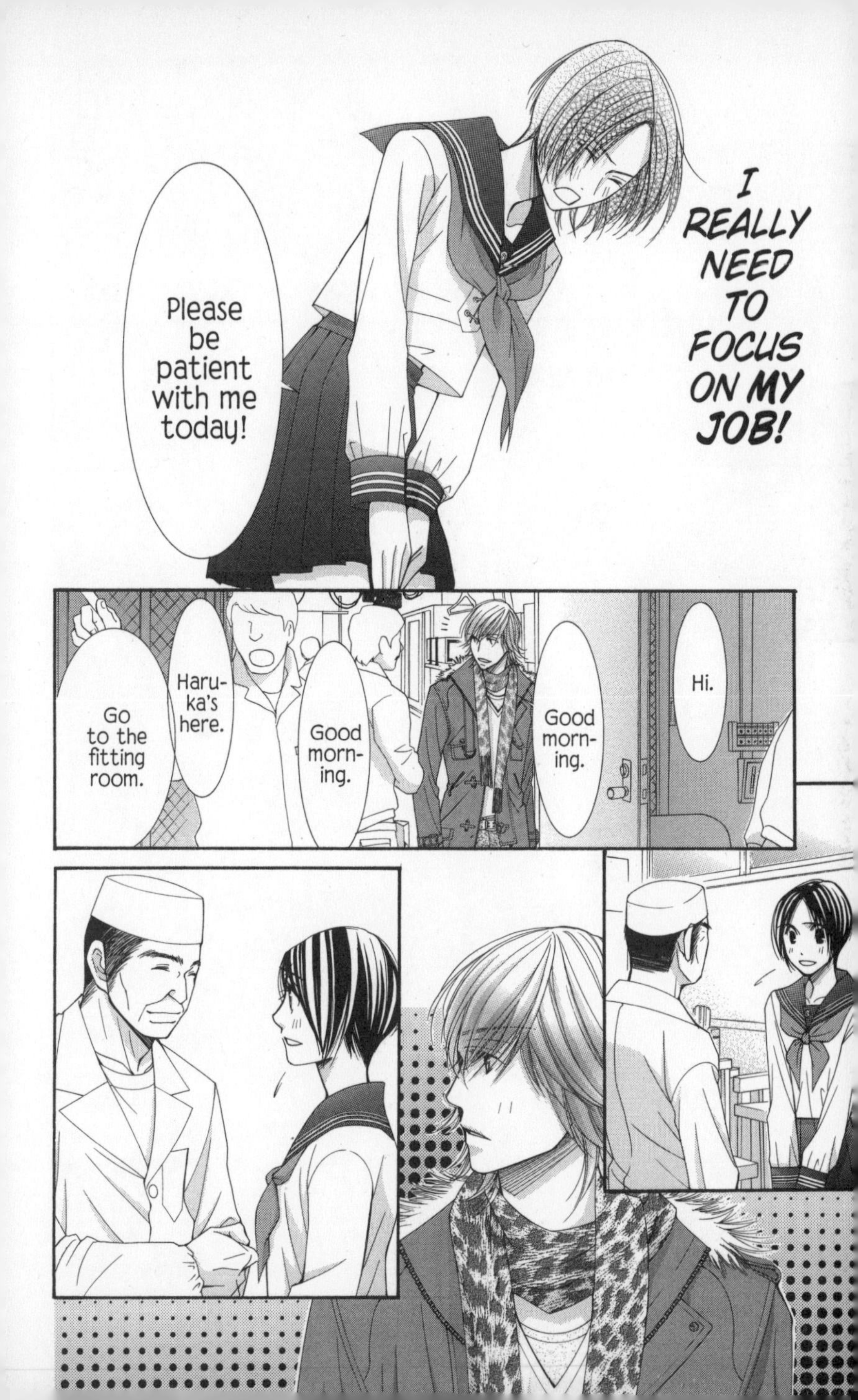
I REALLY NEED TO FOCUS ON MY JOB!
Please be patient with me today!
Hi.
Good morning.
Good morning.
Haru-ka's here.
Go to the fitting room.

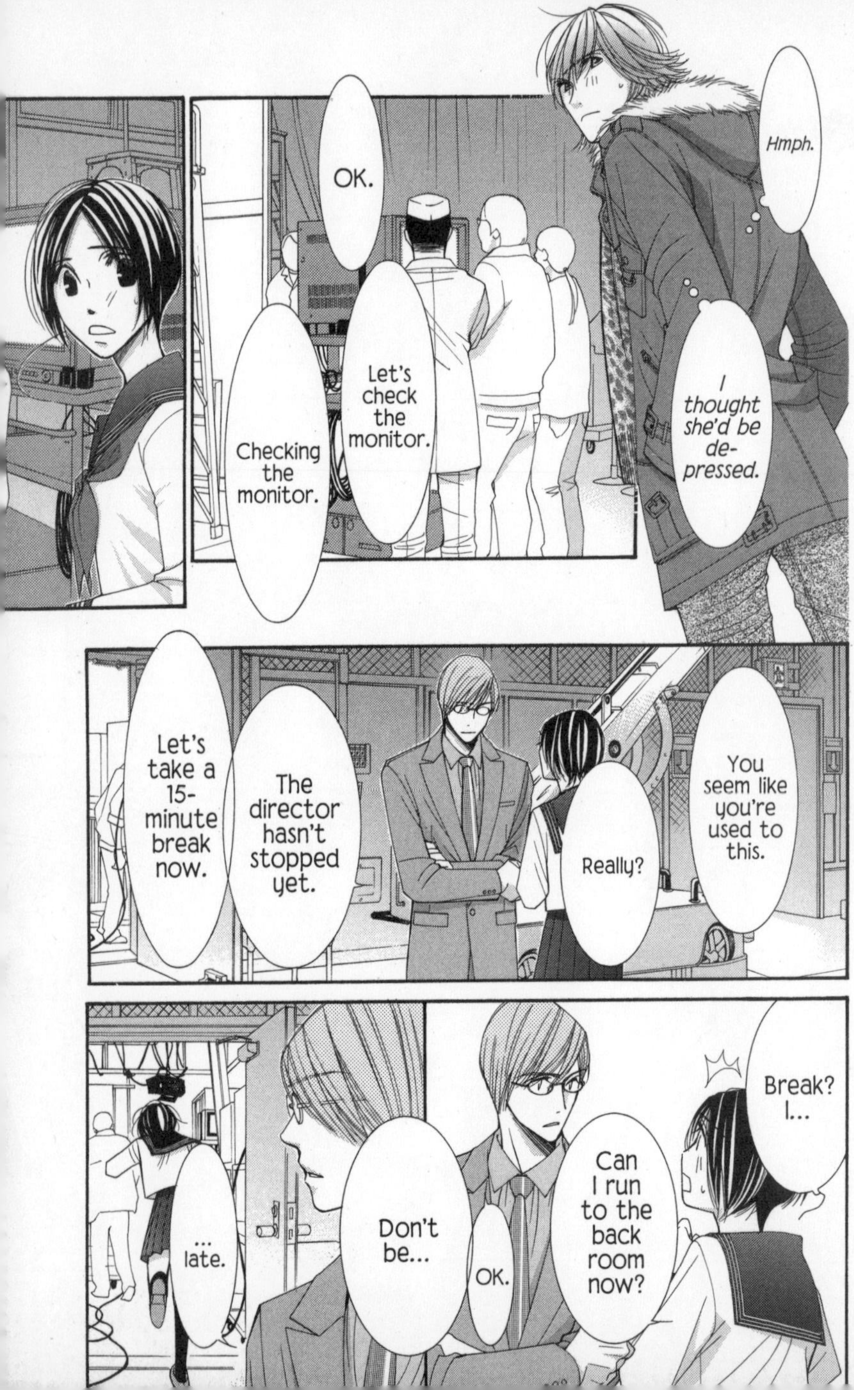
Hmph.
I thought she'd be de-pressed.
OK.
Let's check the monitor.
Checking the monitor.
You seem like you're used to this.
Really?
The director hasn't stopped yet.
Let's take a 15-minute break now.
Break? I...
Can I run to the back room now?
OK.
Don't be...
...late.

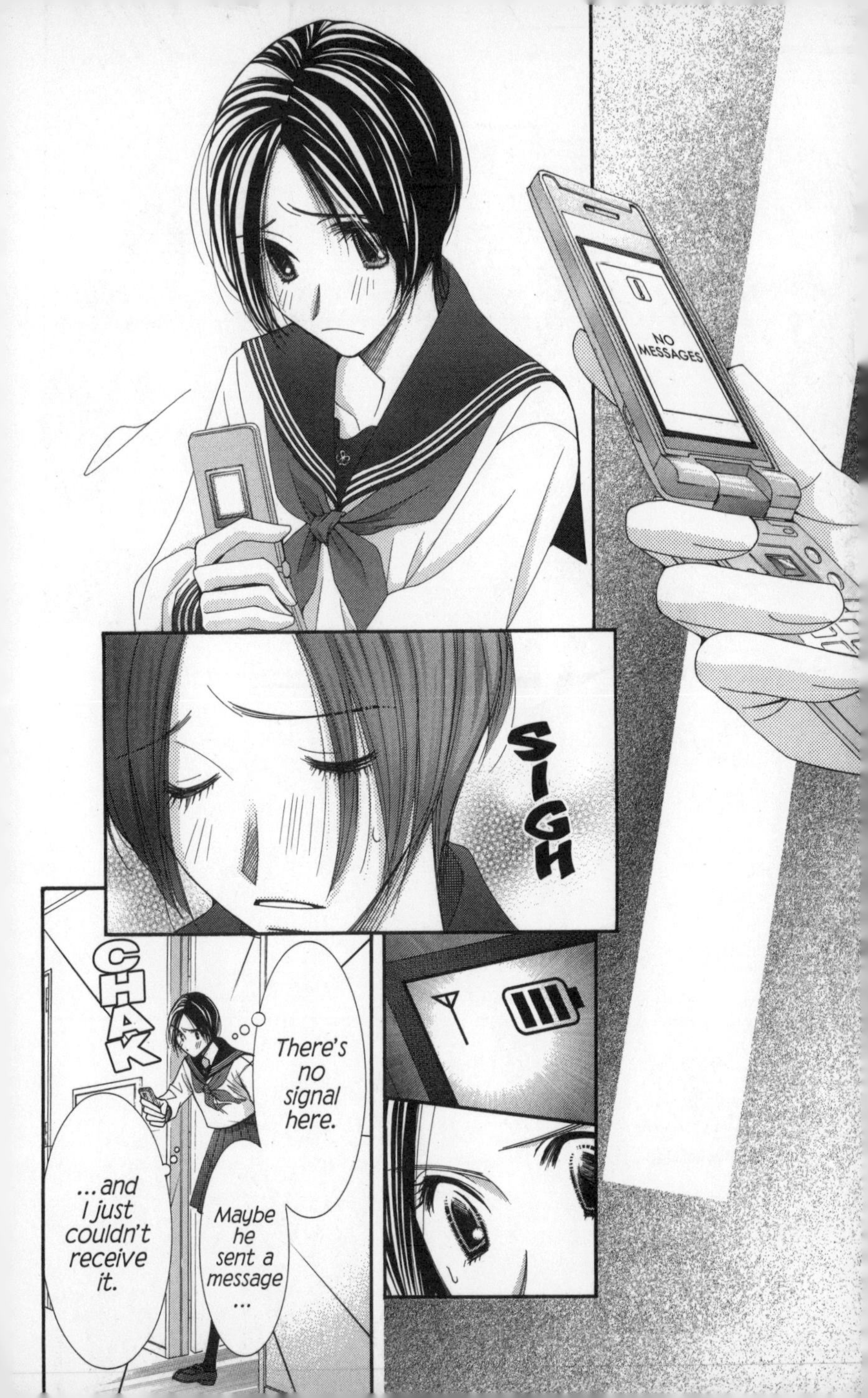
NO MESSAGES
SIGH
There's no signal here.
CHAK
Maybe he sent a message...
...and I just couldn't receive it.

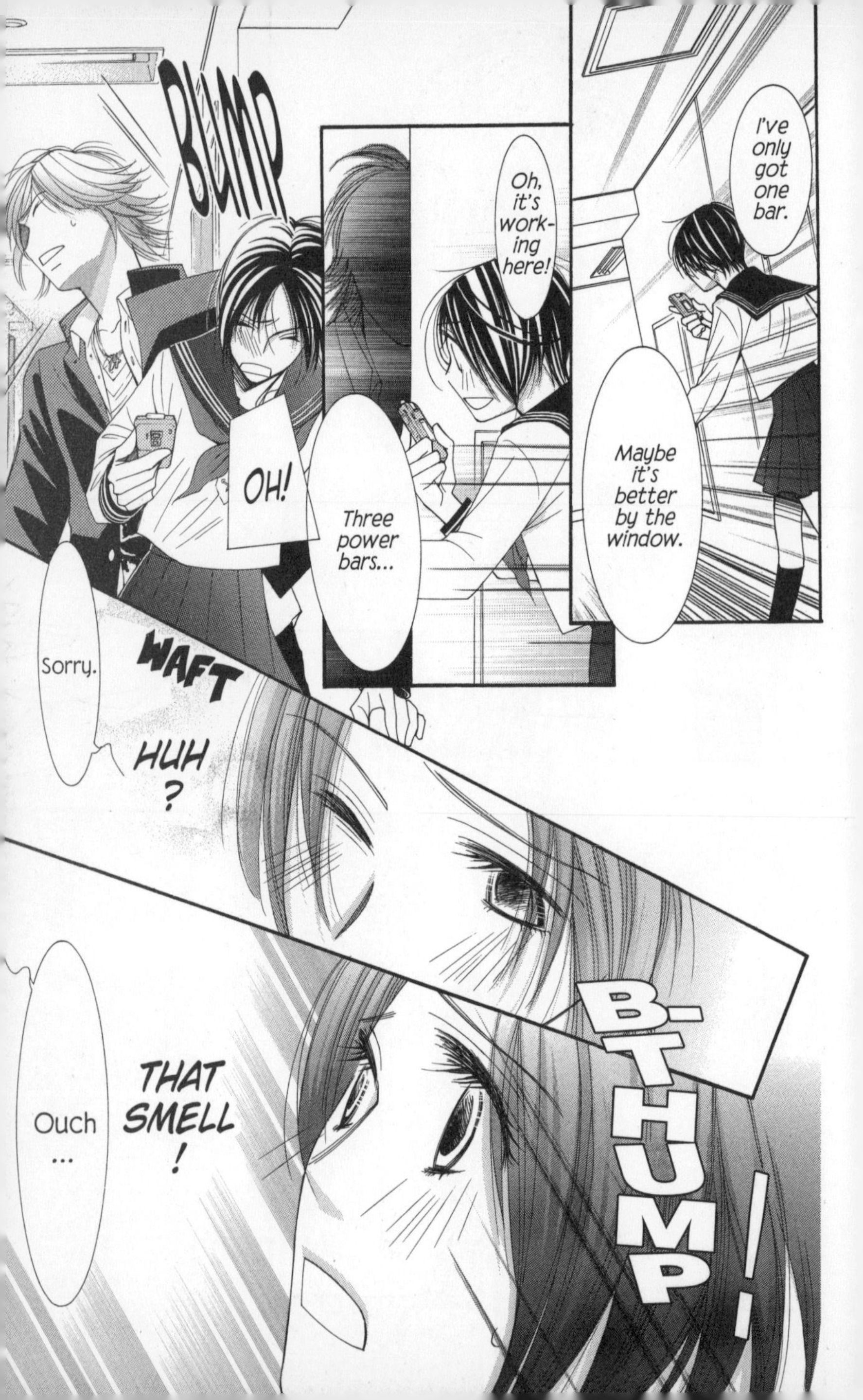
I've only got one bar.
Maybe it's better by the window.
Oh, it's working here!
Three power bars...
BUMP
OH!
Sorry.
WAFT
HUH?
B-THUMP!!
THAT SMELL!
Ouch...

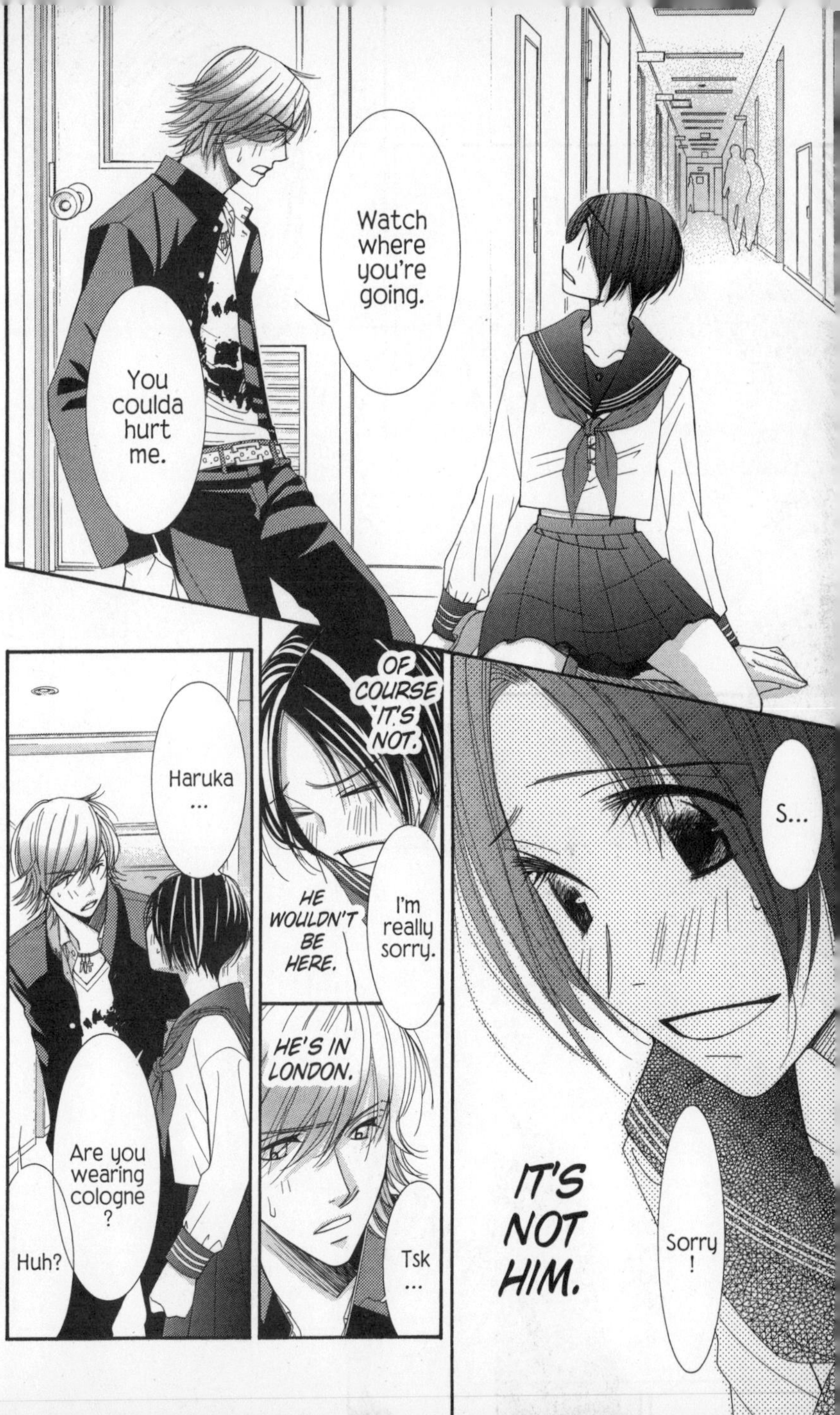
Watch where you're going.
You coulda hurt me.
S...
Sorry!
IT'S NOT HIM.
OF COURSE IT'S NOT.
I'm really sorry.
HE WOULDN'T BE HERE.
HE'S IN LONDON.
Tsk ...
Haruka ...
Are you wearing cologne?
Huh?

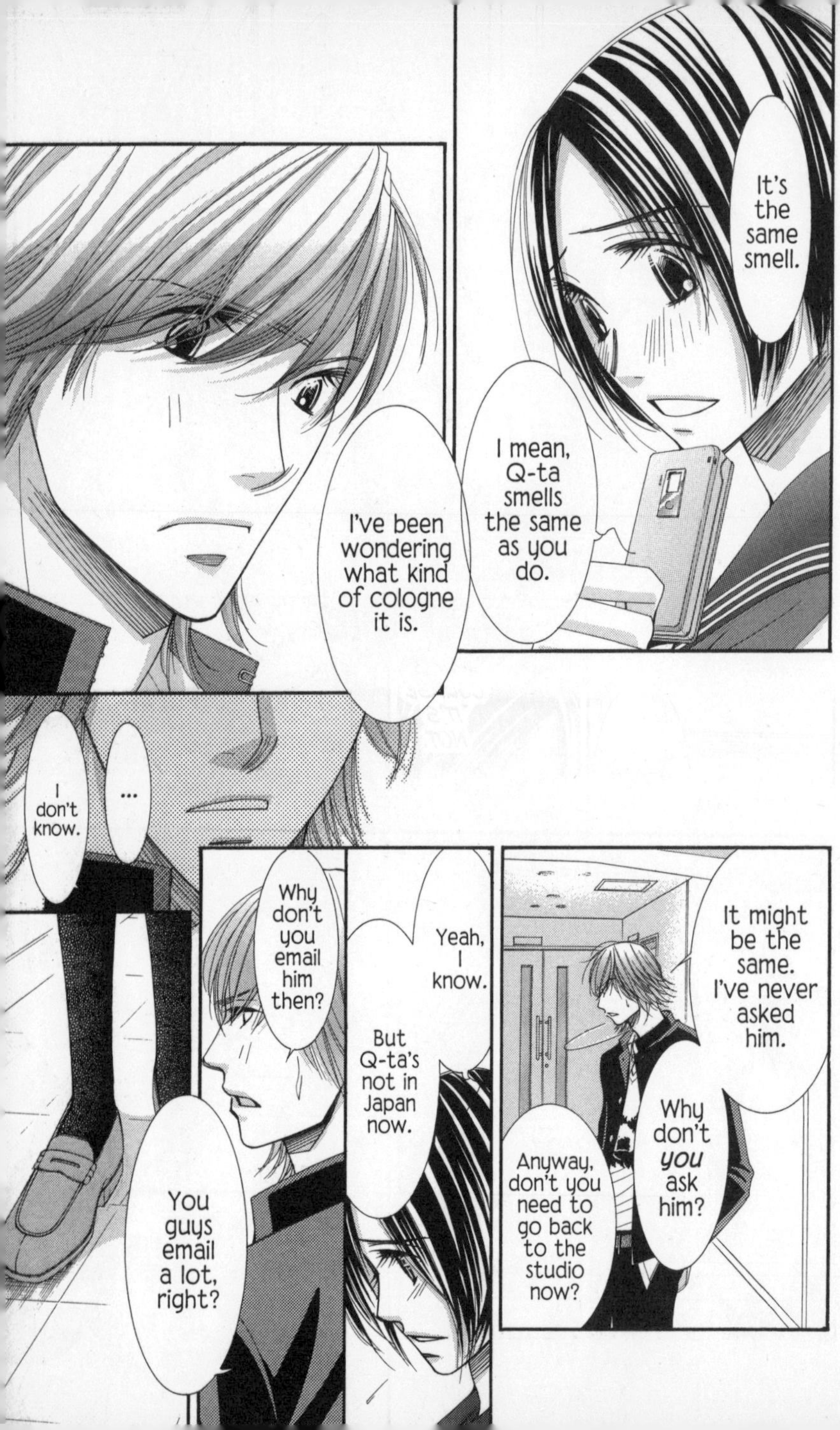
It's the same smell.
I mean, Q-ta smells the same as you do.
I've been wondering what kind of cologne it is.
...
I don't know.
It might be the same. I've never asked him.
Why don't *you* ask him?
Anyway, don't you need to go back to the studio now?
Yeah, I know.
But Q-ta's not in Japan now.
Why don't you email him then?
You guys email a lot, right?

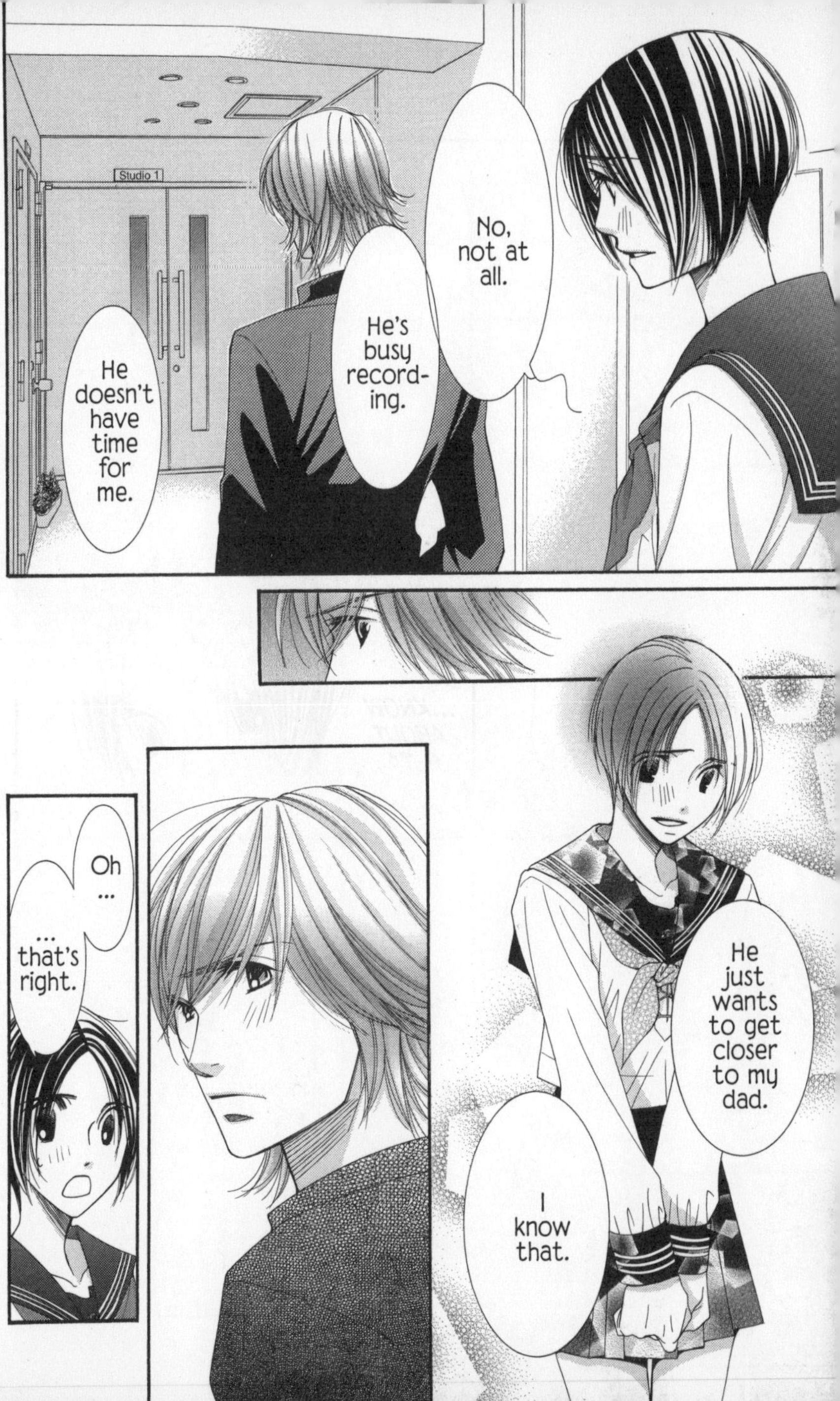
No, not at all.
He's busy recording.
He doesn't have time for me.
Studio 1
He just wants to get closer to my dad.
I know that.
Oh ...
... that's right.

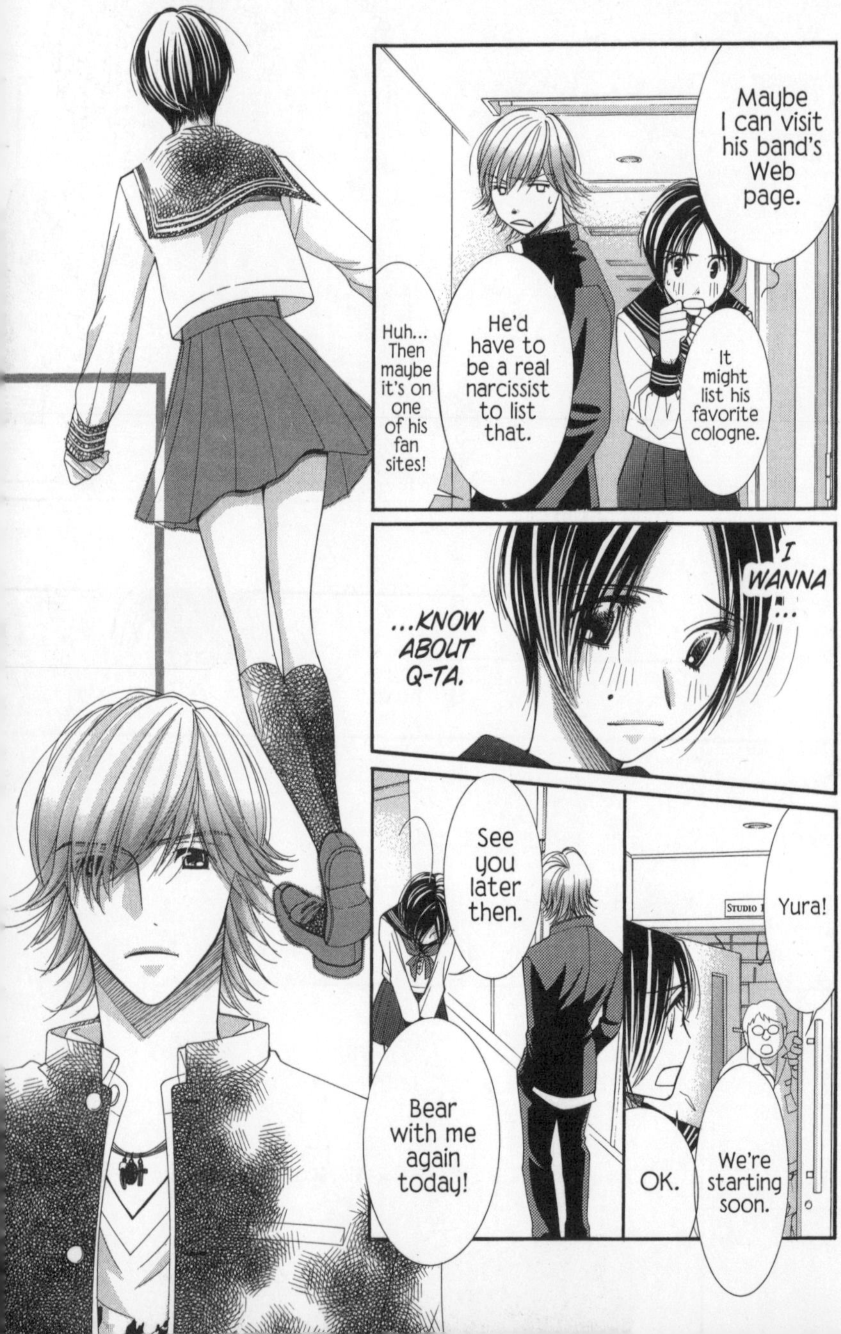

Maybe I can visit his band's Web page.
It might list his favorite cologne.
He'd have to be a real narcissist to list that.
Huh... Then maybe it's on one of his fan sites!
I WANNA...
...KNOW ABOUT Q-TA.
Yura!
STUDIO 1
We're starting soon.
OK.
See you later then.
Bear with me again today!

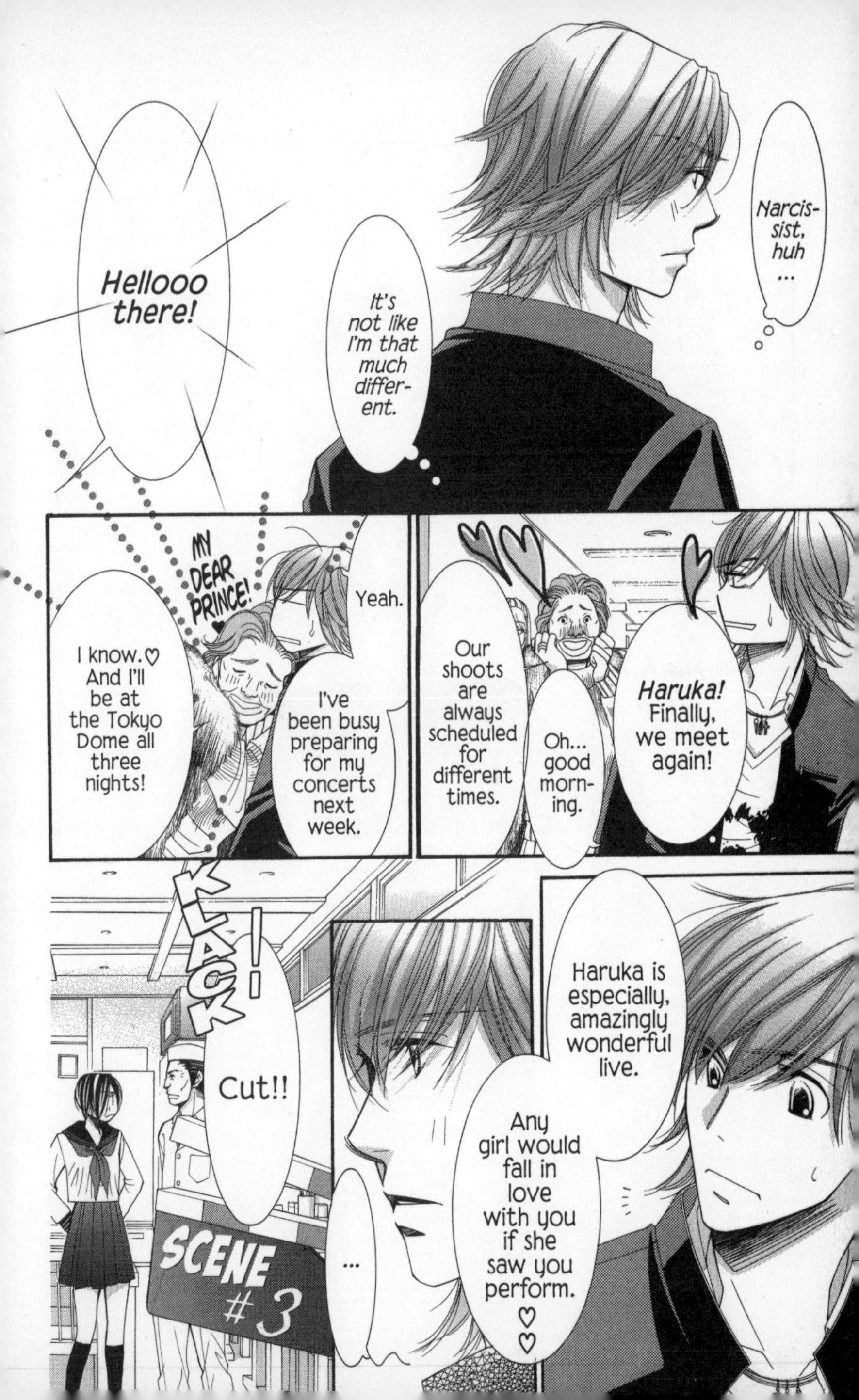
Narcis-sist, huh ...
It's not like I'm that much differ-ent.
Hellooo there!
Haruka! Finally, we meet again!
Oh... good morn-ing.
Our shoots are always scheduled for different times.
Yeah.
I've been busy preparing for my concerts next week.
MY DEAR PRINCE! ♥
I know. ♡ And I'll be at the Tokyo Dome all three nights!
Haruka is especially, amazingly wonderful live.
Any girl would fall in love with you if she saw you perform. ♡ ♡
...
KLACK
!!
Cut!!
SCENE #3

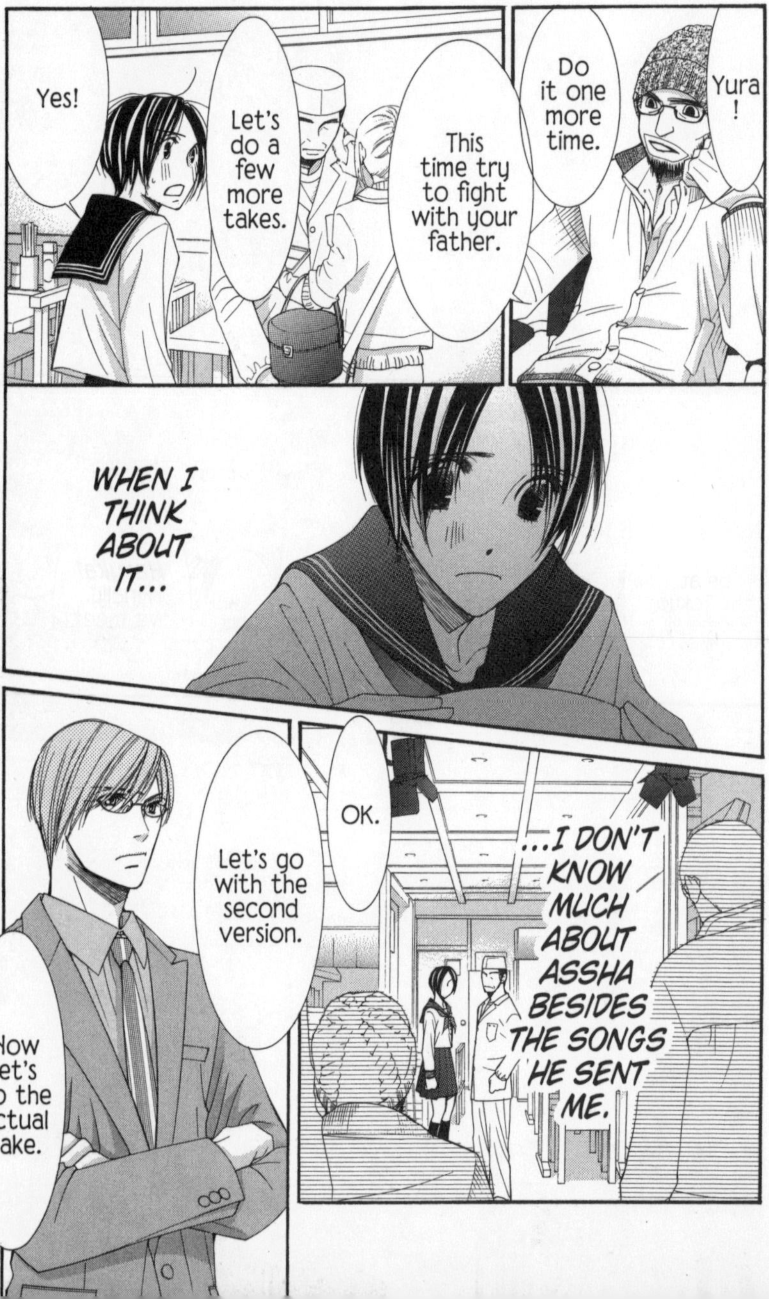
Yura!
Do it one more time.
This time try to fight with your father.
Let's do a few more takes.
Yes!
WHEN I THINK ABOUT IT...
...I DON'T KNOW MUCH ABOUT ASSHA BESIDES THE SONGS HE SENT ME.
OK.
Let's go with the second version.
Now let's do the actual take.

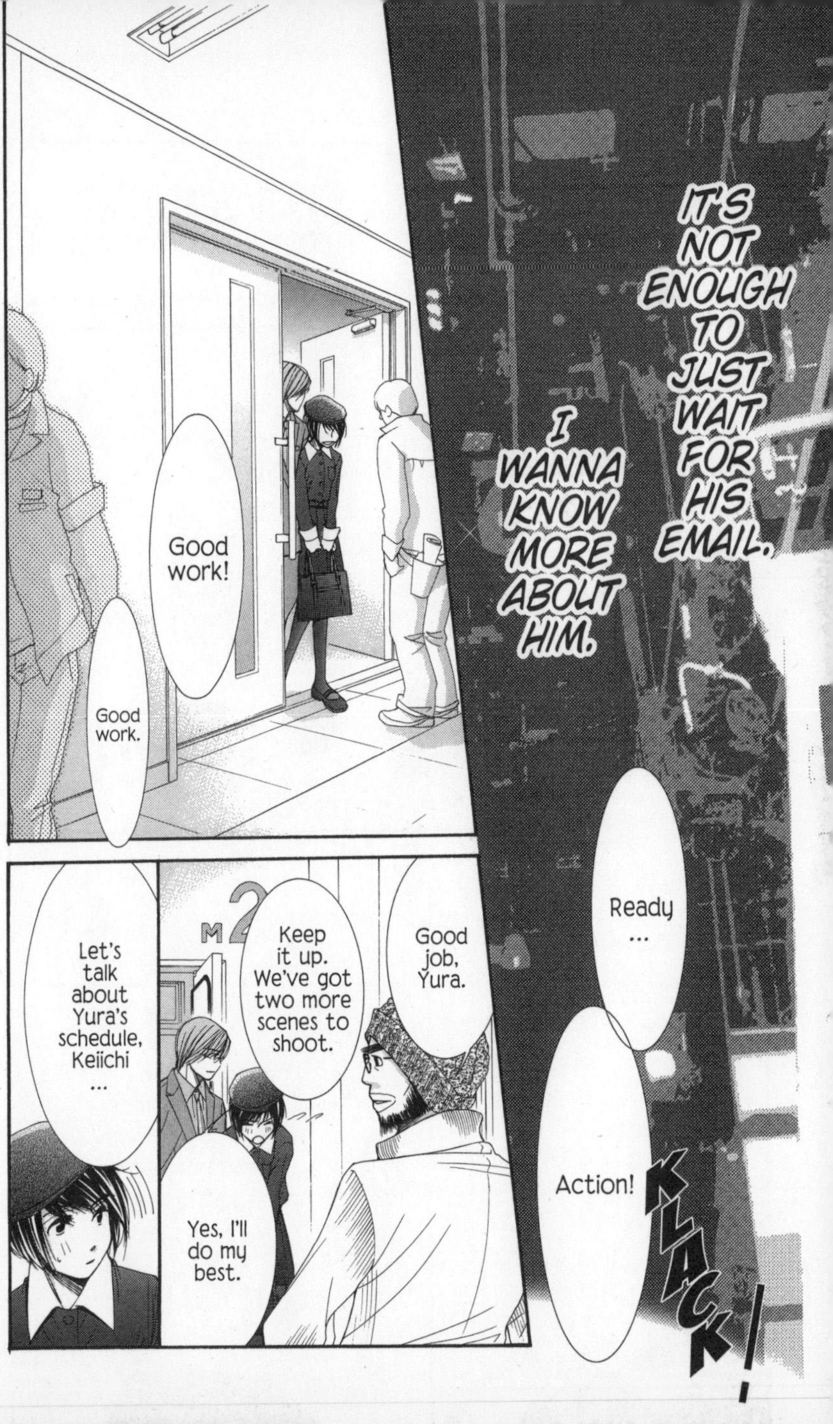
IT'S NOT ENOUGH TO JUST WAIT FOR HIS EMAIL.
I WANNA KNOW MORE ABOUT HIM.
Ready ...
Action!
KLACK!
Good work!
Good work.
Good job, Yura.
Keep it up. We've got two more scenes to shoot.
Let's talk about Yura's schedule, Keiichi ...
Yes, I'll do my best.

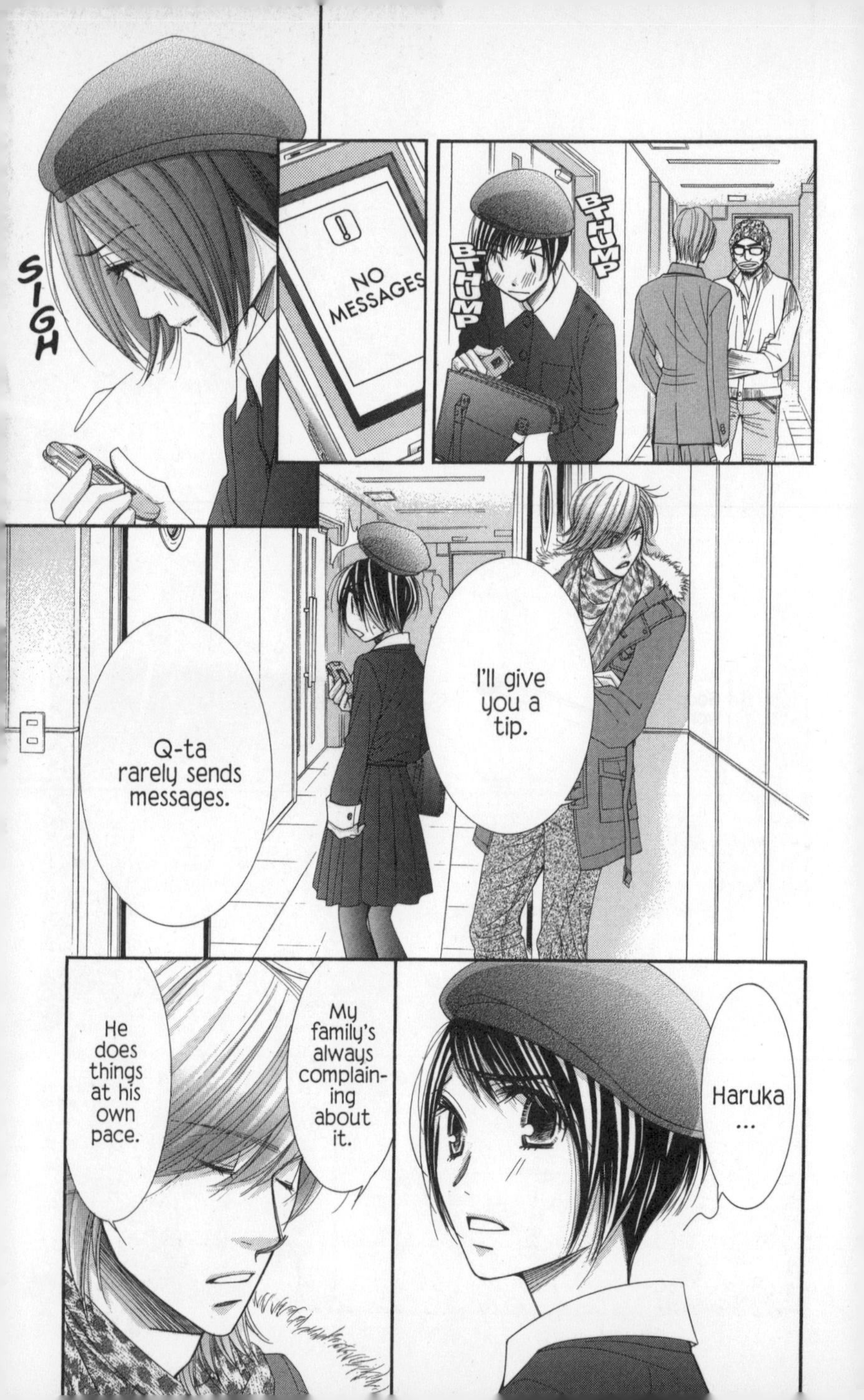
B-THUMP
B-THUMP
NO MESSAGES
SIGH
I'll give you a tip.
Q-ta rarely sends messages.
Haruka ...
My family's always complaining about it.
He does things at his own pace.

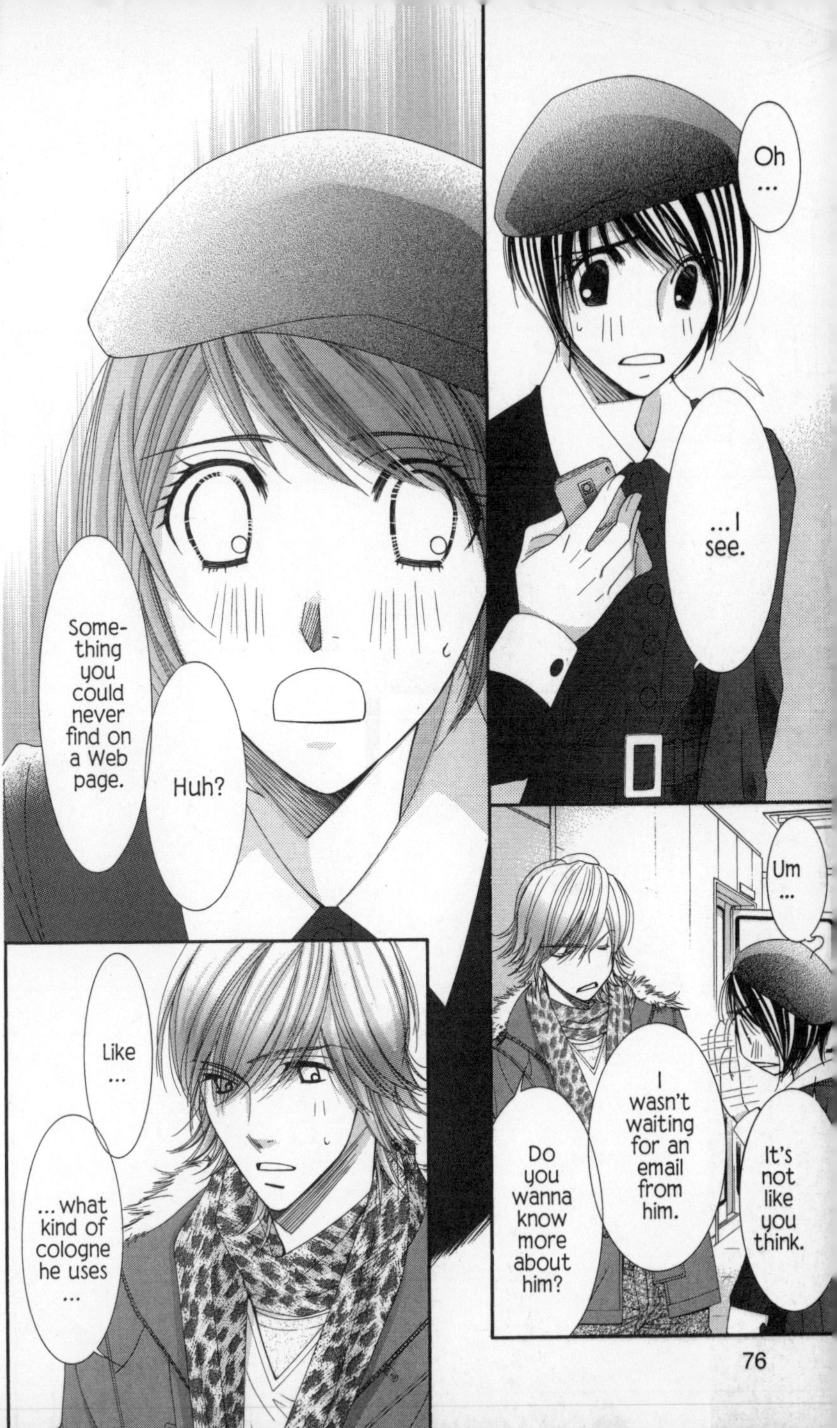
Oh ...
...I see.
Um ...
It's not like you think.
I wasn't waiting for an email from him.
Do you wanna know more about him?
Huh?
Something you could never find on a Web page.
Like ...
...what kind of cologne he uses ...

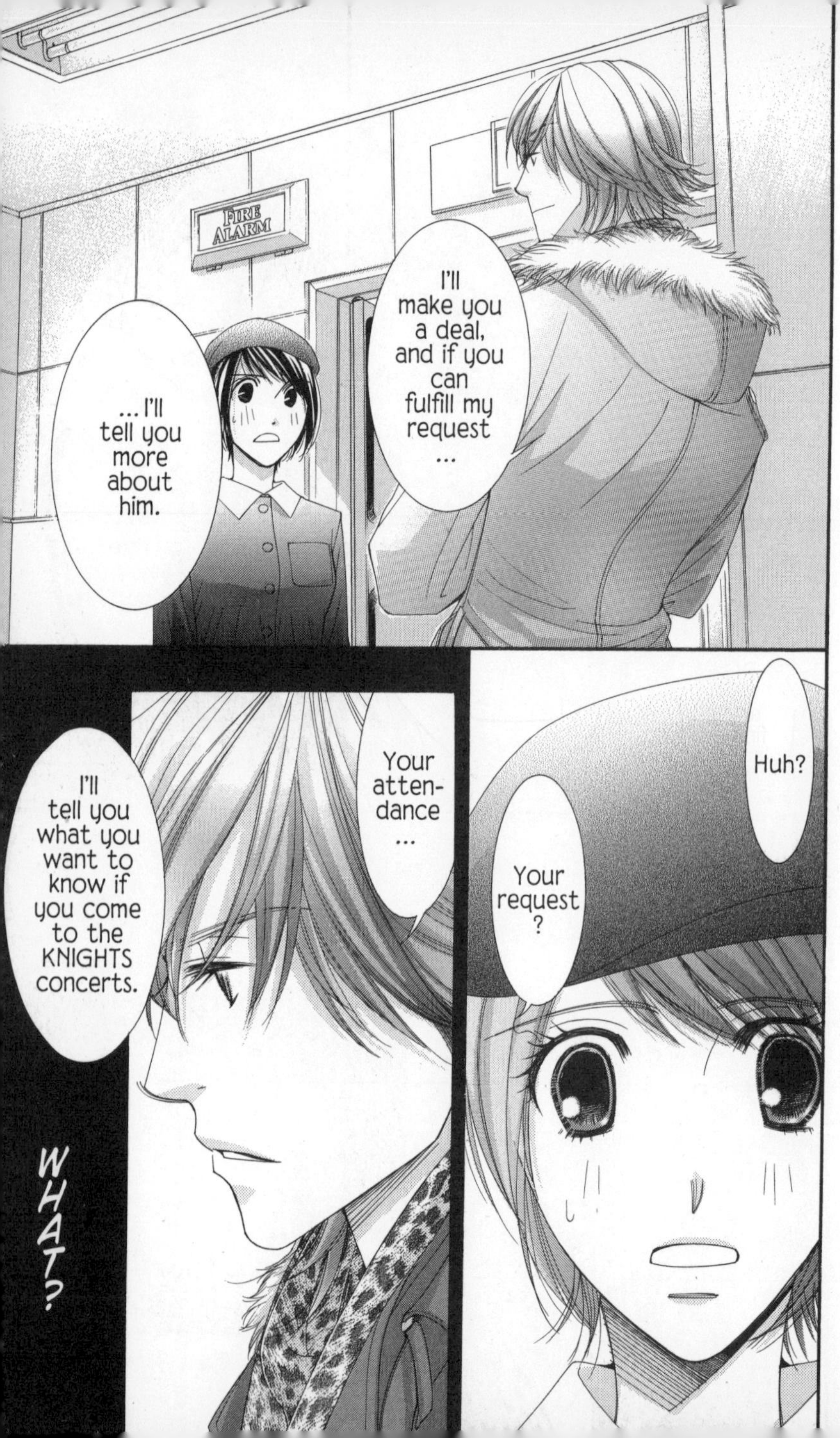
FIRE ALARM
I'll make you a deal, and if you can fulfill my request ...
...I'll tell you more about him.
Huh?
Your request?
Your attendance ...
I'll tell you what you want to know if you come to the KNIGHTS concerts.
WHAT?

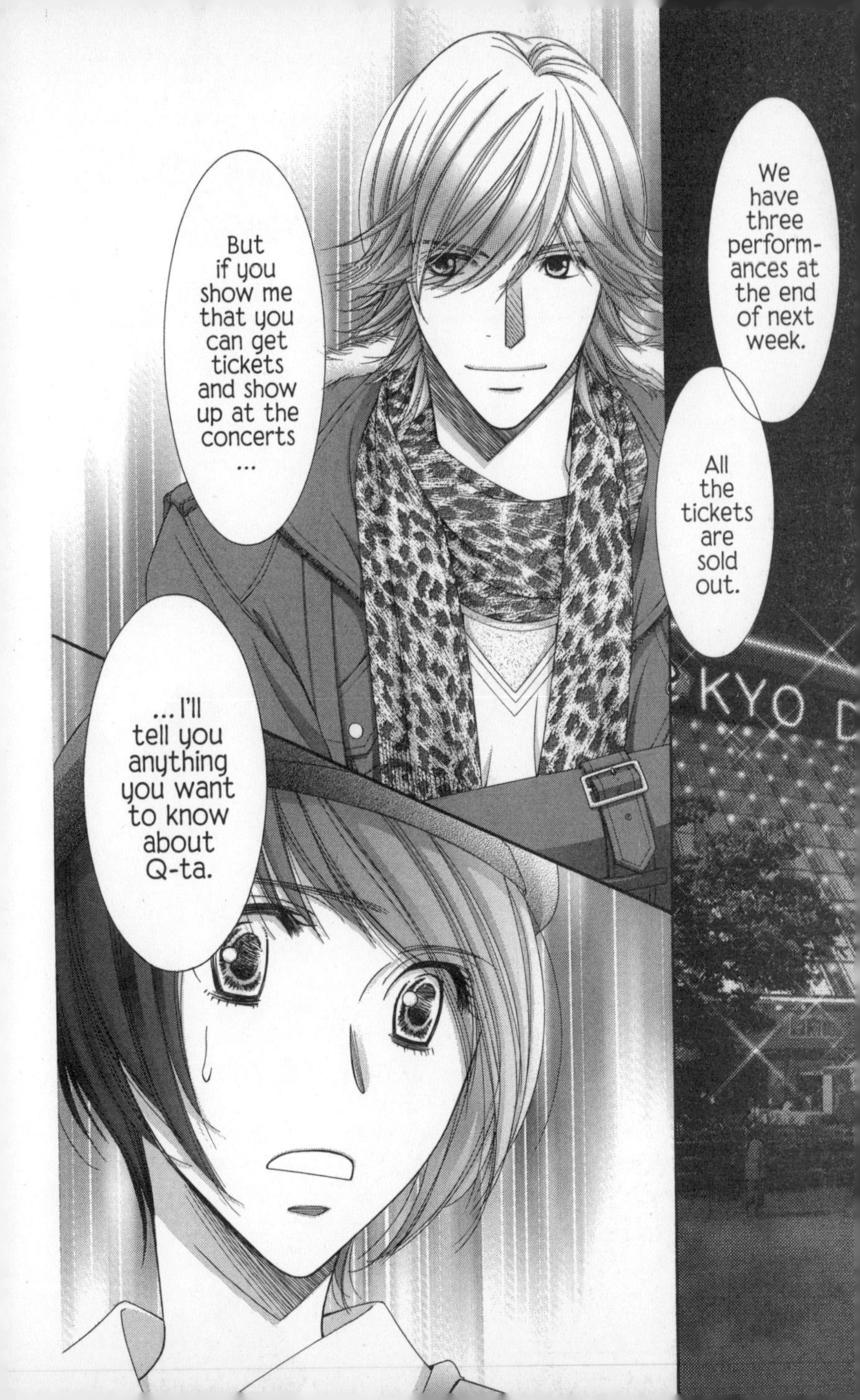
We have three performances at the end of next week.
All the tickets are sold out.
But if you show me that you can get tickets and show up at the concerts ...
... I'll tell you anything you want to know about Q-ta.

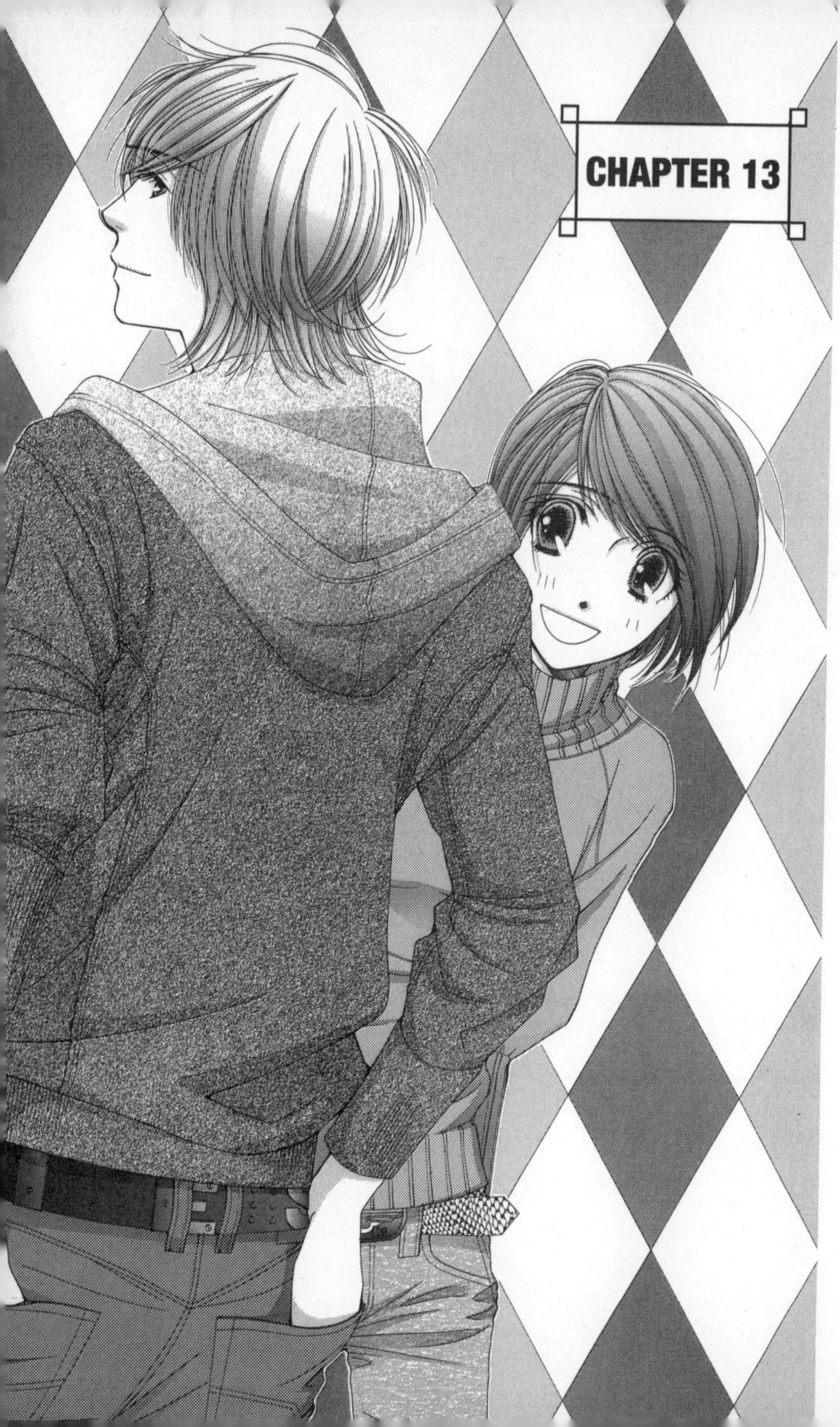
CHAPTER 13

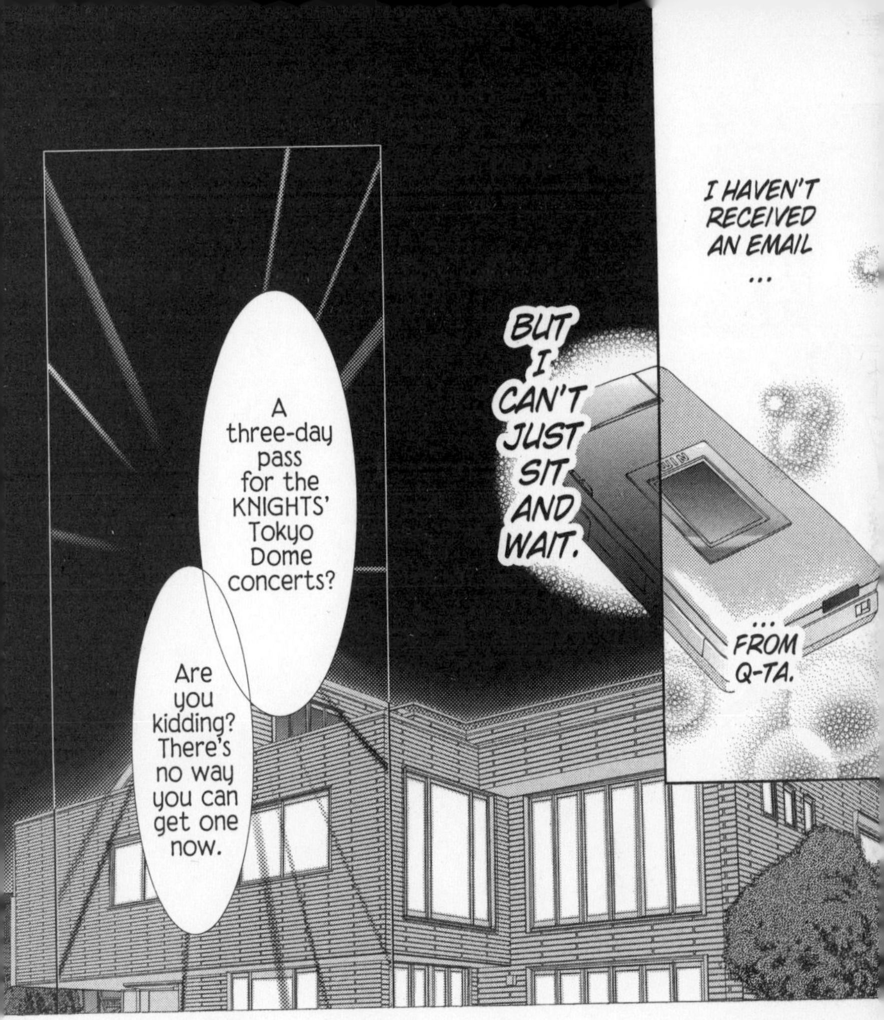
I HAVEN'T RECEIVED AN EMAIL ...
... FROM Q-TA.
BUT I CAN'T JUST SIT AND WAIT.
A three-day pass for the KNIGHTS' Tokyo Dome concerts?
Are you kidding? There's no way you can get one now.

Honey Hunt

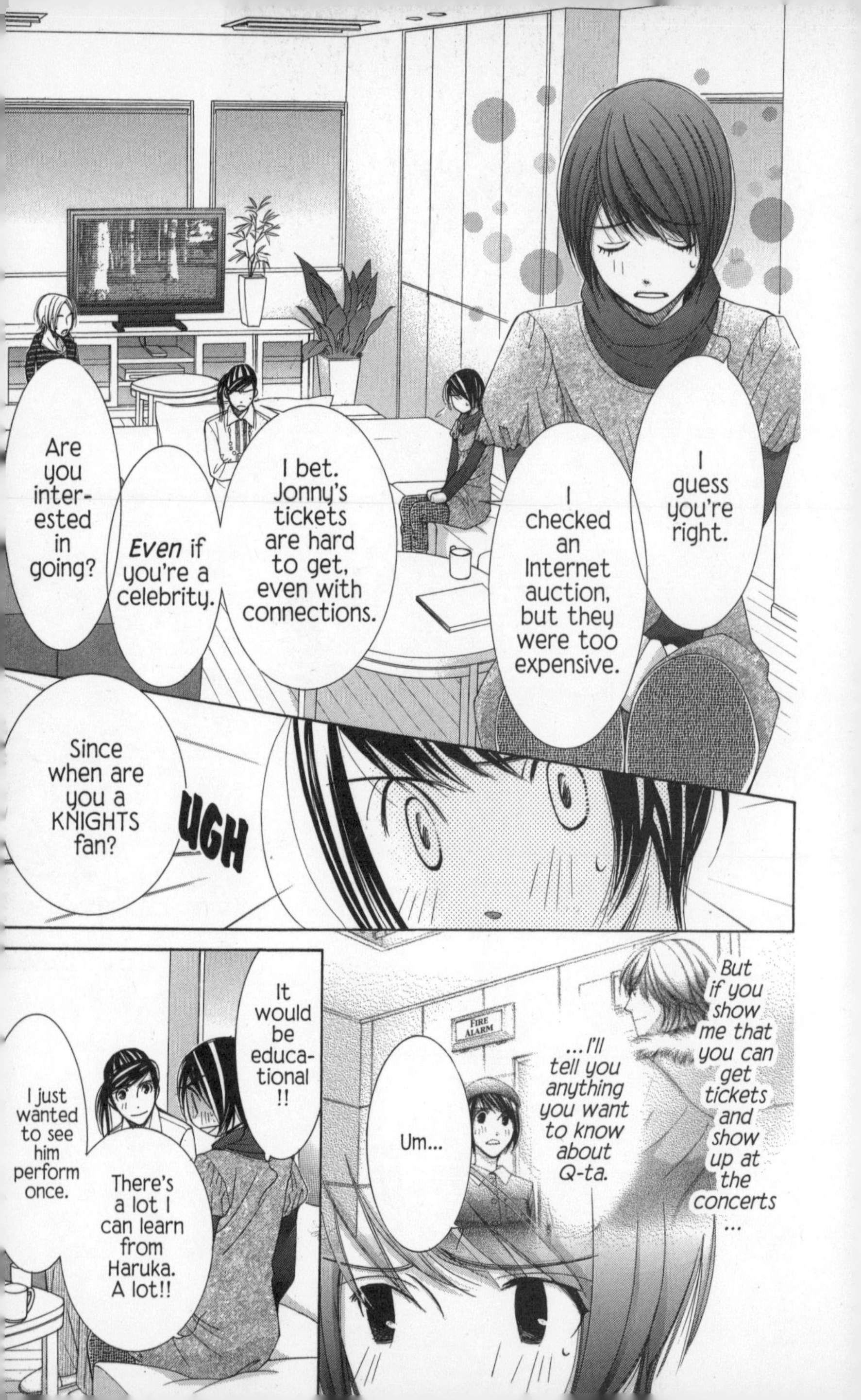
I guess you're right.
I checked an Internet auction, but they were too expensive.
I bet. Jonny's tickets are hard to get, even with connections.
Even if you're a celebrity.
Are you interested in going?
UGH
Since when are you a KNIGHTS fan?
But if you show me that you can get tickets and show up at the concerts...
...I'll tell you anything you want to know about Q-ta.
FIRE ALARM
Um...
It would be educational!!
I just wanted to see him perform once.
There's a lot I can learn from Haruka. A lot!!

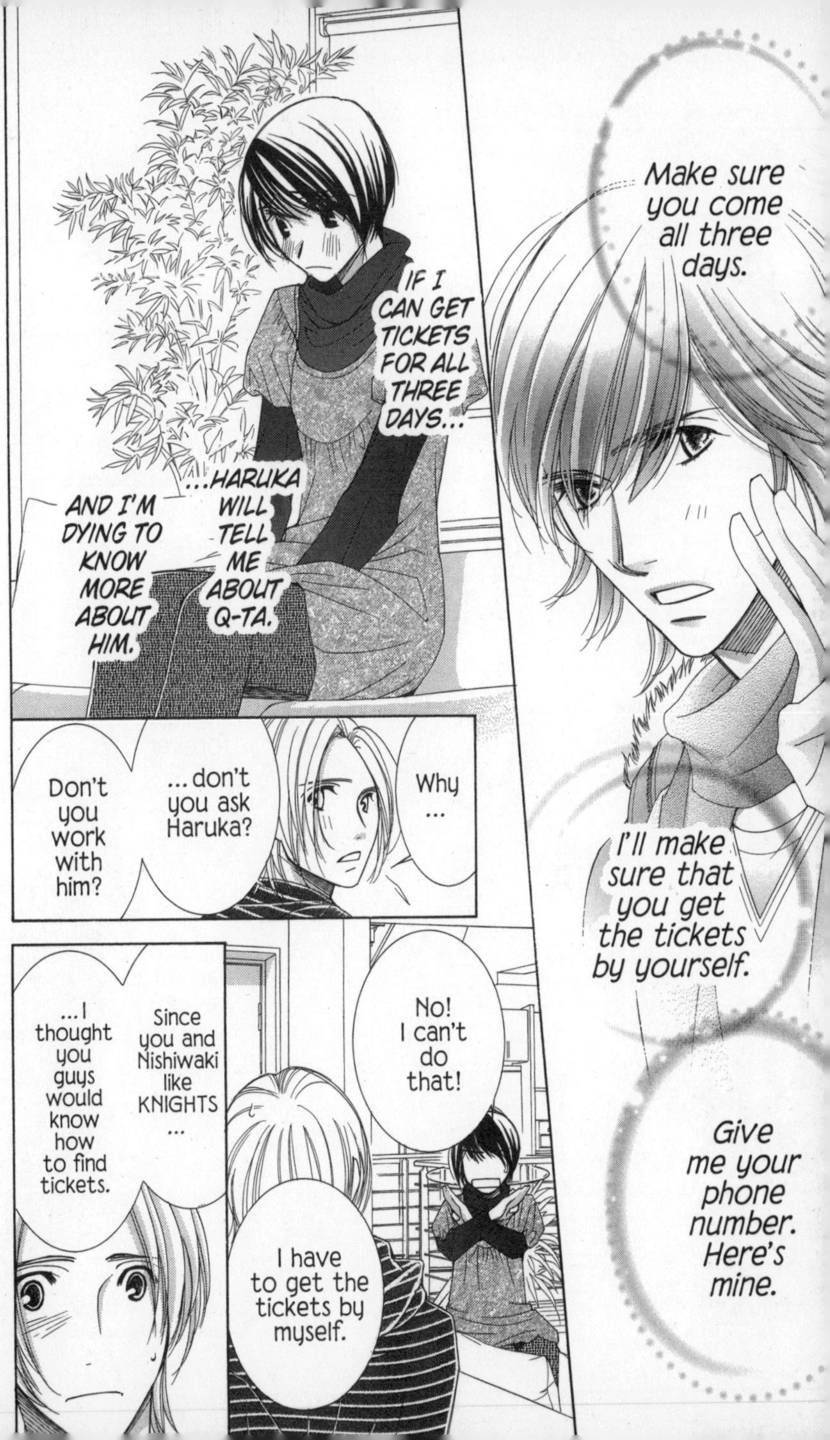
Make sure you come all three days.
I'll make sure that you get the tickets by yourself.
Give me your phone number. Here's mine.
IF I CAN GET TICKETS FOR ALL THREE DAYS...
...HARUKA WILL TELL ME ABOUT Q-TA.
AND I'M DYING TO KNOW MORE ABOUT HIM.
Why ...
...don't you ask Haruka?
Don't you work with him?
No! I can't do that!
Since you and Nishiwaki like KNIGHTS ...
...I thought you guys would know how to find tickets.
I have to get the tickets by myself.

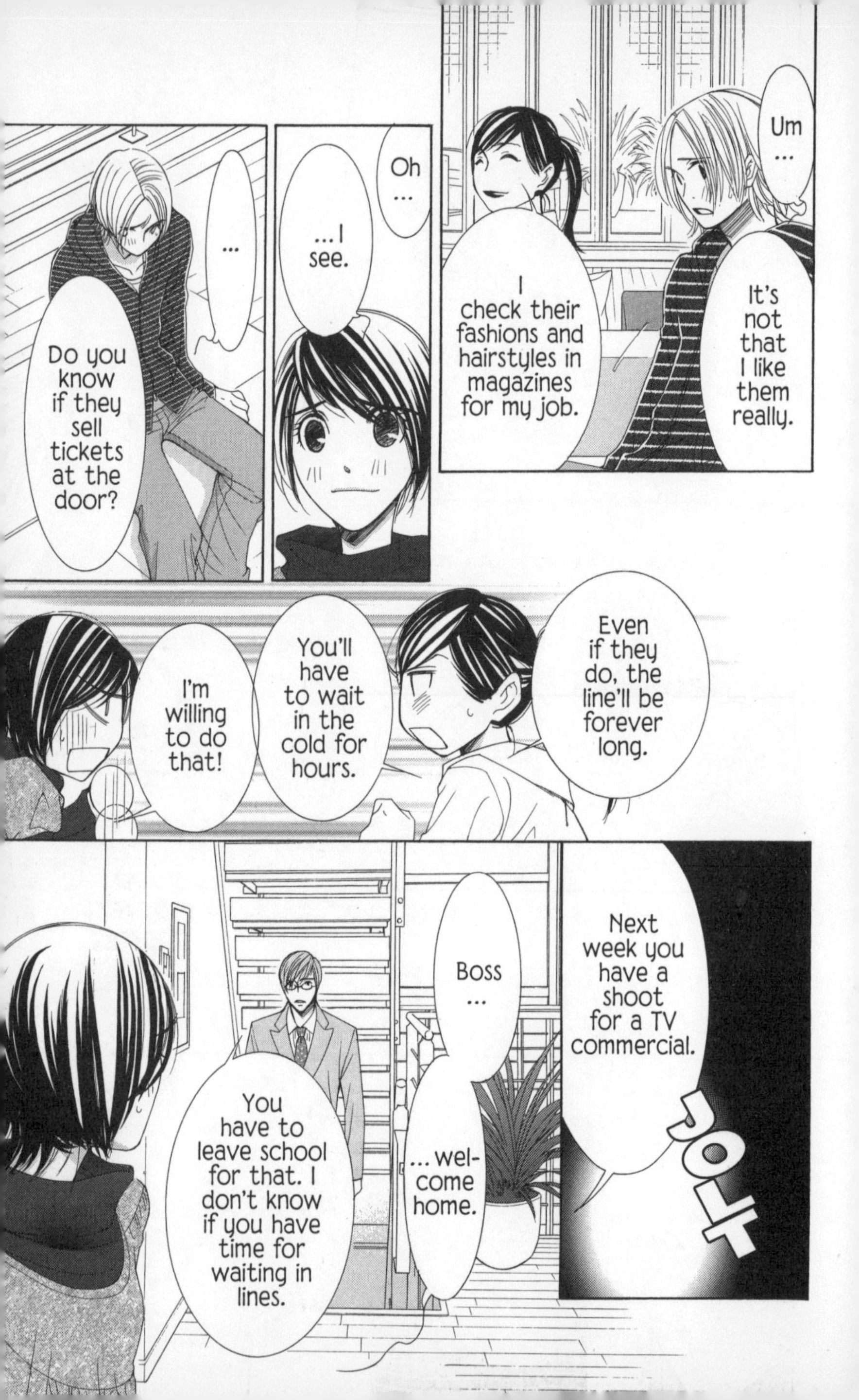
Um ...
It's not that I like them really.
I check their fashions and hairstyles in magazines for my job.
Oh ...
...I see.
...
Do you know if they sell tickets at the door?
Even if they do, the line'll be forever long.
You'll have to wait in the cold for hours.
I'm willing to do that!
Next week you have a shoot for a TV commercial.
JOLT
Boss ...
...wel-come home.
You have to leave school for that. I don't know if you have time for waiting in lines.

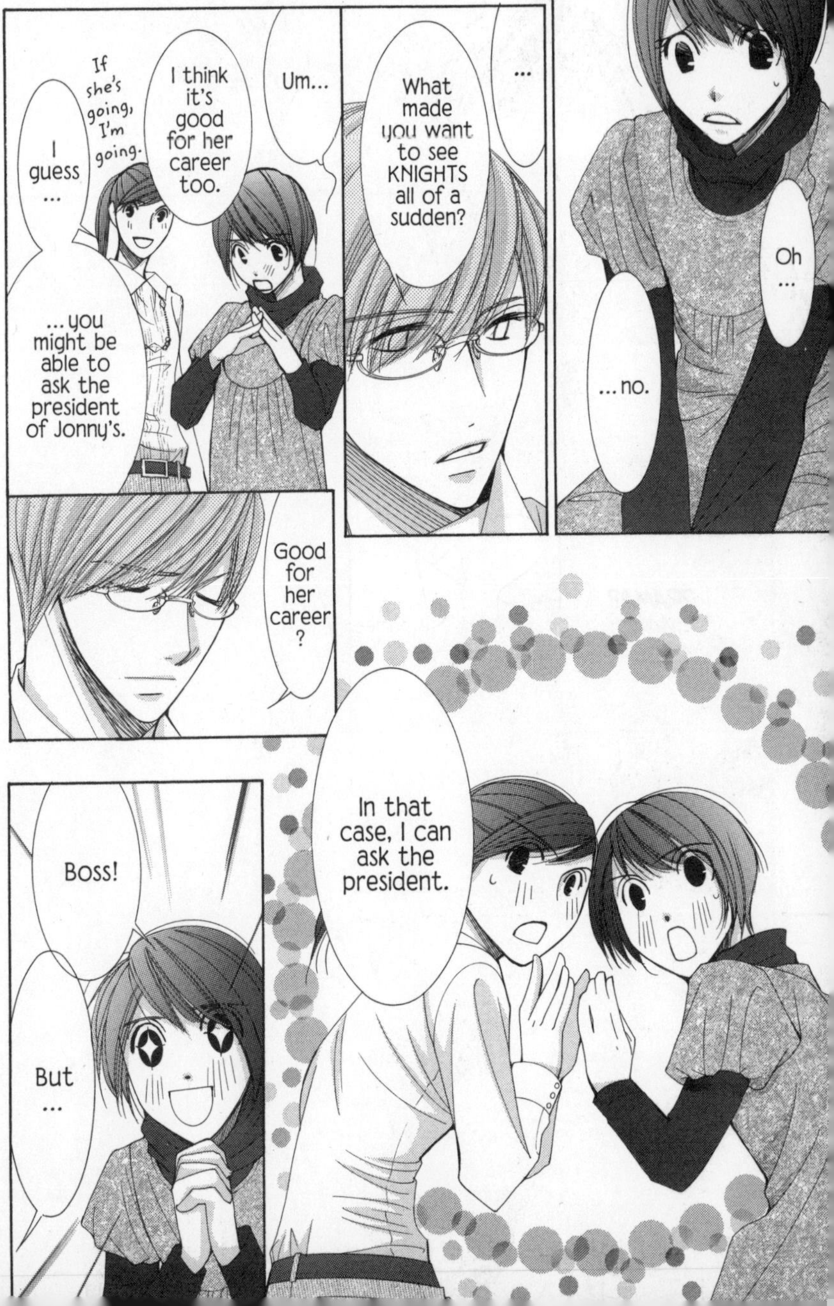

Oh ...
... no.
...
What made you want to see KNIGHTS all of a sudden?
Um...
I think it's good for her career too.
If she's going, I'm going.
I guess ...
... you might be able to ask the president of Jonny's.
Good for her career?
In that case, I can ask the president.
Boss!
But ...

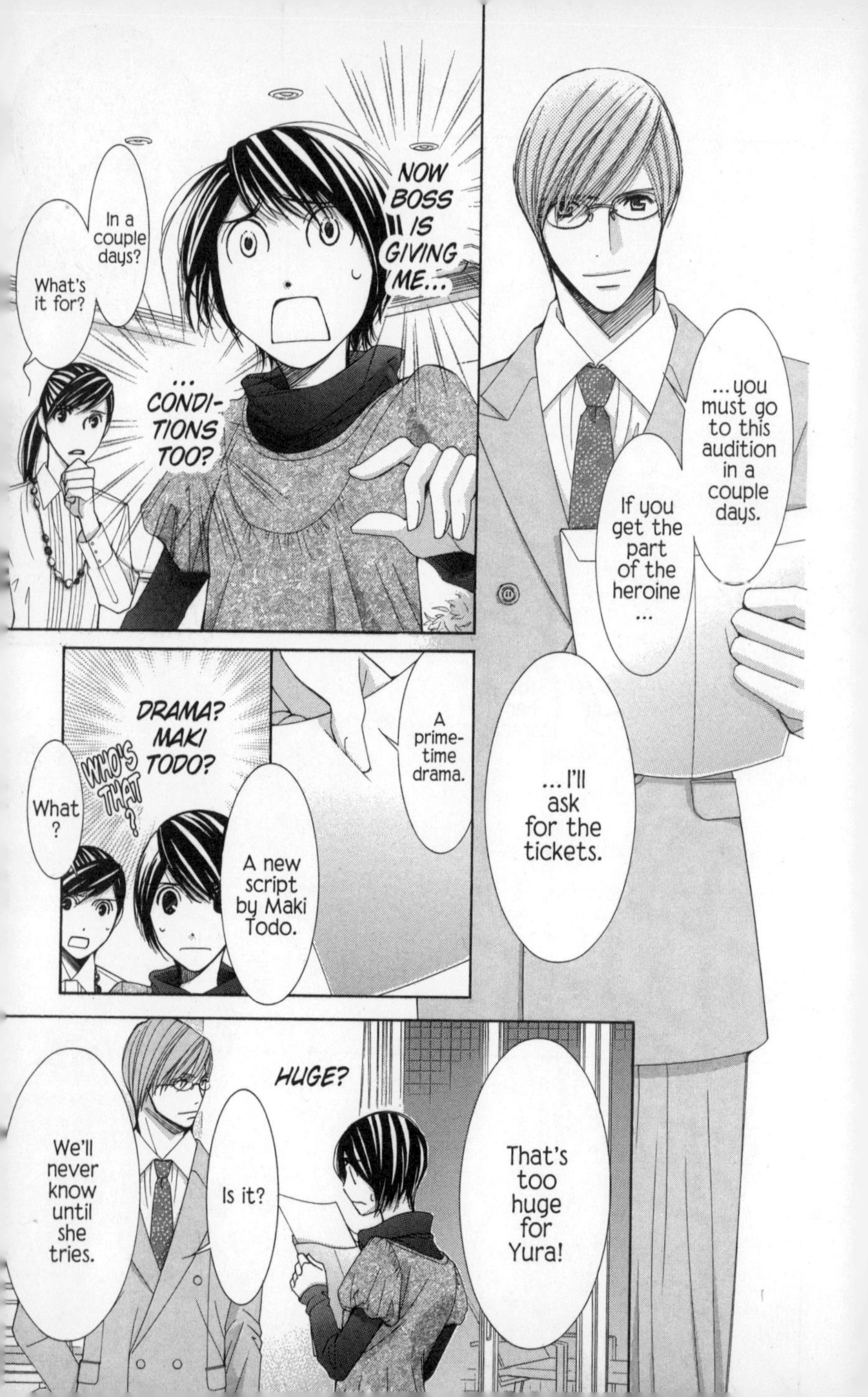
...you must go to this audition in a couple days.
If you get the part of the heroine ...
... I'll ask for the tickets.
NOW BOSS IS GIVING ME...
... CONDITIONS TOO?
In a couple days?
What's it for?
A prime-time drama.
A new script by Maki Todo.
DRAMA? MAKI TODO?
WHO'S THAT?
What?
That's too huge for Yura!
HUGE?
Is it?
We'll never know until she tries.

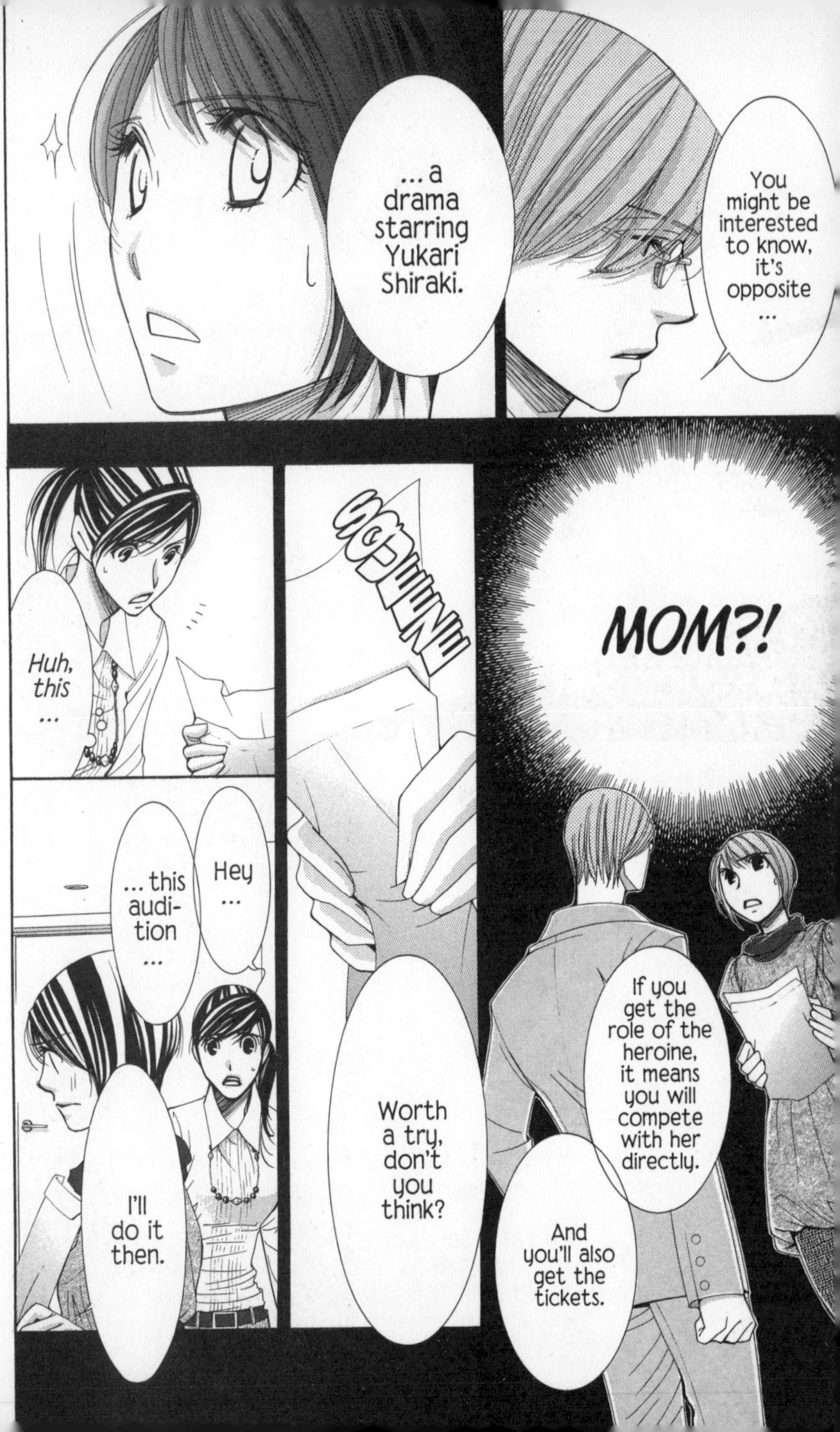
You might be interested to know, it's opposite ...
... a drama starring Yukari Shiraki.
MOM?!
If you get the role of the heroine, it means you will compete with her directly.
And you'll also get the tickets.
SQUEEZE
Worth a try, don't you think?
Huh, this ...
Hey ...
... this audition ...
I'll do it then.

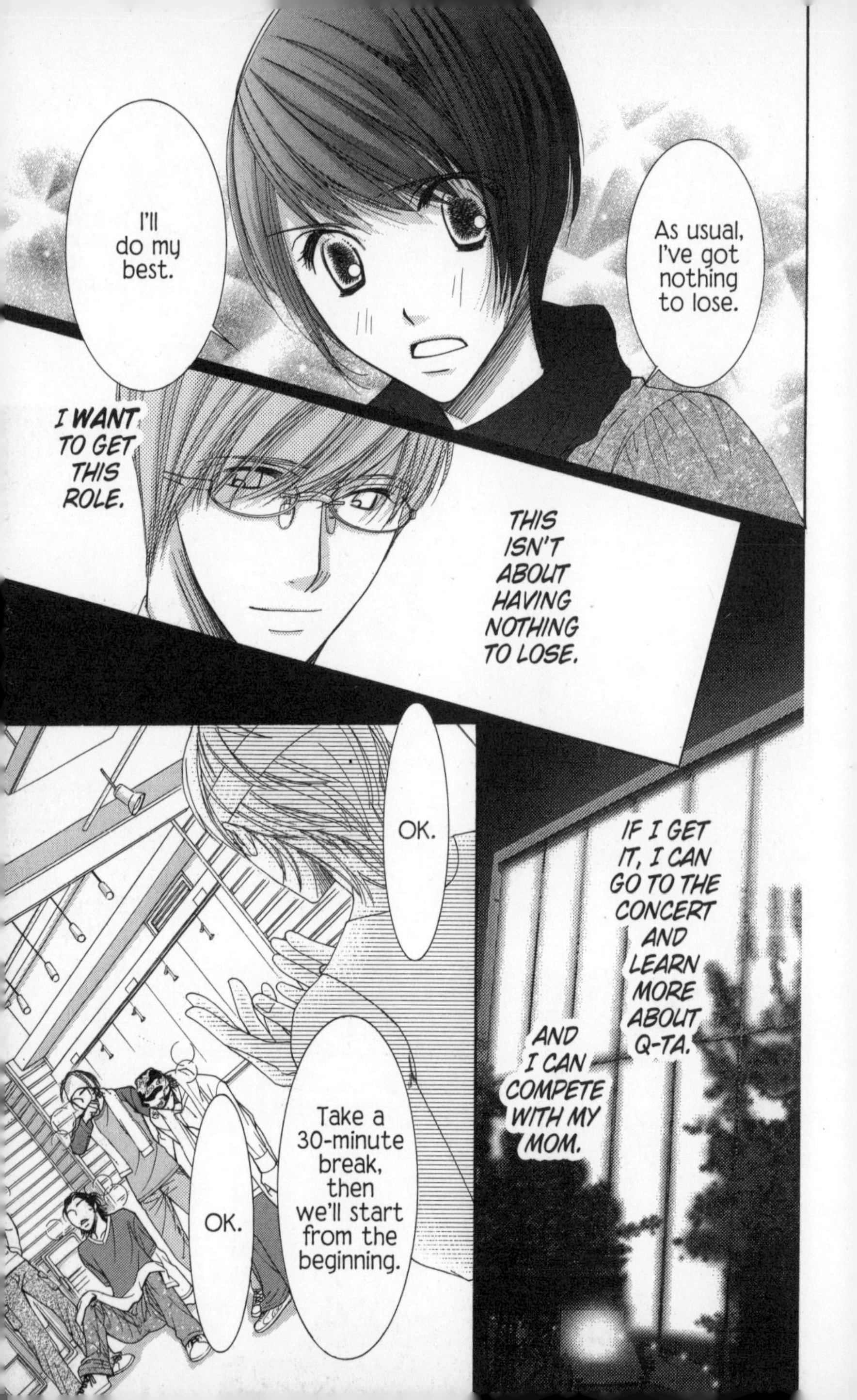
As usual, I've got nothing to lose.
I'll do my best.
THIS ISN'T ABOUT HAVING NOTHING TO LOSE.
I WANT TO GET THIS ROLE.
IF I GET IT, I CAN GO TO THE CONCERT AND LEARN MORE ABOUT Q-TA.
AND I CAN COMPETE WITH MY MOM.
OK.
Take a 30-minute break, then we'll start from the beginning.
OK.

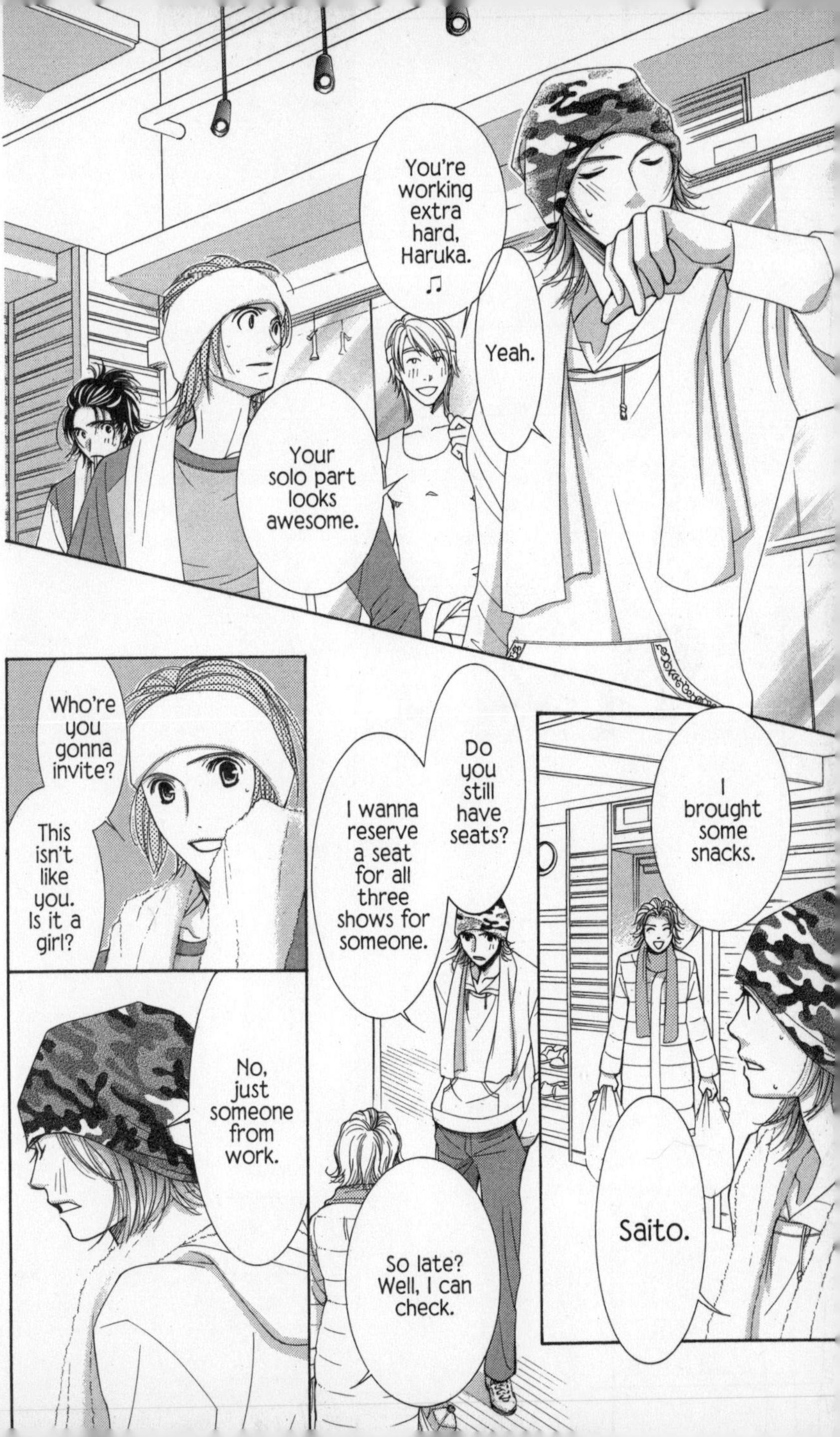
You're working extra hard, Haruka. ♫
Yeah.
Your solo part looks awesome.
I brought some snacks.
Saito.
Do you still have seats?
I wanna reserve a seat for all three shows for someone.
So late? Well, I can check.
Who're you gonna invite?
This isn't like you. Is it a girl?
No, just someone from work.

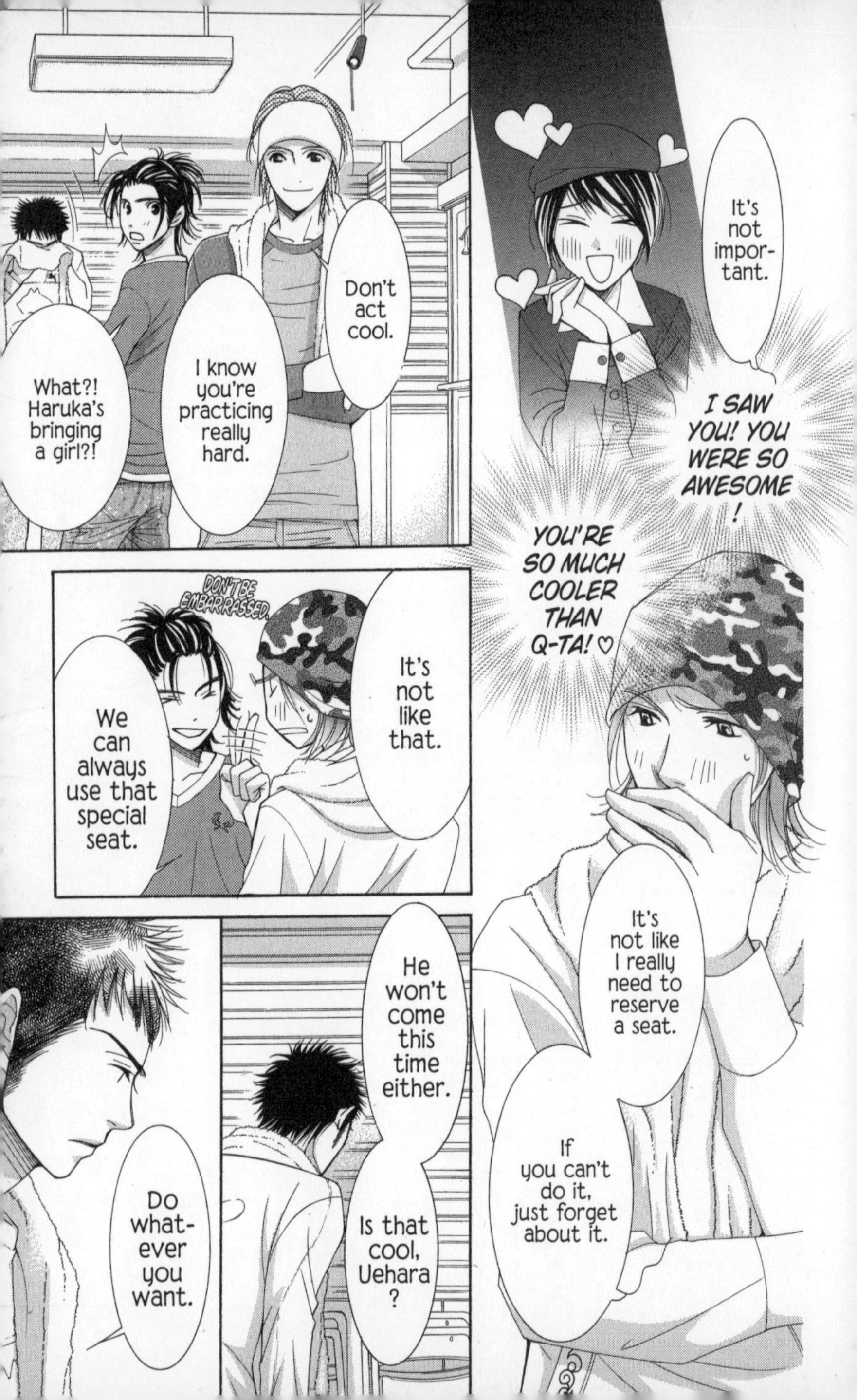
It's not impor-tant.
I SAW YOU! YOU WERE SO AWESOME!
YOU'RE SO MUCH COOLER THAN Q-TA! ♡
It's not like I really need to reserve a seat.
If you can't do it, just forget about it.
Don't act cool.
I know you're practicing really hard.
What?! Haruka's bringing a girl?!
It's not like that.
DON'T BE EMBARRASSED.
We can always use that special seat.
He won't come this time either.
Is that cool, Uehara?
Do what-ever you want.

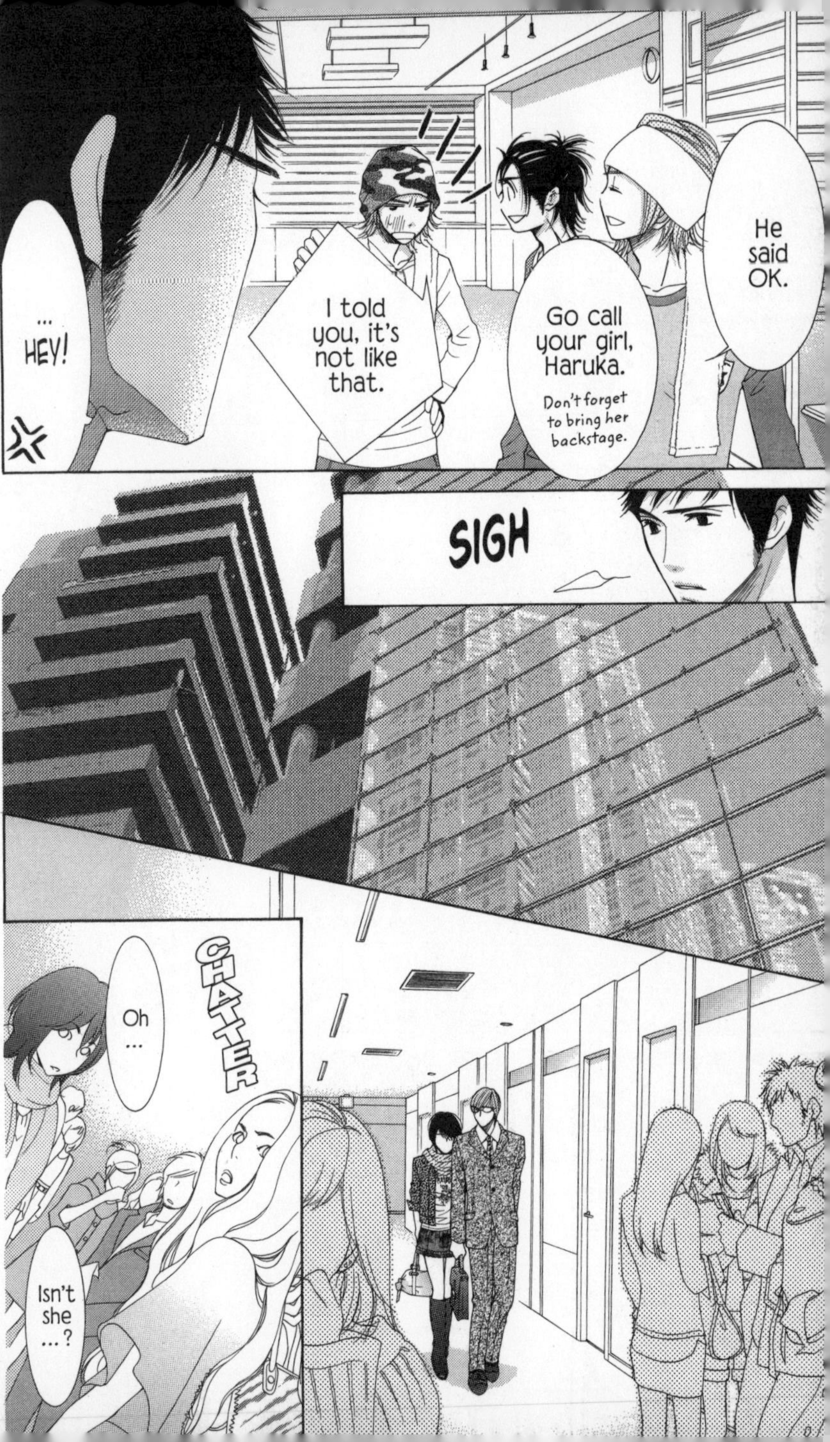
He said OK.
Go call your girl, Haruka.
Don't forget to bring her backstage.
I told you, it's not like that.
... HEY!
SIGH
CHATTER
Oh ...
Isn't she ...?

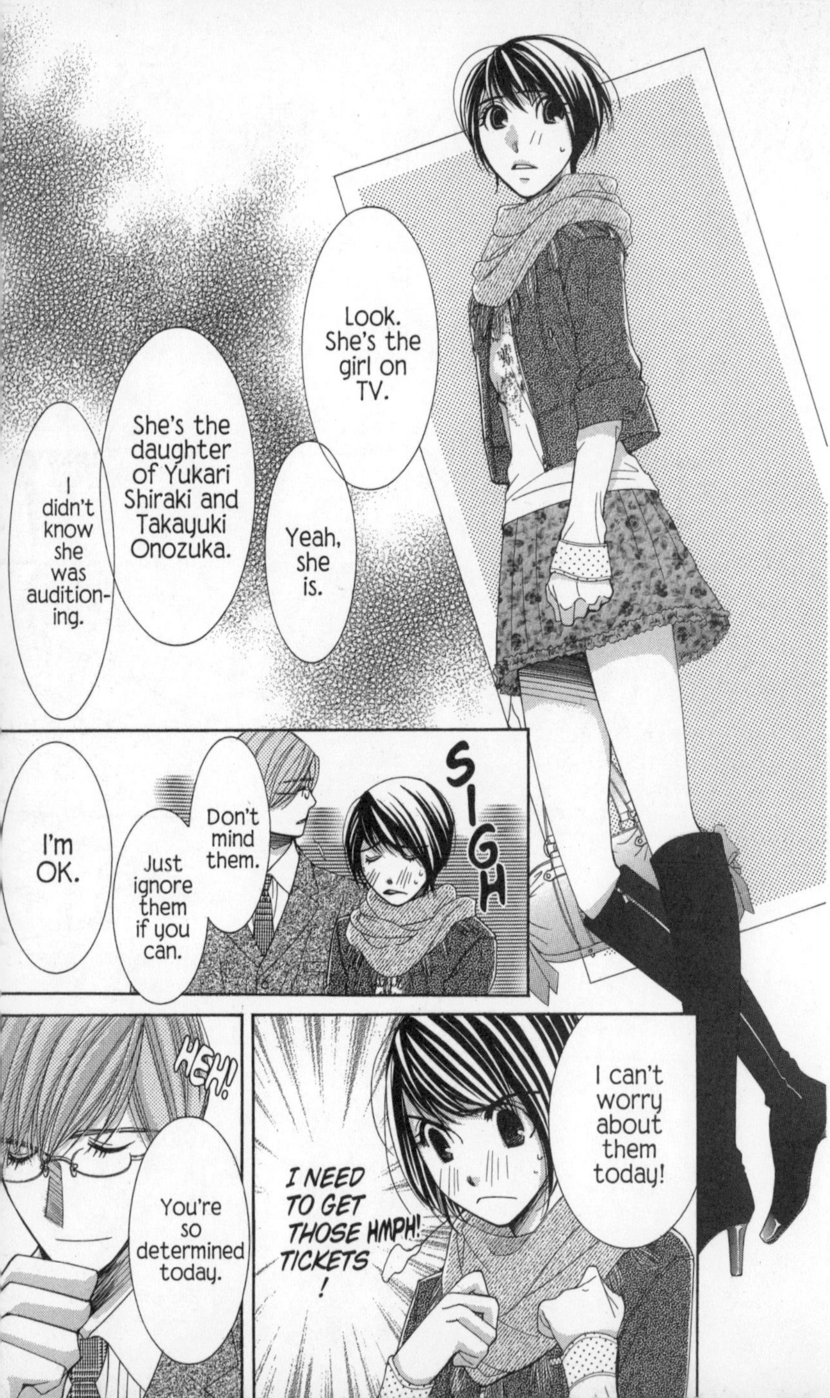
Look. She's the girl on TV.
Yeah, she is.
She's the daughter of Yukari Shiraki and Takayuki Onozuka.
I didn't know she was auditioning.
SIGH
Don't mind them.
Just ignore them if you can.
I'm OK.
I can't worry about them today!
I NEED TO GET THOSE TICKETS!
HMPH!
HEH!
You're so determined today.

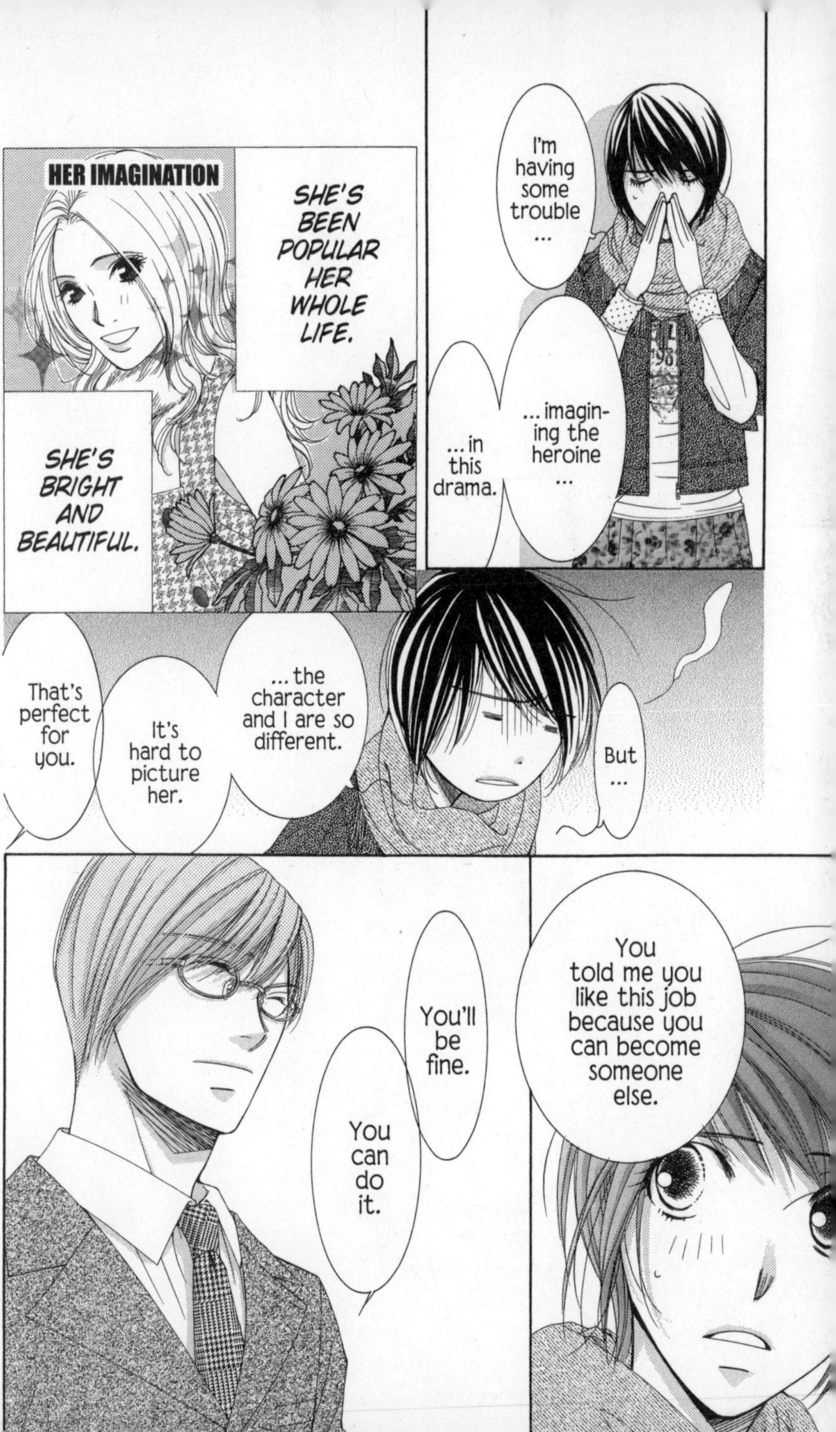

I'm having some trouble...
...imagining the heroine...
...in this drama.
HER IMAGINATION
SHE'S BEEN POPULAR HER WHOLE LIFE.
SHE'S BRIGHT AND BEAUTIFUL.
But...
...the character and I are so different.
It's hard to picture her.
That's perfect for you.
You told me you like this job because you can become someone else.
You'll be fine.
You can do it.

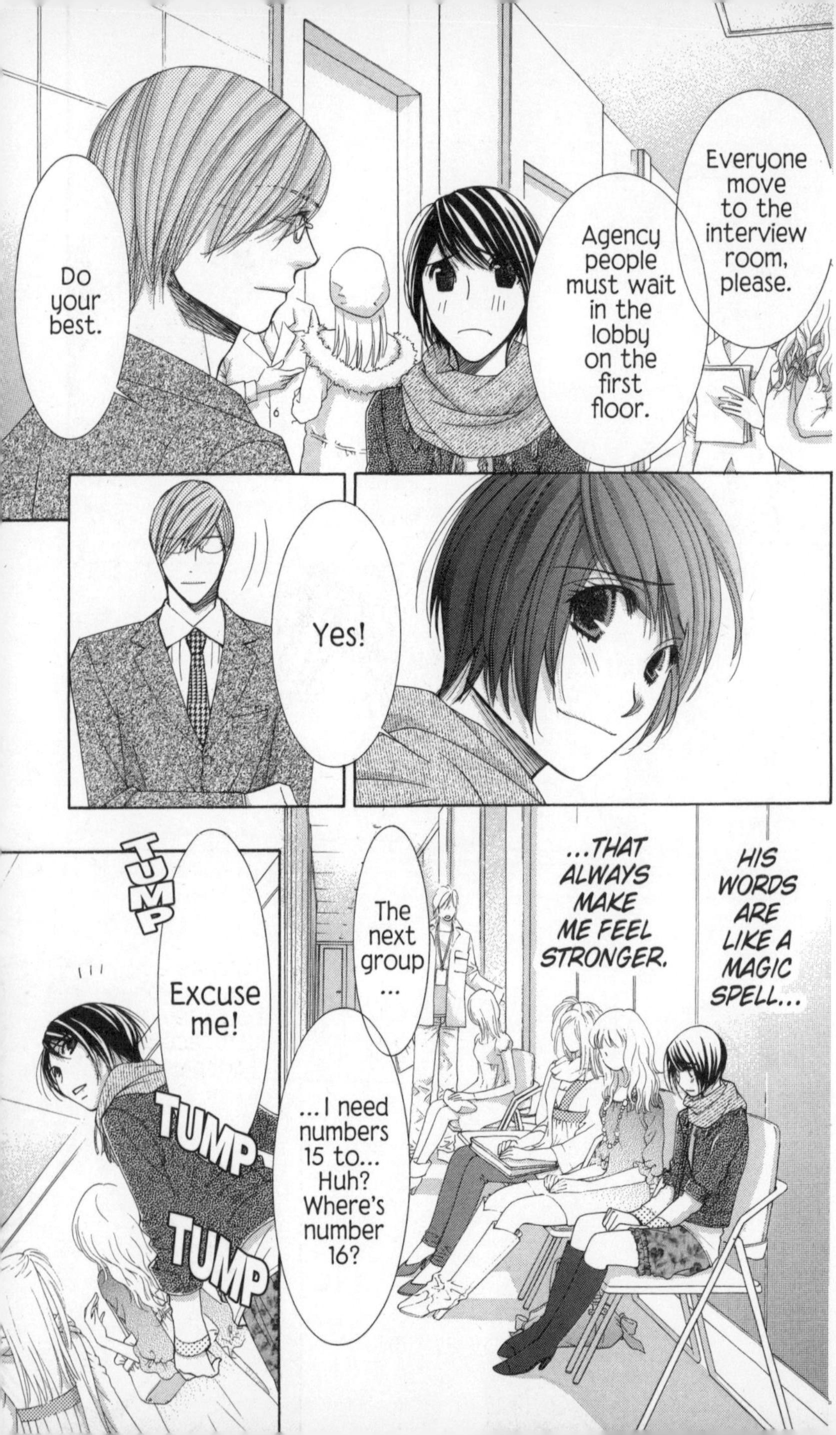
Everyone move to the interview room, please.
Agency people must wait in the lobby on the first floor.
Do your best.
Yes!
HIS WORDS ARE LIKE A MAGIC SPELL...
...THAT ALWAYS MAKE ME FEEL STRONGER.
The next group...
...I need numbers 15 to... Huh? Where's number 16?
Excuse me!
TUMP
TUMP
TUMP
TUMP

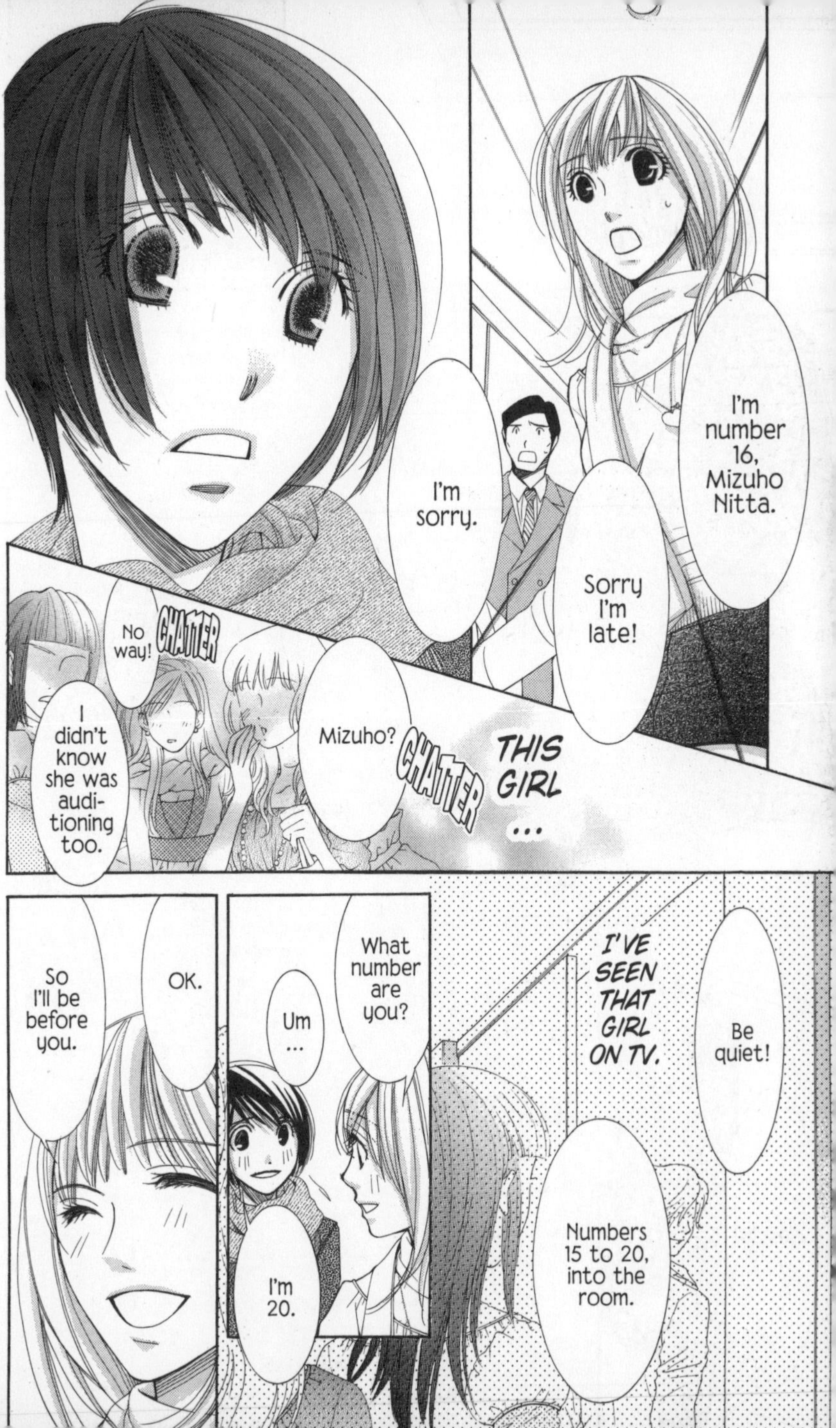
I'm number 16, Mizuho Nitta.
Sorry I'm late!
I'm sorry.
THIS GIRL ...
CHATTER
Mizuho?
CHATTER
No way!
I didn't know she was audi-tioning too.
Be quiet!
I'VE SEEN THAT GIRL ON TV.
Numbers 15 to 20, into the room.
What number are you?
Um ...
I'm 20.
OK.
So I'll be before you.

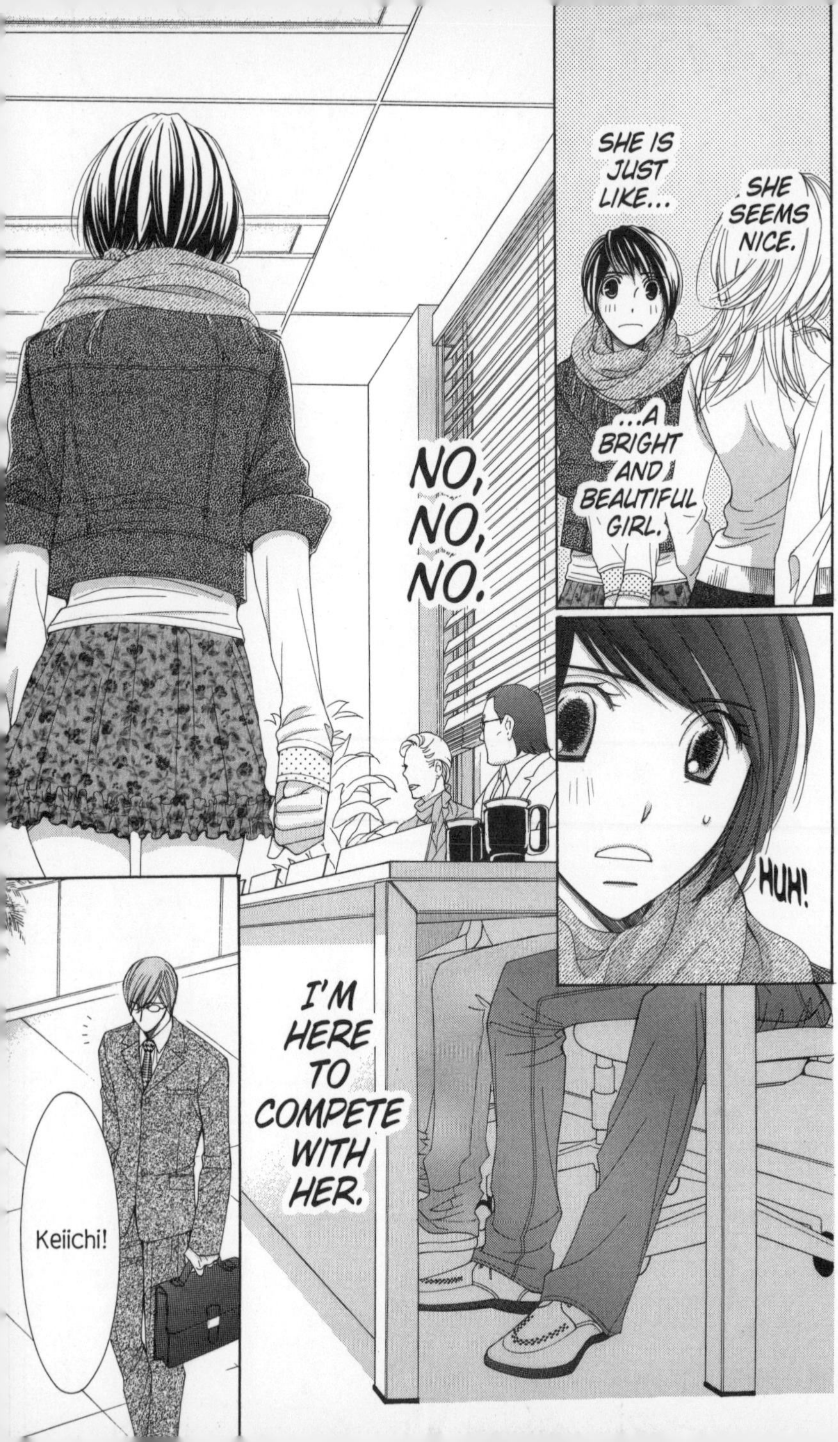
SHE SEEMS NICE.
SHE IS JUST LIKE...
...A BRIGHT AND BEAUTIFUL GIRL.
HUH!
NO, NO, NO.
I'M HERE TO COMPETE WITH HER.
Keiichi!

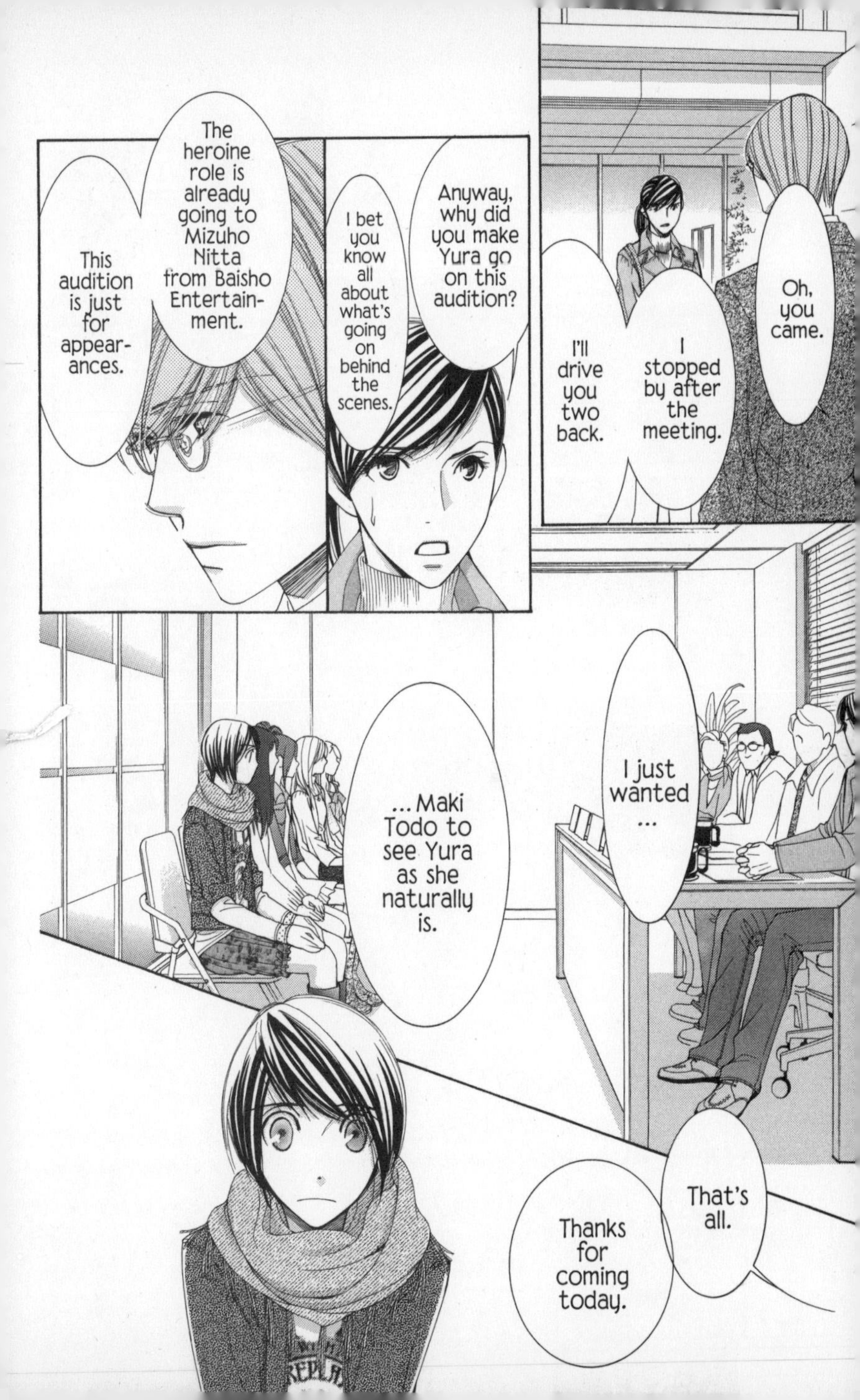
Oh, you came.
I stopped by after the meeting.
I'll drive you two back.
Anyway, why did you make Yura go on this audition?
I bet you know all about what's going on behind the scenes.
The heroine role is already going to Mizuho Nitta from Baisho Entertainment.
This audition is just for appearances.
I just wanted...
...Maki Todo to see Yura as she naturally is.
That's all.
Thanks for coming today.

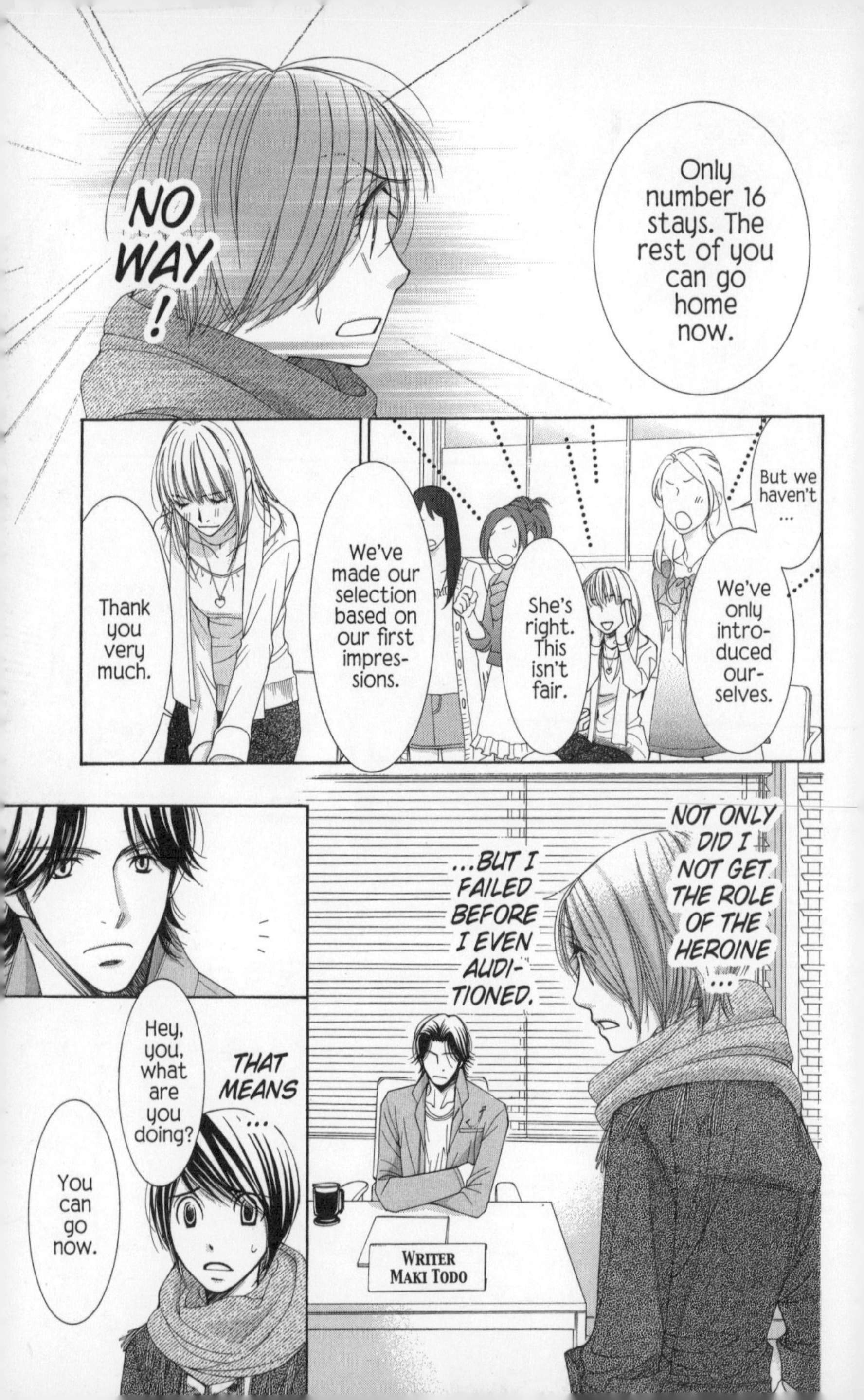
Only number 16 stays. The rest of you can go home now.
NO WAY!
But we haven't...
We've only introduced ourselves.
She's right. This isn't fair.
We've made our selection based on our first impressions.
Thank you very much.
NOT ONLY DID I NOT GET THE ROLE OF THE HEROINE...
...BUT I FAILED BEFORE I EVEN AUDITIONED.
WRITER MAKI TODO
Hey, you, what are you doing?
THAT MEANS...
You can go now.

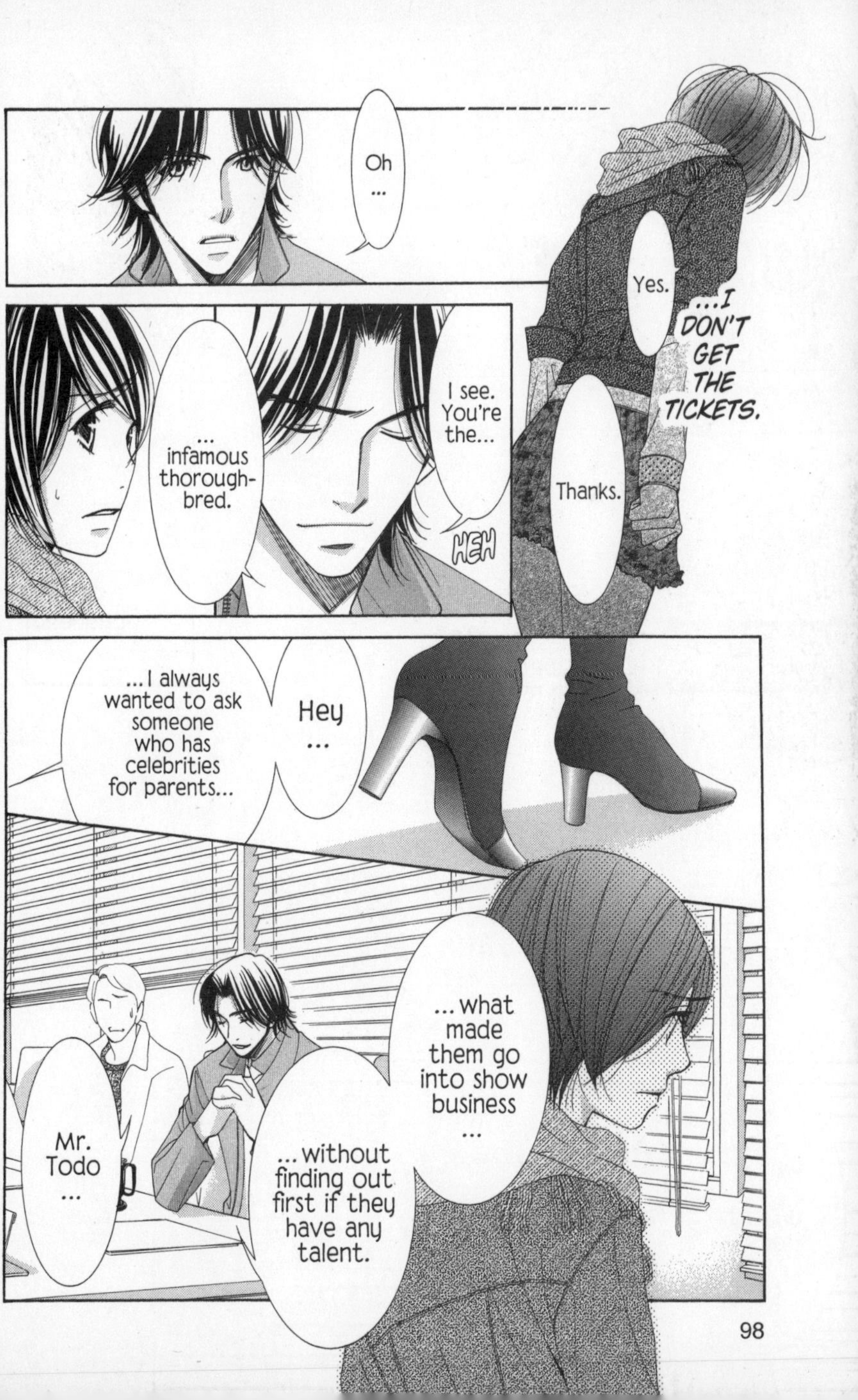
Yes.
...I DON'T GET THE TICKETS.
Thanks.
Oh ...
I see. You're the...
HEH
... infamous thoroughbred.
Hey ...
...I always wanted to ask someone who has celebrities for parents...
...what made them go into show business ...
...without finding out first if they have any talent.
Mr. Todo ...

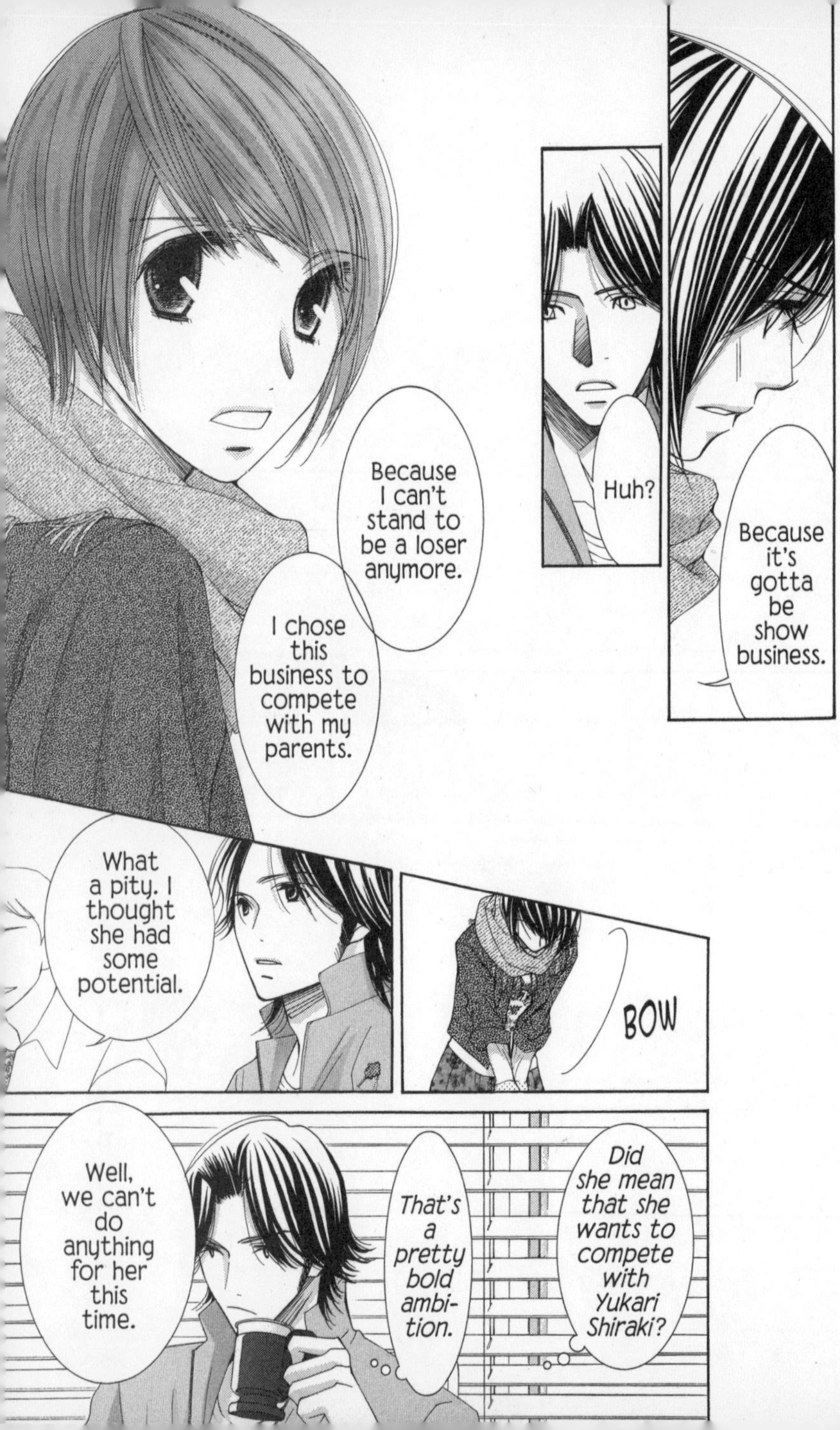
Because it's gotta be show business.
Huh?
Because I can't stand to be a loser anymore.
I chose this business to compete with my parents.
BOW
What a pity. I thought she had some potential.
Did she mean that she wants to compete with Yukari Shiraki?
That's a pretty bold ambition.
Well, we can't do anything for her this time.

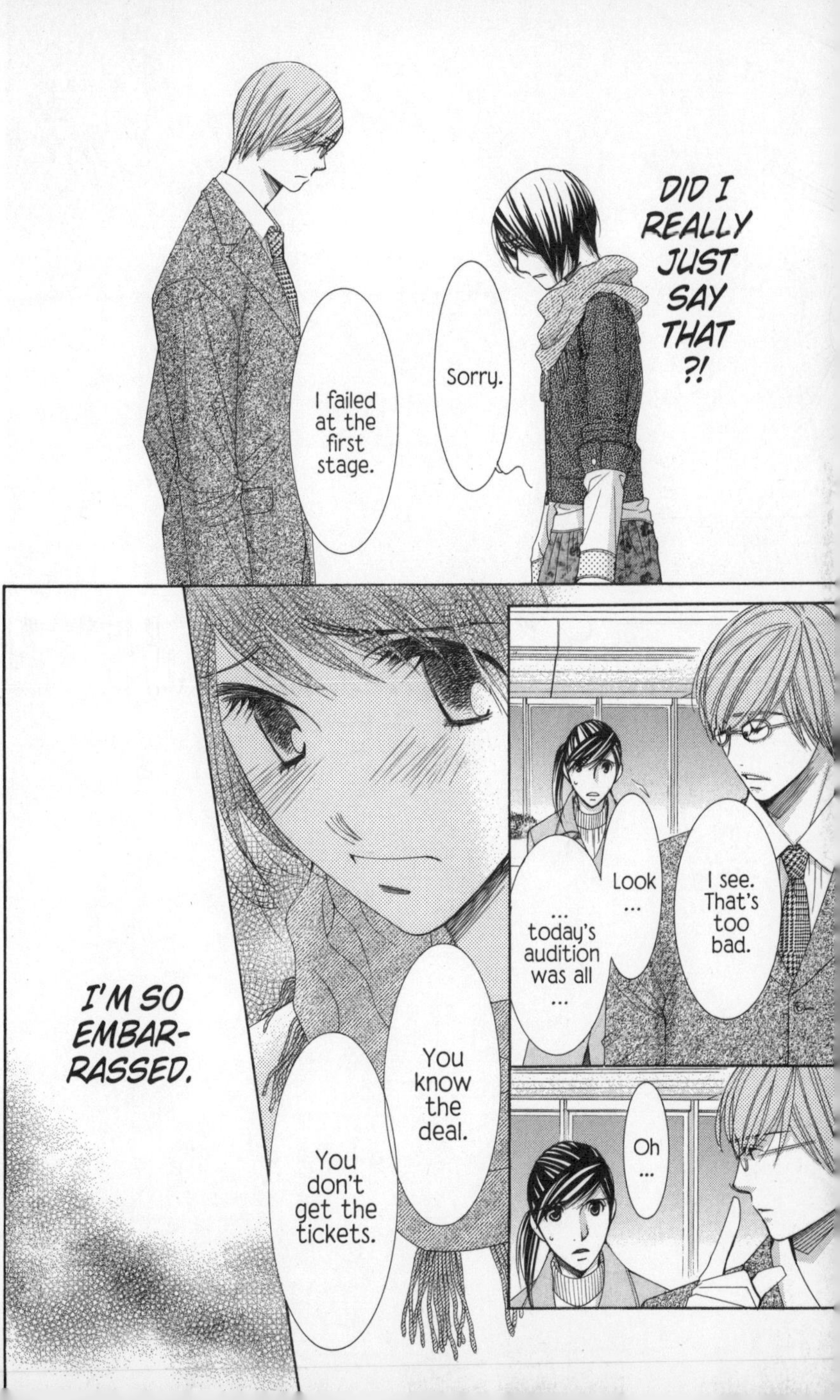
DID I REALLY JUST SAY THAT?!
Sorry.
I failed at the first stage.
I see. That's too bad.
Look ...
... today's audition was all ...
Oh ...
You know the deal.
You don't get the tickets.
I'M SO EMBARRASSED.

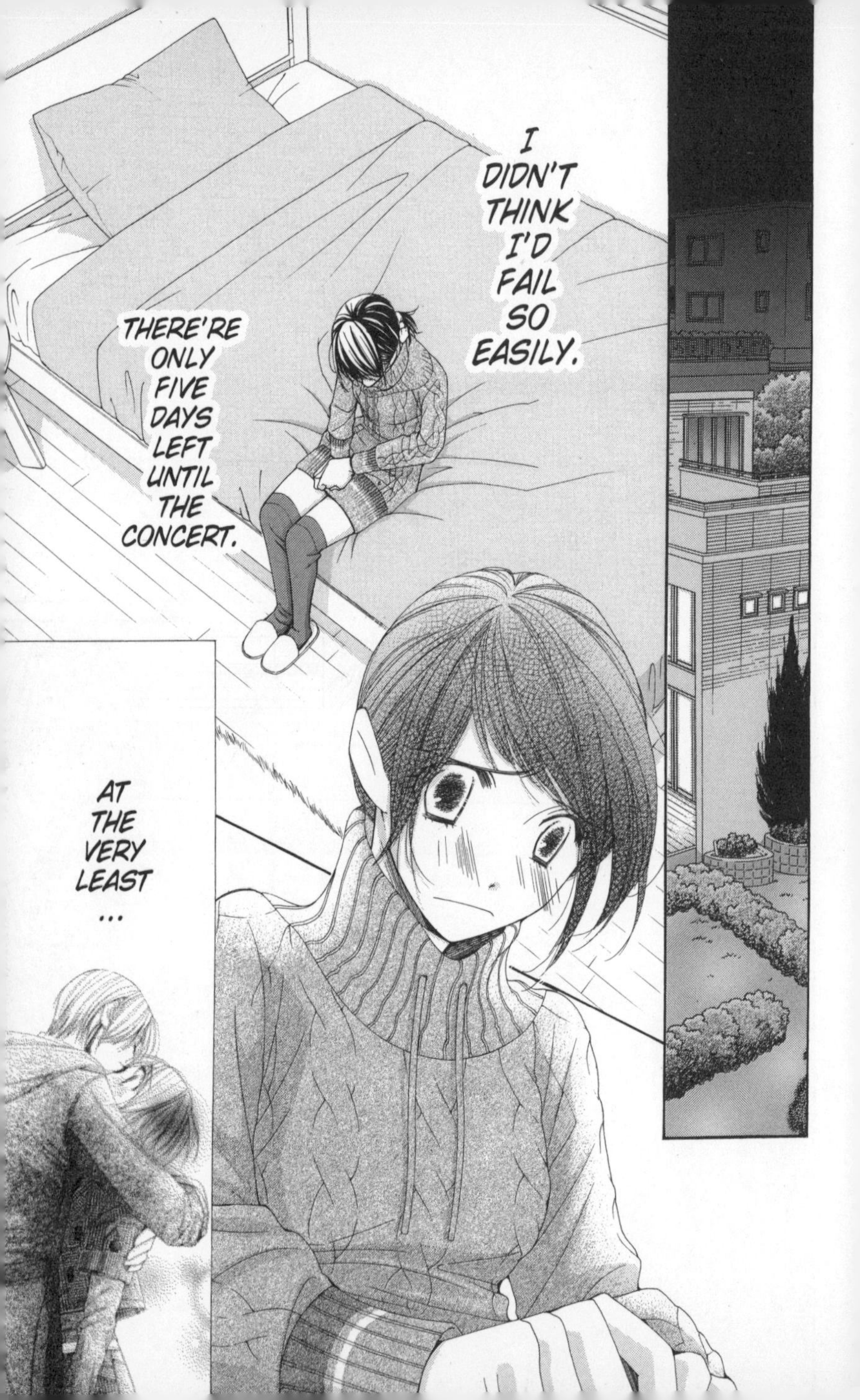
I DIDN'T THINK I'D FAIL SO EASILY.
THERE'RE ONLY FIVE DAYS LEFT UNTIL THE CONCERT.
AT THE VERY LEAST ...

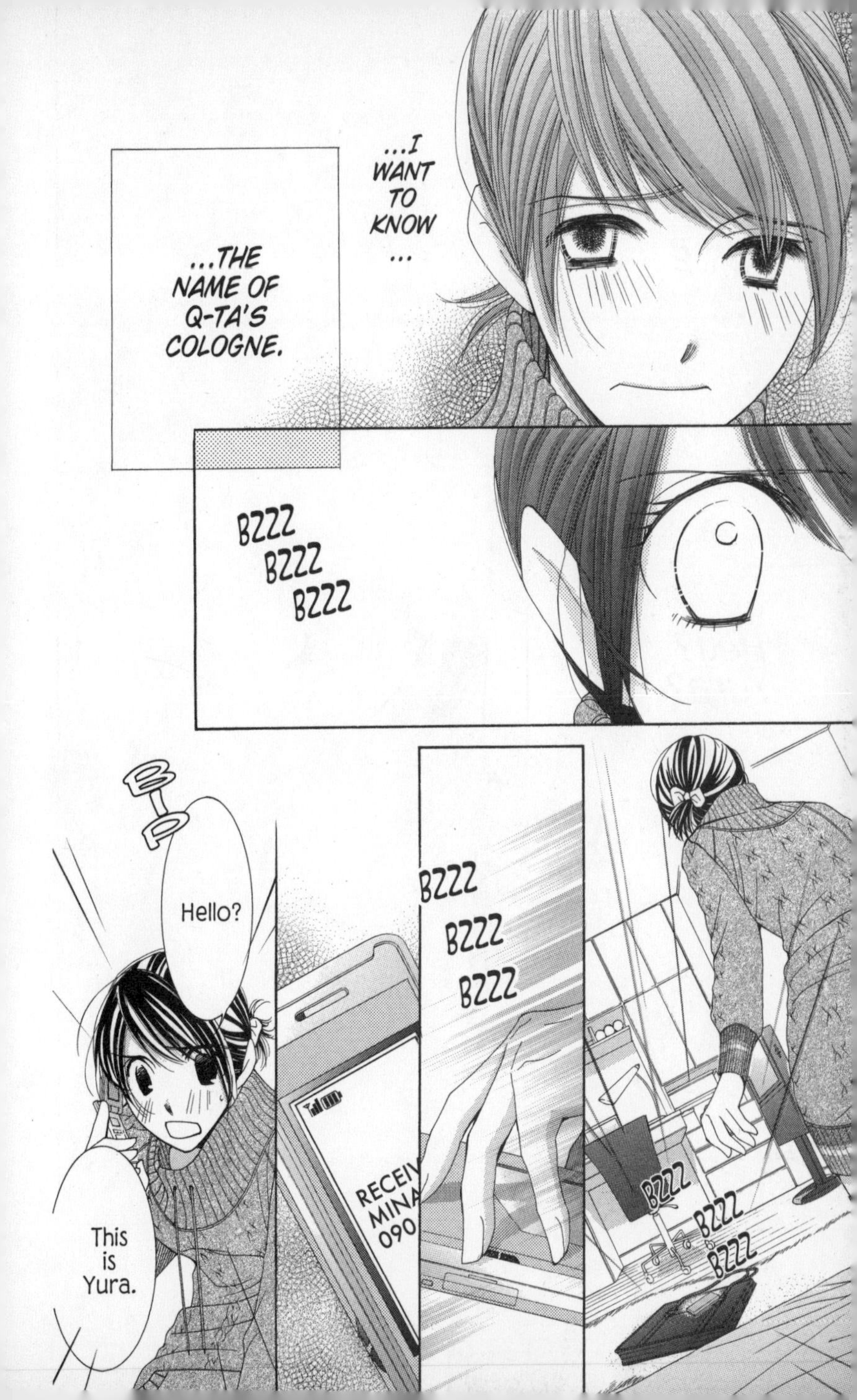
...I WANT TO KNOW ...
...THE NAME OF Q-TA'S COLOGNE.
BZZZ BZZZ BZZZ
BZZZ BZZZ BZZZ
BZZZ BZZZ BZZZ
RECEIV
MINA
090
BIP
Hello?
This is Yura.

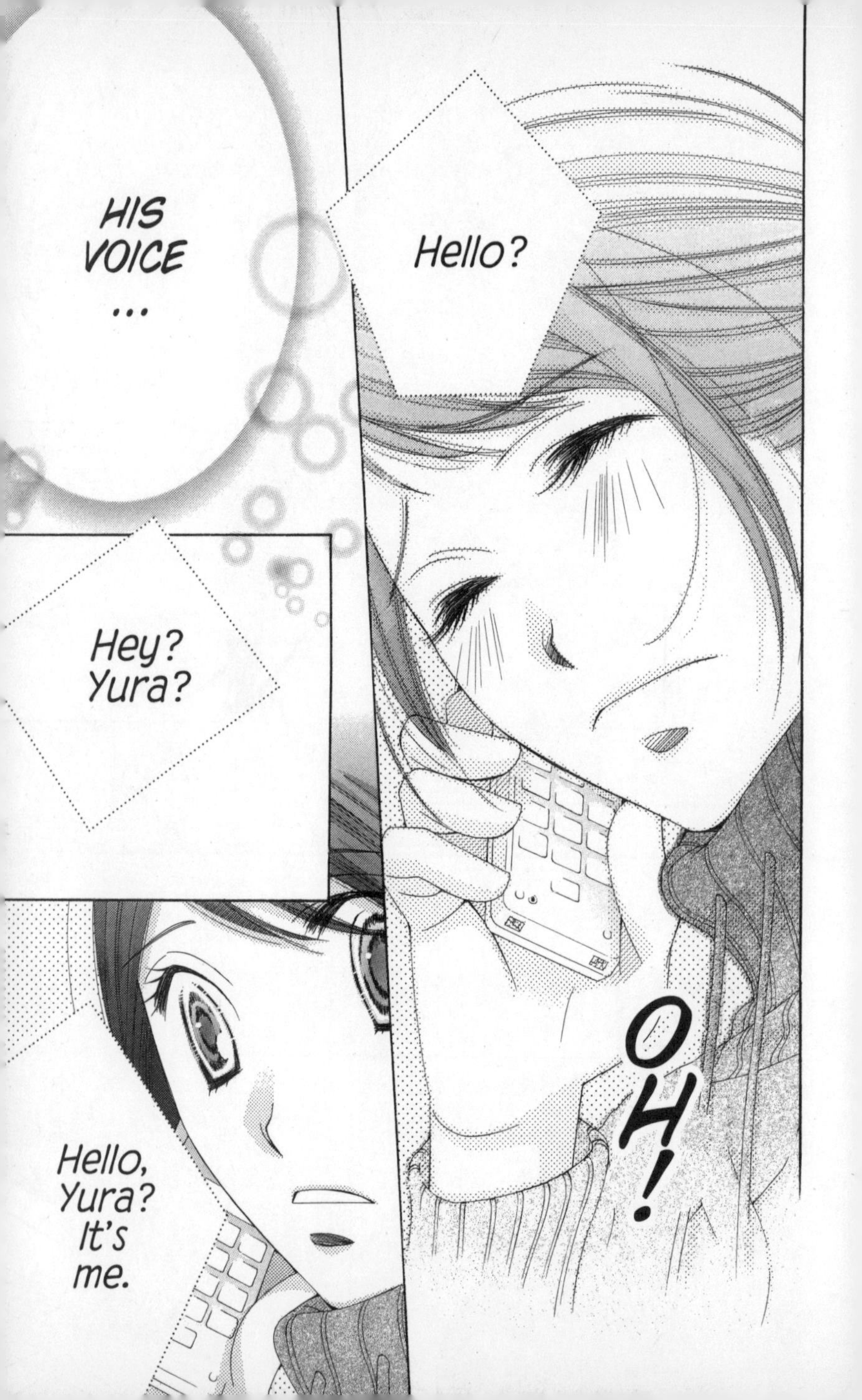
Hello?
OH!
HIS VOICE ...
Hey? Yura?
Hello, Yura? It's me.

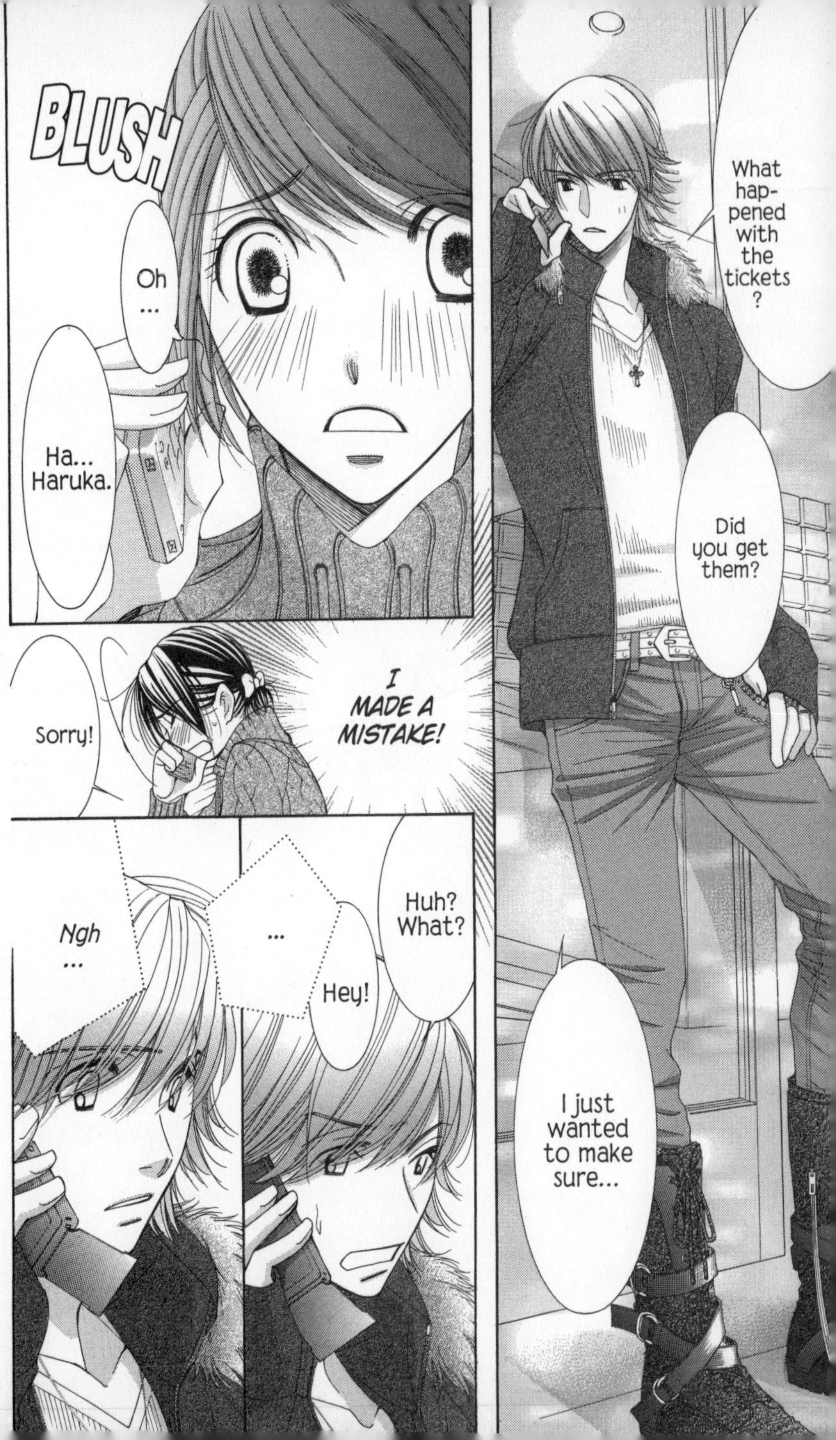
What hap-pened with the tickets?
Did you get them?
I just wanted to make sure...
BLUSH
Oh ...
Ha... Haruka.
I MADE A MISTAKE!
Sorry!
Huh? What?
Hey!
...
Ngh ...

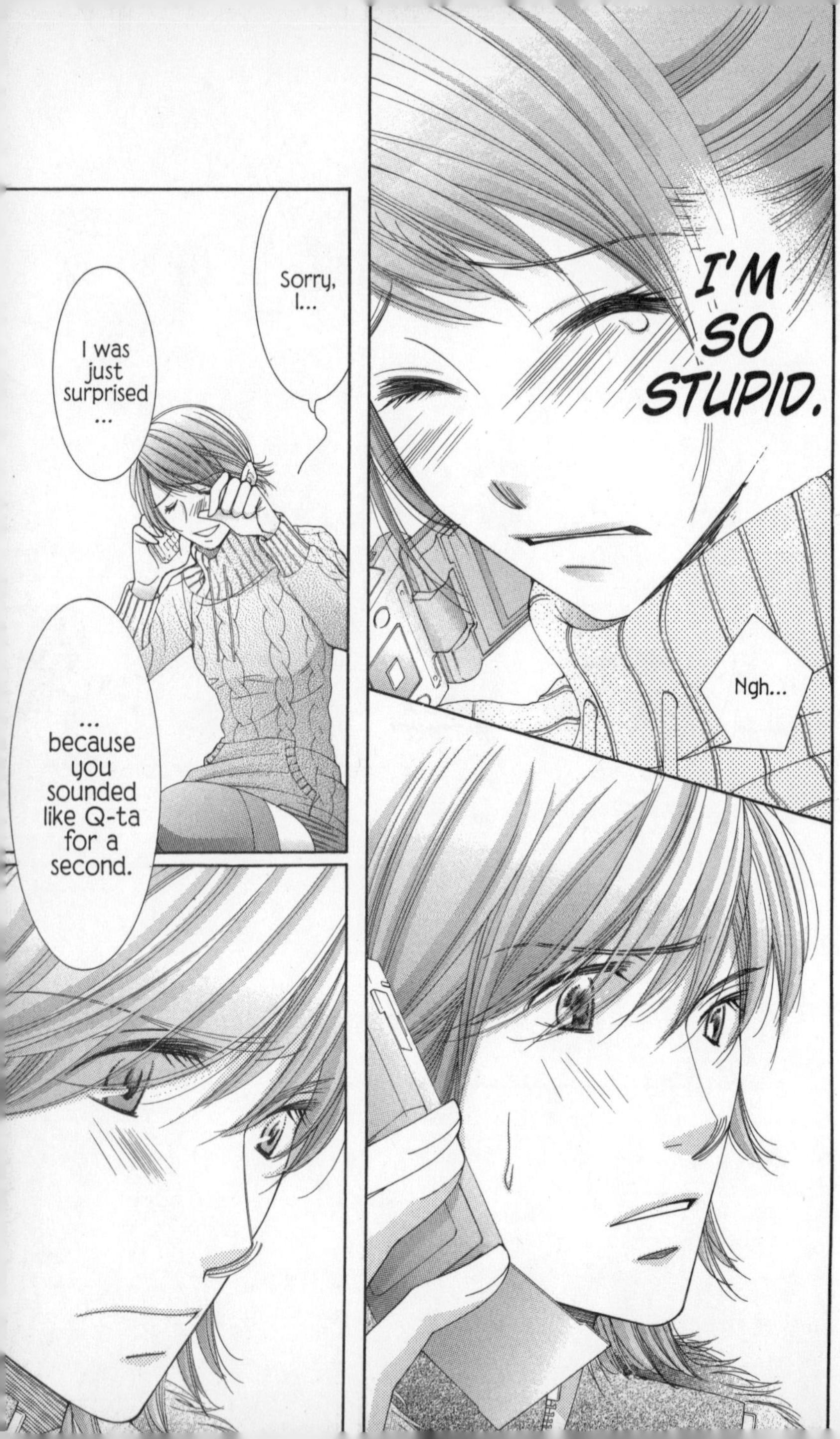
I'M SO STUPID.
Sorry, I...
I was just surprised...
...because you sounded like Q-ta for a second.
Ngh...

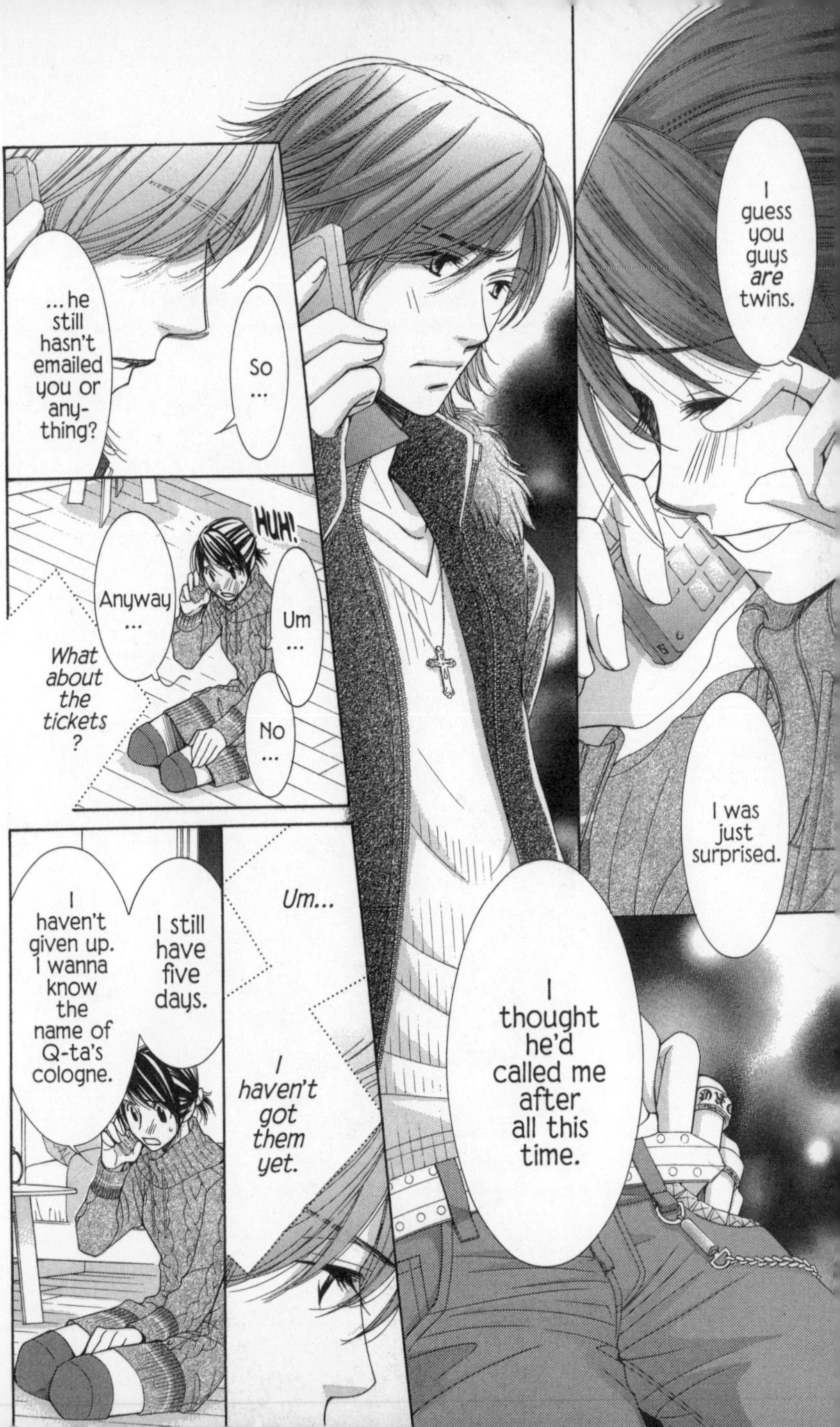

I guess you guys are twins.
I was just surprised.
I thought he'd called me after all this time.
So...
...he still hasn't emailed you or anything?
HUH!
Um...
No...
Anyway...
What about the tickets?
Um...
I haven't got them yet.
I still have five days.
I haven't given up. I wanna know the name of Q-ta's cologne.

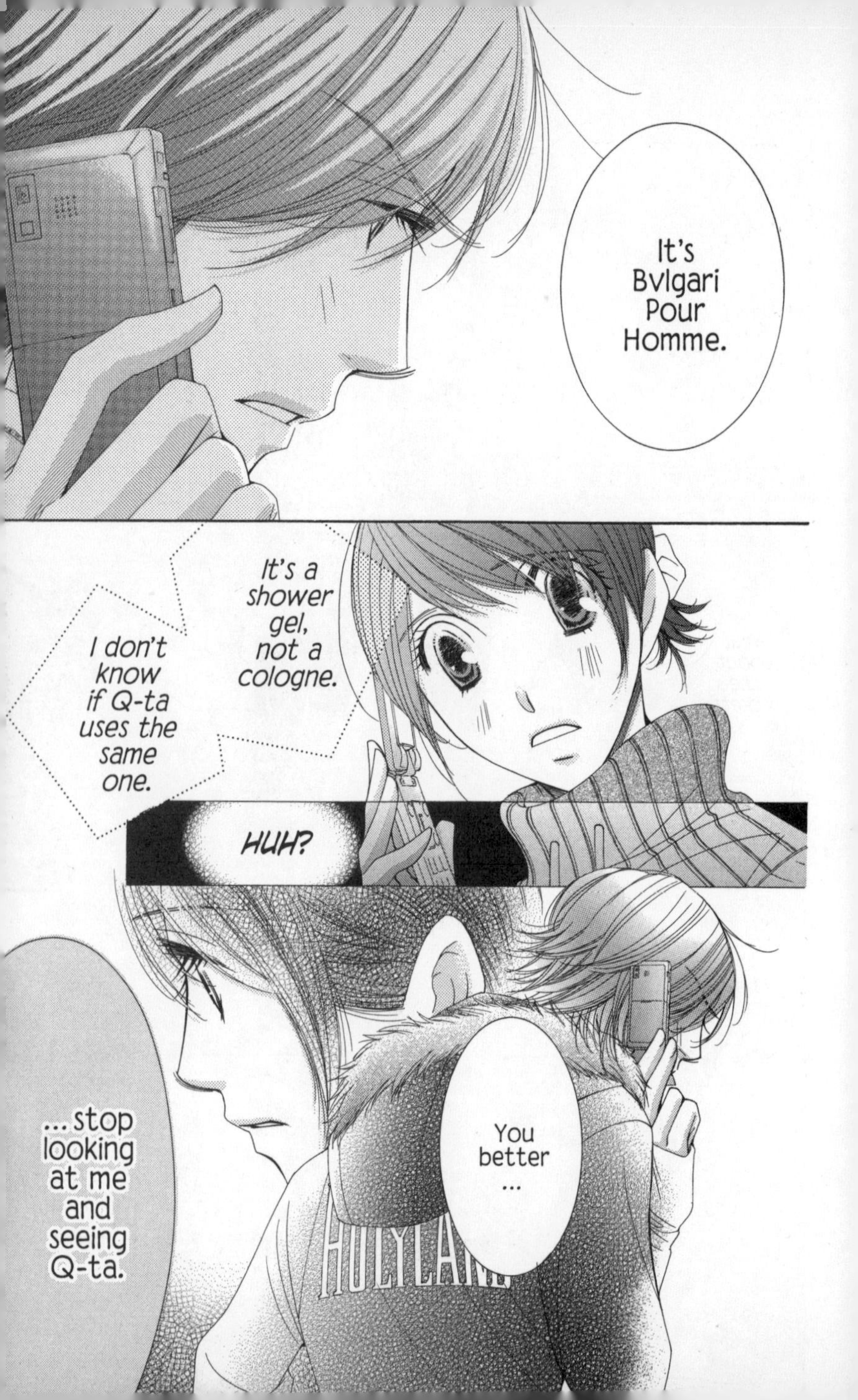
It's Bvlgari Pour Homme.
It's a shower gel, not a cologne.
I don't know if Q-ta uses the same one.
HUH?
You better...
...stop looking at me and seeing Q-ta.
HOLYLAND

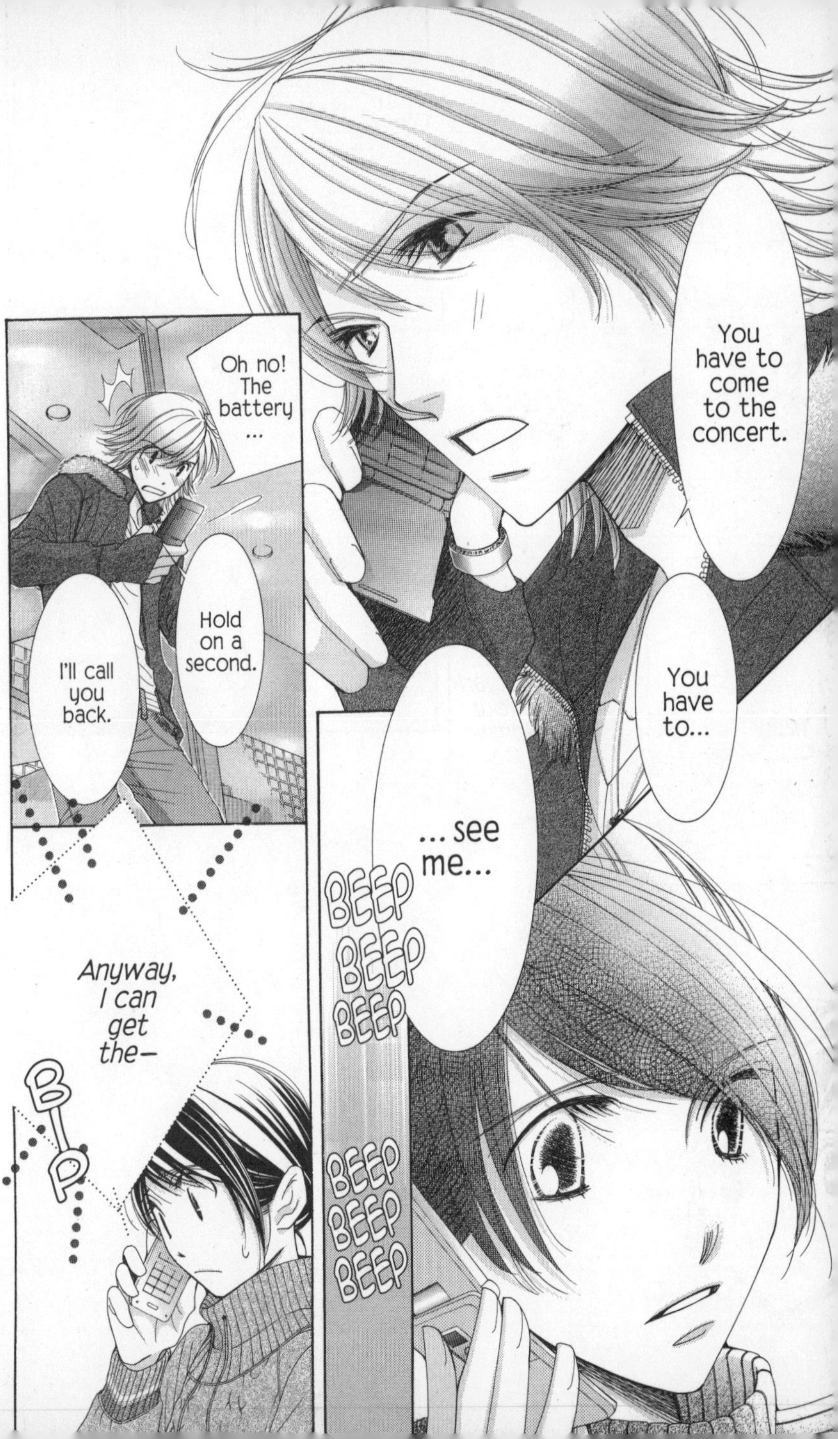

You have to come to the concert.
You have to...
... see me...
BEEP BEEP BEEP
BEEP BEEP BEEP
Oh no! The battery ...
Hold on a second.
I'll call you back.
Anyway, I can get the–
BIP

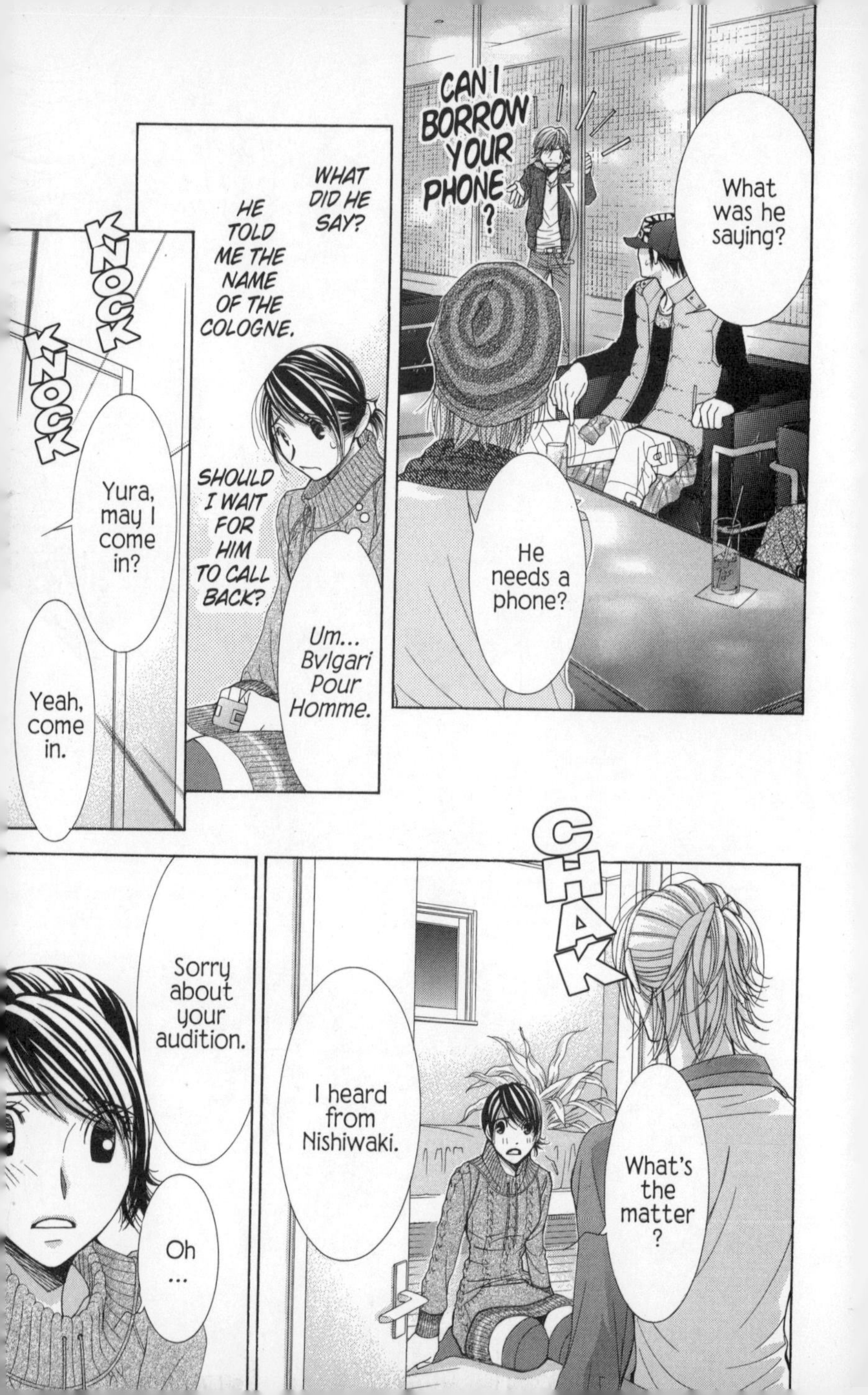
CAN I BORROW YOUR PHONE?
What was he saying?
He needs a phone?
WHAT DID HE SAY?
HE TOLD ME THE NAME OF THE COLOGNE.
Um... Bvlgari Pour Homme.
SHOULD I WAIT FOR HIM TO CALL BACK?
KNOCK
KNOCK
Yura, may I come in?
Yeah, come in.
CHAK
What's the matter?
I heard from Nishiwaki.
Sorry about your audition.
Oh...

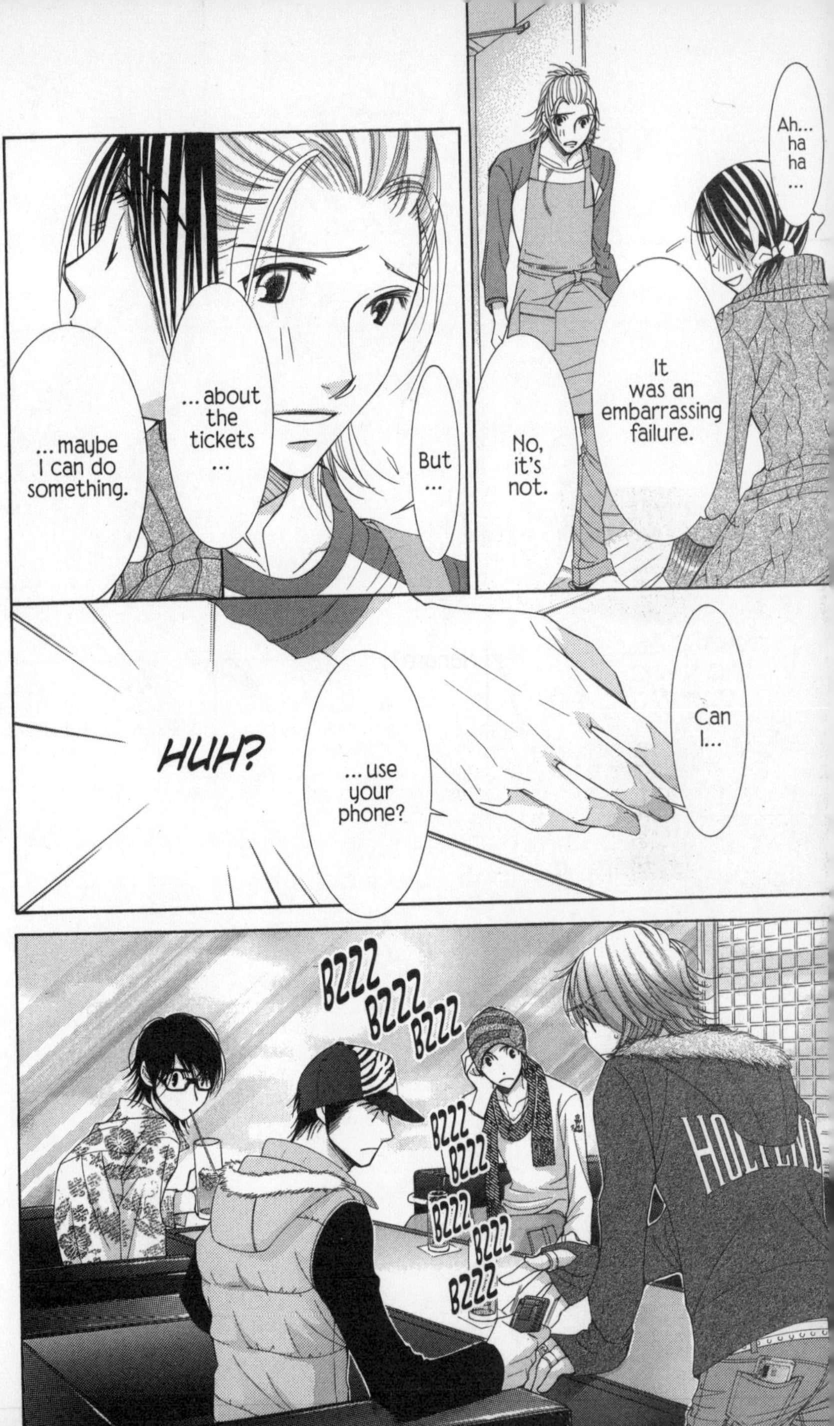
Ah... ha ha...
It was an embarrassing failure.
No, it's not.
But...
...about the tickets...
...maybe I can do something.
Can I...
...use your phone?
HUH?
BZZZ BZZZ BZZZ
BZZZ BZZZ BZZZ BZZZ BZZZ

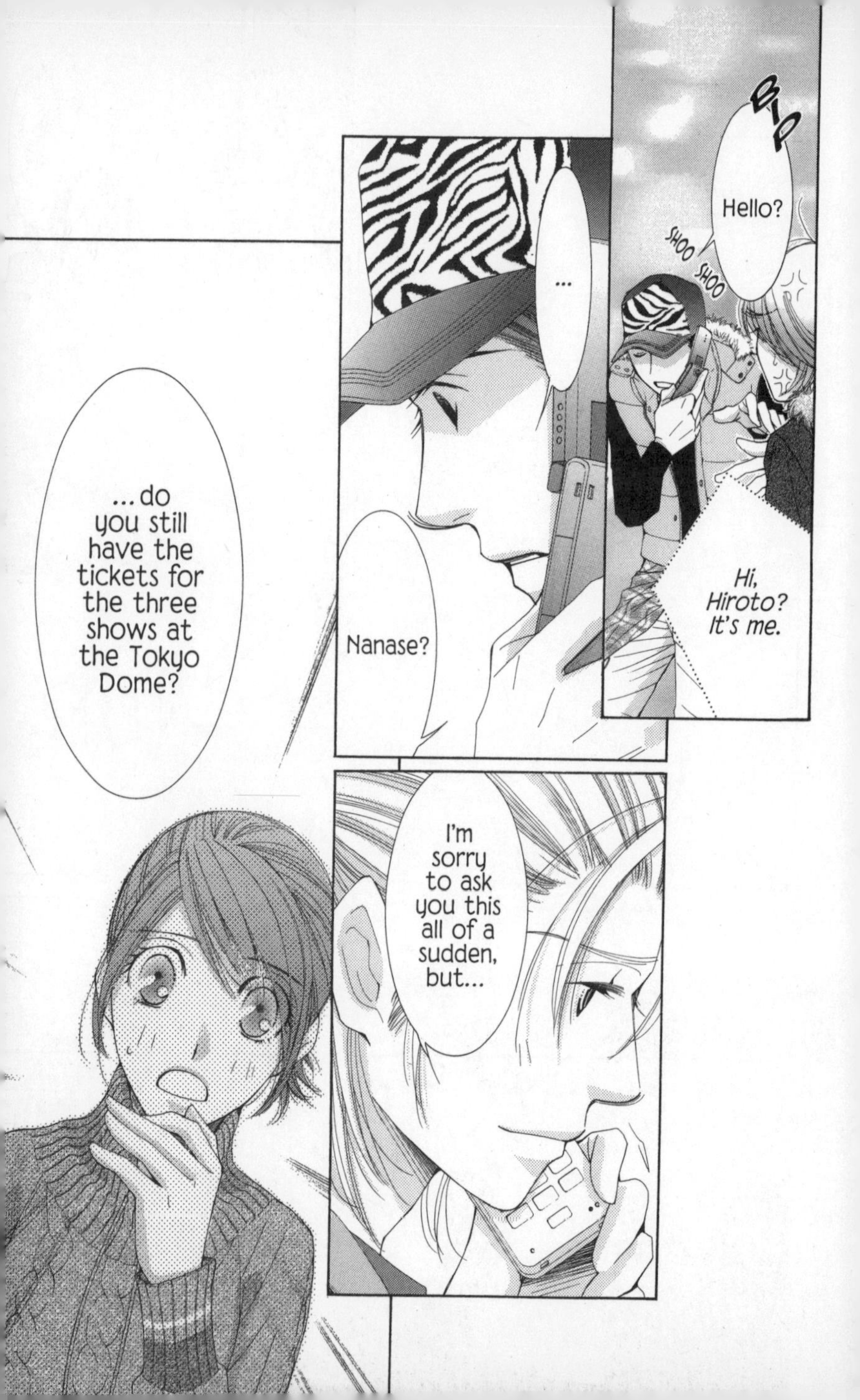

BIP
Hello?
SHOO SHOO
Hi, Hiroto? It's me.
...
Nanase?
I'm sorry to ask you this all of a sudden, but...
...do you still have the tickets for the three shows at the Tokyo Dome?

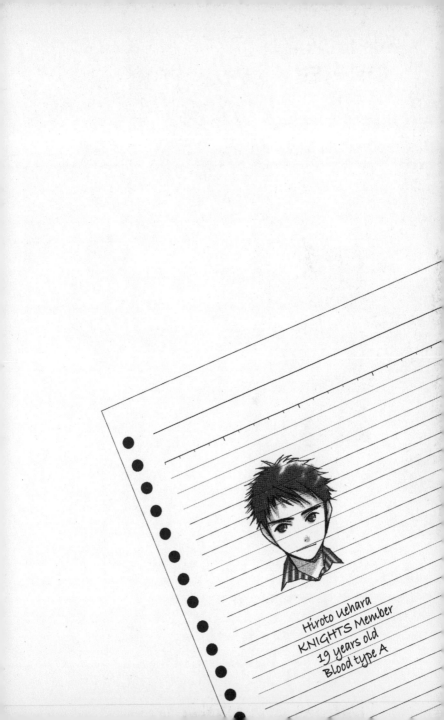

Hiroto Uehara
KNIGHTS Member
19 years old
Blood type A

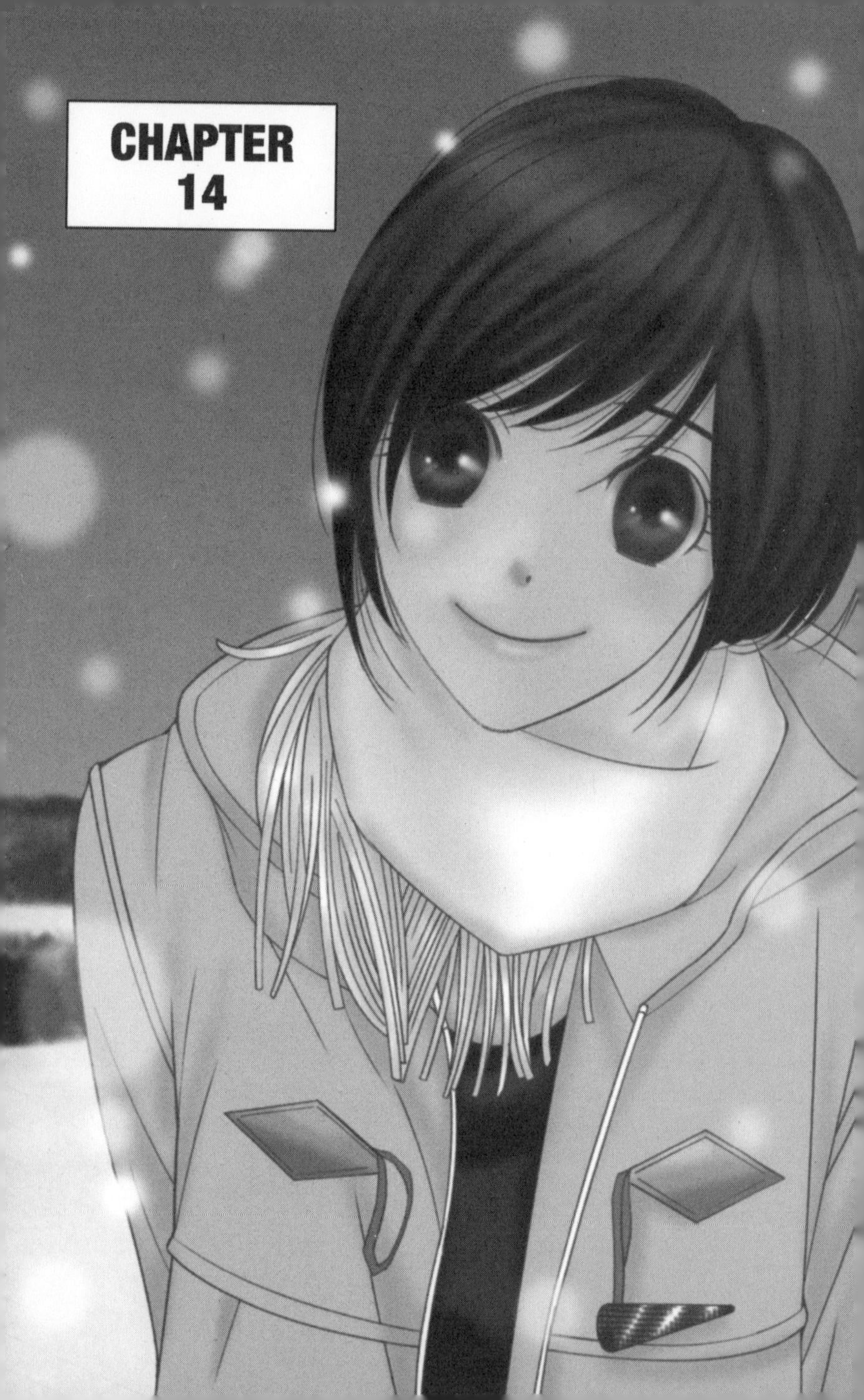
CHAPTER 14

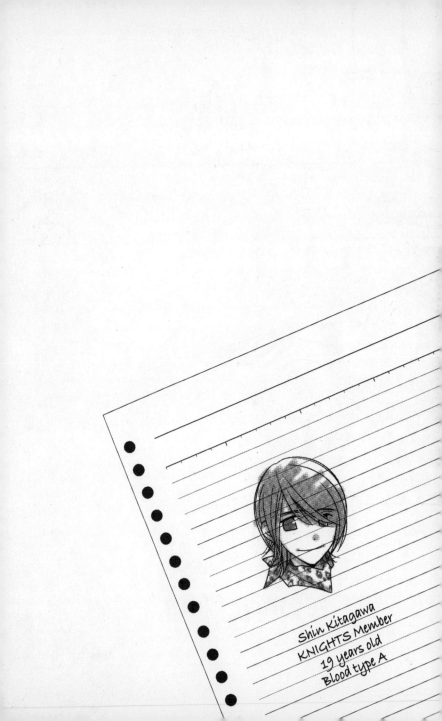

Shin Kitagawa
KNIGHTS Member
19 years old
Blood type A

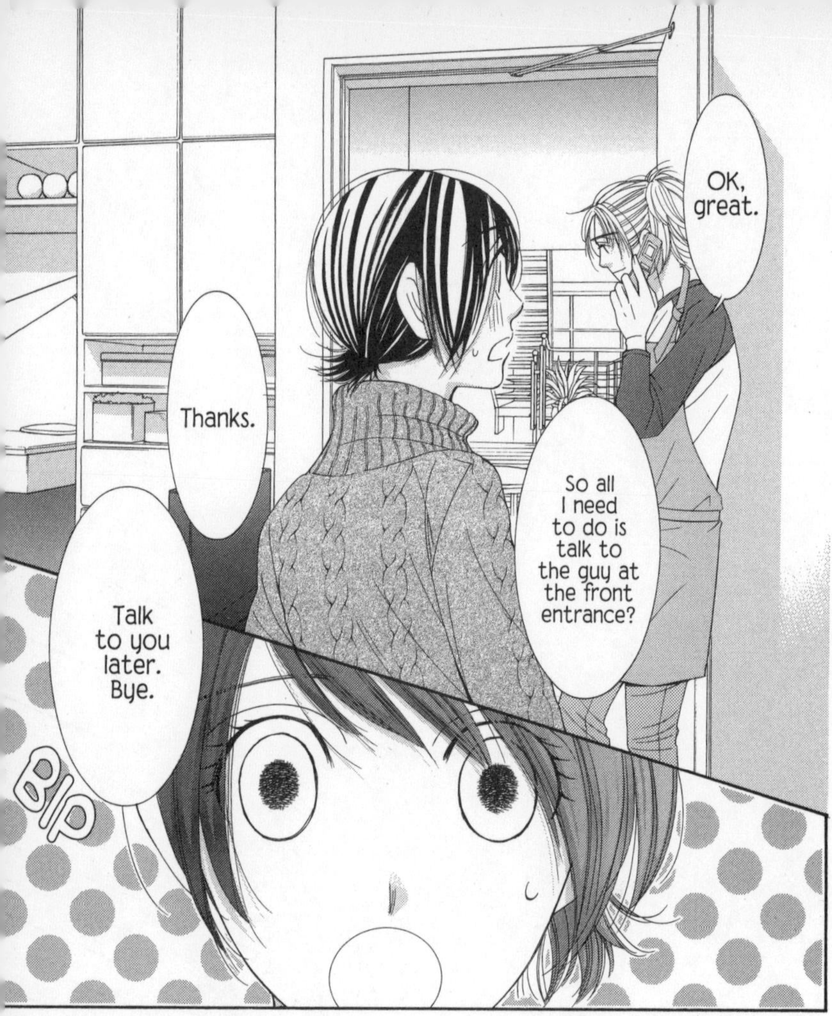
OK, great.
So all I need to do is talk to the guy at the front entrance?
Thanks.
Talk to you later. Bye.
BIP

Honey Hunt

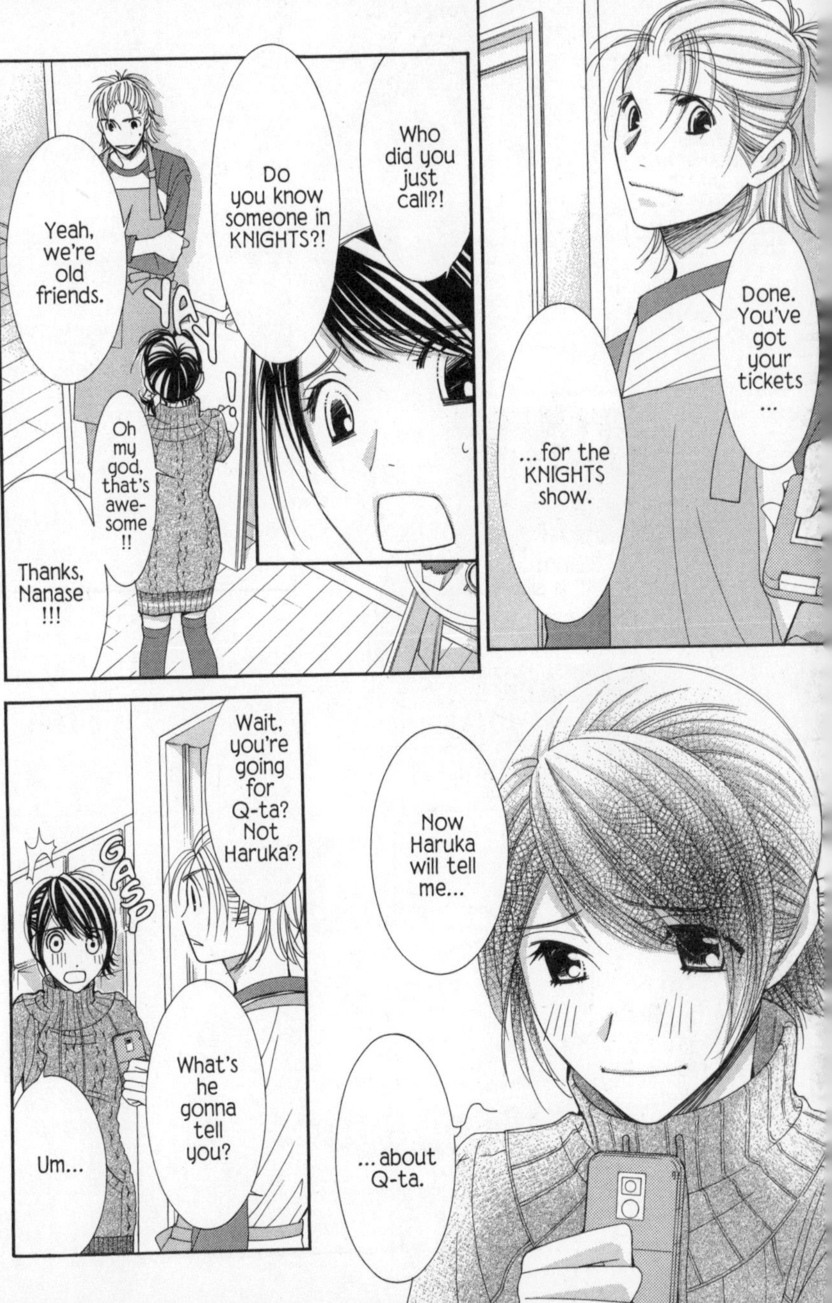

Done. You've got your tickets ...
...for the KNIGHTS show.
Who did you just call?!
Do you know someone in KNIGHTS?!
Yeah, we're old friends.
YAY!
Oh my god, that's awe-some!!
Thanks, Nanase!!!
Now Haruka will tell me...
...about Q-ta.
Wait, you're going for Q-ta? Not Haruka?
GASP
What's he gonna tell you?
Um...

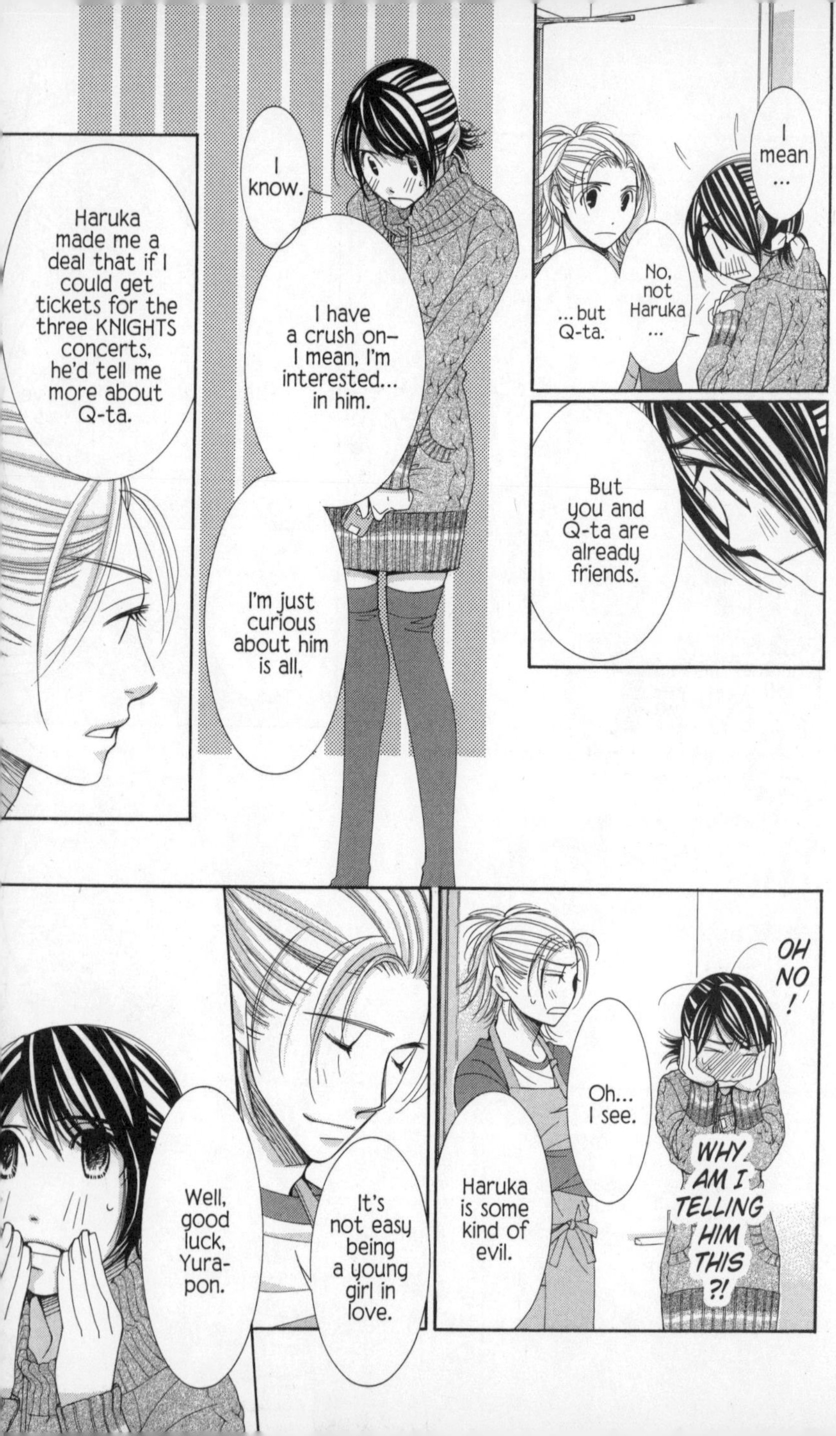
I mean...
No, not Haruka...
...but Q-ta.
But you and Q-ta are already friends.
I know.
I have a crush on— I mean, I'm interested... in him.
I'm just curious about him is all.
Haruka made me a deal that if I could get tickets for the three KNIGHTS concerts, he'd tell me more about Q-ta.
OH NO!
WHY AM I TELLING HIM THIS?!
Oh... I see.
Haruka is some kind of evil.
It's not easy being a young girl in love.
Well, good luck, Yura-pon.

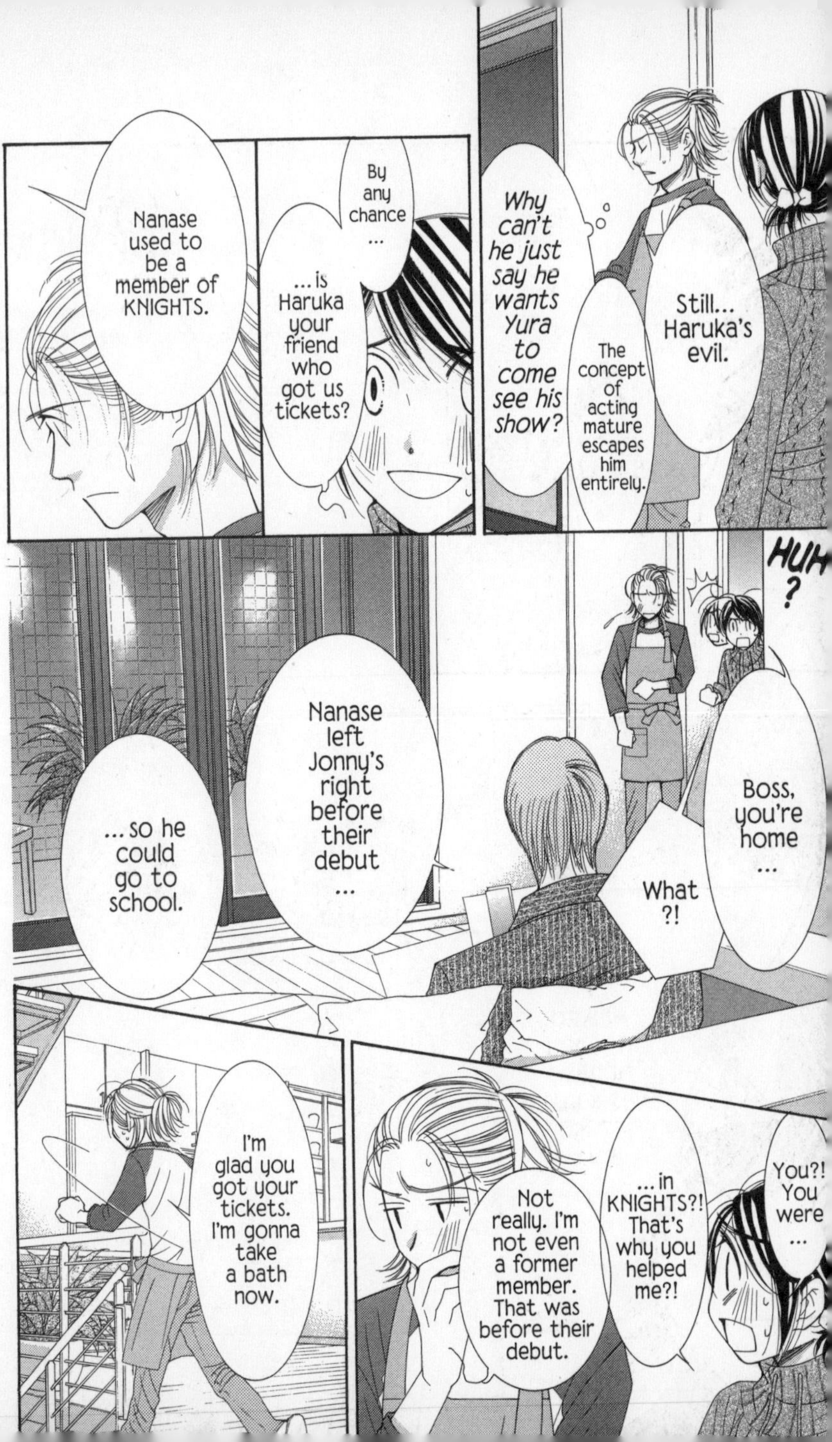

Still... Haruka's evil.
The concept of acting mature escapes him entirely.
Why can't he just say he wants Yura to come see his show?
By any chance ...
... is Haruka your friend who got us tickets?
Nanase used to be a member of KNIGHTS.
HUH ?
Boss, you're home ...
What ?!
Nanase left Jonny's right before their debut ...
... so he could go to school.
You?! You were ...
... in KNIGHTS?! That's why you helped me?!
Not really. I'm not even a former member. That was before their debut.
I'm glad you got your tickets. I'm gonna take a bath now.

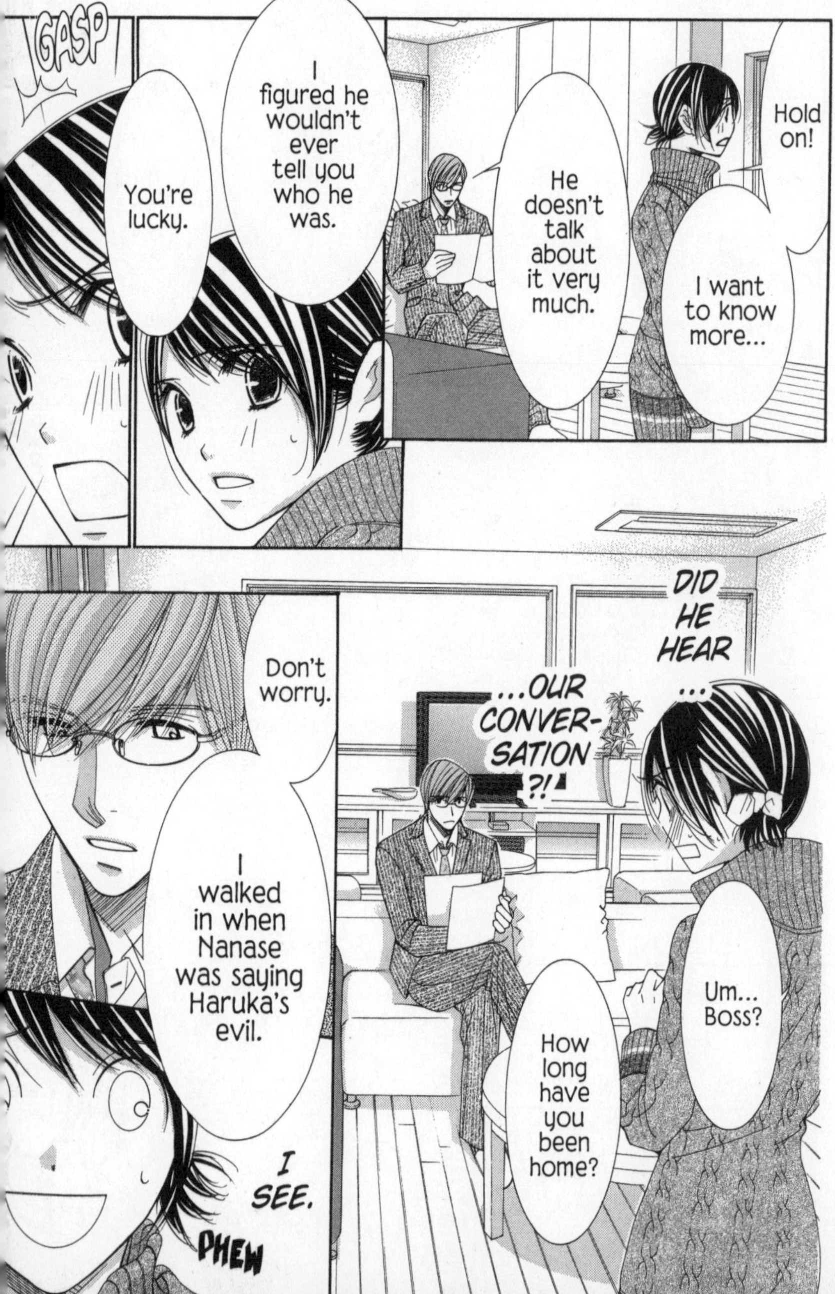
Hold on!
I want to know more...
He doesn't talk about it very much.
I figured he wouldn't ever tell you who he was.
GASP
You're lucky.
DID HE HEAR ...
...OUR CONVERSATION?!
Um... Boss?
How long have you been home?
Don't worry.
I walked in when Nanase was saying Haruka's evil.
I SEE.
PHEW

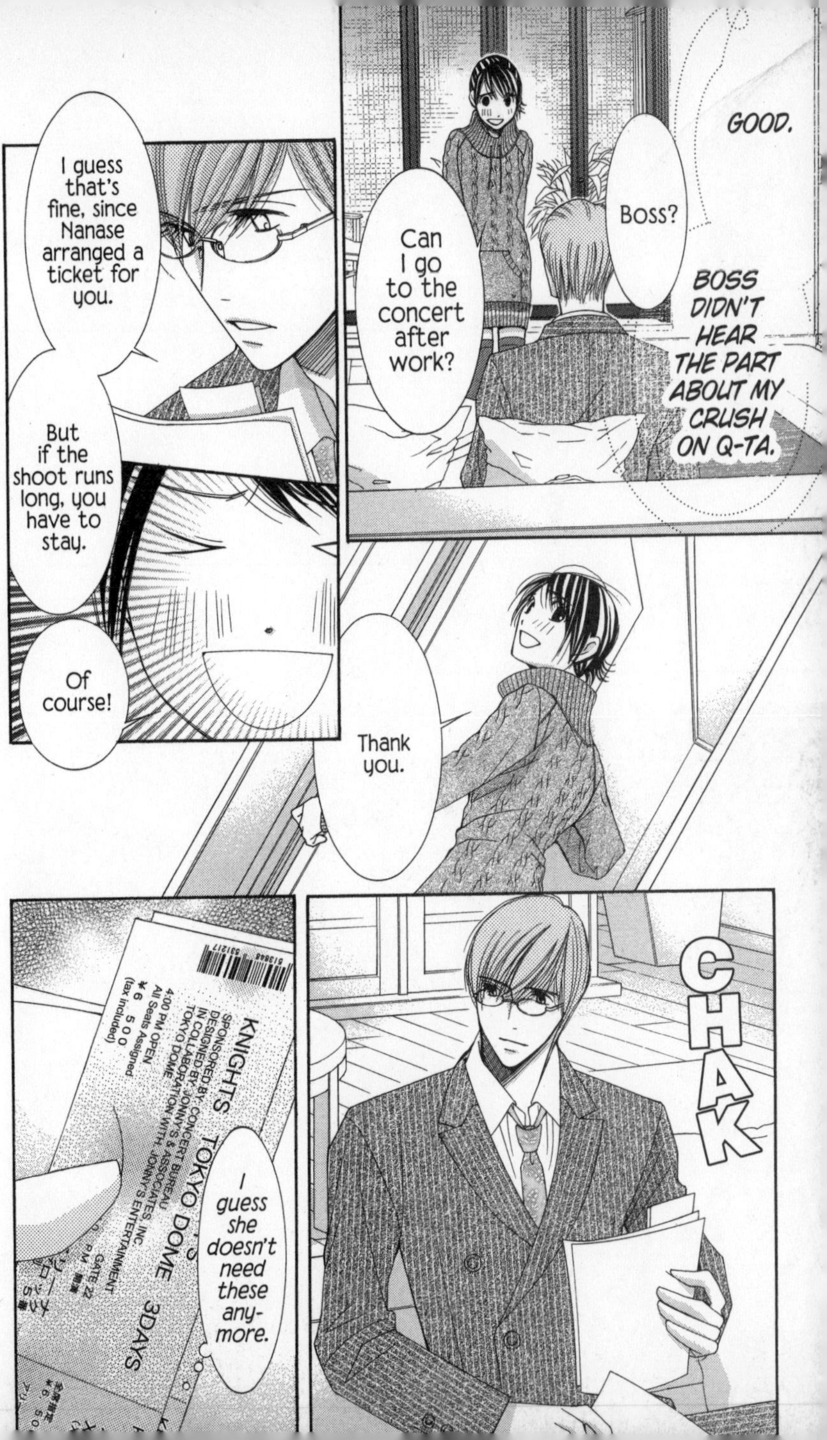
GOOD.
BOSS DIDN'T HEAR THE PART ABOUT MY CRUSH ON Q-TA.
Boss?
Can I go to the concert after work?
I guess that's fine, since Nanase arranged a ticket for you.
But if the shoot runs long, you have to stay.
Of course!
Thank you.
CHAK
KNIGHTS TOKYO DOME 3DAYS
SPONSORED BY: CONCERT BUREAU
DESIGNED BY: JOHNNY'S & ASSOCIATES, INC
IN COLLABORATION WITH JOHNNY'S ENTERTAINMENT
TOKYO DOME
4:00 PM OPEN
All Seats Assigned
¥6 500
(tax included)
GATE 22
I guess she doesn't need these anymore.

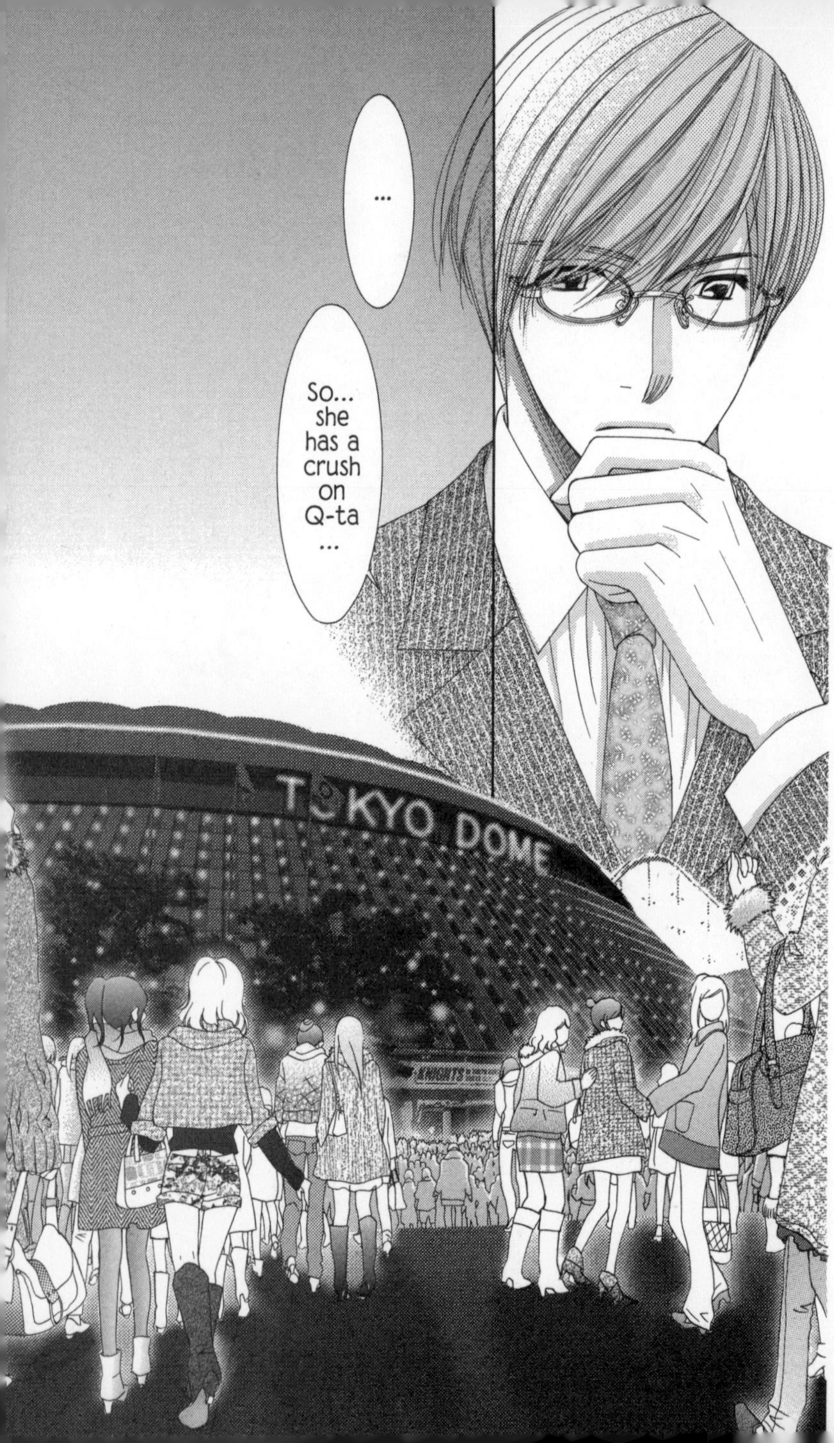
...
So... she has a crush on Q-ta ...
TOKYO DOME

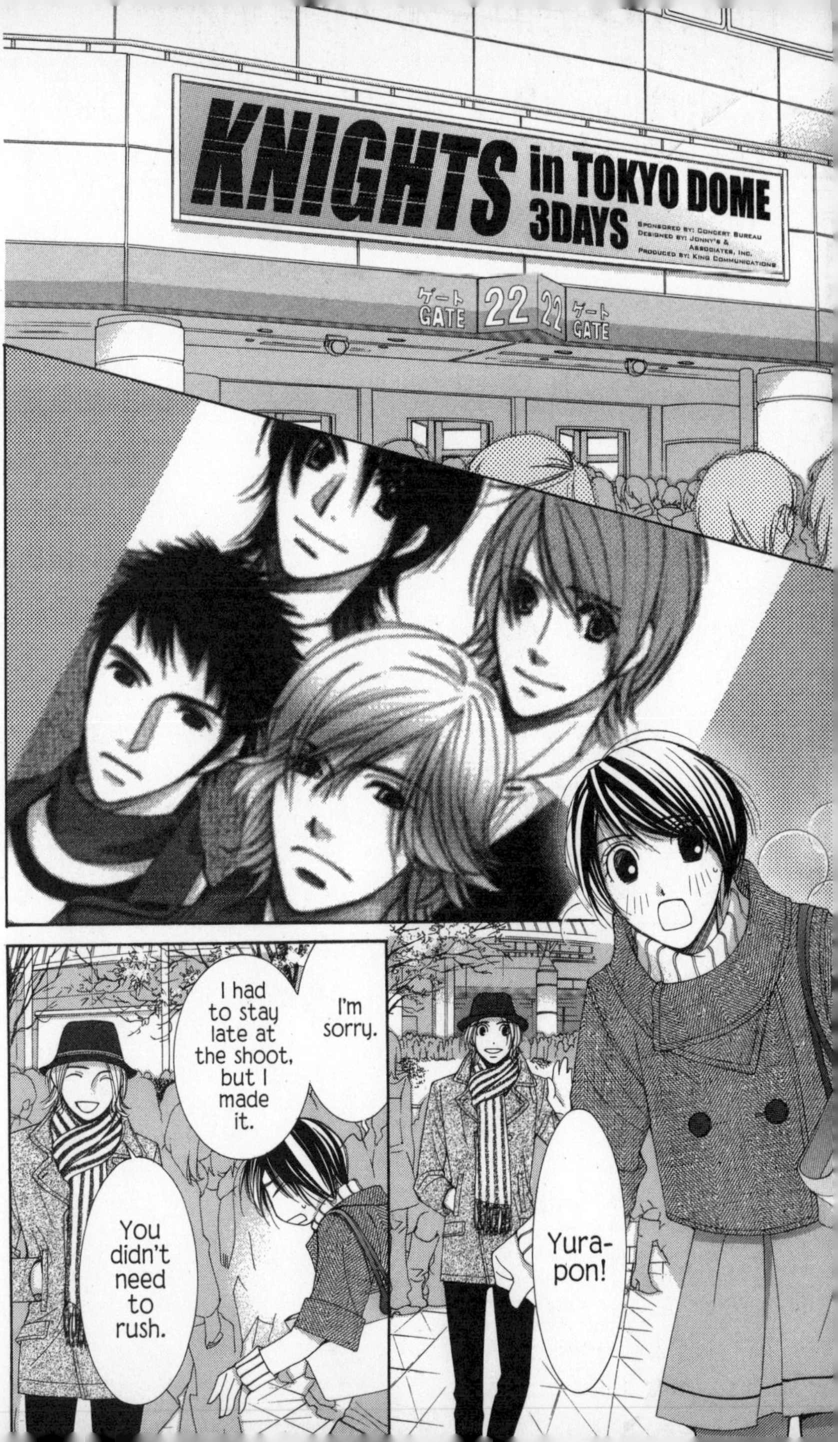
KNIGHTS in TOKYO DOME 3DAYS
SPONSORED BY: CONCERT BUREAU
DESIGNED BY: JONNY'S & ASSOCIATES, INC.
PRODUCED BY: KING COMMUNICATIONS
ゲート GATE 22
22 ゲート GATE
Yura-pon!
I'm sorry.
I had to stay late at the shoot, but I made it.
You didn't need to rush.

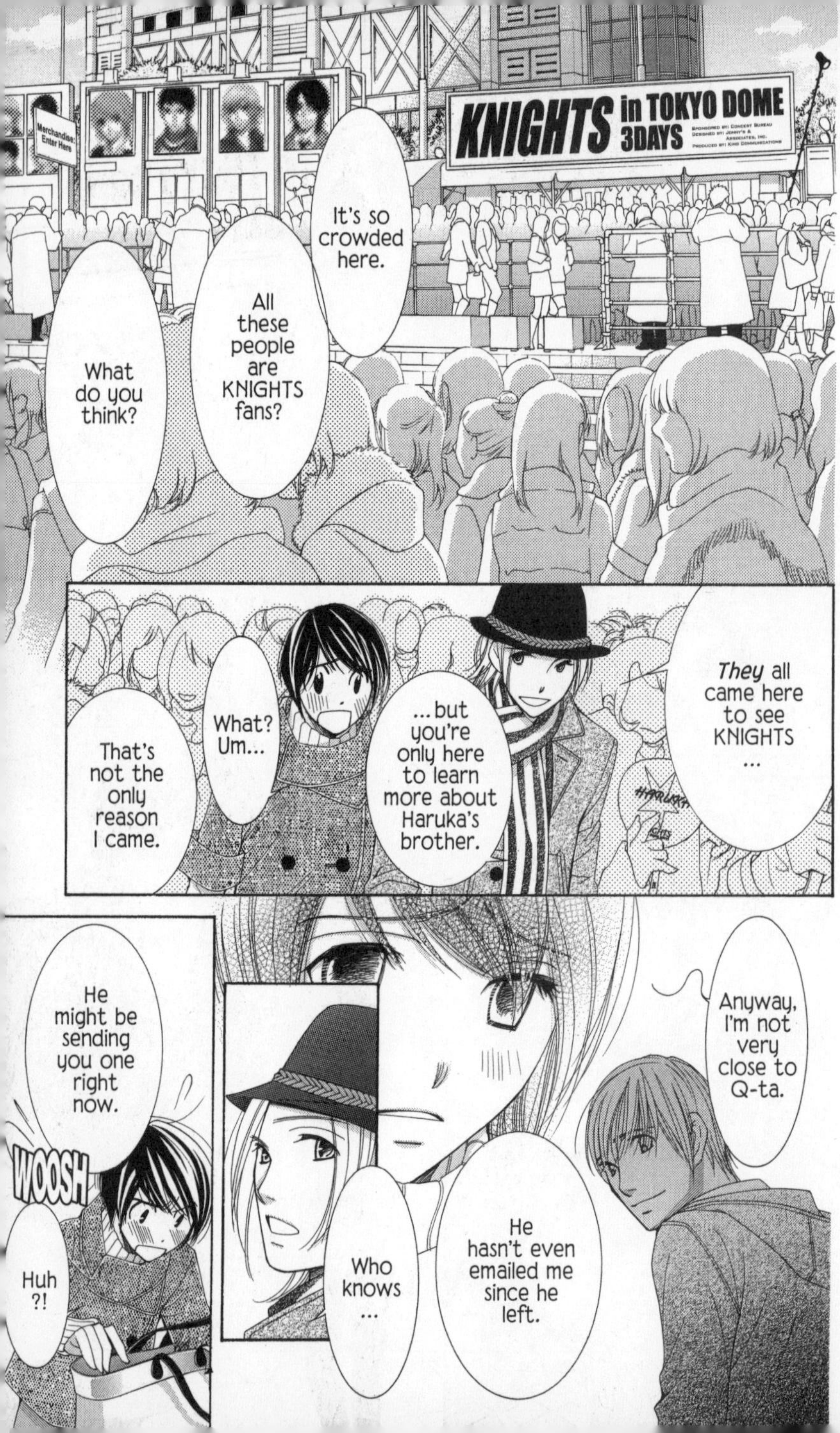

KNIGHTS in TOKYO DOME 3DAYS
SPONSORED BY: CONCERT BUREAU
DESIGNED BY: JOHNY'S & ASSOCIATES, INC.
PRODUCED BY: KING COMMUNICATIONS
Merchandise: Enter Here
It's so crowded here.
All these people are KNIGHTS fans?
What do you think?
They all came here to see KNIGHTS ...
...but you're only here to learn more about Haruka's brother.
What? Um...
That's not the only reason I came.
Anyway, I'm not very close to Q-ta.
He hasn't even emailed me since he left.
Who knows ...
He might be sending you one right now.
WOOSH
Huh ?!

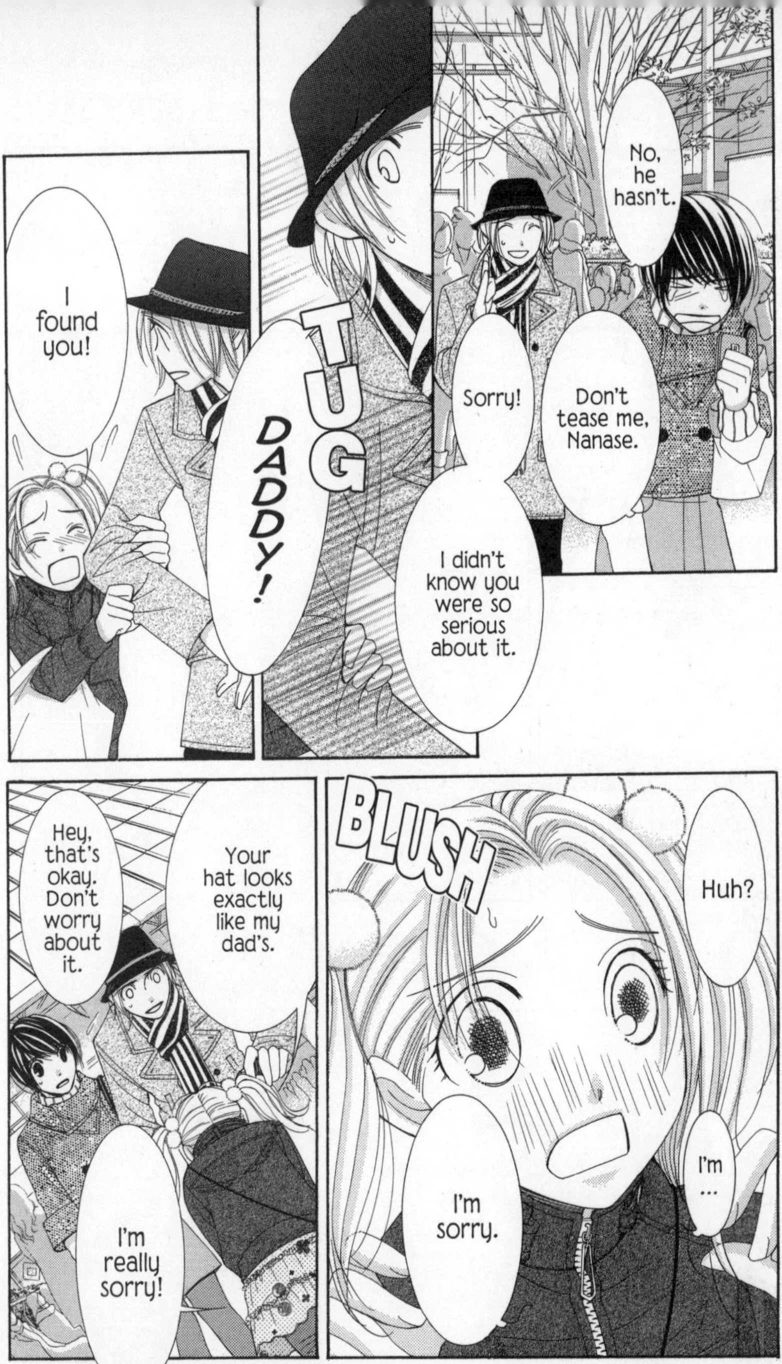
No, he hasn't.
Don't tease me, Nanase.
Sorry!
I didn't know you were so serious about it.
TUG
DADDY!
I found you!
BLUSH
Huh?
I'm...
I'm sorry.
Your hat looks exactly like my dad's.
Hey, that's okay. Don't worry about it.
I'm really sorry!

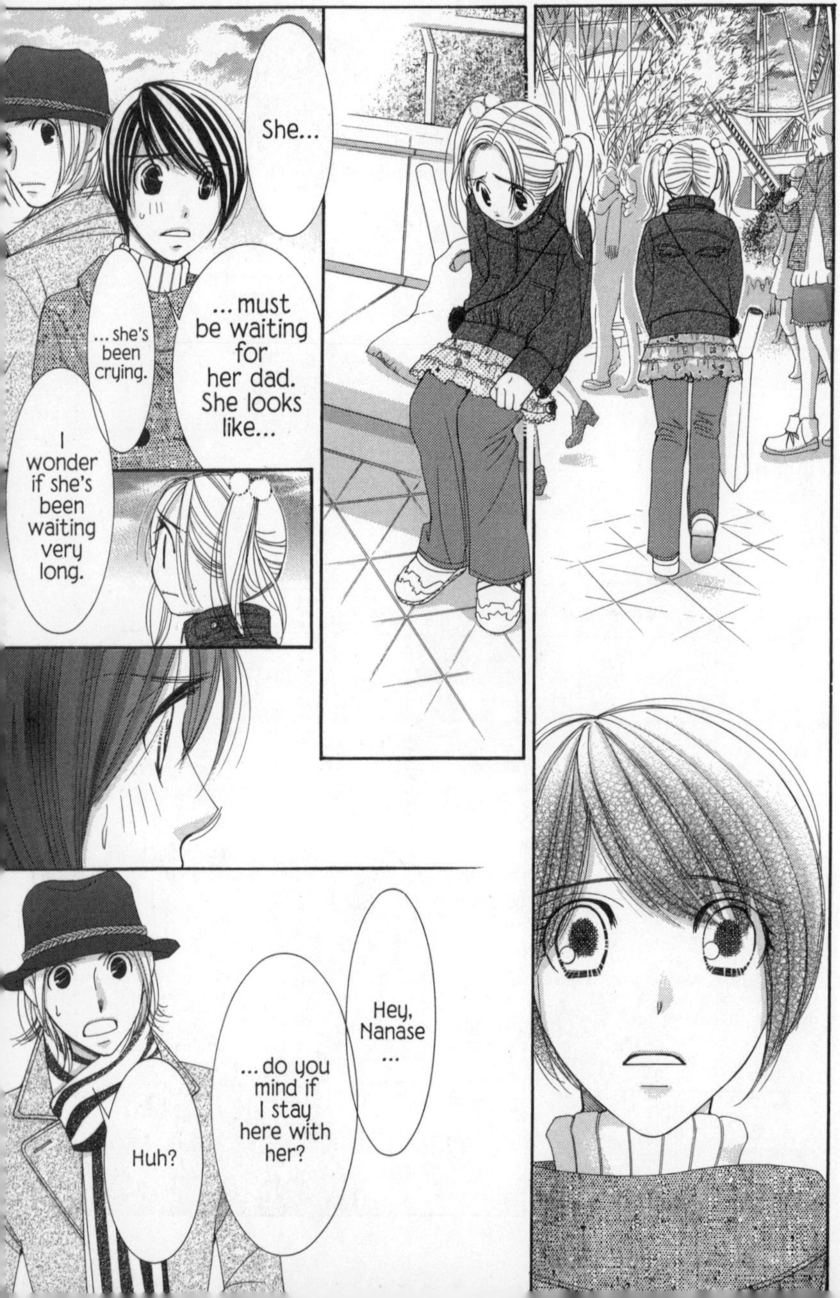
She...
...must be waiting for her dad. She looks like...
...she's been crying.
I wonder if she's been waiting very long.
Hey, Nanase...
...do you mind if I stay here with her?
Huh?

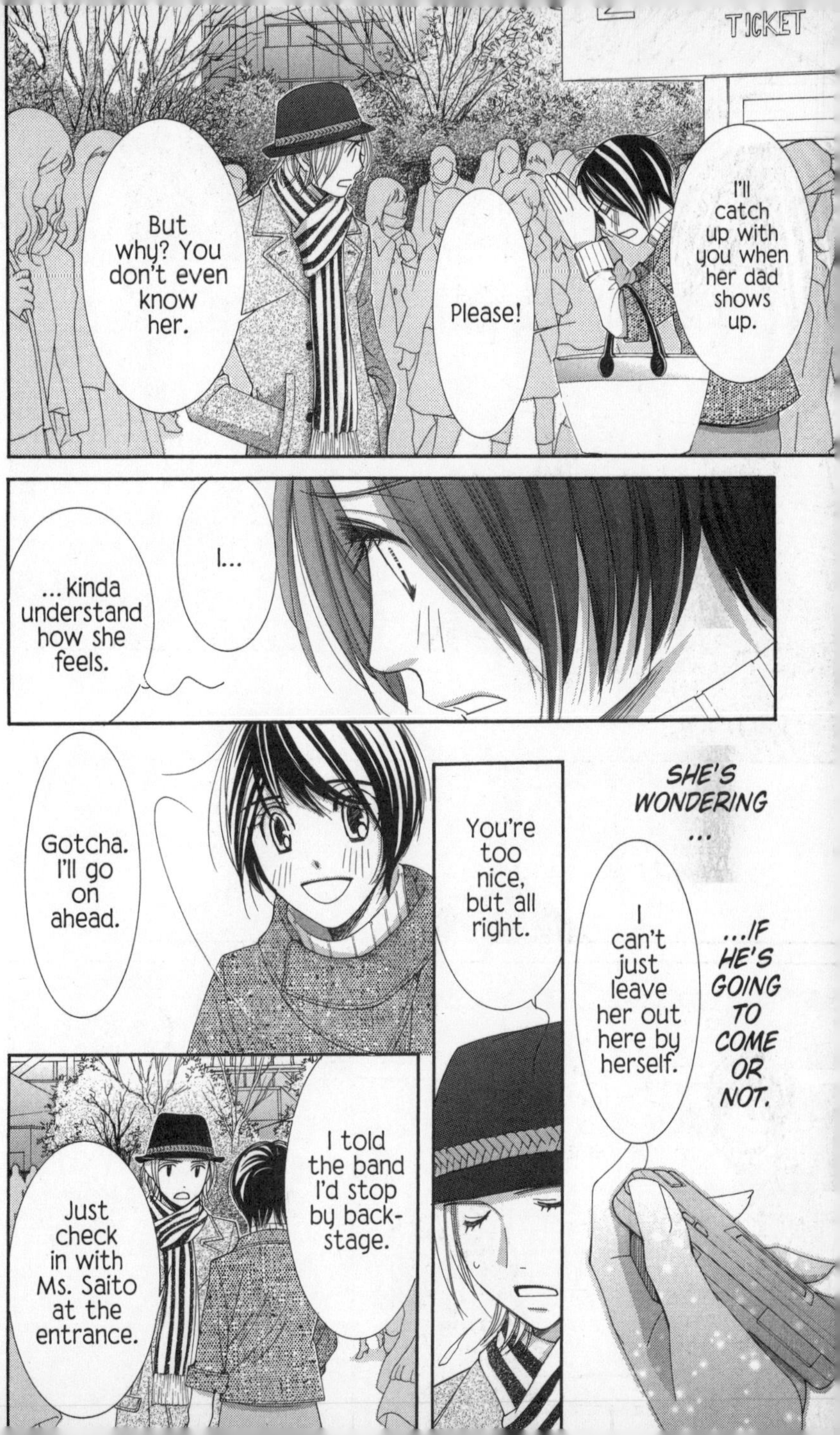
TICKET
I'll catch up with you when her dad shows up.
Please!
But why? You don't even know her.
I...
...kinda understand how she feels.
SHE'S WONDERING...
I can't just leave her out here by herself.
...IF HE'S GOING TO COME OR NOT.
You're too nice, but all right.
Gotcha. I'll go on ahead.
I told the band I'd stop by back-stage.
Just check in with Ms. Saito at the entrance.

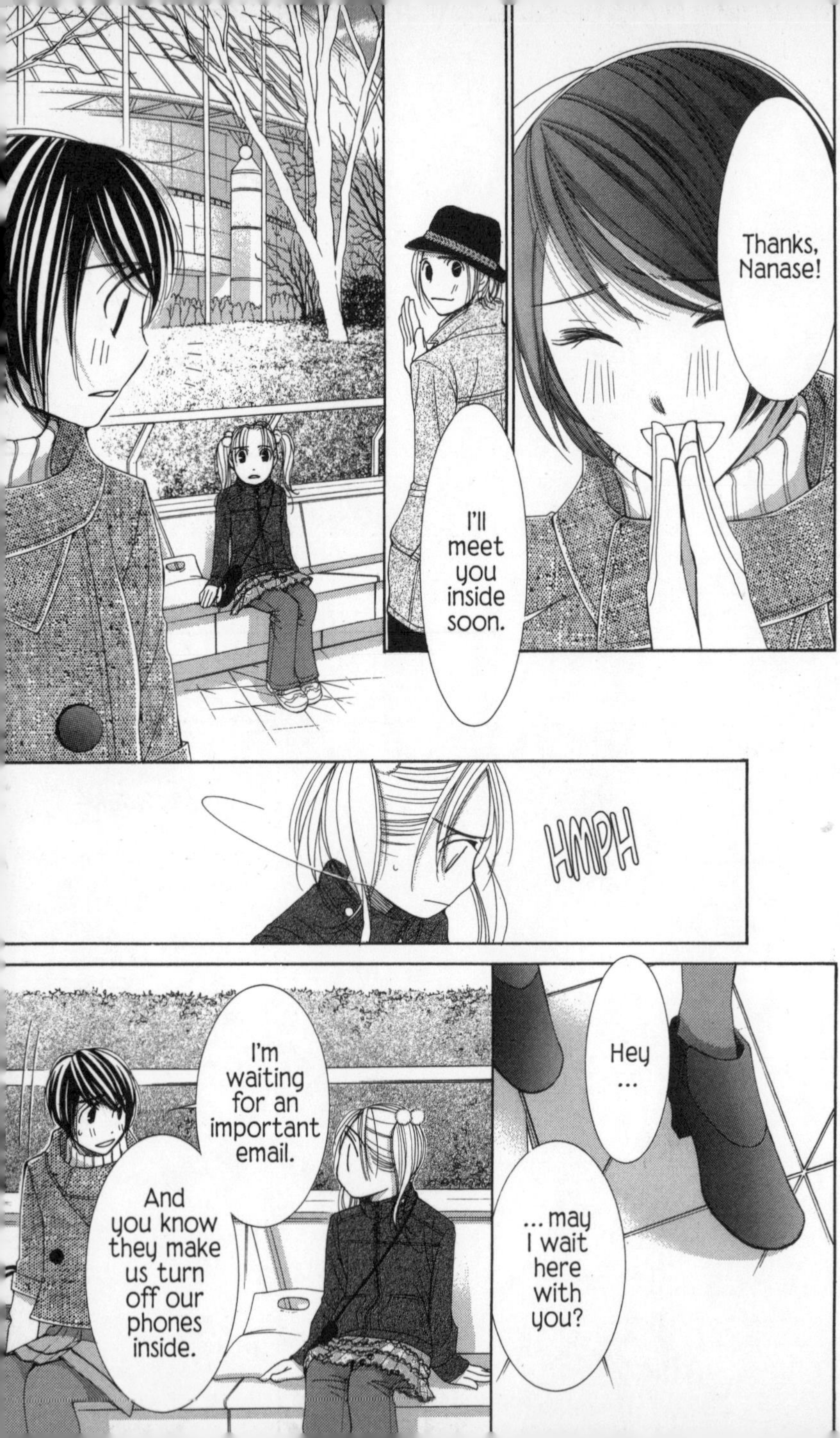
Thanks, Nanase!
I'll meet you inside soon.
HMPH
Hey ...
... may I wait here with you?
I'm waiting for an important email.
And you know they make us turn off our phones inside.

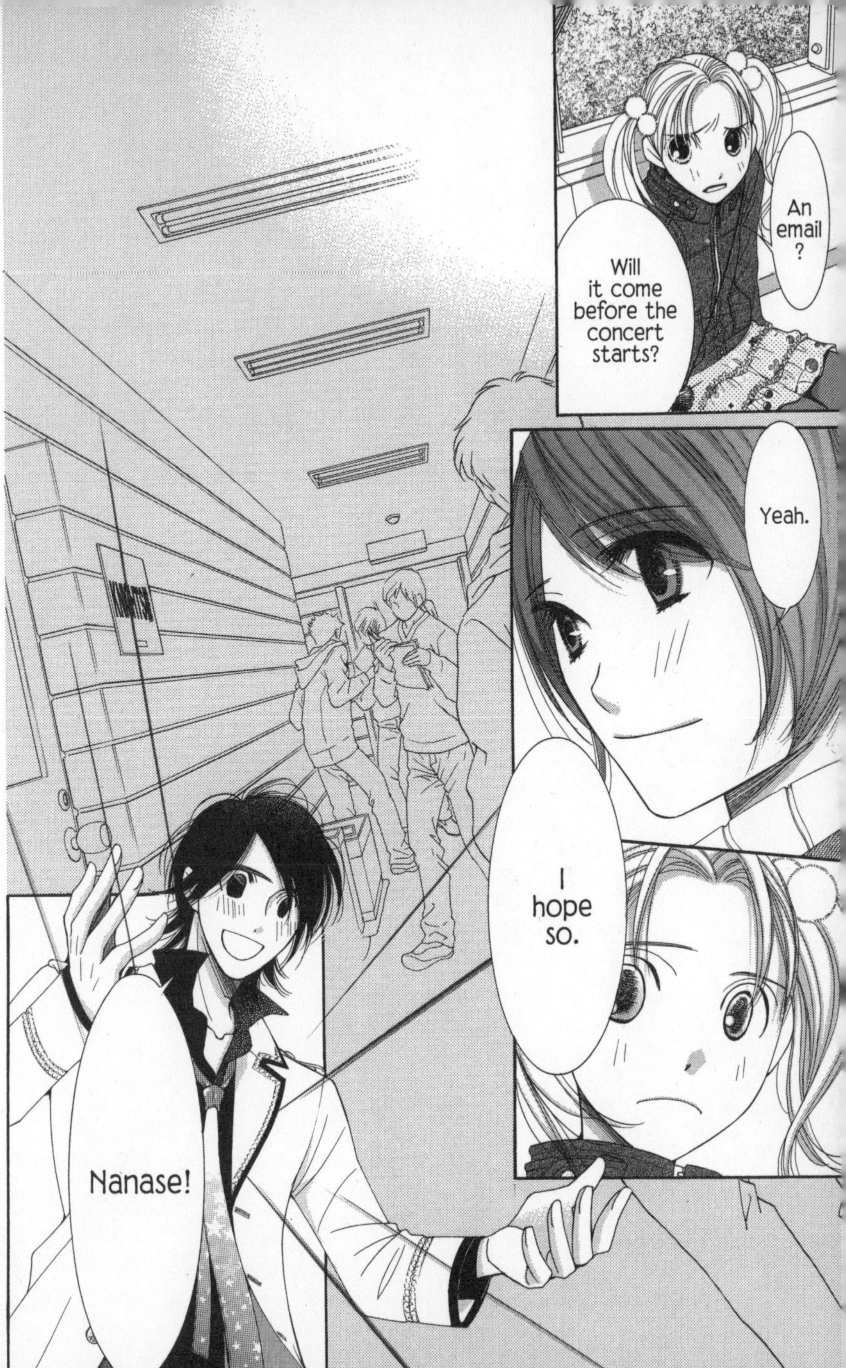
An email?
Will it come before the concert starts?
Yeah.
I hope so.
Nanase!

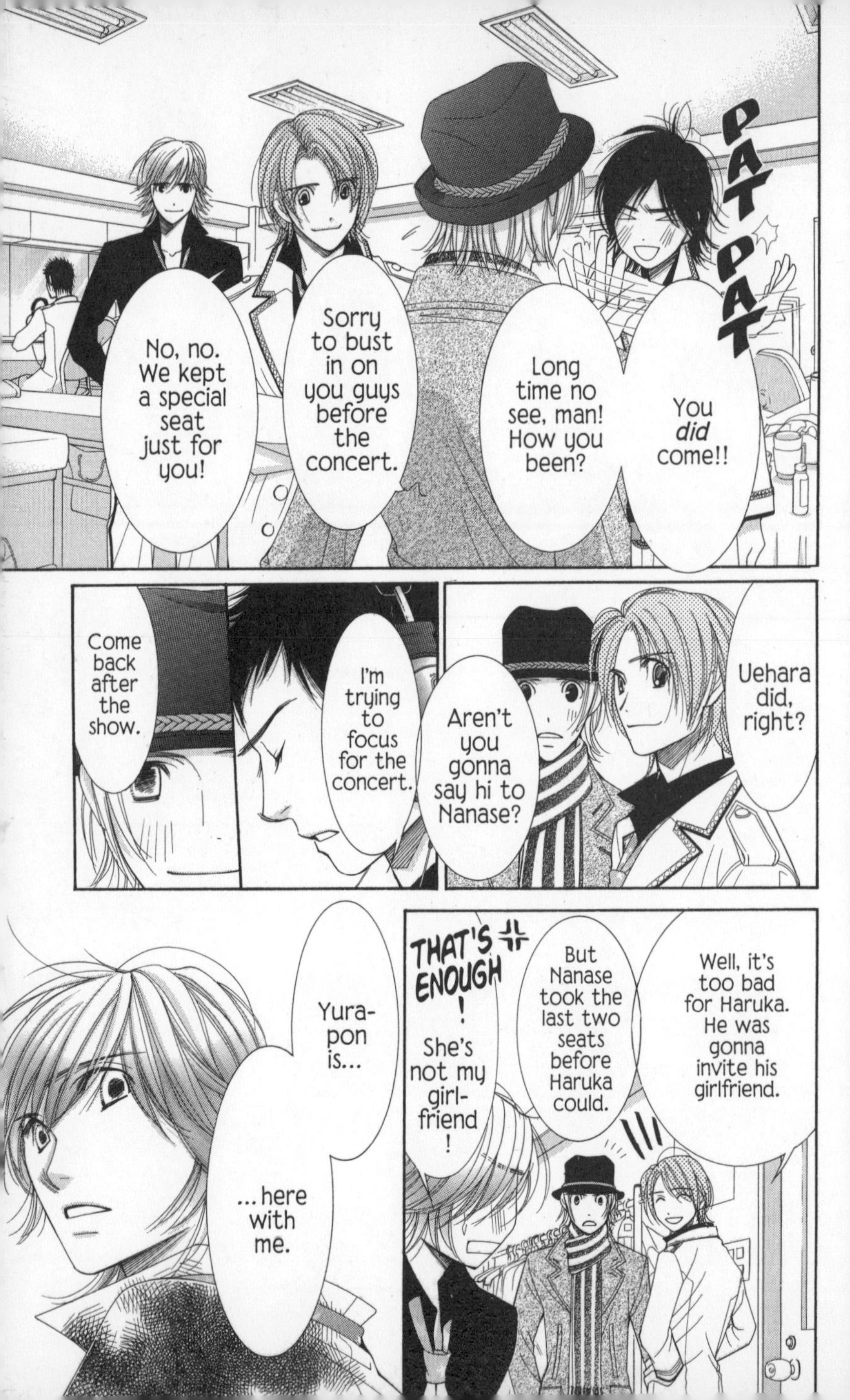
PAT PAT
You *did* come!!
Long time no see, man! How you been?
Sorry to bust in on you guys before the concert.
No, no. We kept a special seat just for you!
Uehara did, right?
Aren't you gonna say hi to Nanase?
I'm trying to focus for the concert.
Come back after the show.
Well, it's too bad for Haruka. He was gonna invite his girlfriend.
But Nanase took the last two seats before Haruka could.
THAT'S ENOUGH!
She's not my girlfriend!
Yura-pon is...
...here with me.

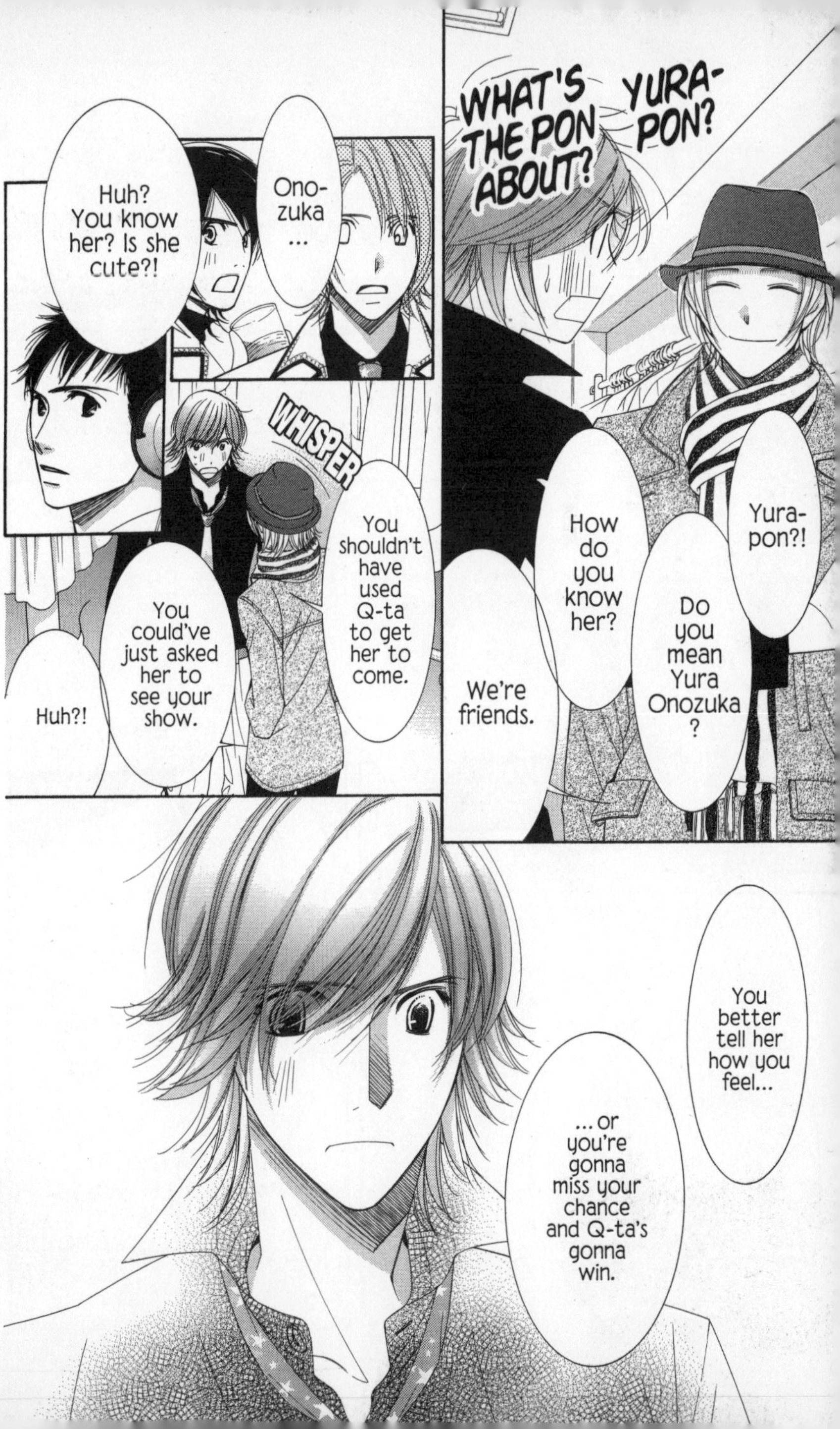
YURA-PON?
WHAT'S THE PON ABOUT?
Yura-pon?!
Do you mean Yura Onozuka?
How do you know her?
We're friends.
Ono-zuka...
Huh? You know her? Is she cute?!
WHISPER
You shouldn't have used Q-ta to get her to come.
You could've just asked her to see your show.
Huh?!
You better tell her how you feel...
...or you're gonna miss your chance and Q-ta's gonna win.

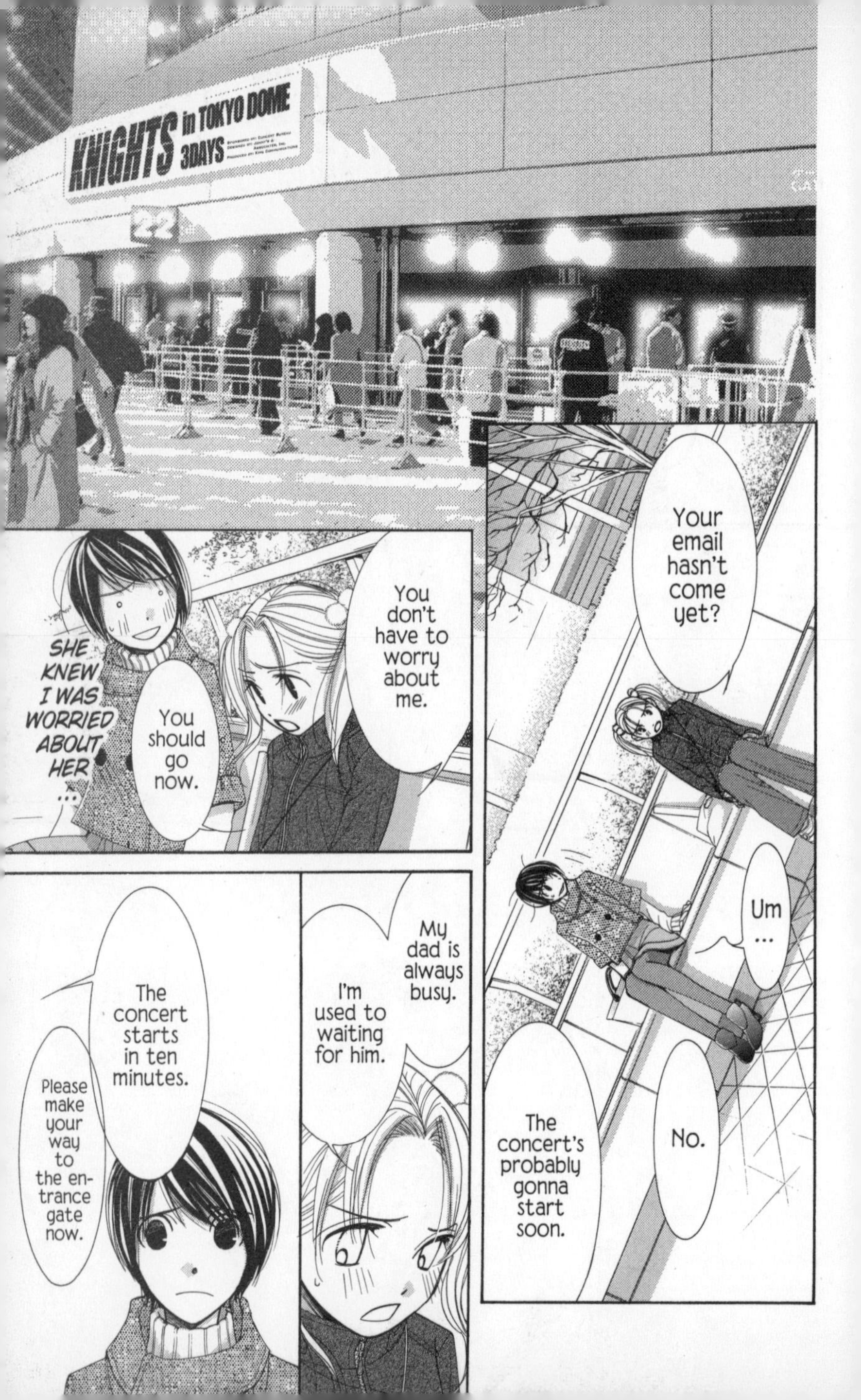
KNIGHTS in TOKYO DOME 3DAYS
22
Your email hasn't come yet?
Um ...
No.
The concert's probably gonna start soon.
You don't have to worry about me.
You should go now.
SHE KNEW I WAS WORRIED ABOUT HER ...
My dad is always busy.
I'm used to waiting for him.
The concert starts in ten minutes.
Please make your way to the entrance gate now.

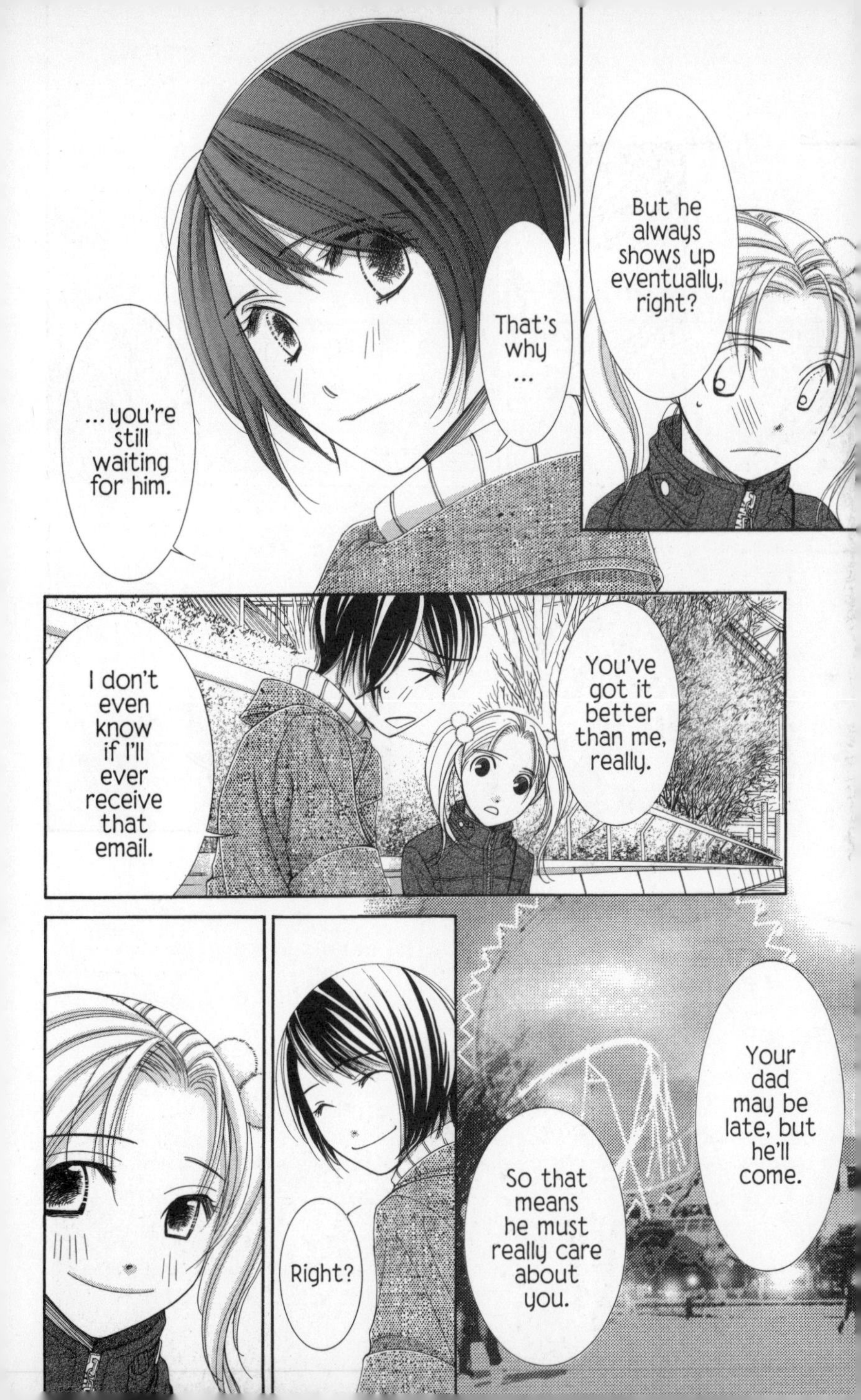
But he always shows up eventually, right?
That's why ...
... you're still waiting for him.
You've got it better than me, really.
I don't even know if I'll ever receive that email.
Your dad may be late, but he'll come.
So that means he must really care about you.
Right?

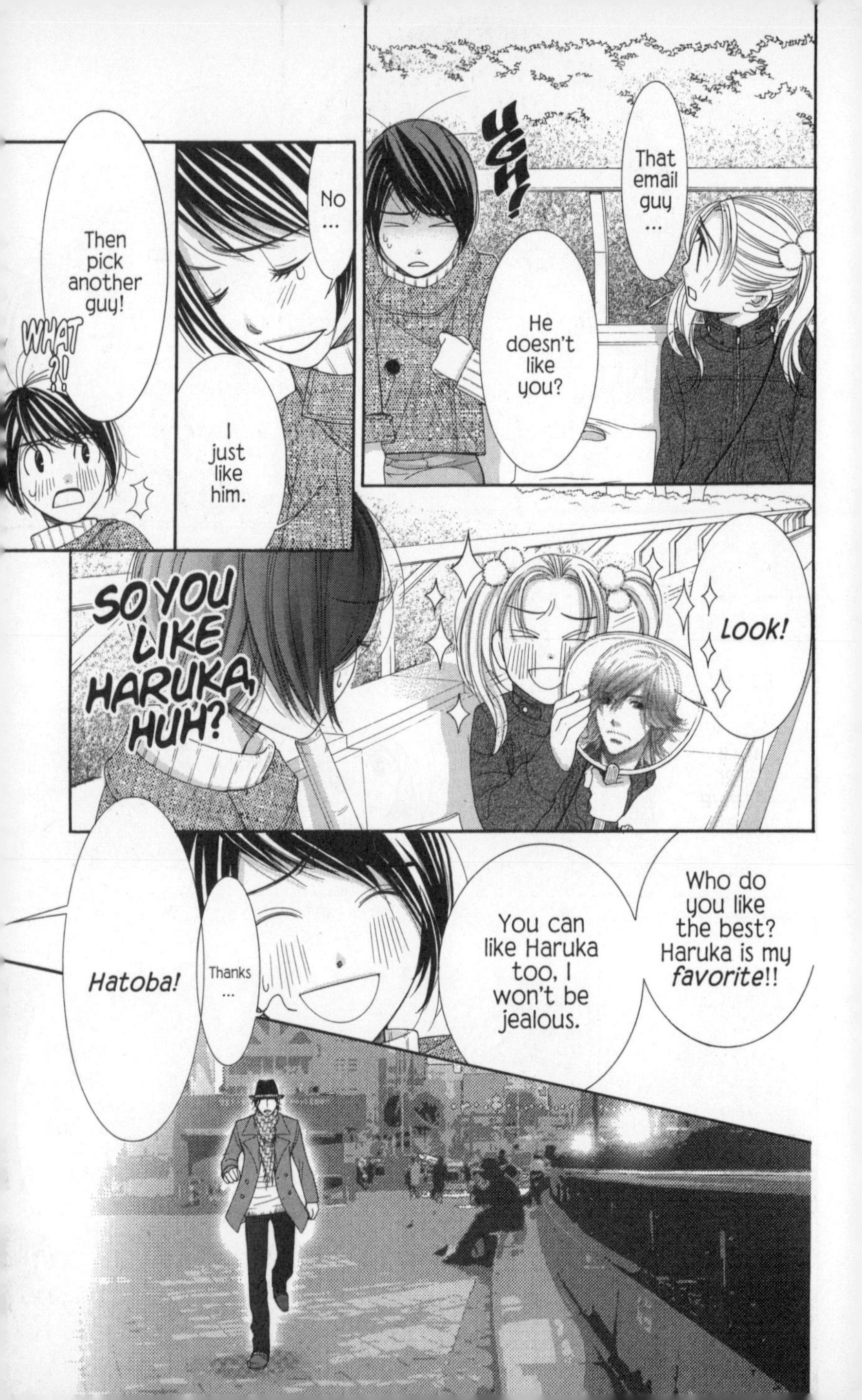

That email guy ...
UGH!
He doesn't like you?
No ...
I just like him.
Then pick another guy!
WHAT ?!
Look!
SO YOU LIKE HARUKA, HUH?
Who do you like the best? Haruka is my *favorite*!!
You can like Haruka too, I won't be jealous.
Thanks ...
Hatoba!

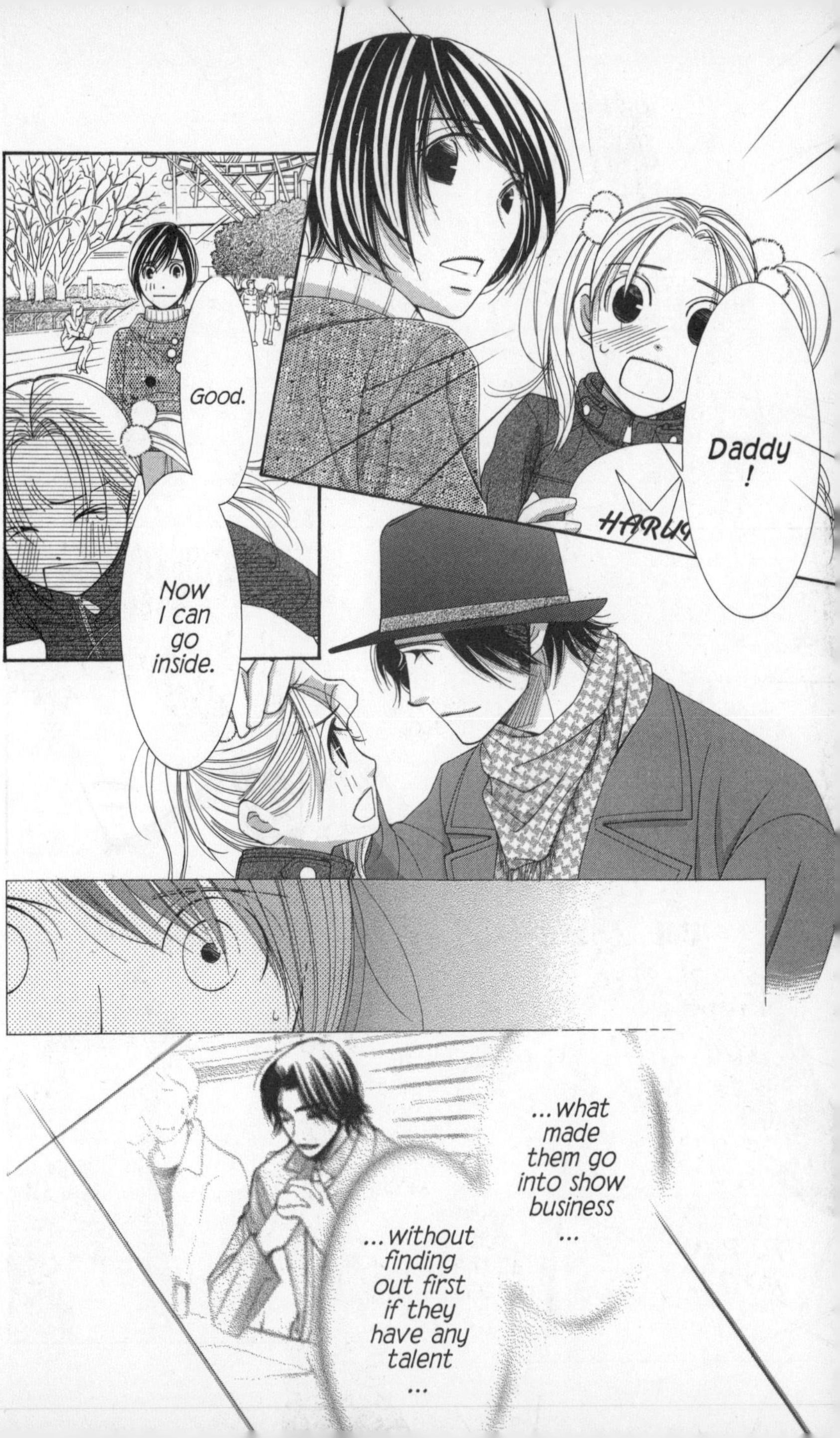
Daddy!
HARUY
Good.
Now I can go inside.
...what made them go into show business...
...without finding out first if they have any talent...

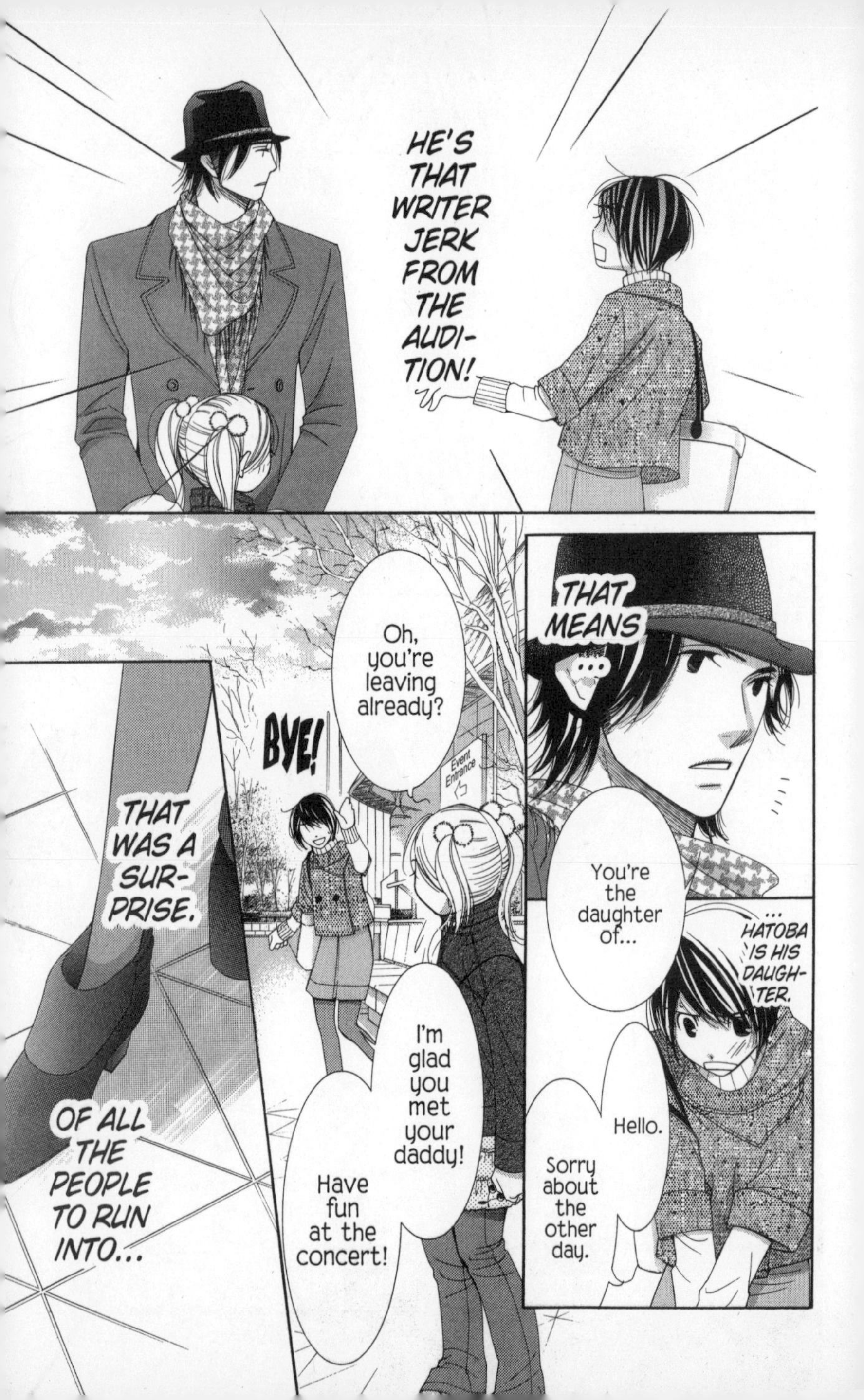
HE'S THAT WRITER JERK FROM THE AUDITION!
THAT MEANS ...
You're the daughter of...
...HATOBA IS HIS DAUGHTER.
Hello.
Sorry about the other day.
Oh, you're leaving already?
BYE!
Event Entrance
I'm glad you met your daddy!
Have fun at the concert!
THAT WAS A SURPRISE.
OF ALL THE PEOPLE TO RUN INTO...

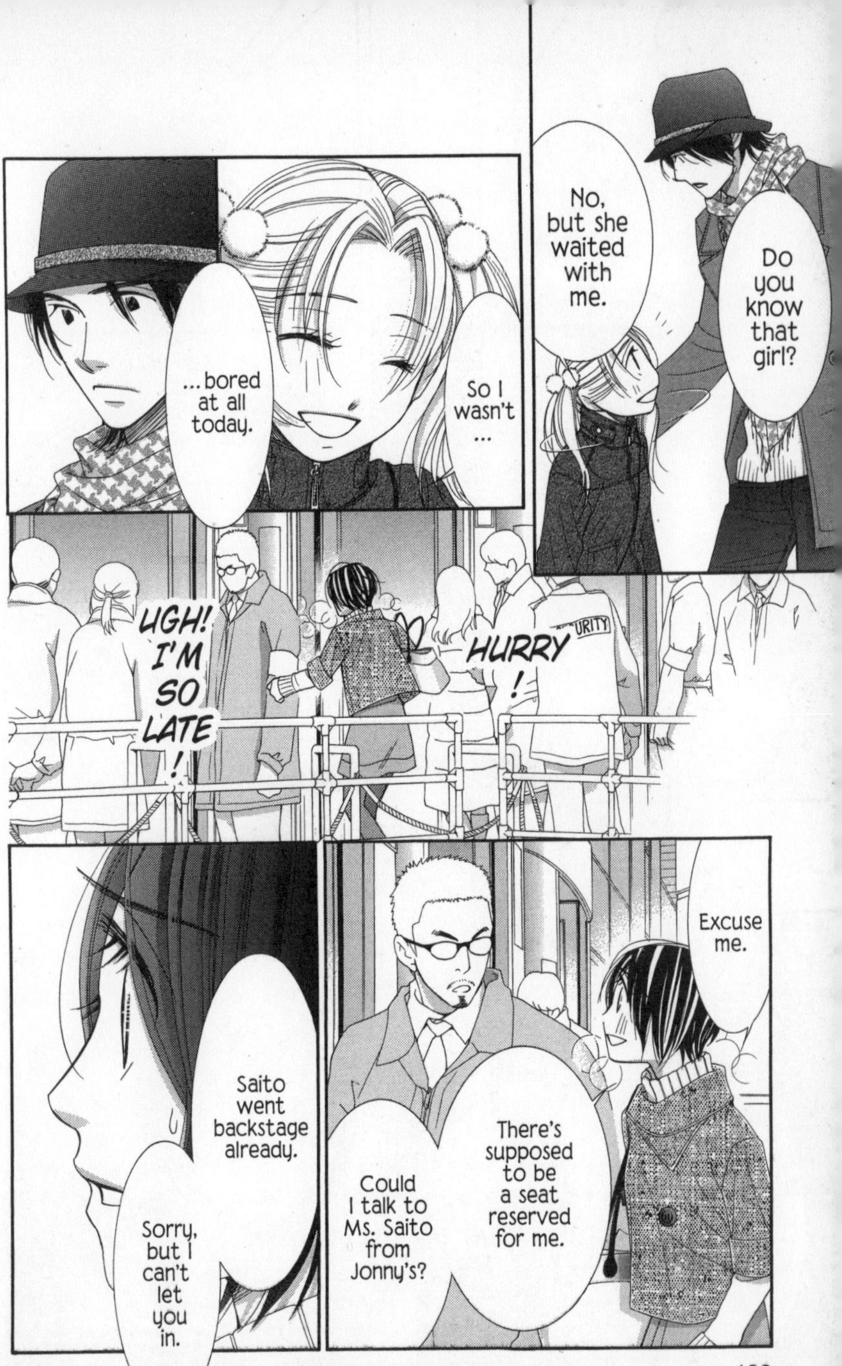
Do you know that girl?
No, but she waited with me.
So I wasn't...
...bored at all today.
HURRY!
UGH! I'M SO LATE!
Excuse me.
There's supposed to be a seat reserved for me.
Could I talk to Ms. Saito from Jonny's?
Saito went backstage already.
Sorry, but I can't let you in.

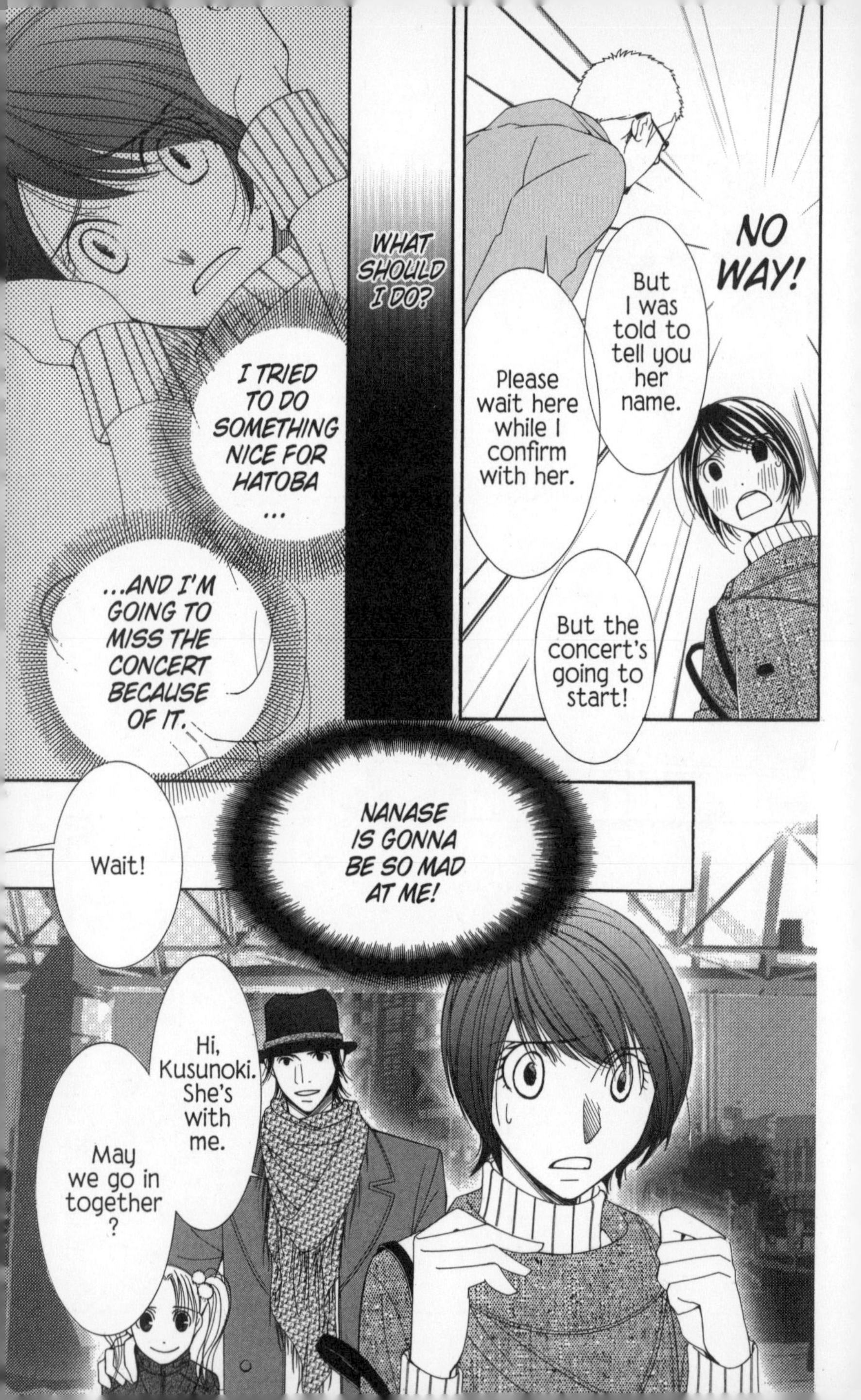
NO WAY!
But I was told to tell you her name.
Please wait here while I confirm with her.
But the concert's going to start!
WHAT SHOULD I DO?
I TRIED TO DO SOMETHING NICE FOR HATOBA ...
...AND I'M GOING TO MISS THE CONCERT BECAUSE OF IT.
NANASE IS GONNA BE SO MAD AT ME!
Wait!
Hi, Kusunoki. She's with me.
May we go in together ?

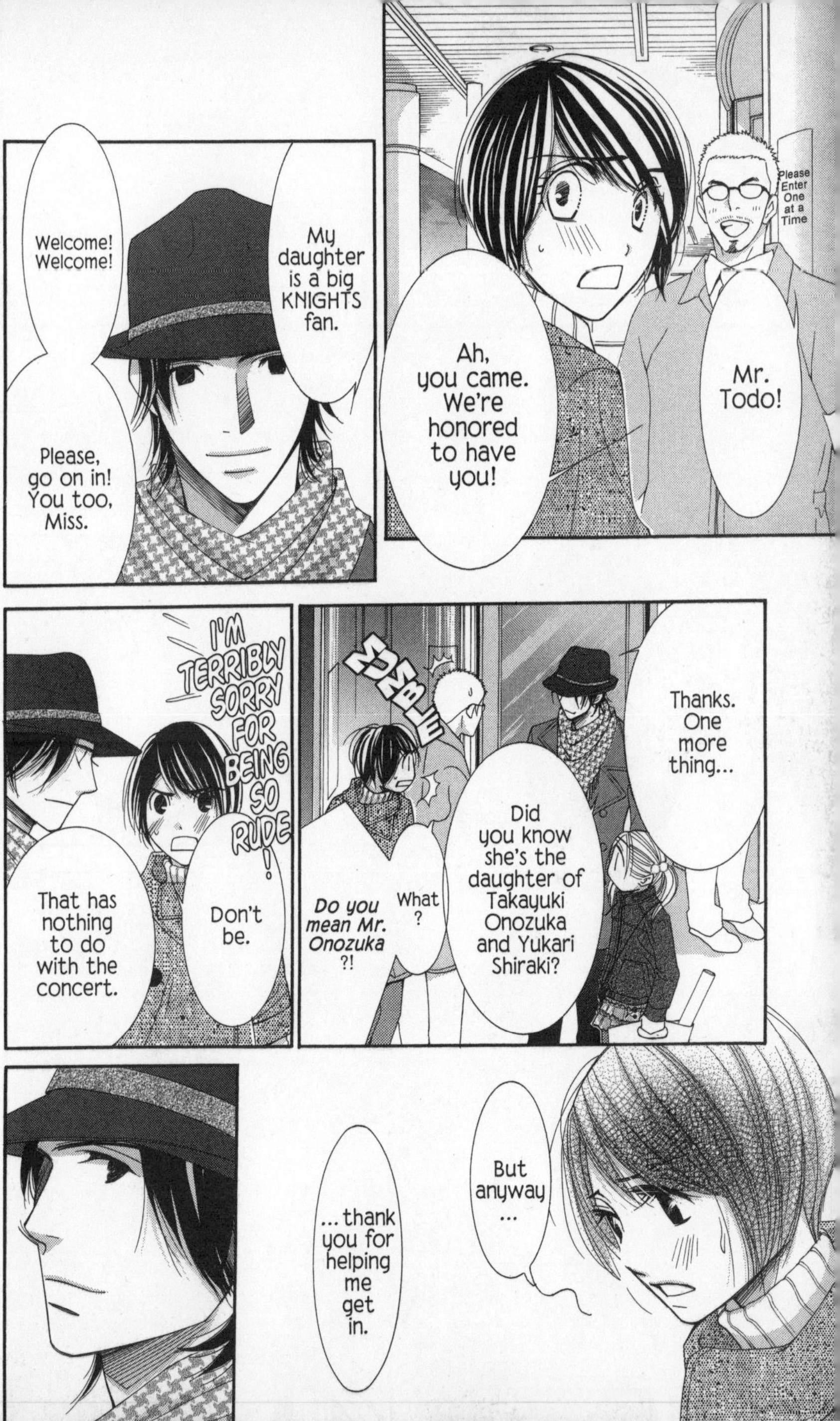
Mr. Todo!
Please Enter One at a Time
Ah, you came. We're honored to have you!
My daughter is a big KNIGHTS fan.
Welcome! Welcome!
Please, go on in! You too, Miss.
Thanks. One more thing...
Did you know she's the daughter of Takayuki Onozuka and Yukari Shiraki?
What?
Do you mean Mr. Onozuka?!
I'M TERRIBLY SORRY FOR BEING SO RUDE!
Don't be.
That has nothing to do with the concert.
But anyway...
...thank you for helping me get in.

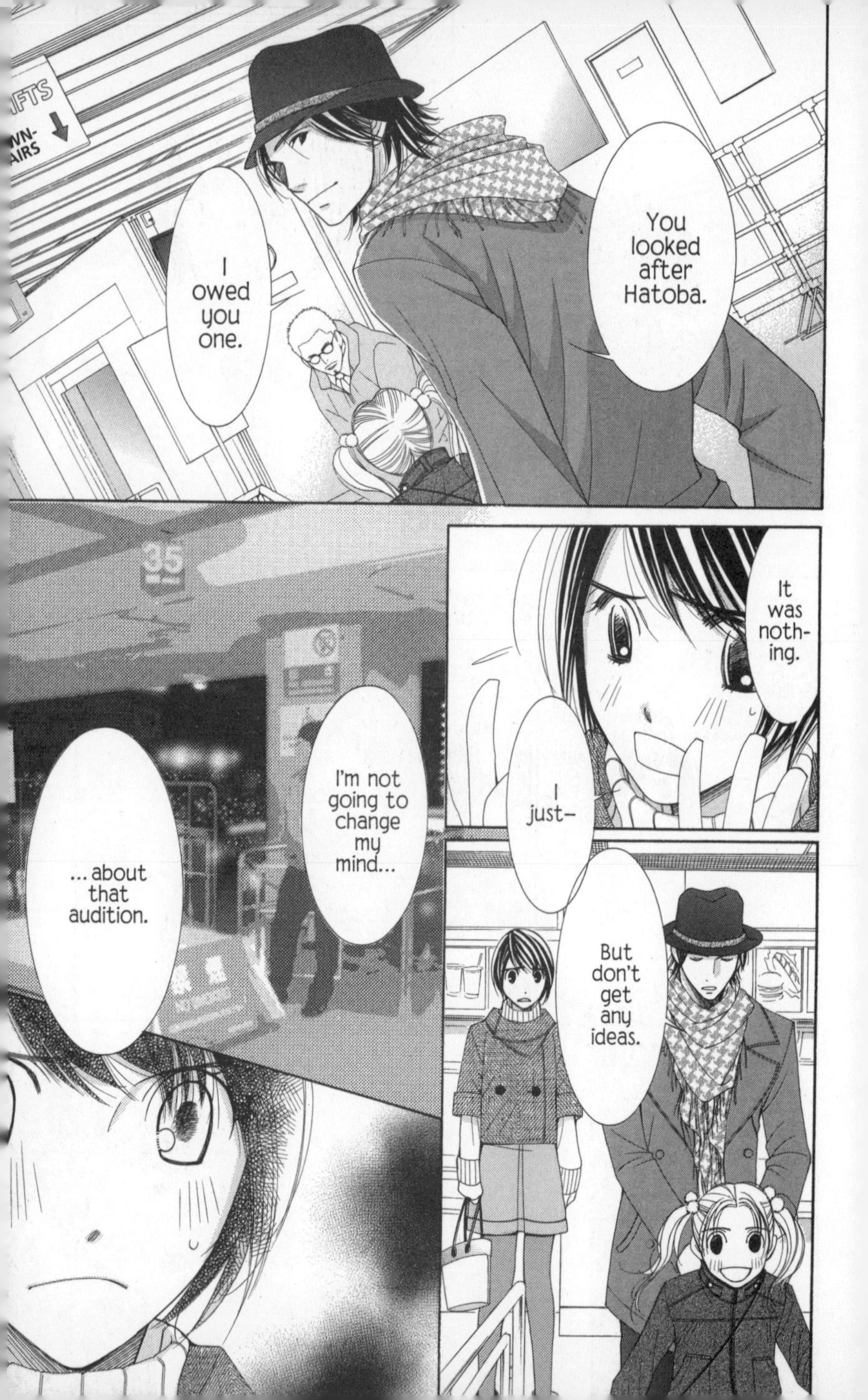
You looked after Hatoba.
I owed you one.
It was noth-ing.
I just—
But don't get any ideas.
I'm not going to change my mind...
...about that audition.

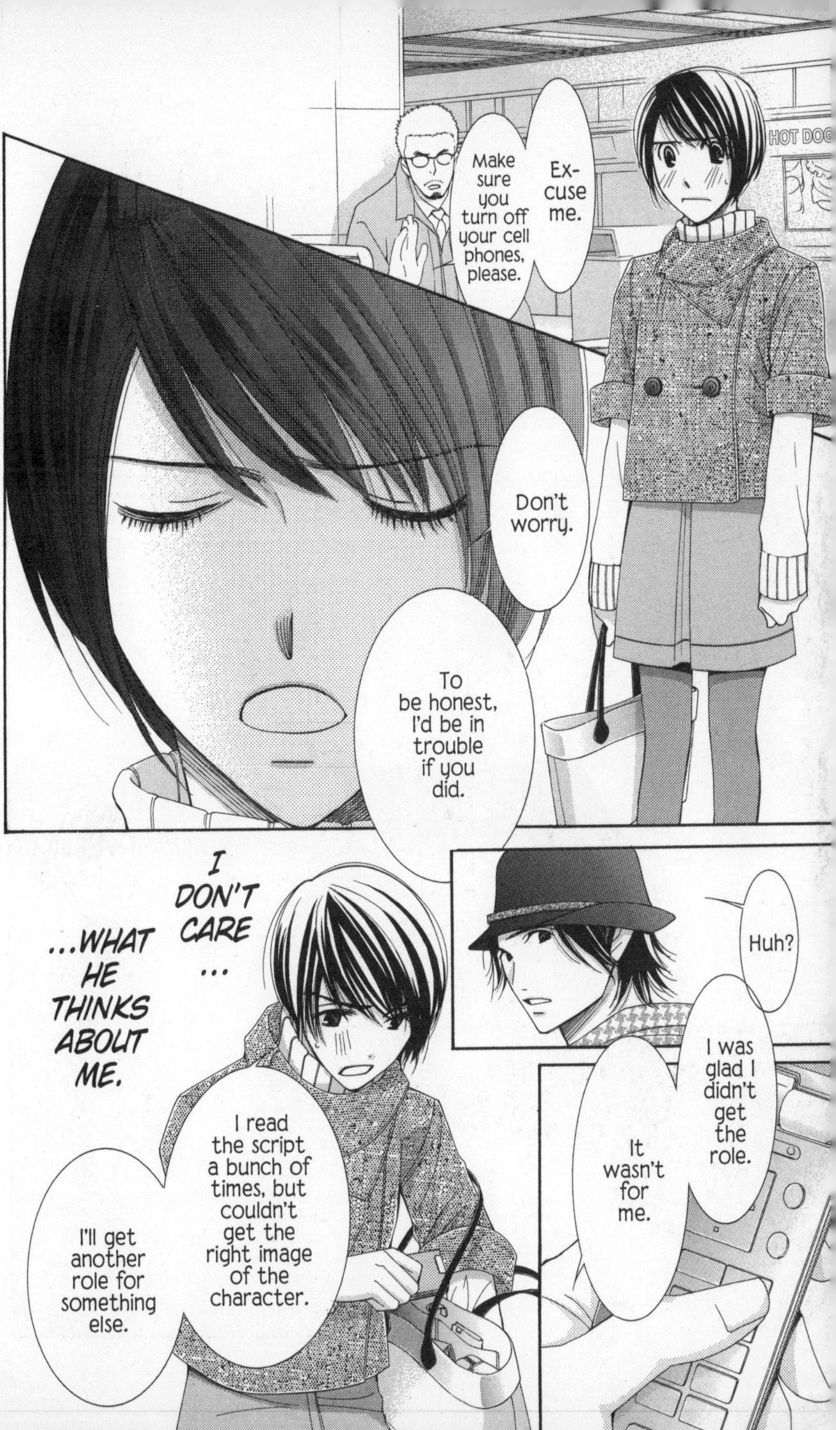
Ex-cuse me.
Make sure you turn off your cell phones, please.
Don't worry.
To be honest, I'd be in trouble if you did.
HOT DOG
Huh?
I was glad I didn't get the role.
It wasn't for me.
I DON'T CARE ...
...WHAT HE THINKS ABOUT ME.
I read the script a bunch of times, but couldn't get the right image of the character.
I'll get another role for something else.

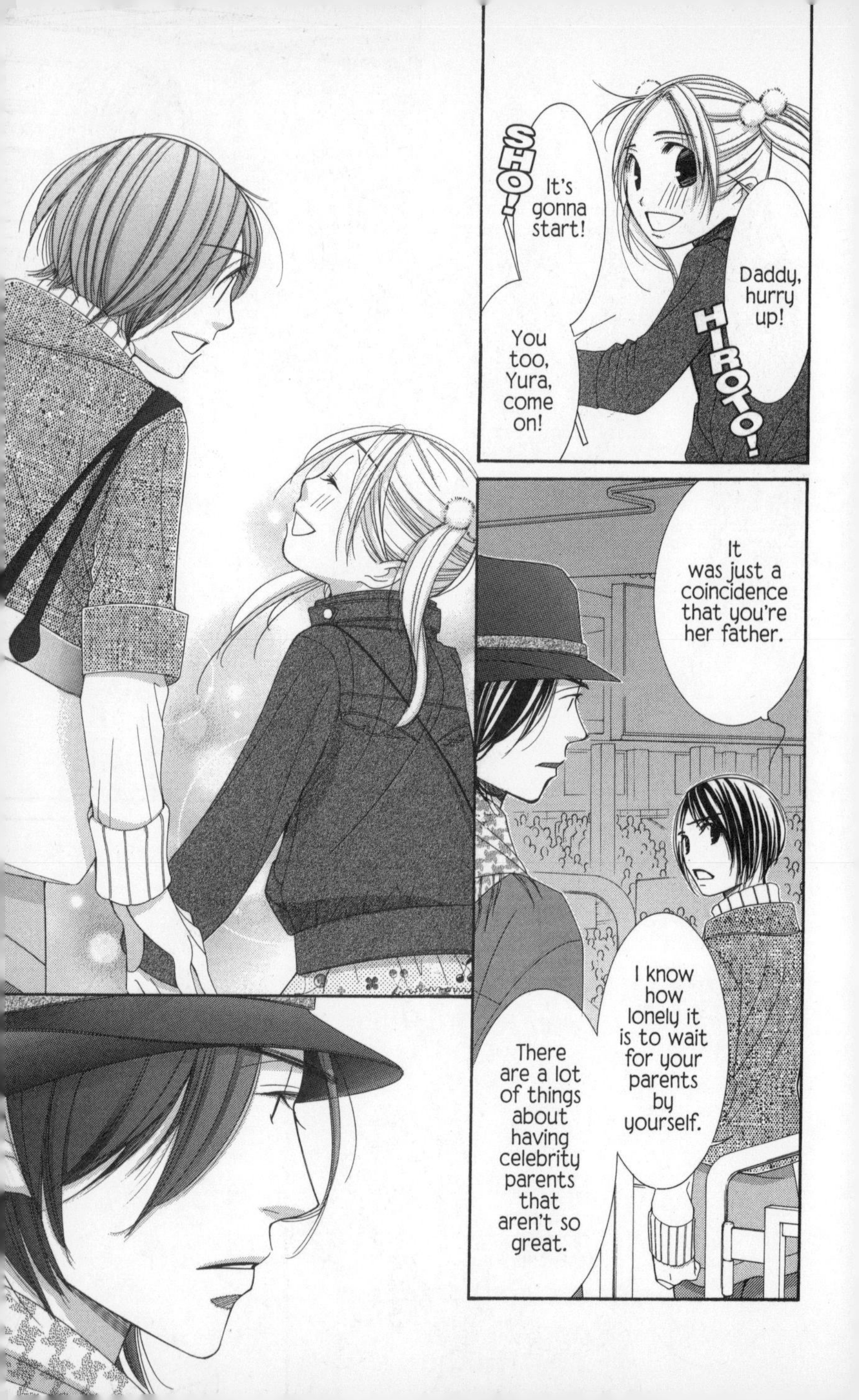
Daddy, hurry up!
HIROTO!
It's gonna start!
SHO!
You too, Yura, come on!
It was just a coincidence that you're her father.
I know how lonely it is to wait for your parents by yourself.
There are a lot of things about having celebrity parents that aren't so great.

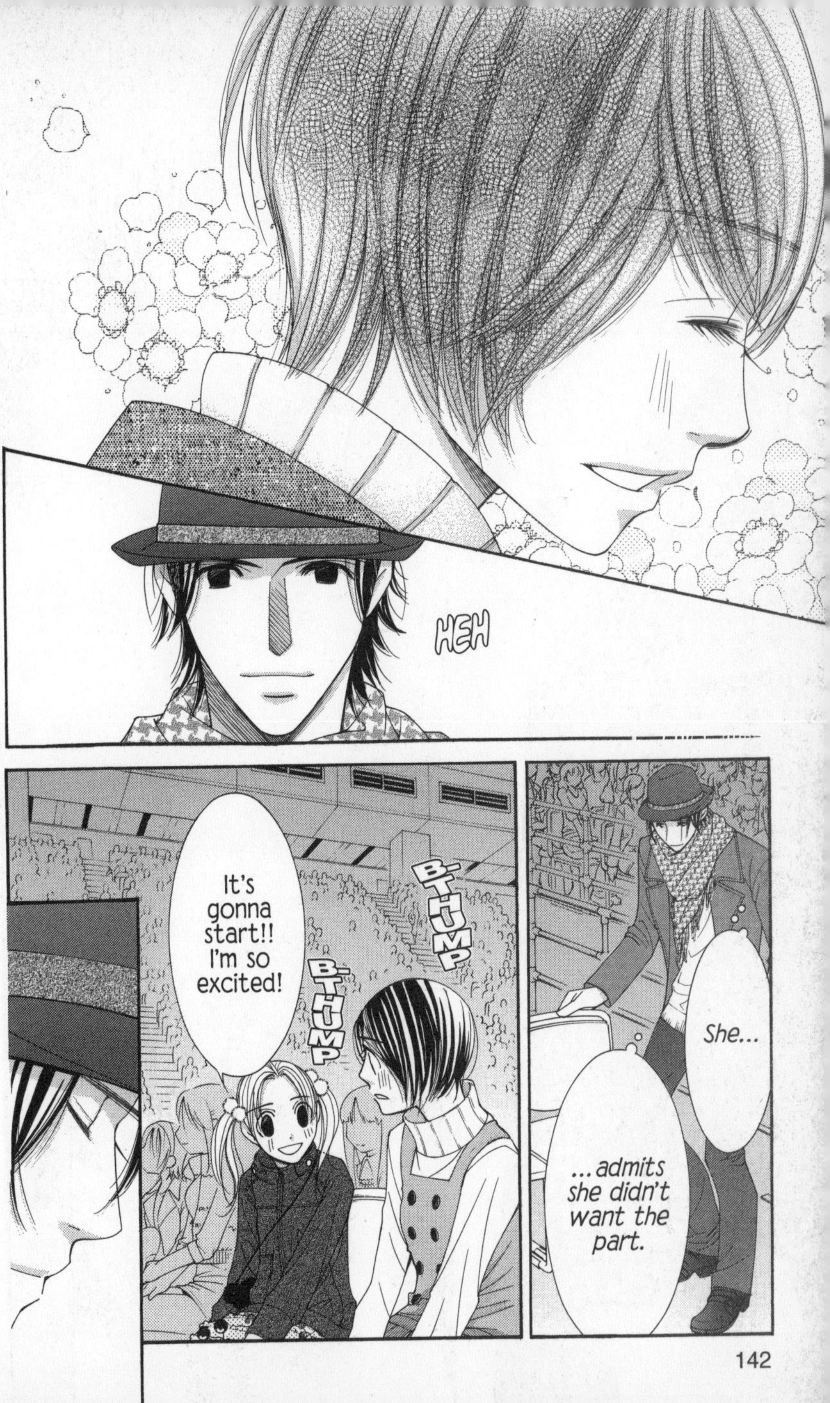
HEH
She...
...admits she didn't want the part.
It's gonna start!! I'm so excited!
B-THUMP
B-THUMP

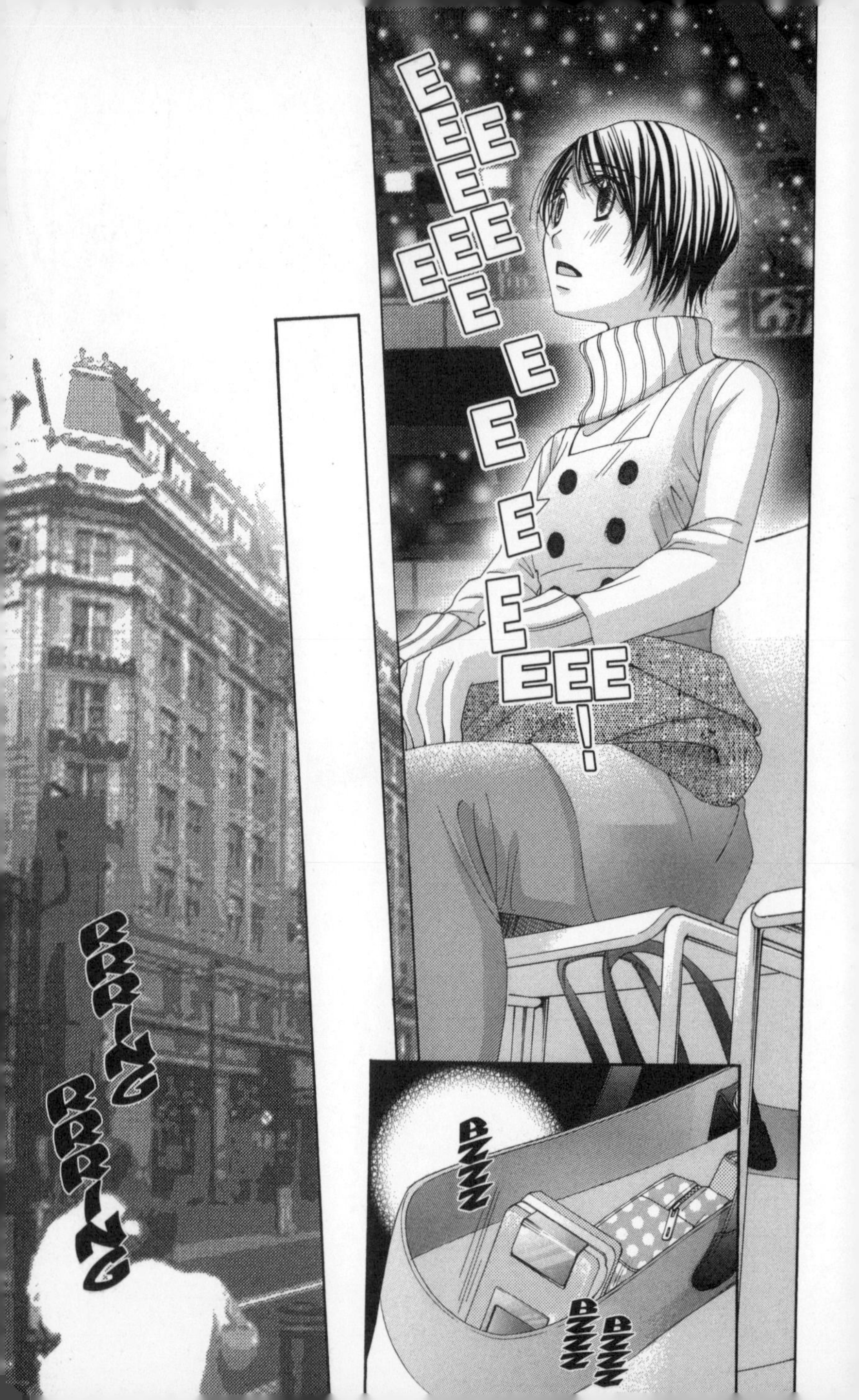
EEEEEEEEEEEEEEEEE!
BZZZ
BZZZ BZZZ
RRRING
RRRING

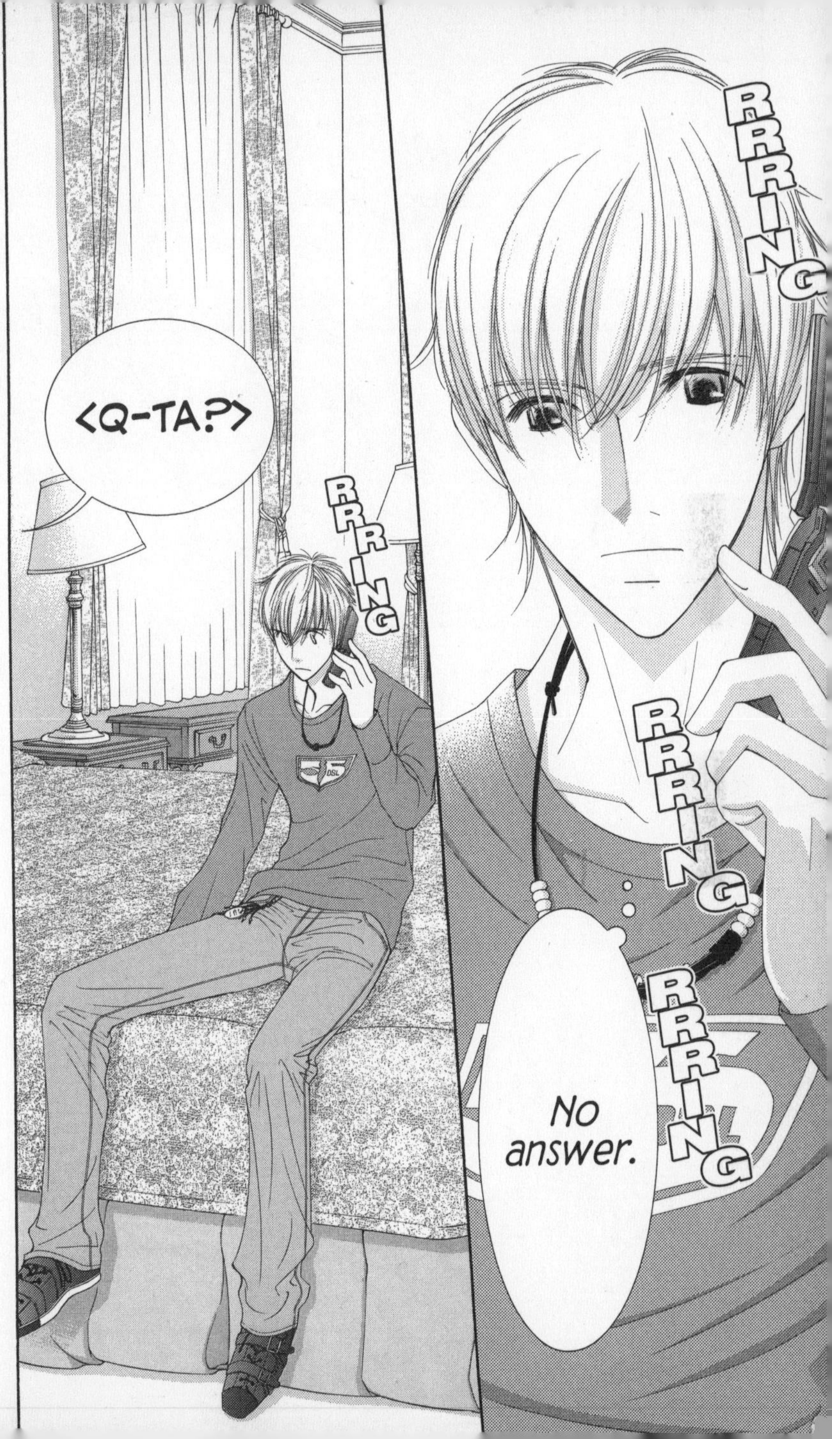
RRRING
RRRING
RRRING
No answer.
<Q-TA?>
RRRING

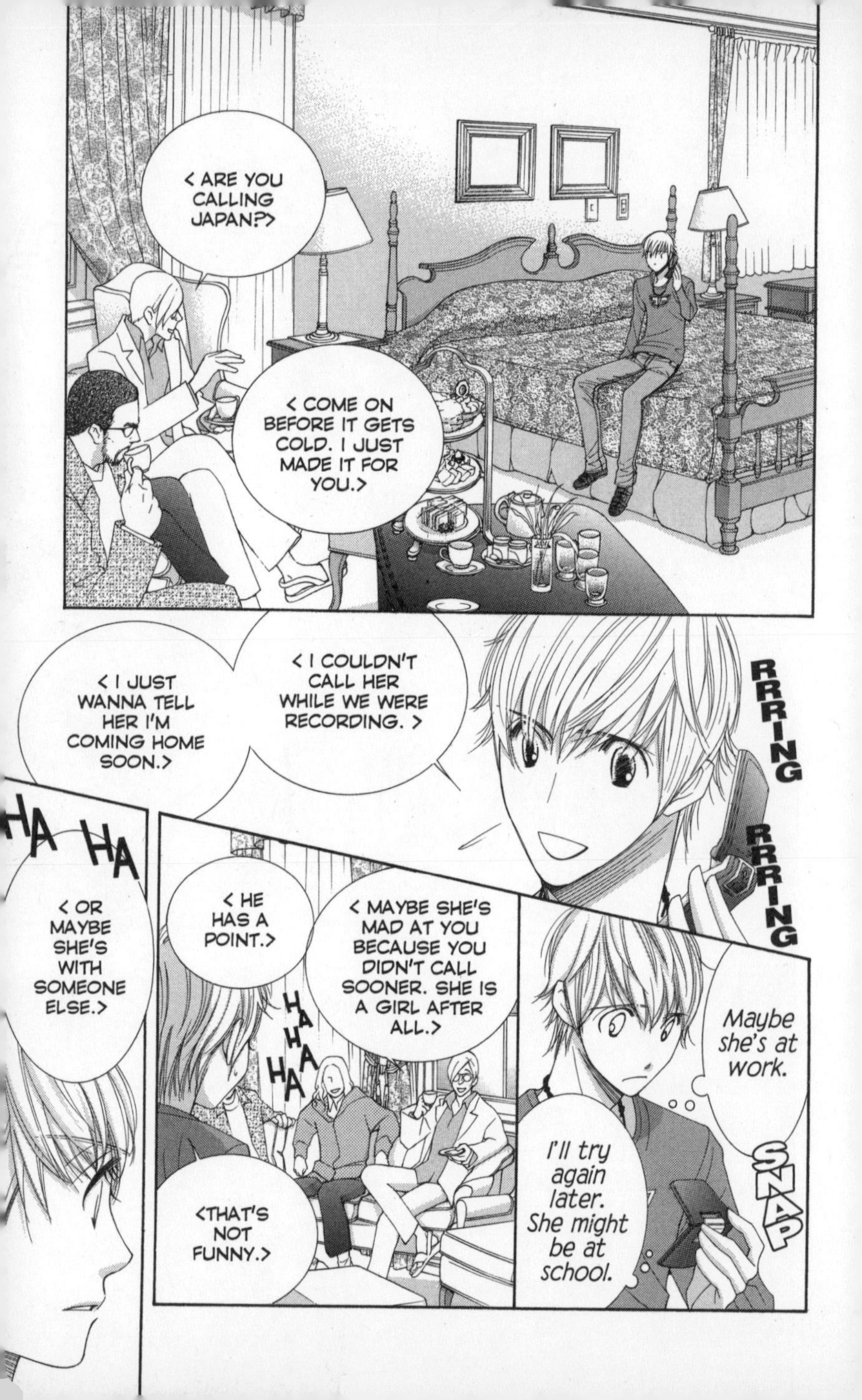
< ARE YOU CALLING JAPAN?>
< COME ON BEFORE IT GETS COLD. I JUST MADE IT FOR YOU.>
RRRING
< I COULDN'T CALL HER WHILE WE WERE RECORDING. >
< I JUST WANNA TELL HER I'M COMING HOME SOON.>
RRRING
Maybe she's at work.
SNAP
I'll try again later. She might be at school.
< MAYBE SHE'S MAD AT YOU BECAUSE YOU DIDN'T CALL SOONER. SHE IS A GIRL AFTER ALL.>
< HE HAS A POINT.>
HA HA HA
<THAT'S NOT FUNNY.>
HA HA
< OR MAYBE SHE'S WITH SOMEONE ELSE.>

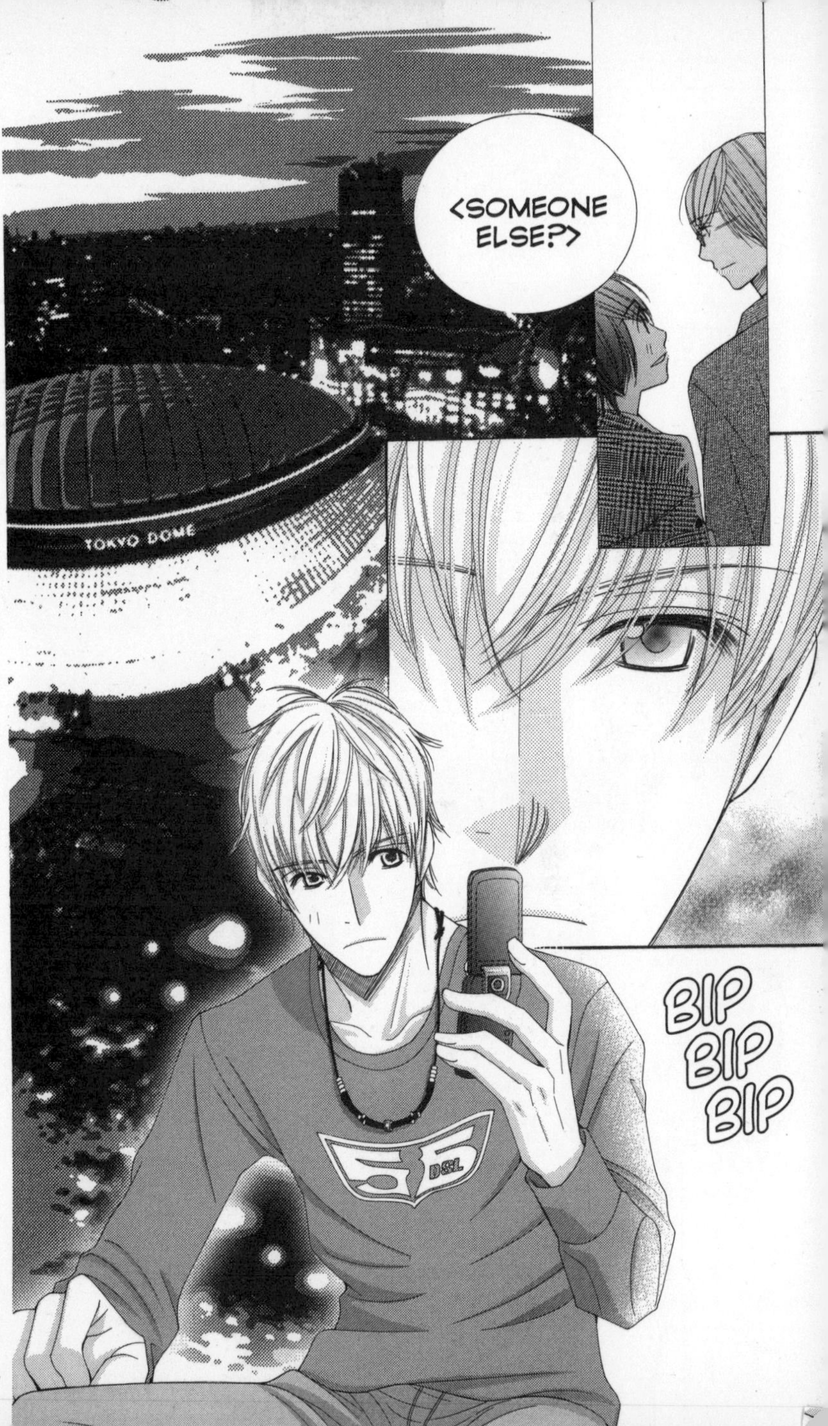
<SOMEONE ELSE?>
TOKYO DOME
BIP BIP BIP

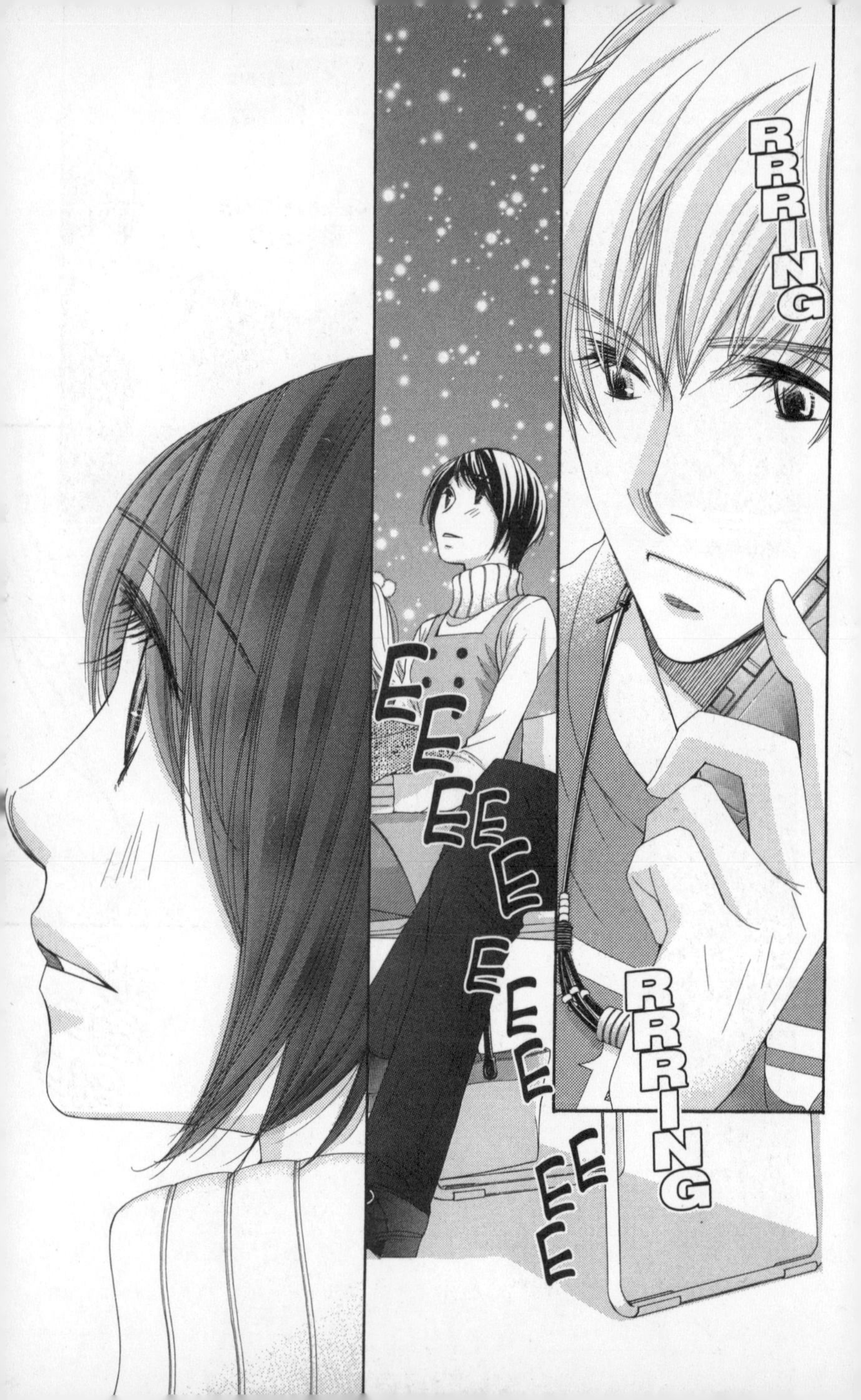
RRRING
RRRING
EEEEEEEEEEE

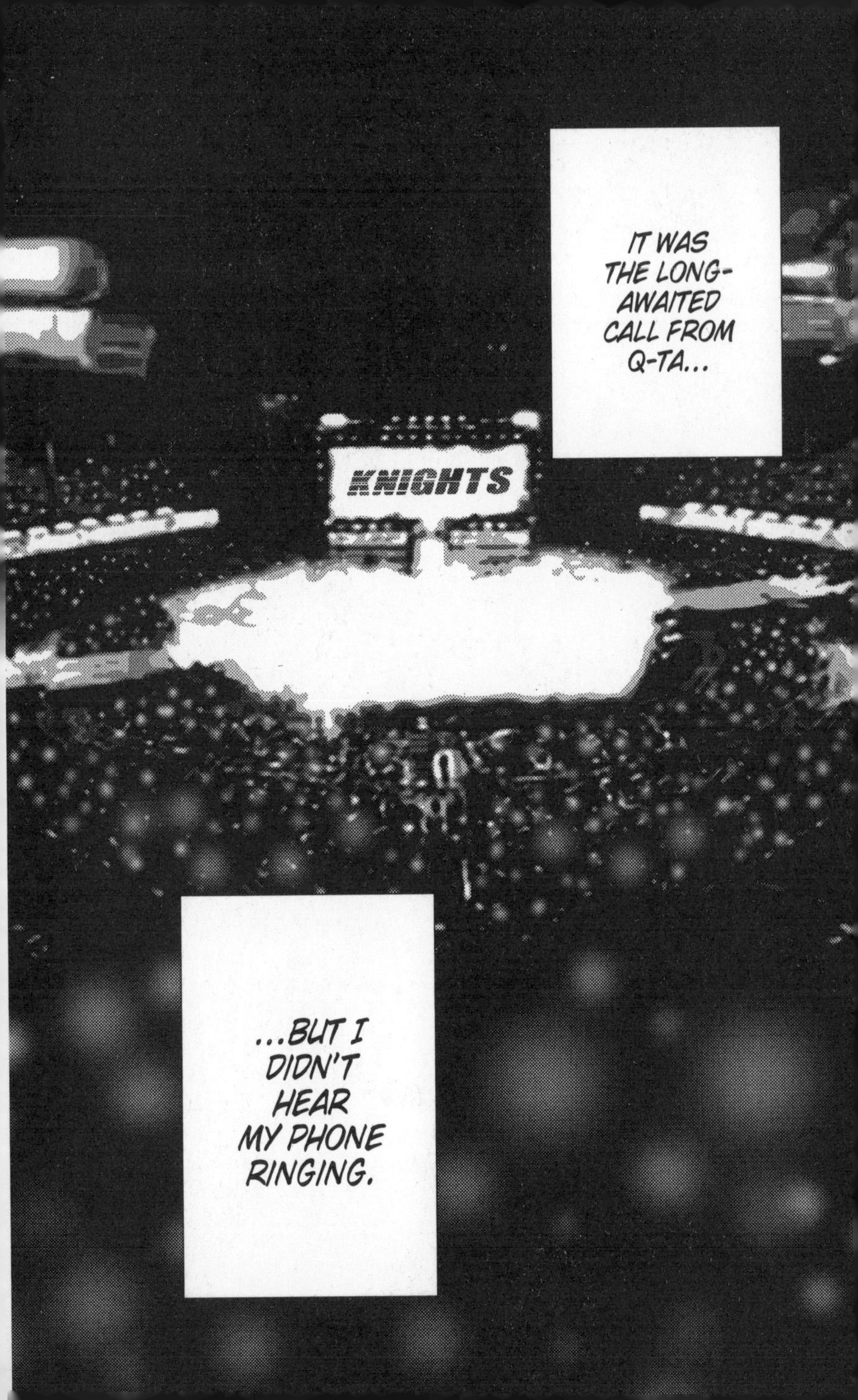
IT WAS THE LONG-AWAITED CALL FROM Q-TA...
KNIGHTS
...BUT I DIDN'T HEAR MY PHONE RINGING.

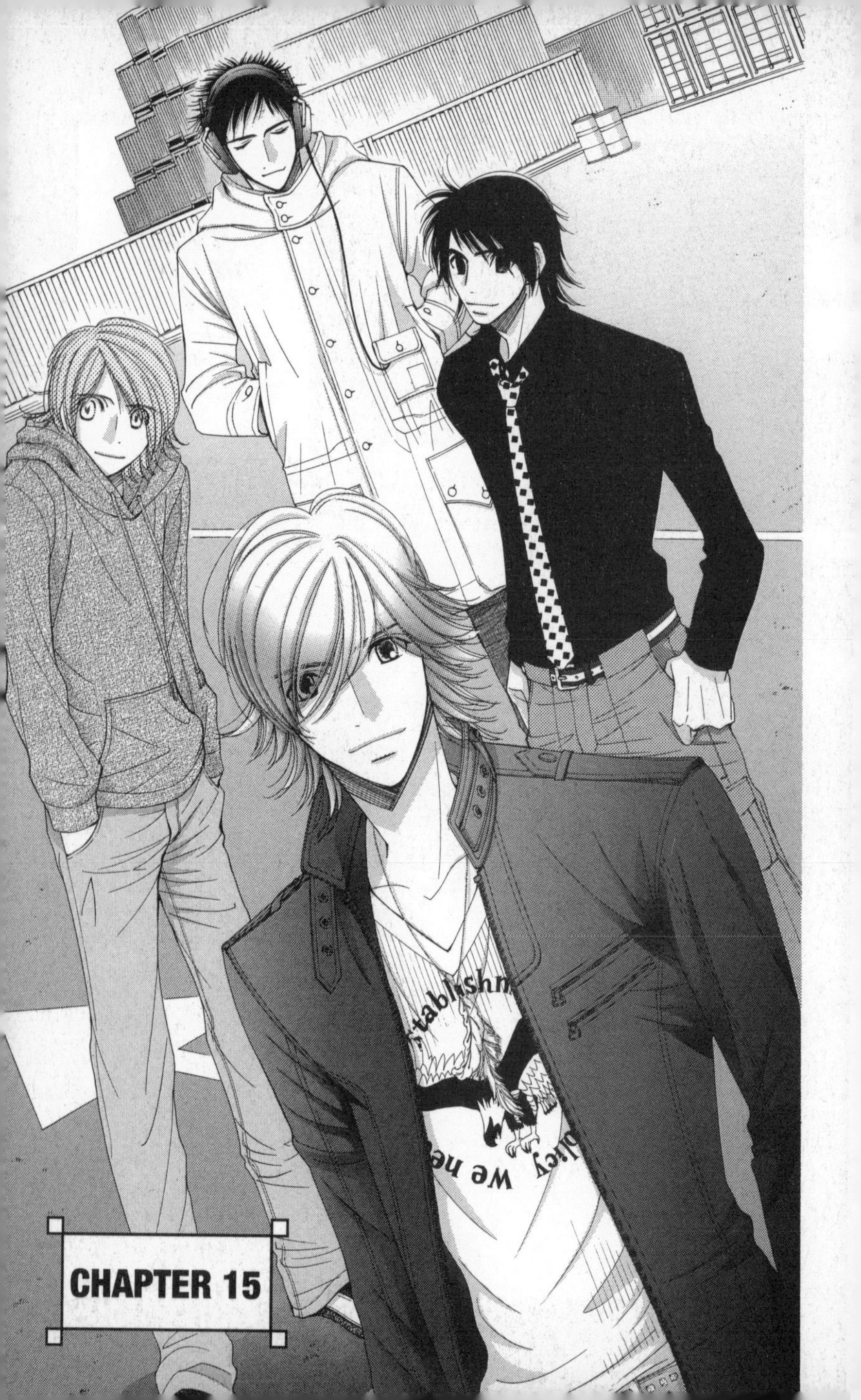

CHAPTER 15

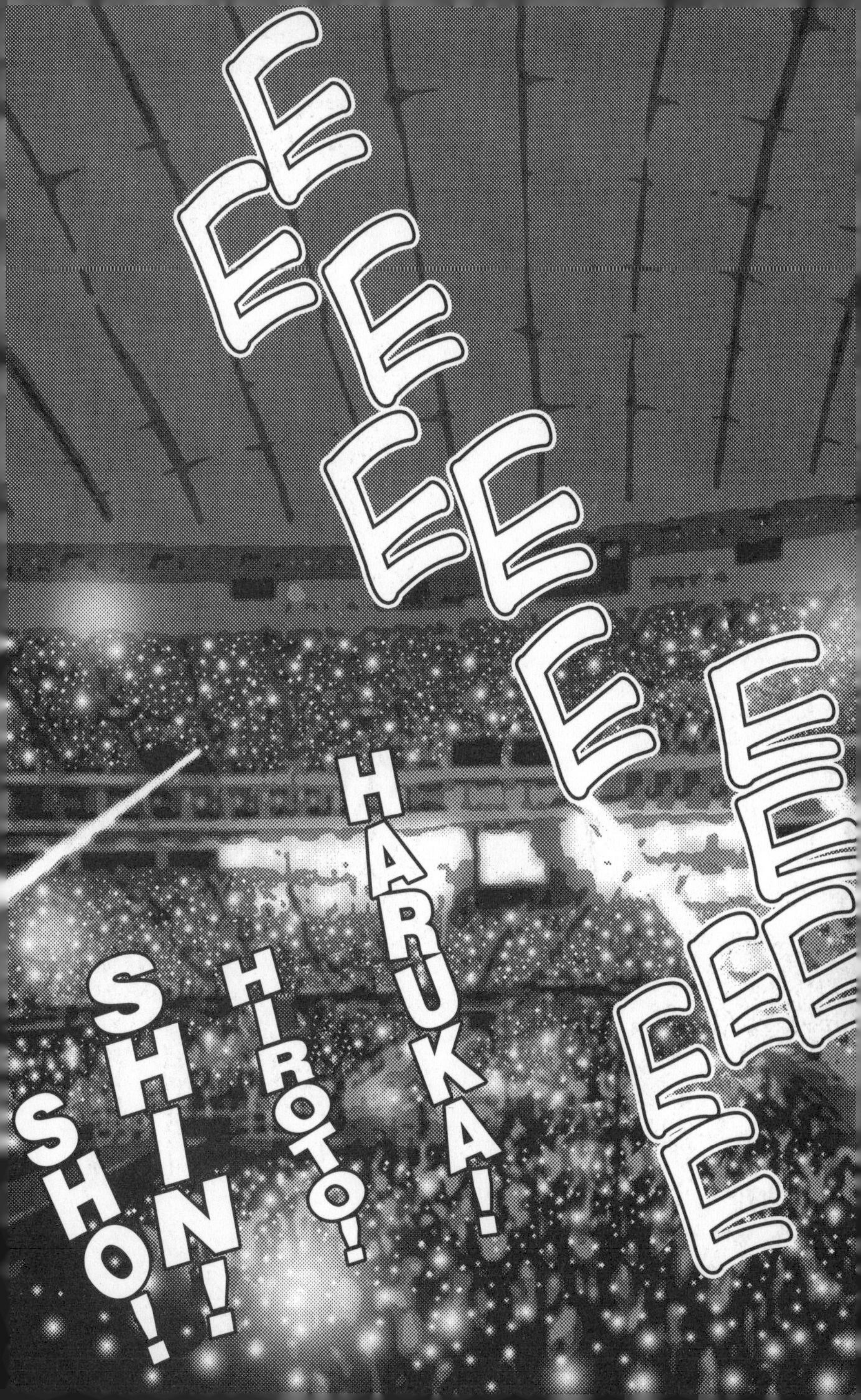
EEEEEEEEEEEEE
HARUKA!
HIROTO!
SHIN!
SHO!

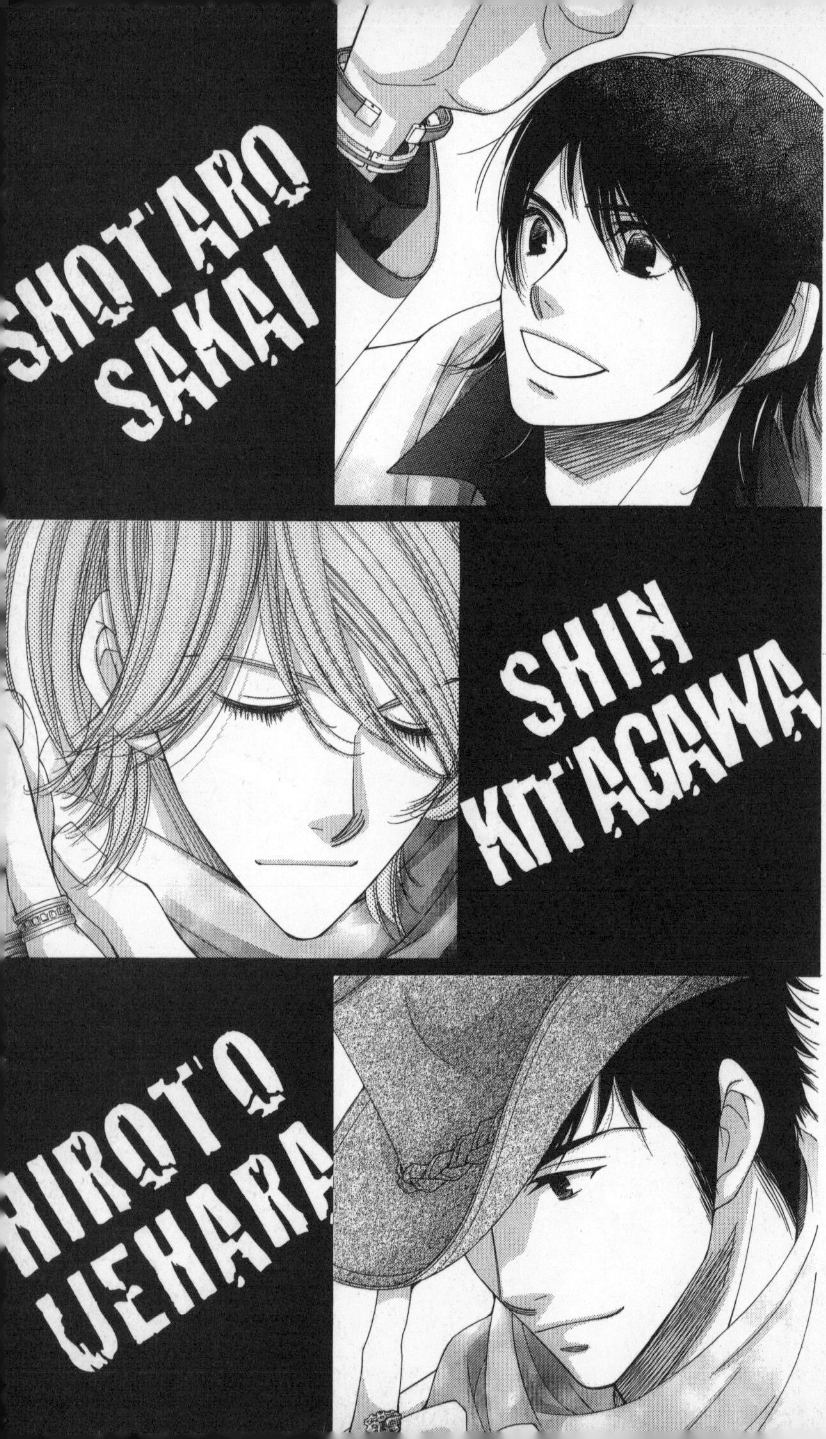
SHOTARO SAKAI
SHIN KITAGAWA
HIROTO UEHARA

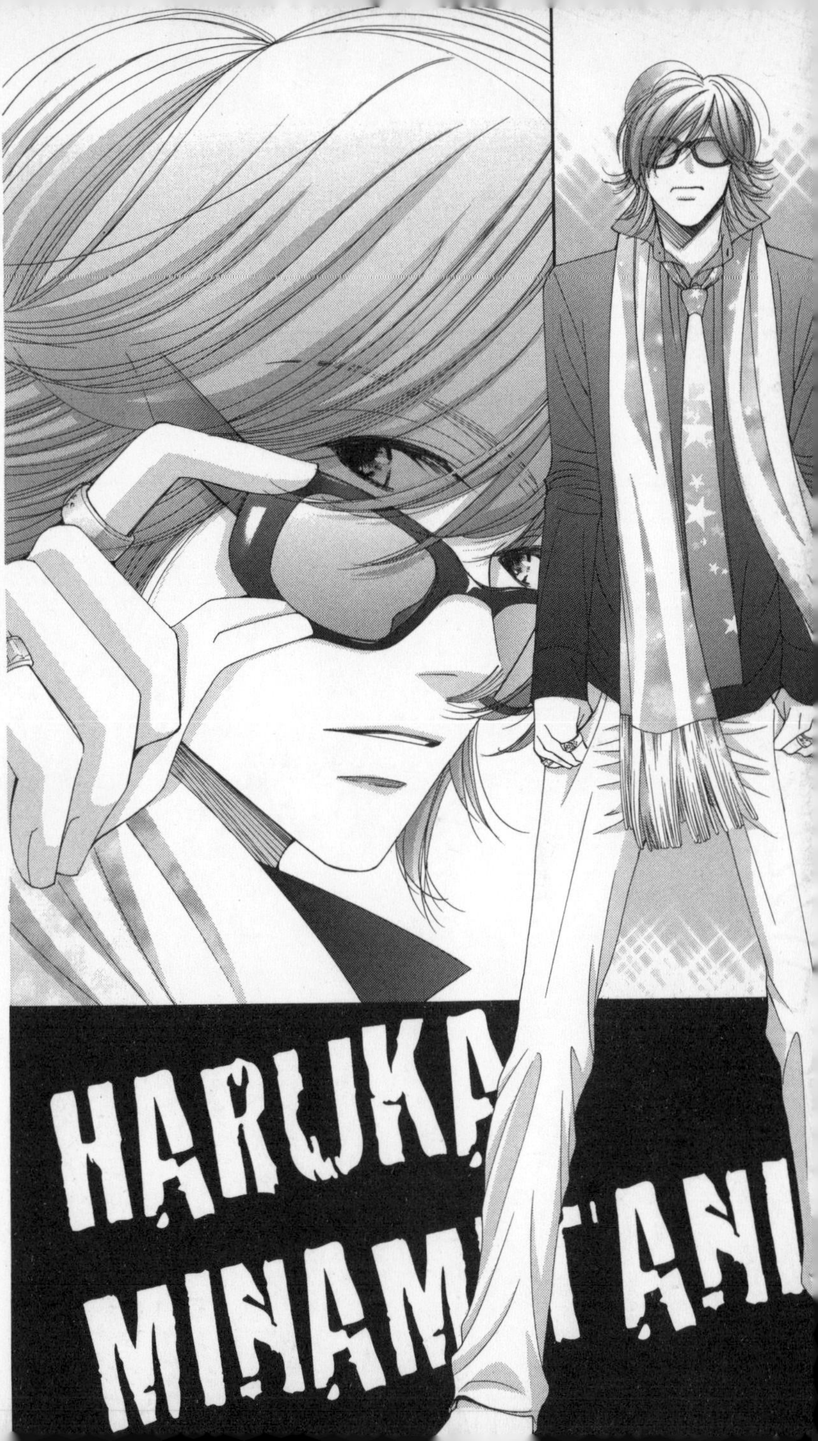
HARUKA
MINAMITANI

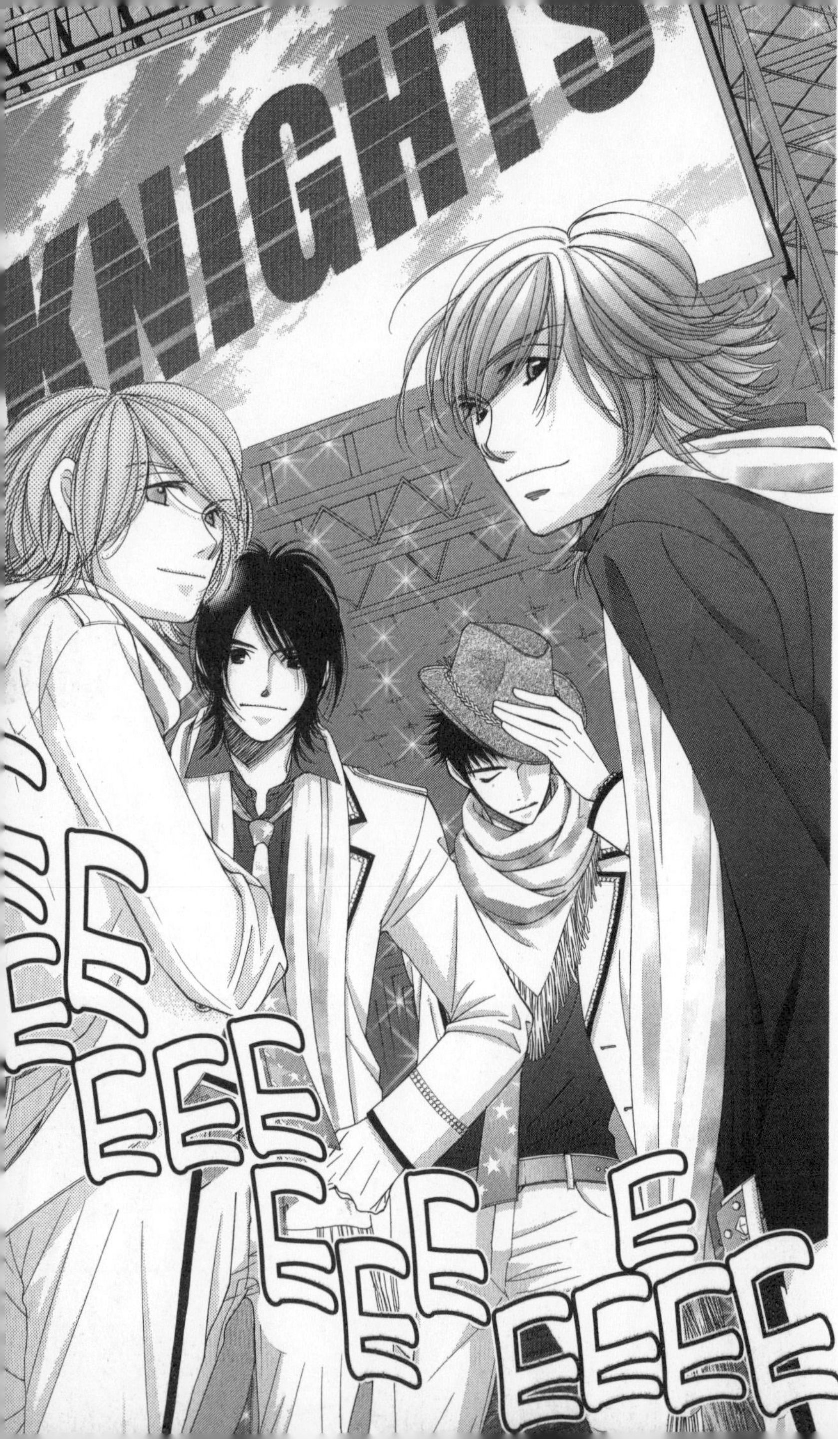
KNIGHTS
KYEEEEEEEEEEEEE

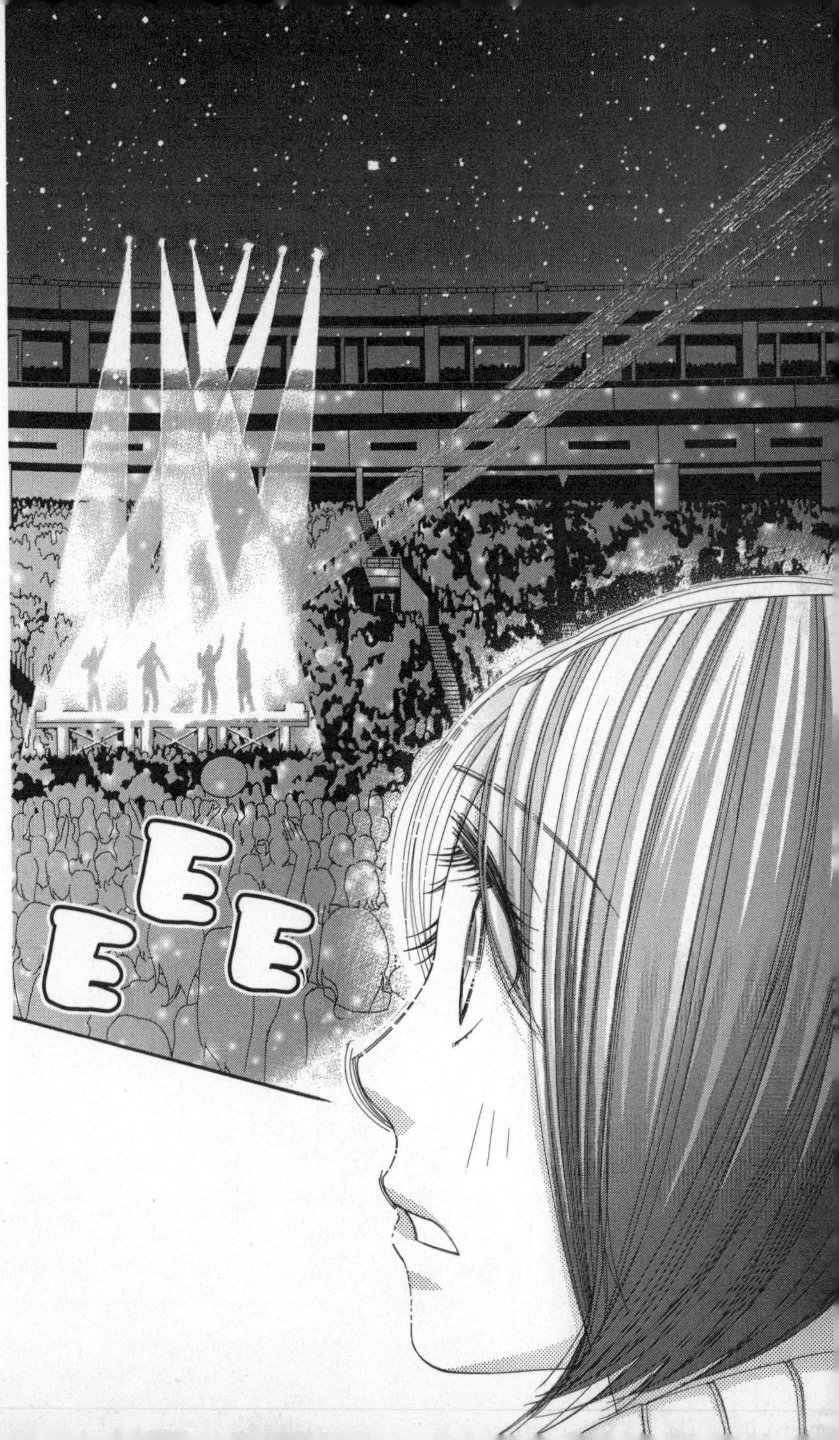
EEEE

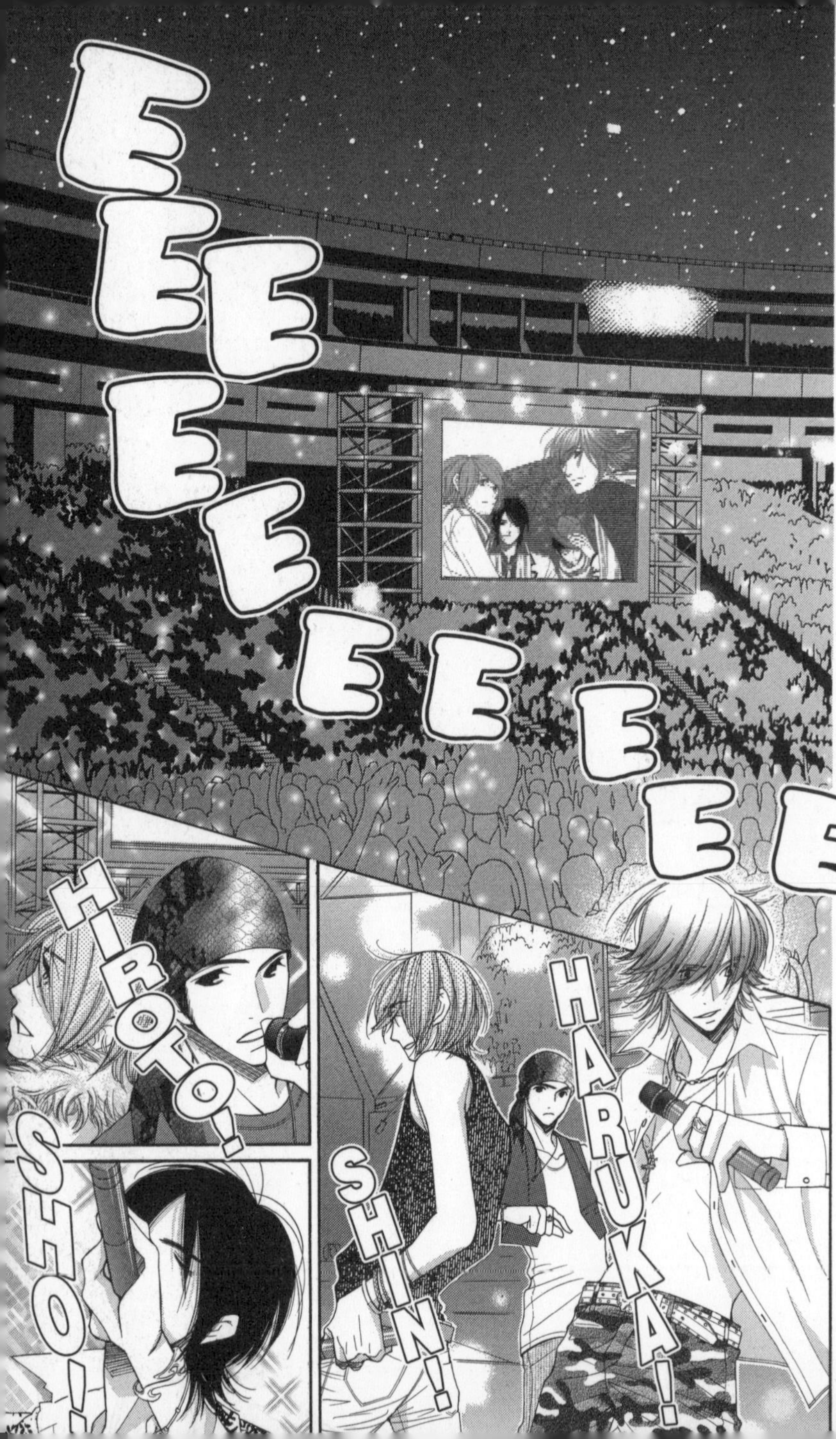
EEEEEEEEEE
HARUKA!
SHIN!
HIROTO!
SHO!

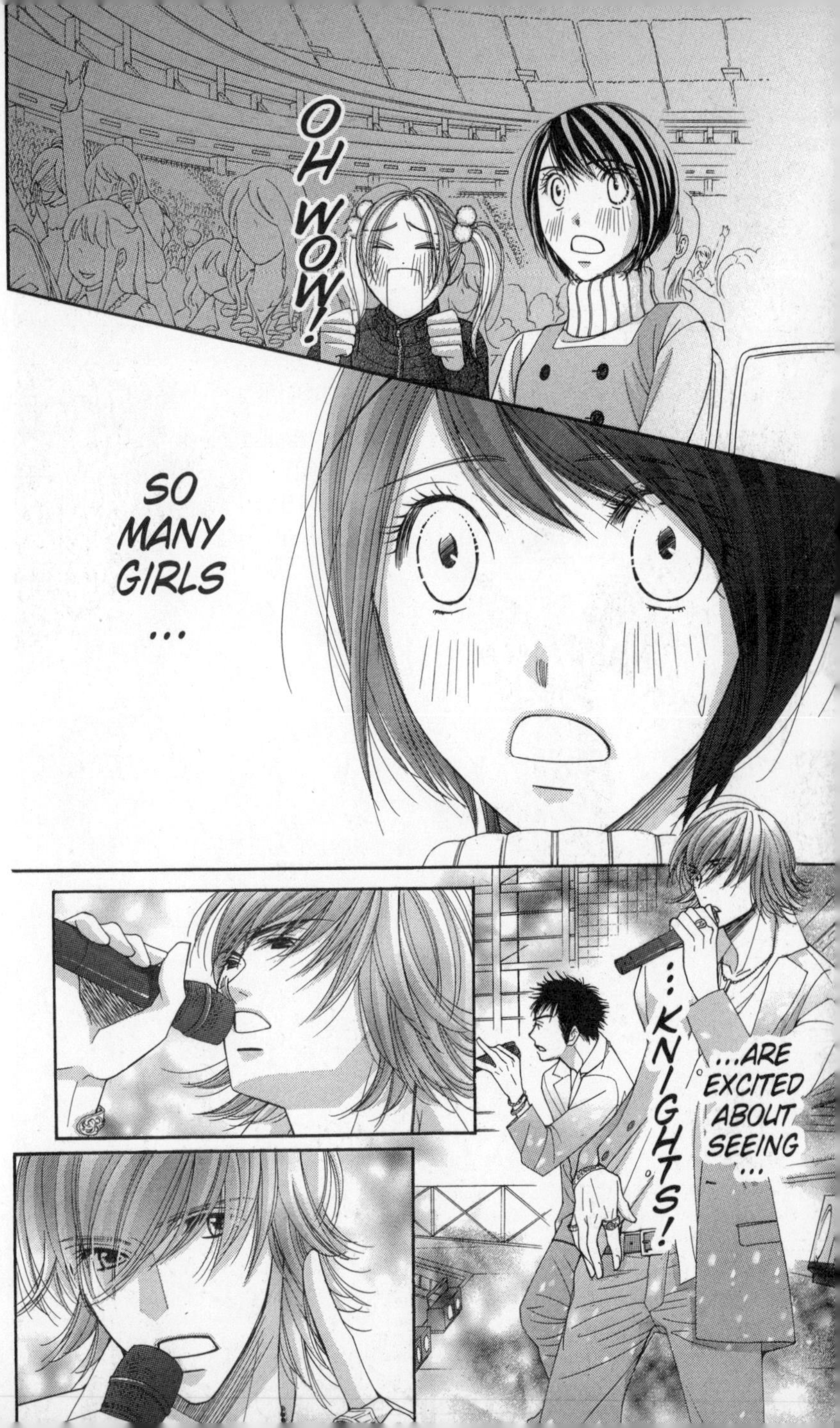
OH WOW!
SO MANY GIRLS ...
...ARE EXCITED ABOUT SEEING ...
...KNIGHTS!

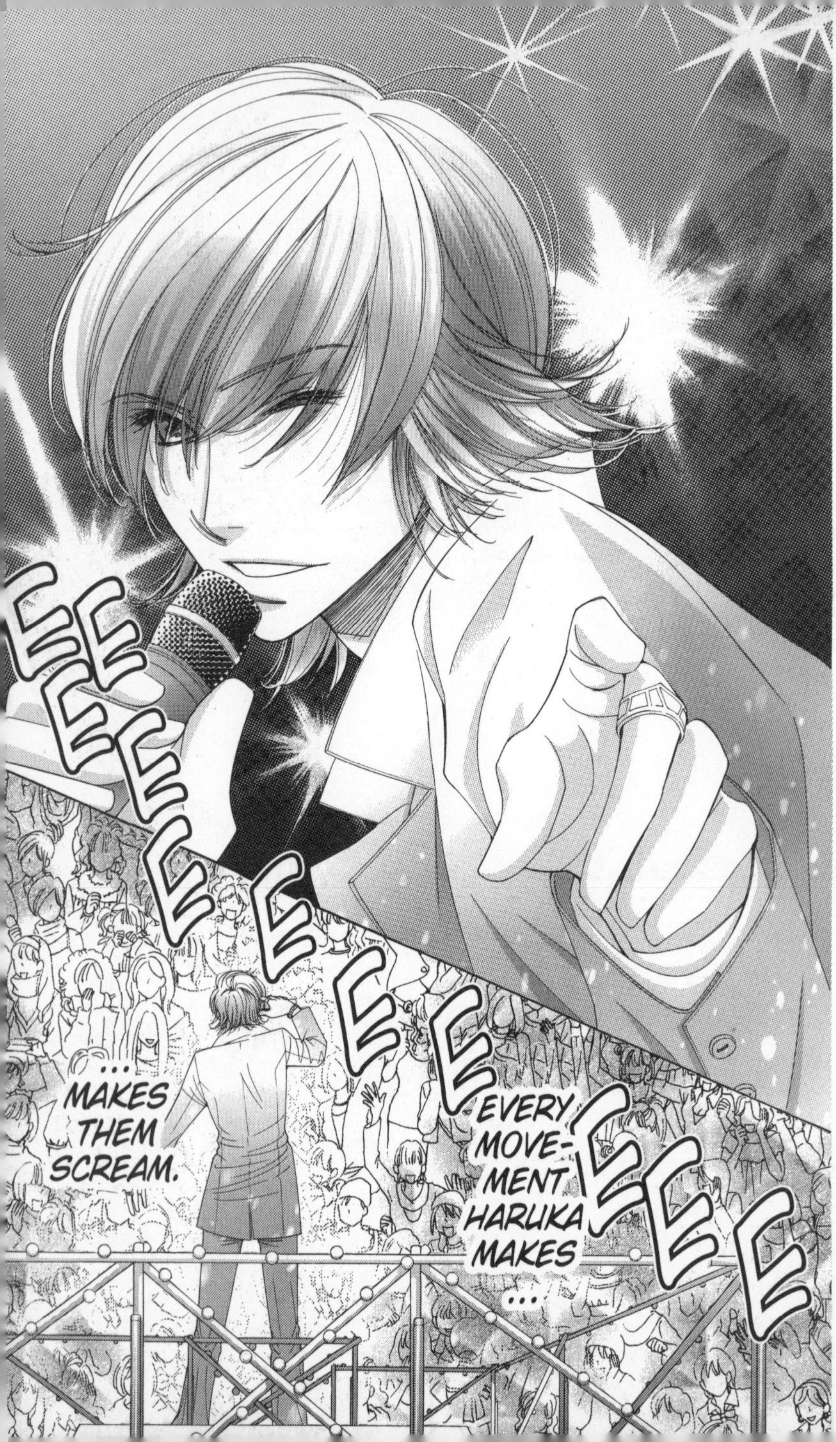
EVERY MOVEMENT HARUKA MAKES...
...MAKES THEM SCREAM.
EEEEEEEEEEEEEE

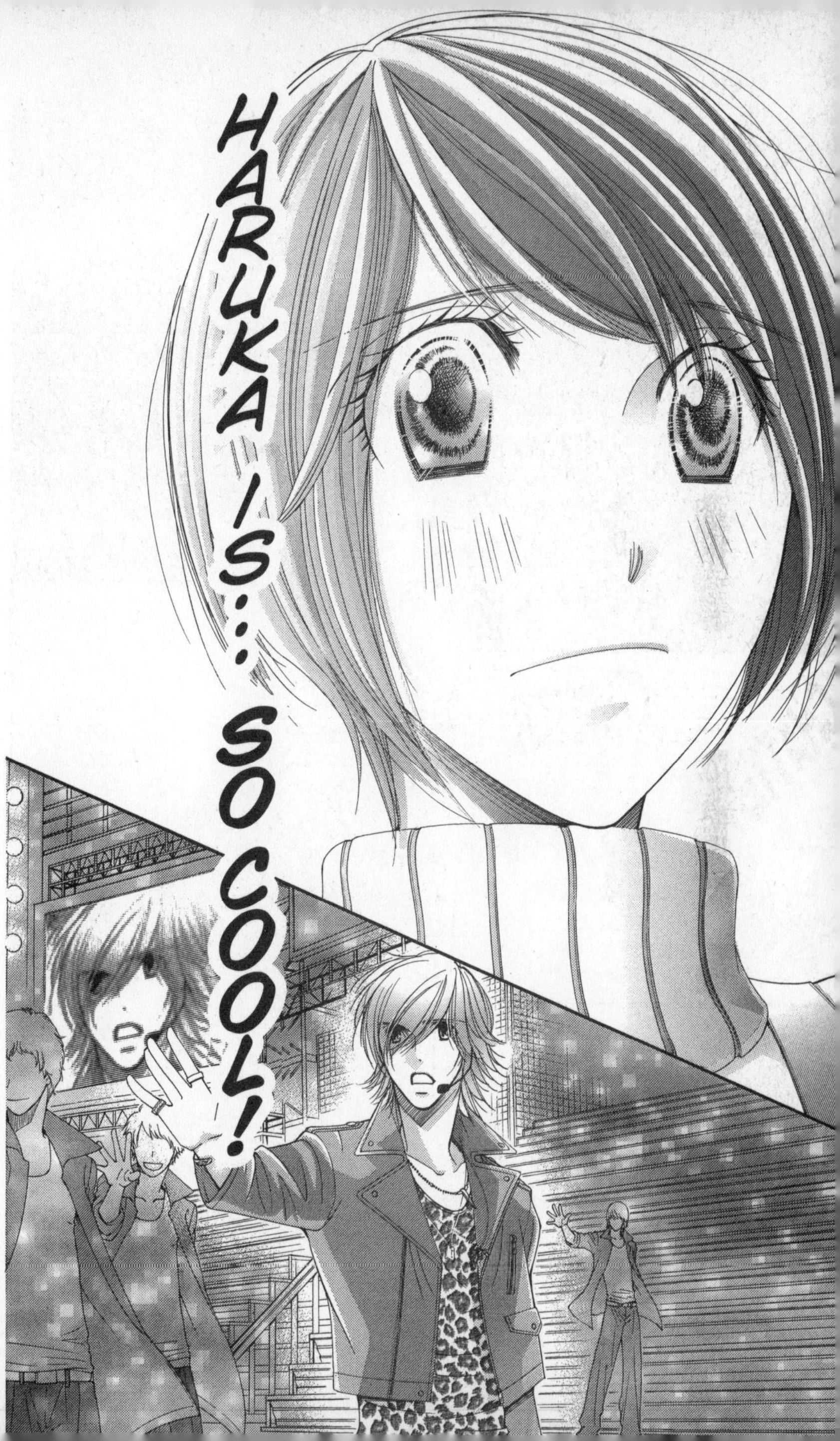
HARUKA IS... SO COOL!

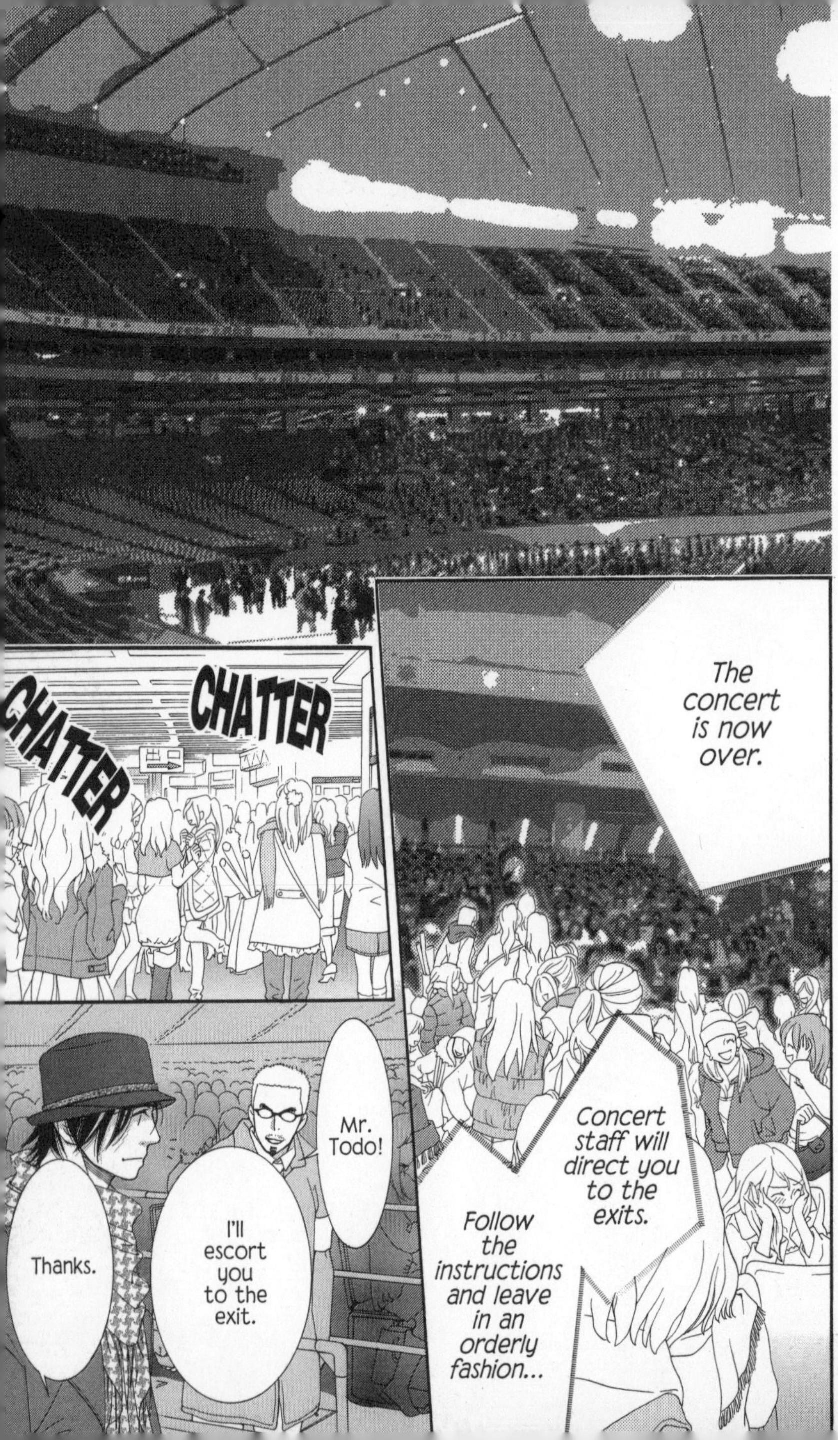
The concert is now over.
Concert staff will direct you to the exits.
Follow the instructions and leave in an orderly fashion...
CHATTER
CHATTER
Mr. Todo!
I'll escort you to the exit.
Thanks.

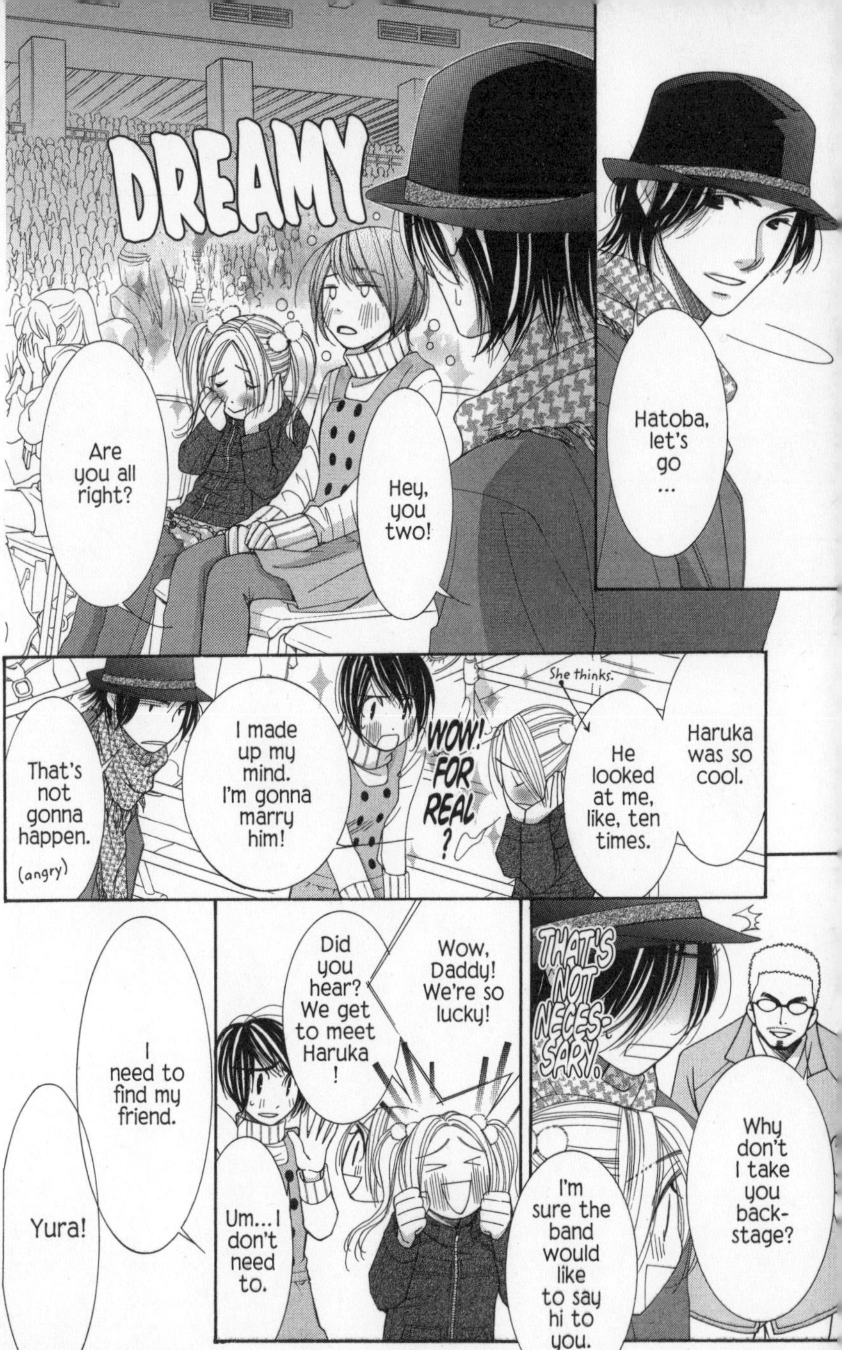
Hatoba, let's go ...
DREAMY
Hey, you two!
Are you all right?
Haruka was so cool.
He looked at me, like, ten times.
She thinks.
WOW! FOR REAL?
I made up my mind. I'm gonna marry him!
That's not gonna happen.
(angry)
Why don't I take you back-stage?
I'm sure the band would like to say hi to you.
THAT'S NOT NECES-SARY.
Wow, Daddy! We're so lucky!
Did you hear? We get to meet Haruka!
Um...I don't need to.
I need to find my friend.
Yura!

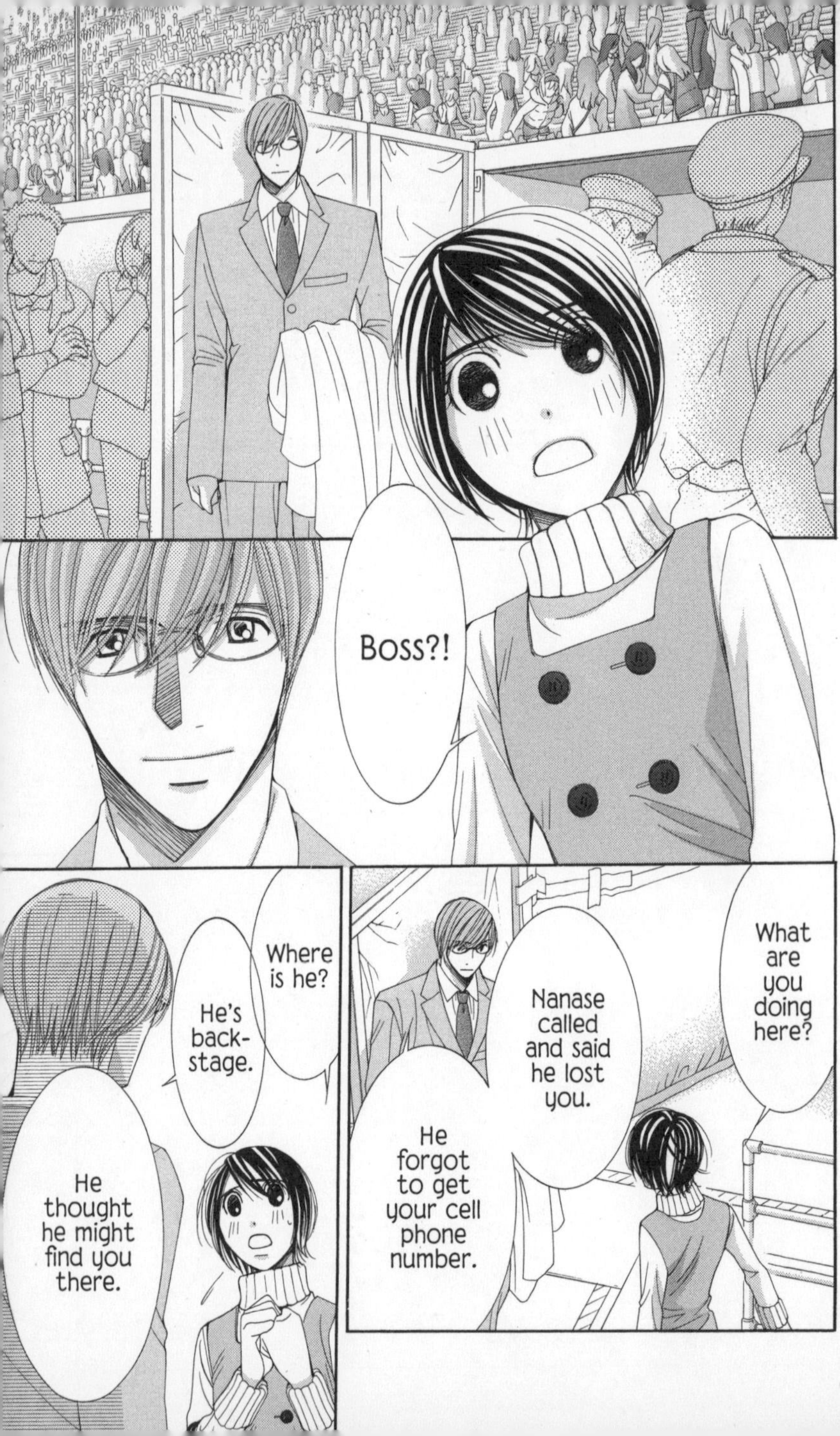
Boss?!
What are you doing here?
Nanase called and said he lost you.
He forgot to get your cell phone number.
Where is he?
He's back-stage.
He thought he might find you there.

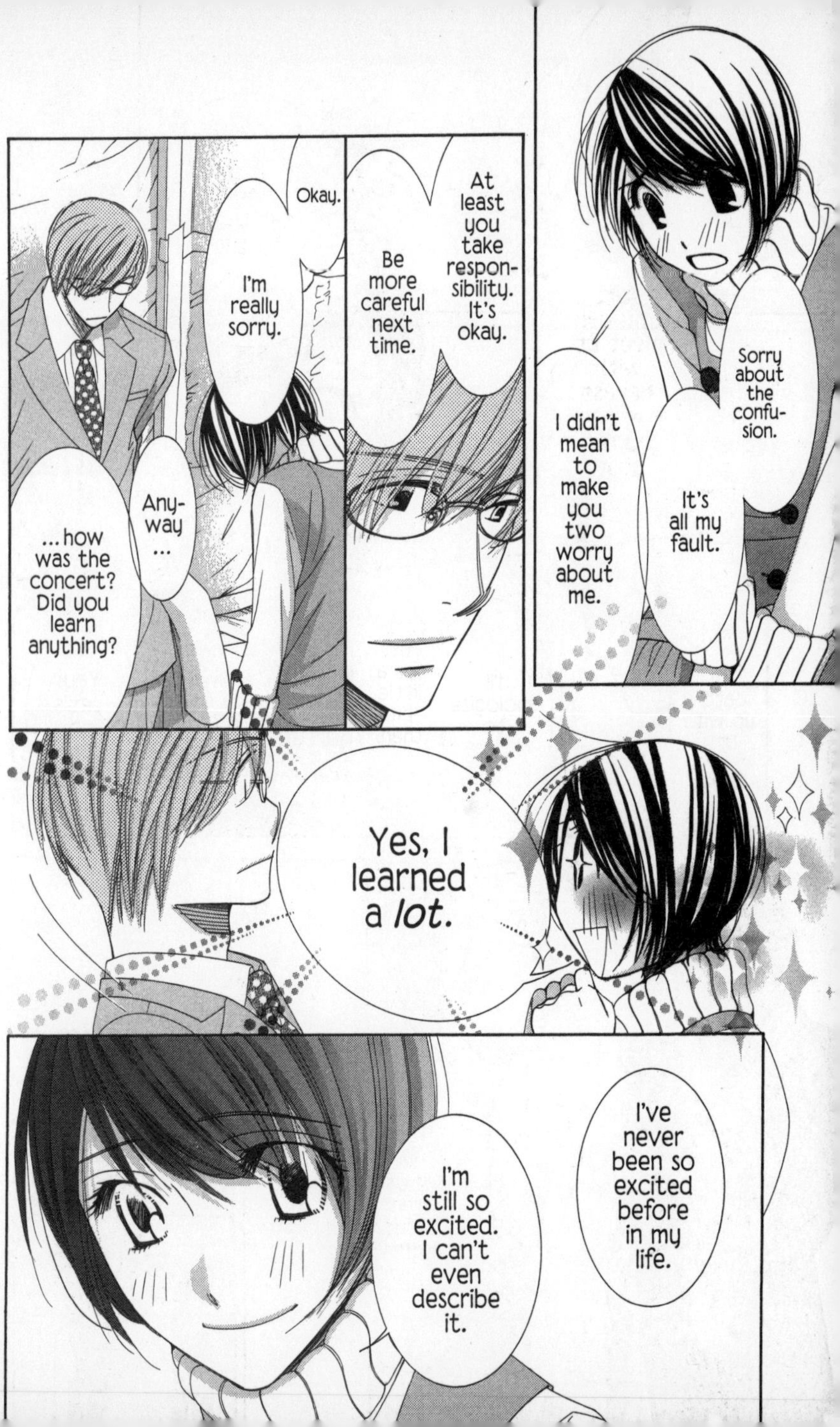
Sorry about the confusion.
It's all my fault.
I didn't mean to make you two worry about me.
At least you take responsibility. It's okay.
Be more careful next time.
Okay.
I'm really sorry.
Any-way...
...how was the concert? Did you learn anything?
Yes, I learned a *lot*.
I've never been so excited before in my life.
I'm still so excited. I can't even describe it.

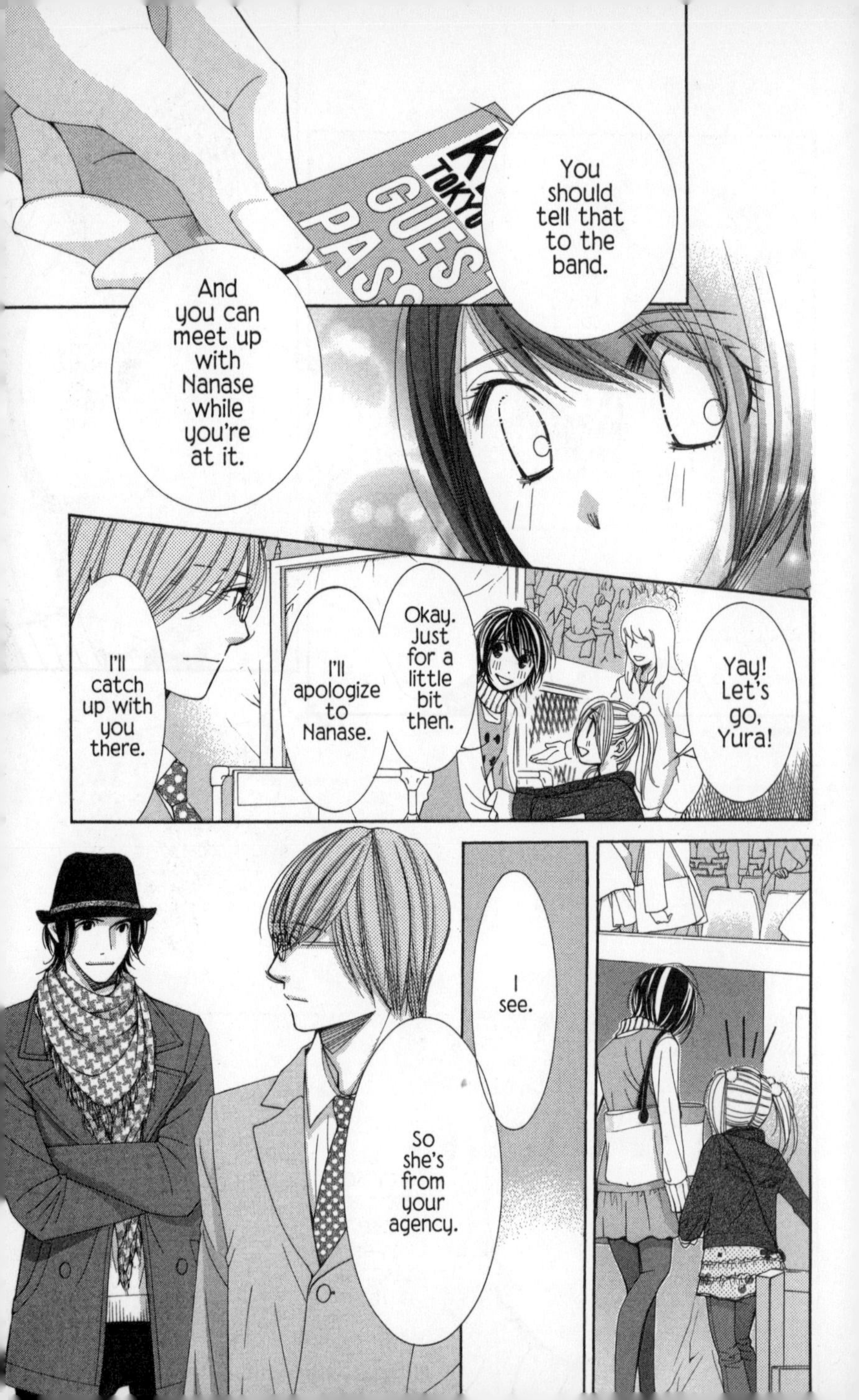
You should tell that to the band.
And you can meet up with Nanase while you're at it.
Yay! Let's go, Yura!
Okay. Just for a little bit then.
I'll apologize to Nanase.
I'll catch up with you there.
I see.
So she's from your agency.

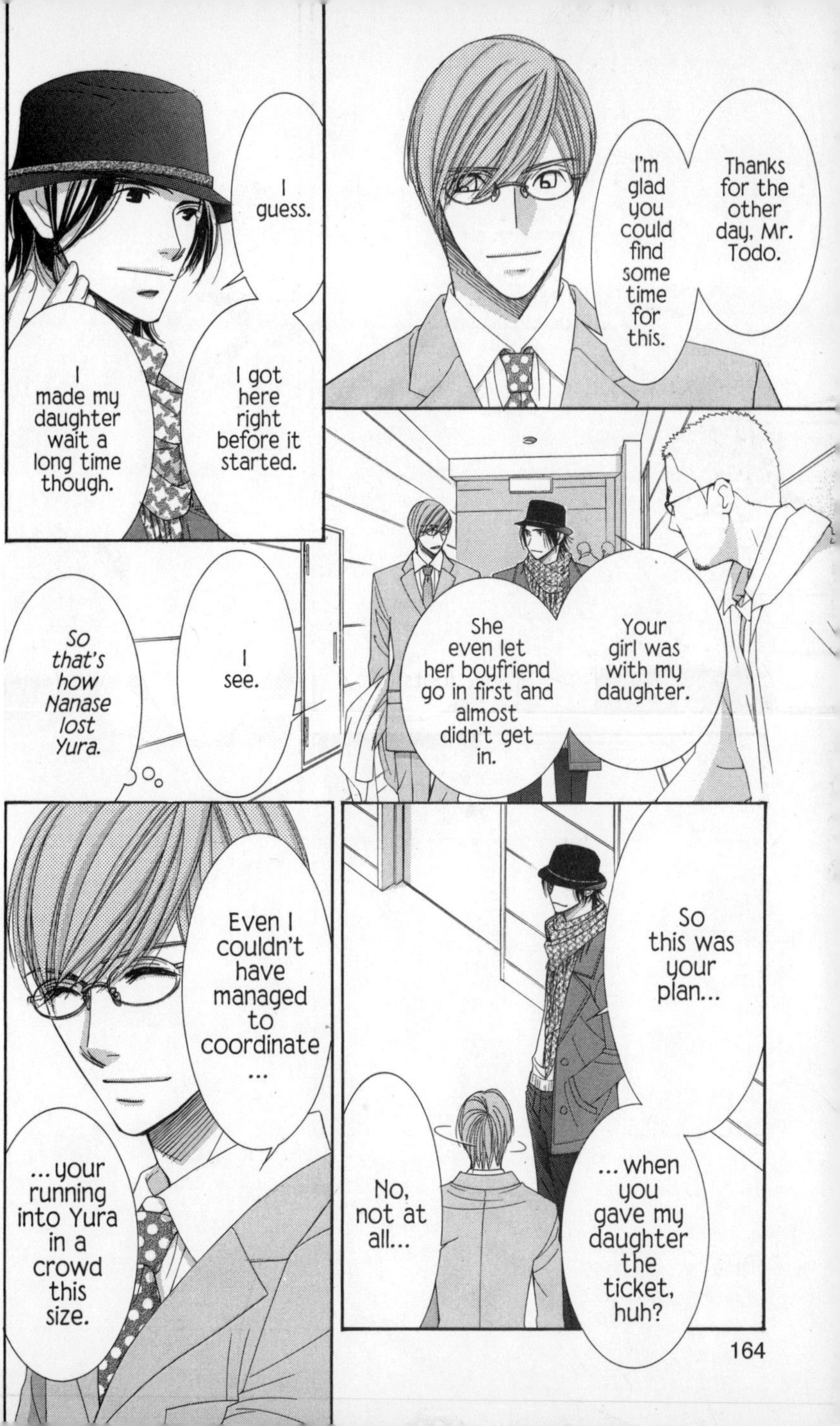
Thanks for the other day, Mr. Todo.
I'm glad you could find some time for this.
I guess.
I got here right before it started.
I made my daughter wait a long time though.
Your girl was with my daughter.
She even let her boyfriend go in first and almost didn't get in.
I see.
So that's how Nanase lost Yura.
So this was your plan...
...when you gave my daughter the ticket, huh?
No, not at all...
Even I couldn't have managed to coordinate...
...your running into Yura in a crowd this size.

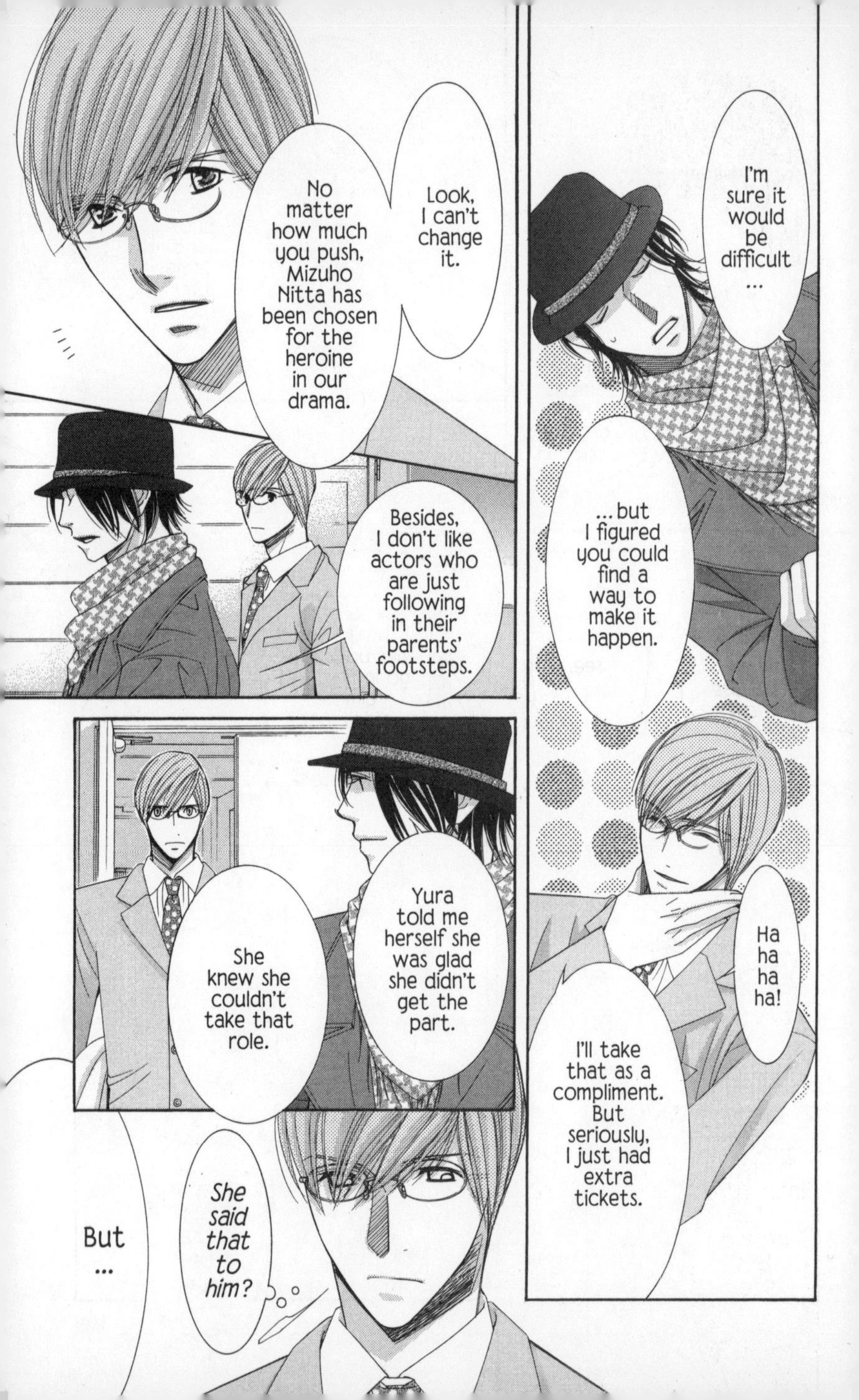
I'm sure it would be difficult...
...but I figured you could find a way to make it happen.
Ha ha ha ha!
I'll take that as a compliment. But seriously, I just had extra tickets.
Look, I can't change it.
No matter how much you push, Mizuho Nitta has been chosen for the heroine in our drama.
Besides, I don't like actors who are just following in their parents' footsteps.
Yura told me herself she was glad she didn't get the part.
She knew she couldn't take that role.
She said that to him?
But...

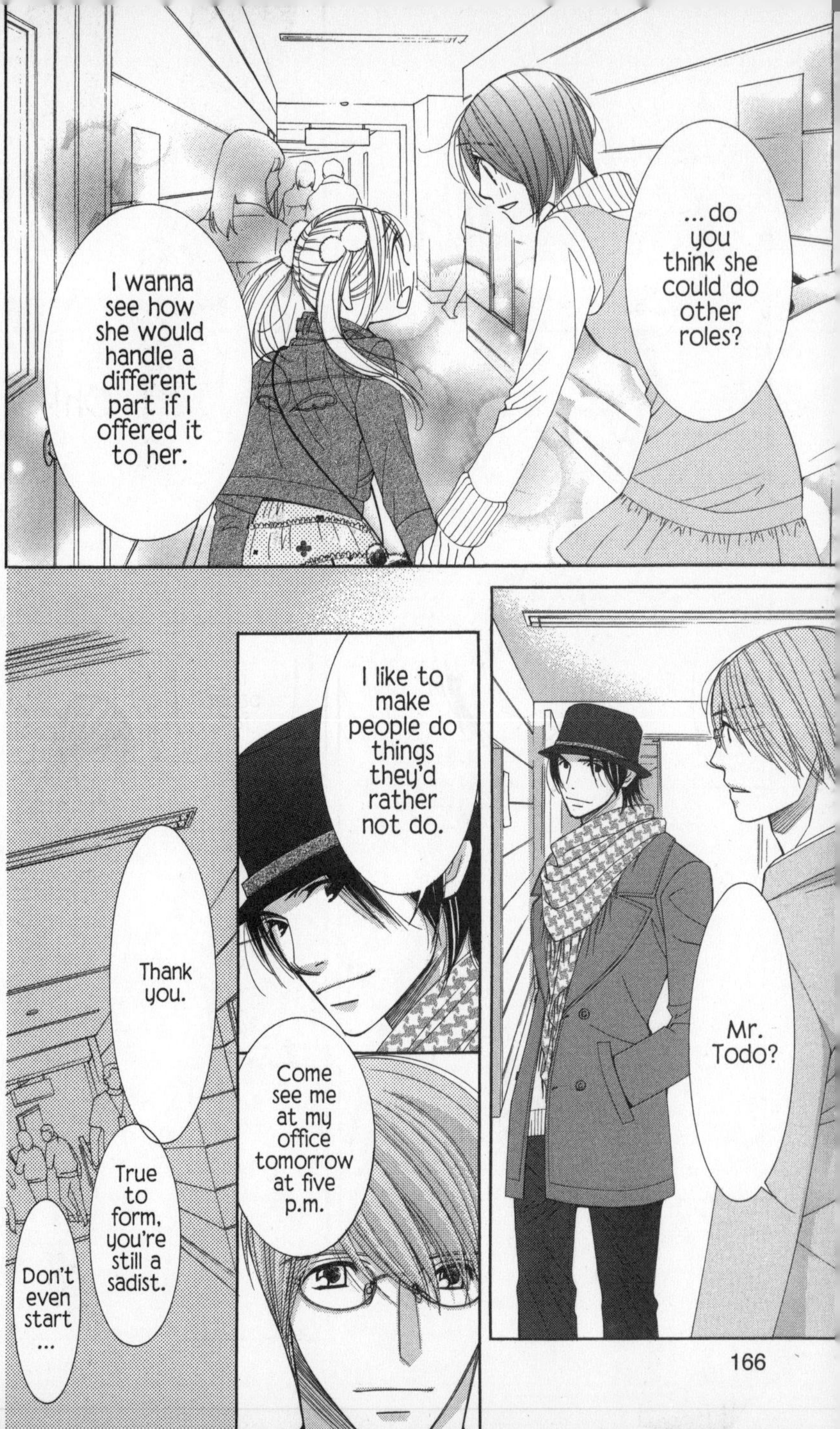
...do you think she could do other roles?
I wanna see how she would handle a different part if I offered it to her.
Mr. Todo?
I like to make people do things they'd rather not do.
Come see me at my office tomorrow at five p.m.
Thank you.
True to form, you're still a sadist.
Don't even start ...

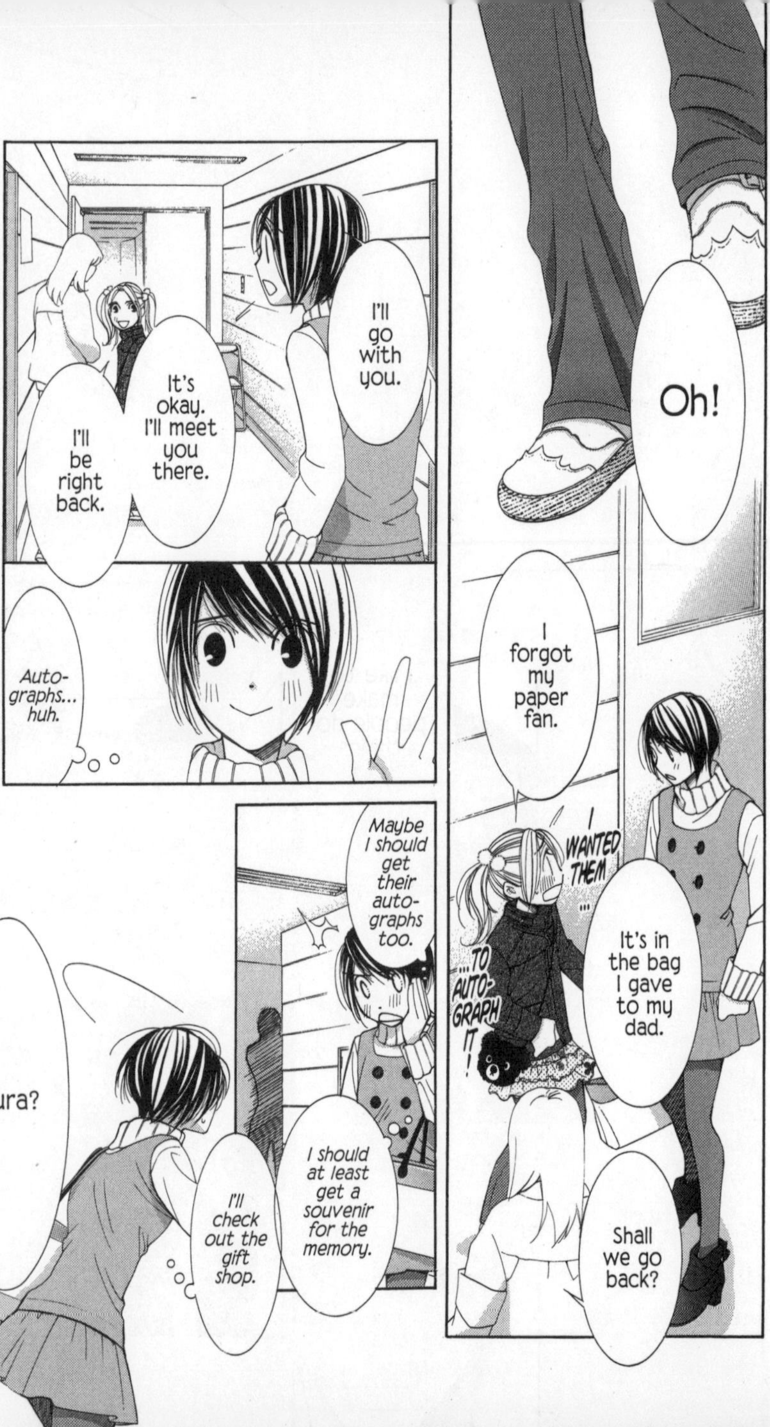
Oh!
I forgot my paper fan.
I WANTED THEM...
...TO AUTOGRAPH IT!
It's in the bag I gave to my dad.
Shall we go back?
I'll go with you.
It's okay. I'll meet you there.
I'll be right back.
Auto-graphs... huh.
Maybe I should get their auto-graphs too.
I should at least get a souvenir for the memory.
I'll check out the gift shop.
Yura?

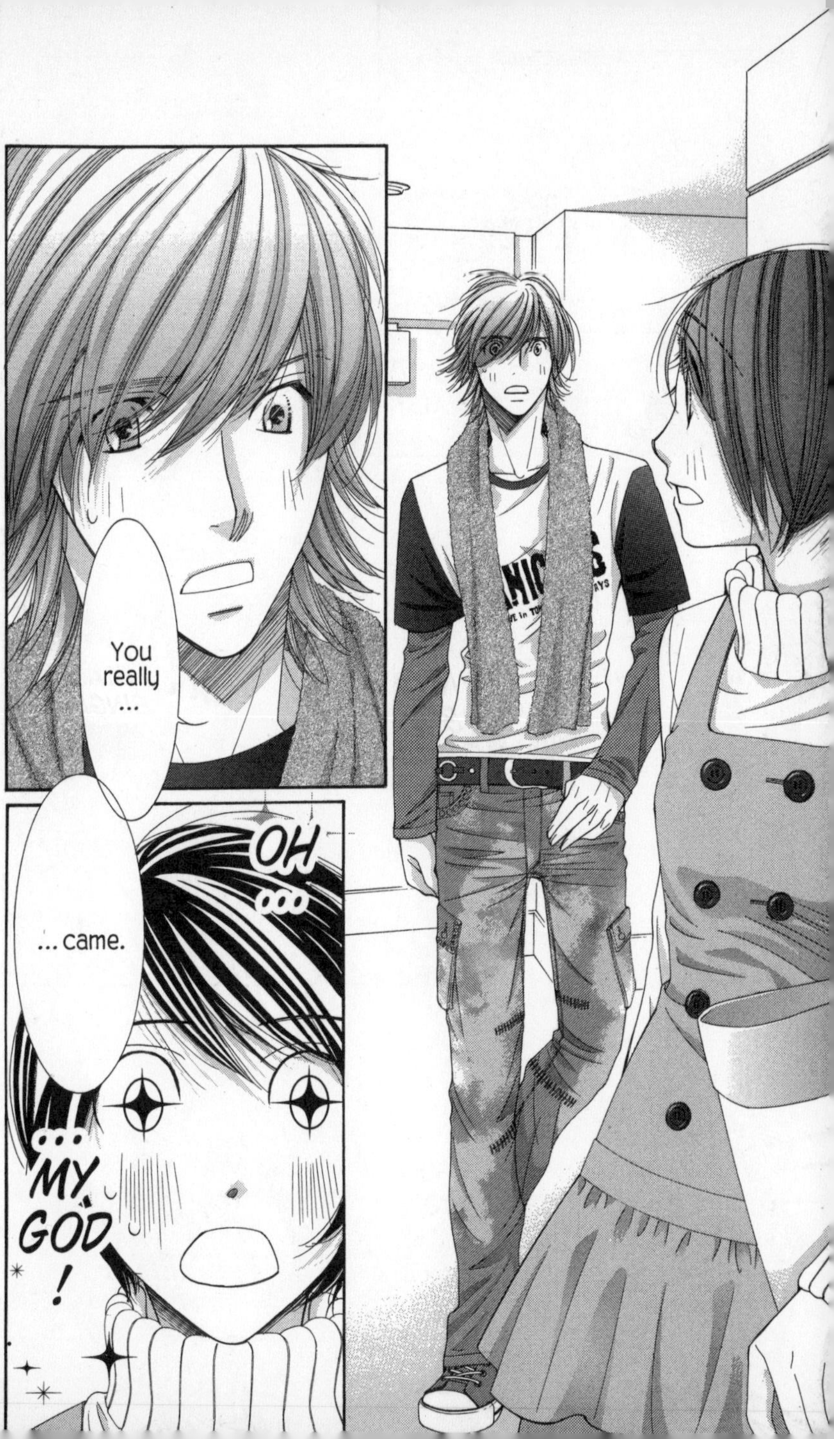
You really ...
... came.
OH ...
... MY GOD !

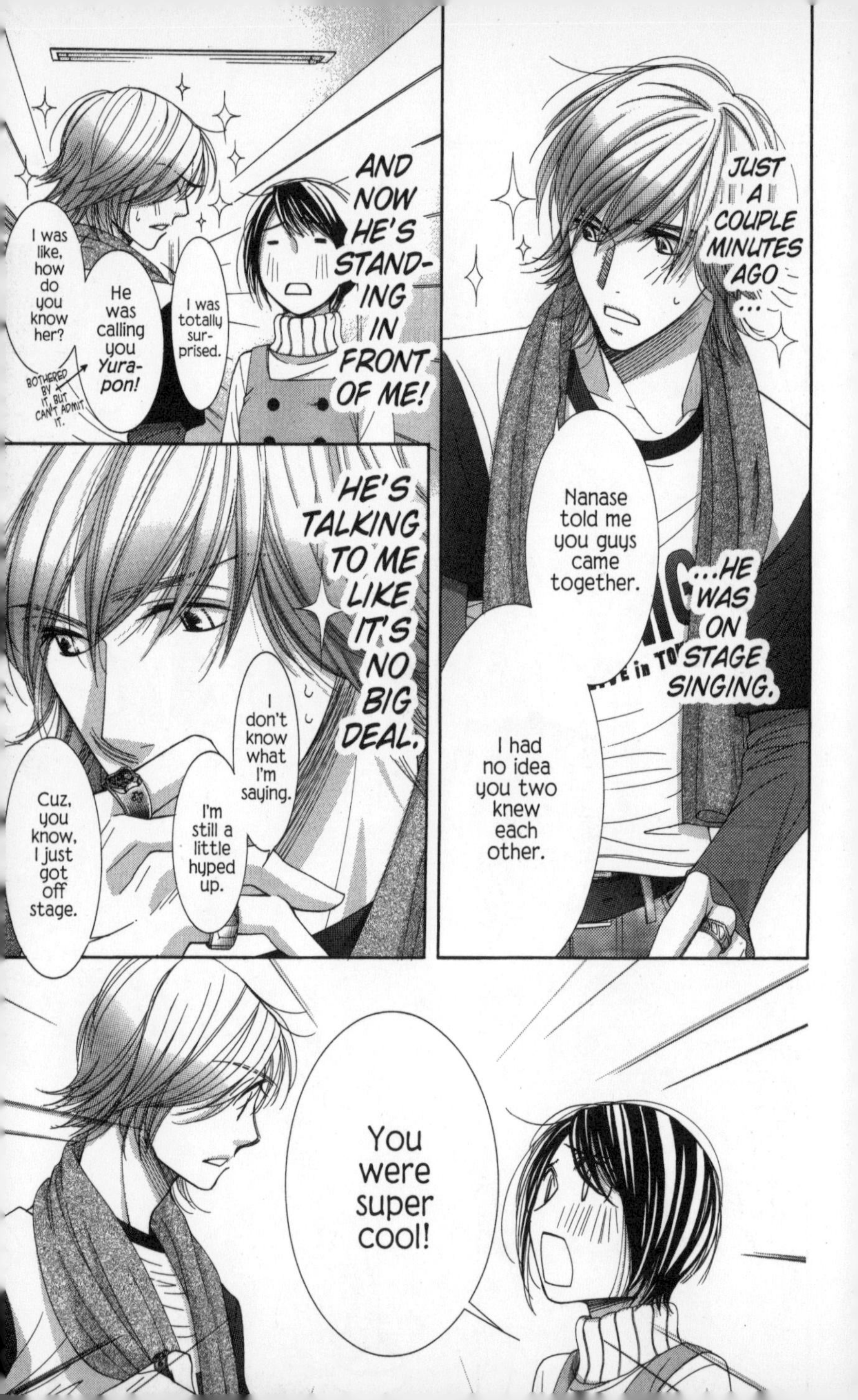
JUST A COUPLE MINUTES AGO...
Nanase told me you guys came together.
...HE WAS ON STAGE SINGING.
I had no idea you two knew each other.
AND NOW HE'S STANDING IN FRONT OF ME!
I was totally surprised.
He was calling you Yura-pon!
I was like, how do you know her?
BOTHERED BY IT, BUT CAN'T ADMIT IT.
HE'S TALKING TO ME LIKE IT'S NO BIG DEAL.
I don't know what I'm saying.
I'm still a little hyped up.
Cuz, you know, I just got off stage.
You were super cool!

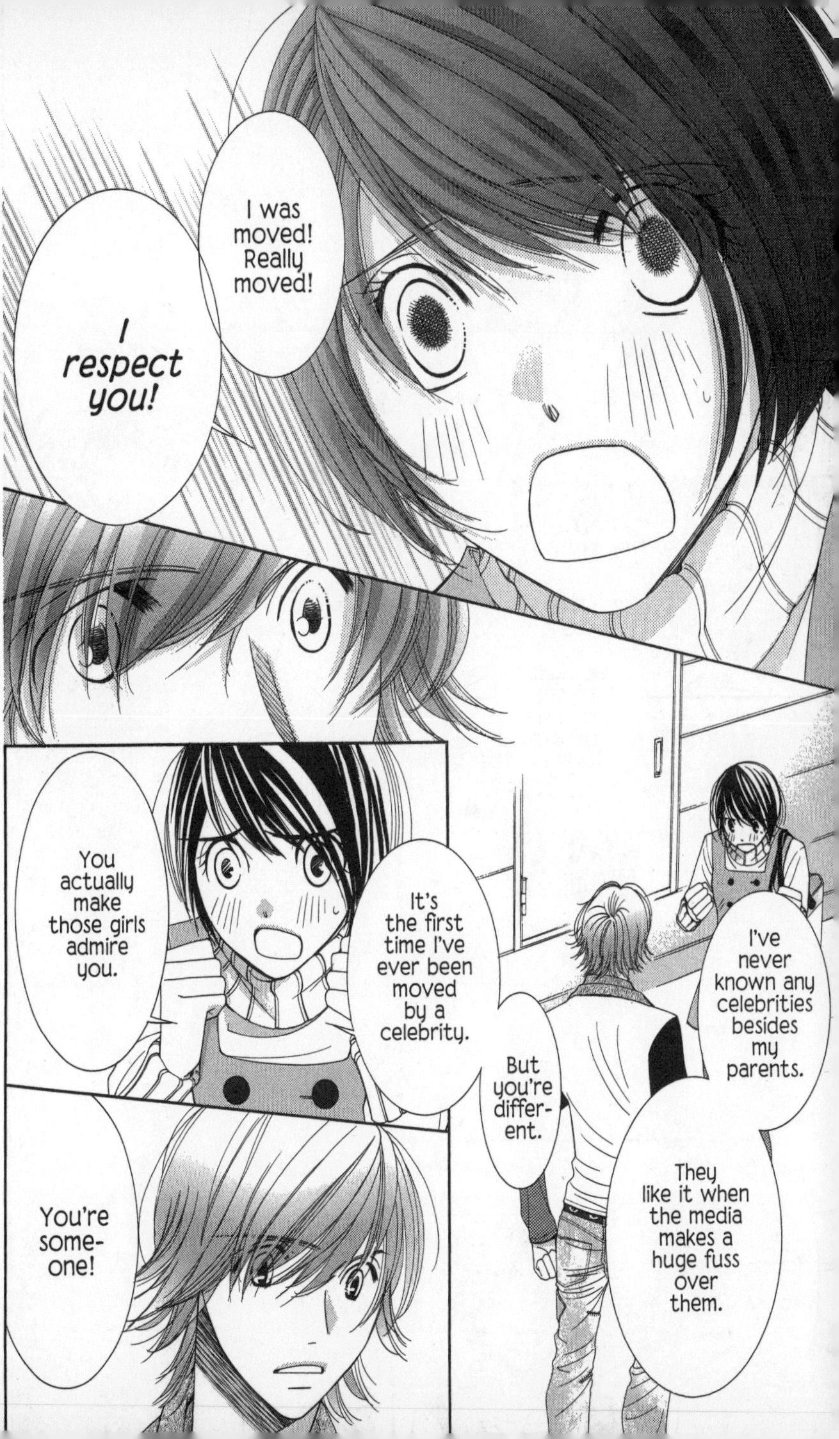
I was moved! Really moved!
I respect you!
I've never known any celebrities besides my parents.
They like it when the media makes a huge fuss over them.
But you're different.
It's the first time I've ever been moved by a celebrity.
You actually make those girls admire you.
You're someone!

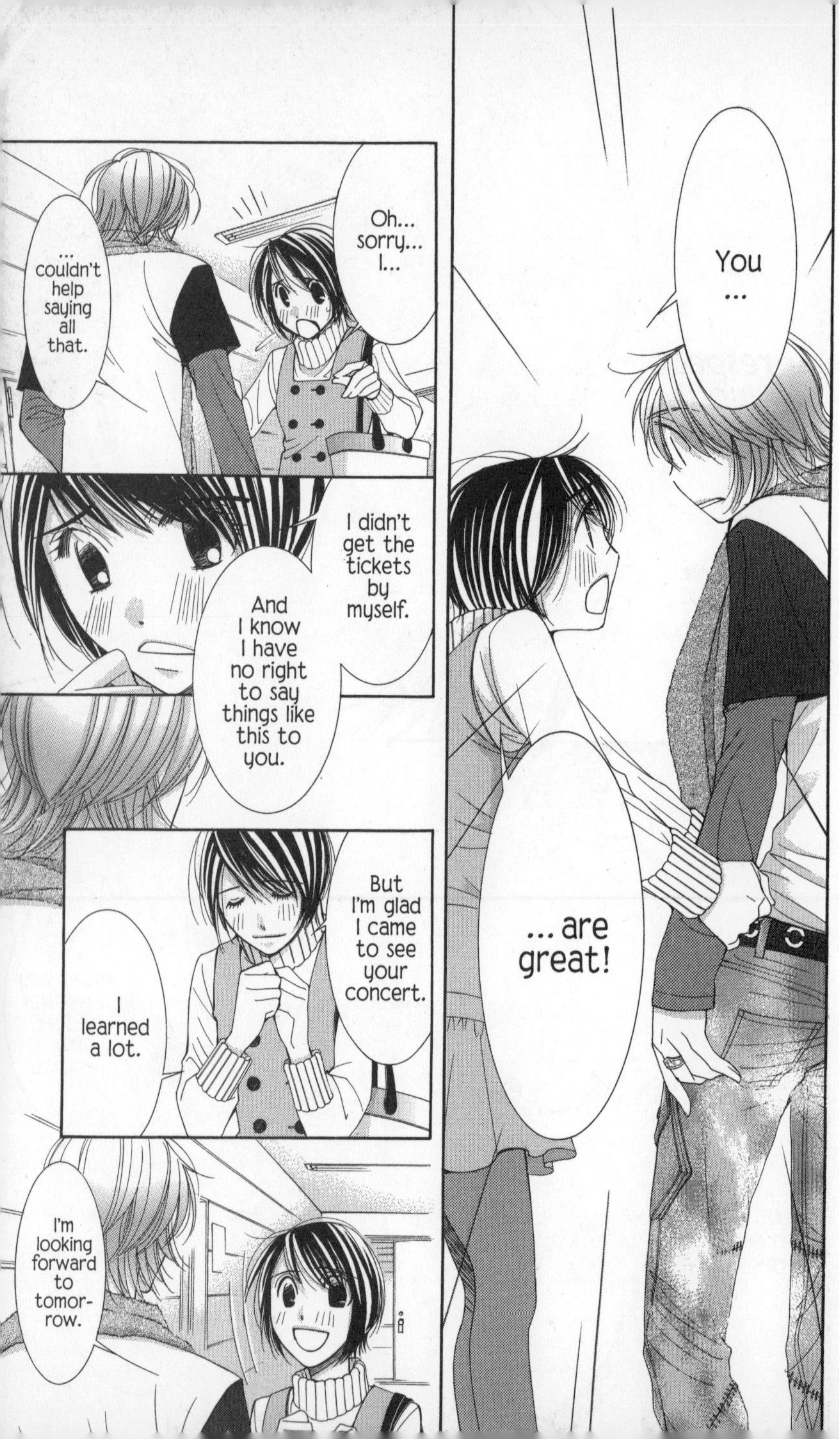
You ...
... are great!
Oh... sorry... I...
... couldn't help saying all that.
I didn't get the tickets by myself.
And I know I have no right to say things like this to you.
But I'm glad I came to see your concert.
I learned a lot.
I'm looking forward to tomorrow.

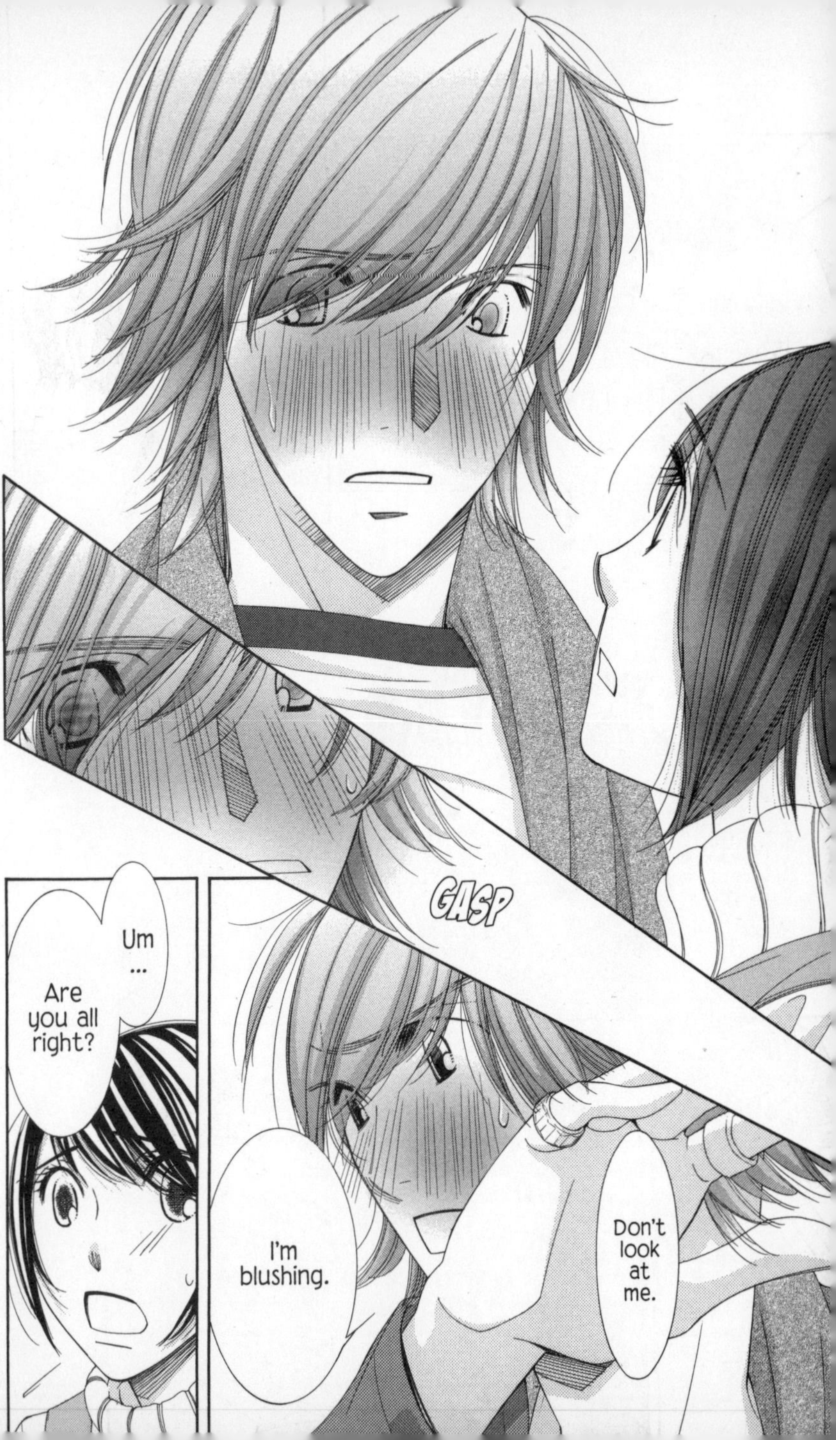
GASP
Don't look at me.
I'm blushing.
Um ...
Are you all right?

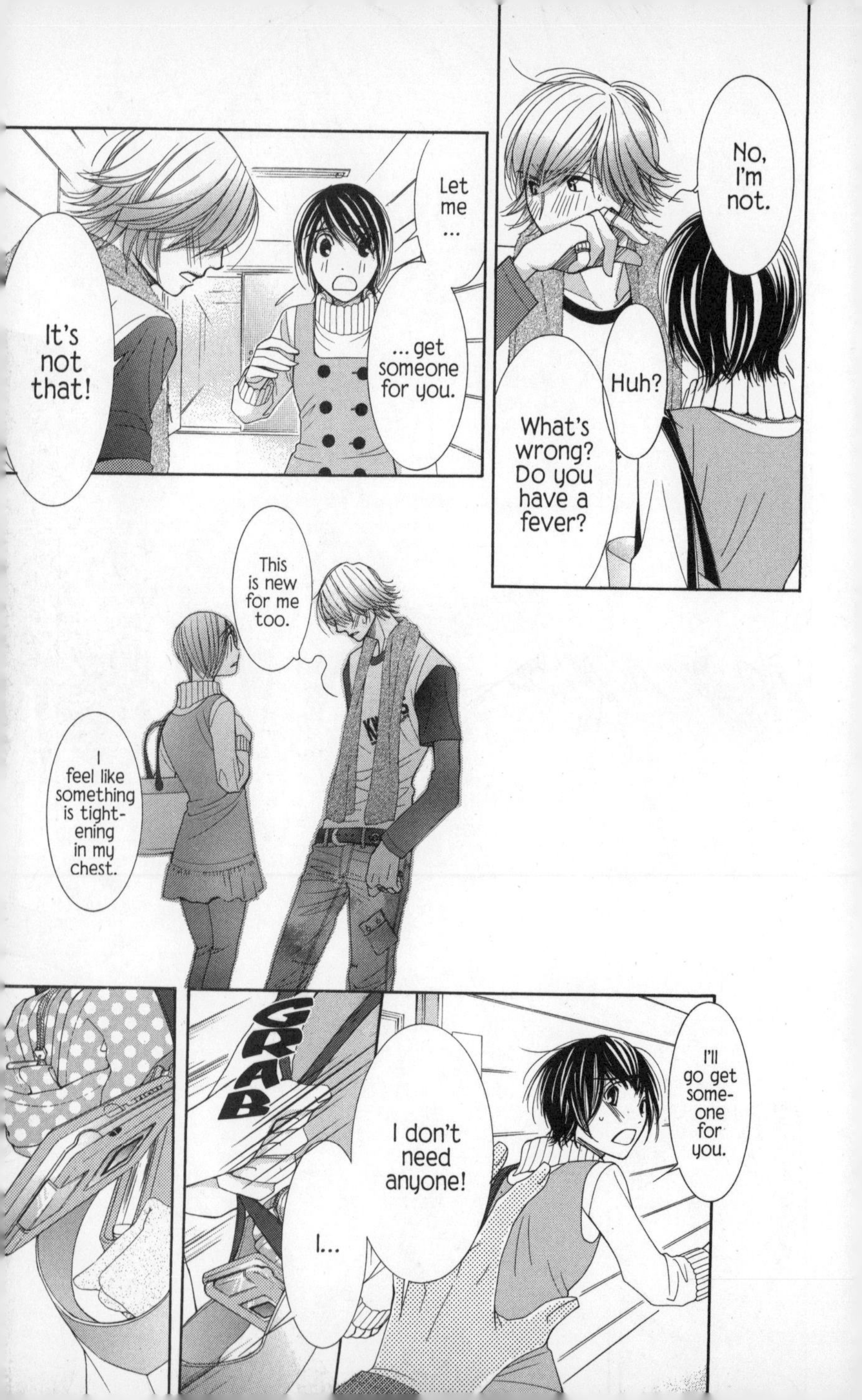
No, I'm not.
Huh?
What's wrong? Do you have a fever?
Let me ...
... get someone for you.
It's not that!
This is new for me too.
I feel like something is tight-ening in my chest.
I'll go get some-one for you.
I don't need anyone!
GRAB
I...

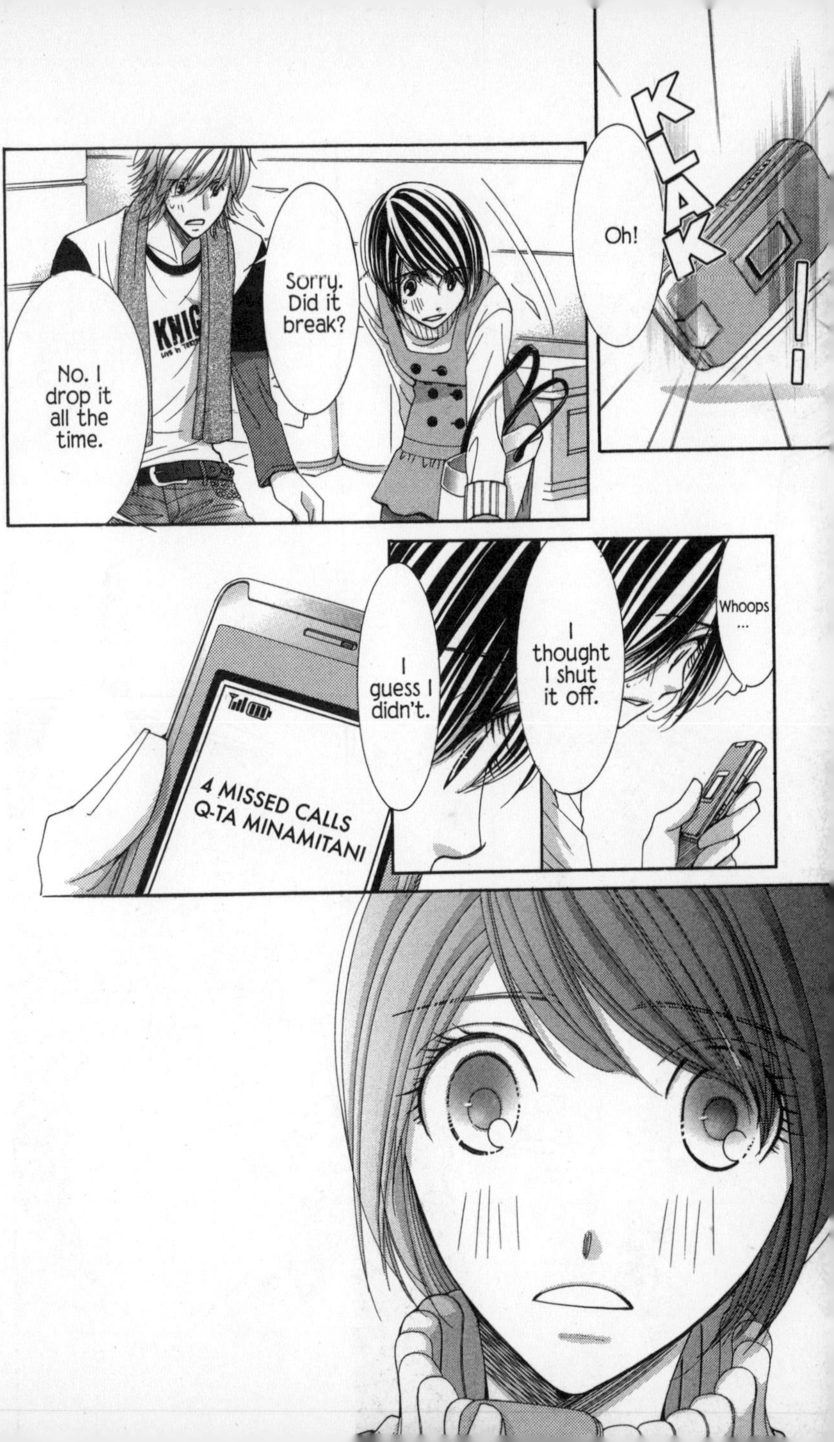
KLAK
Oh!
!!
Sorry. Did it break?
No. I drop it all the time.
Whoops...
I thought I shut it off.
I guess I didn't.
4 MISSED CALLS
Q-TA MINAMITANI

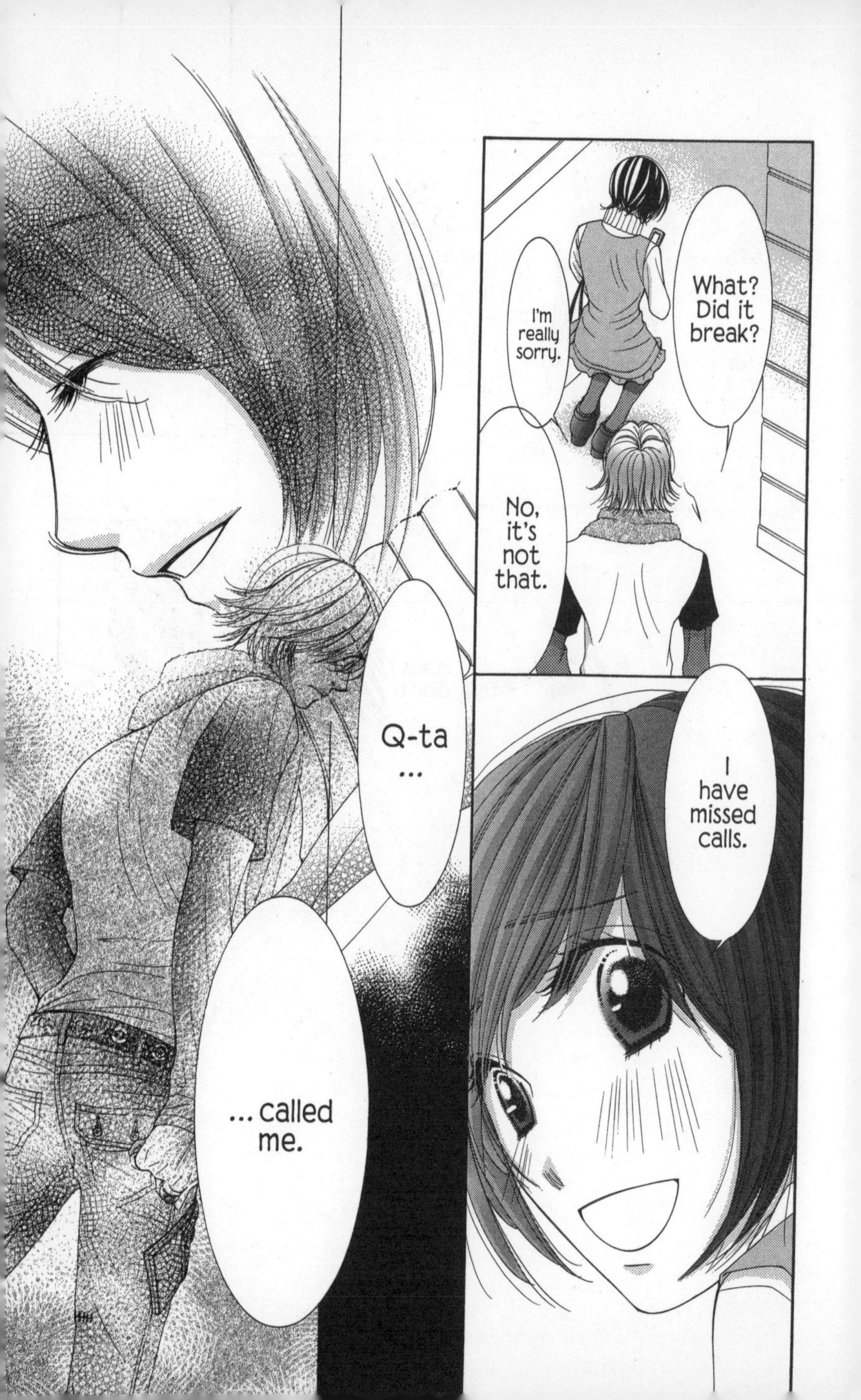
What? Did it break?
I'm really sorry.
No, it's not that.
I have missed calls.
Q-ta ...
... called me.

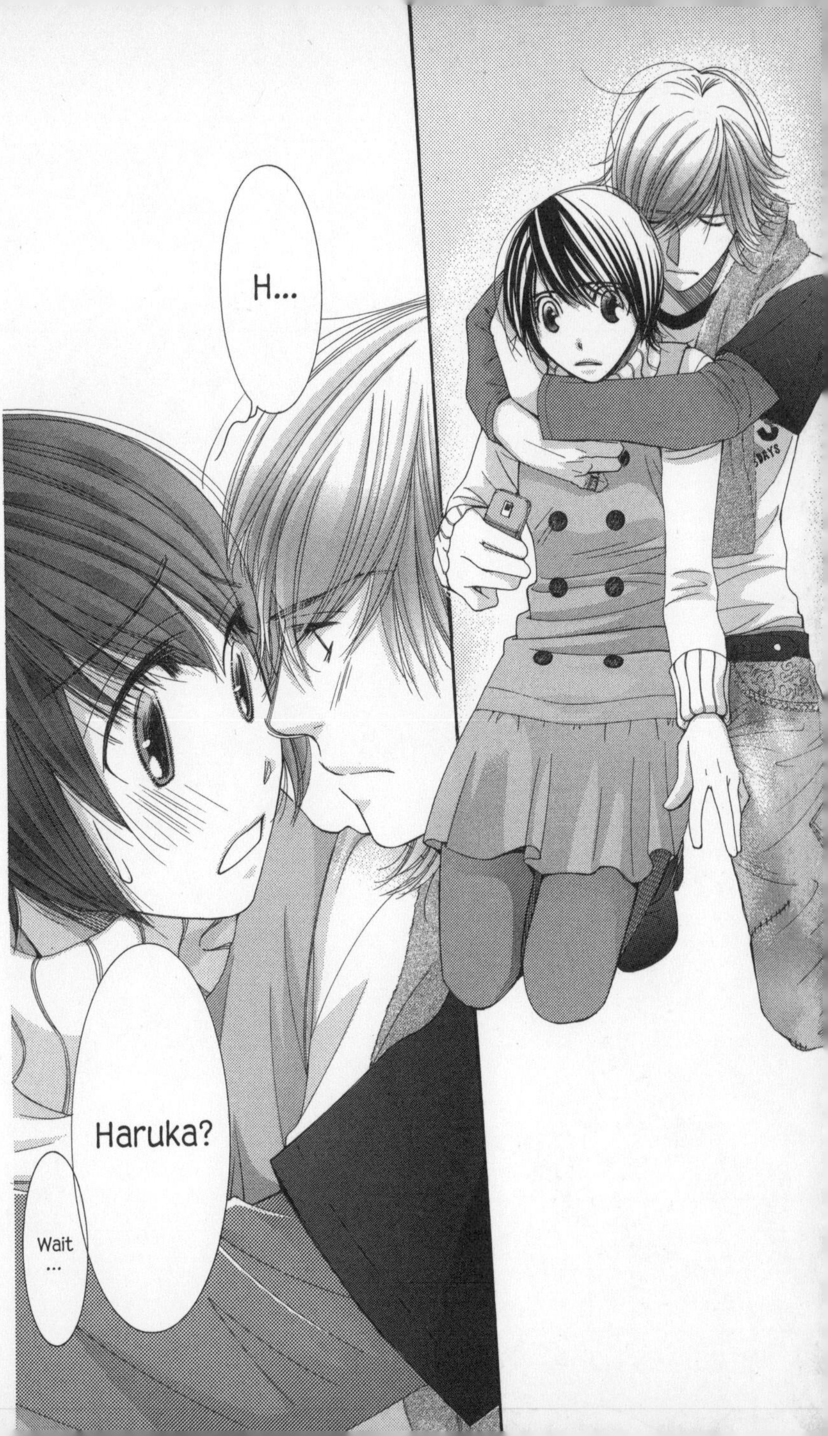
H...
Haruka?
Wait ...

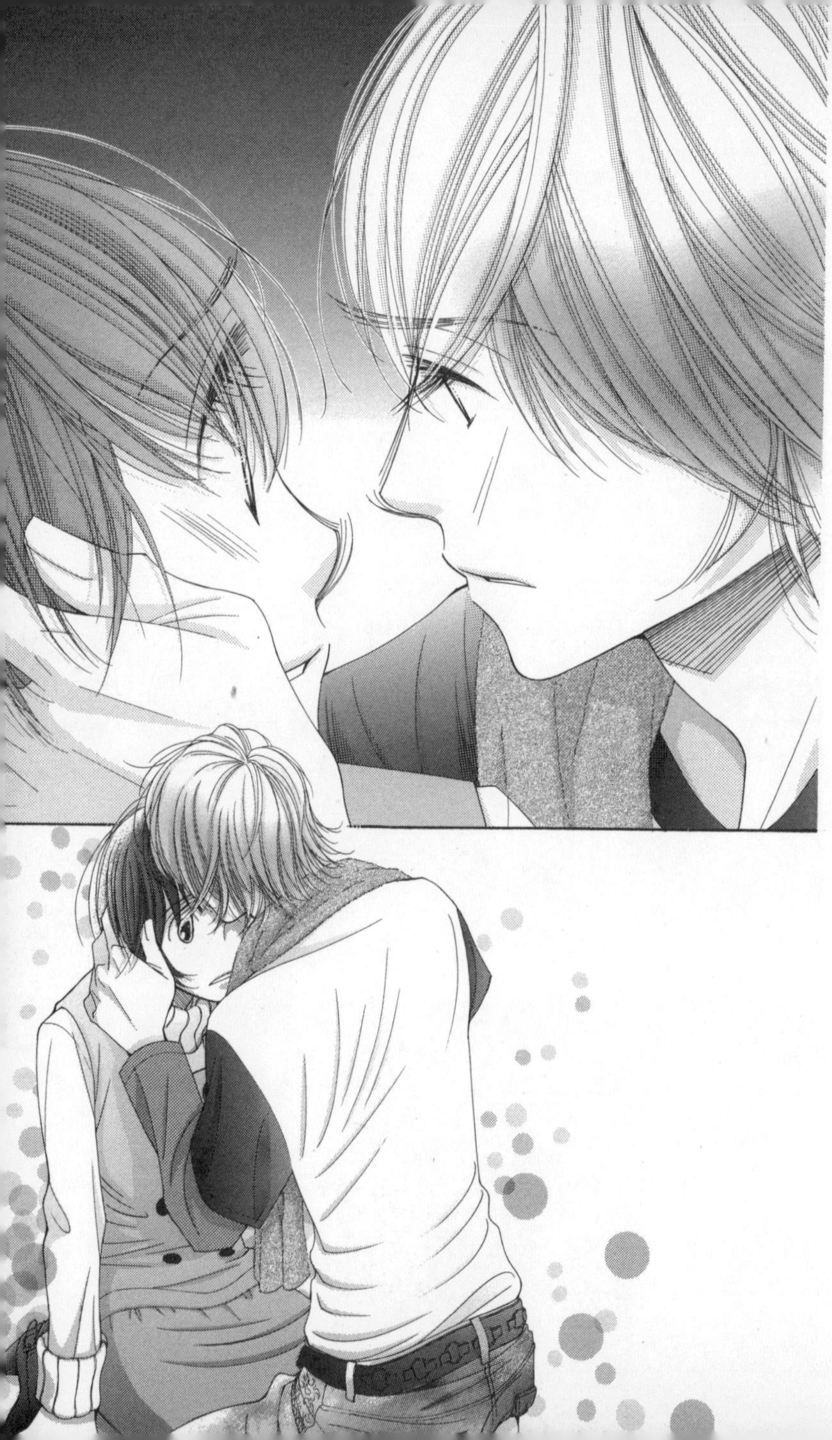

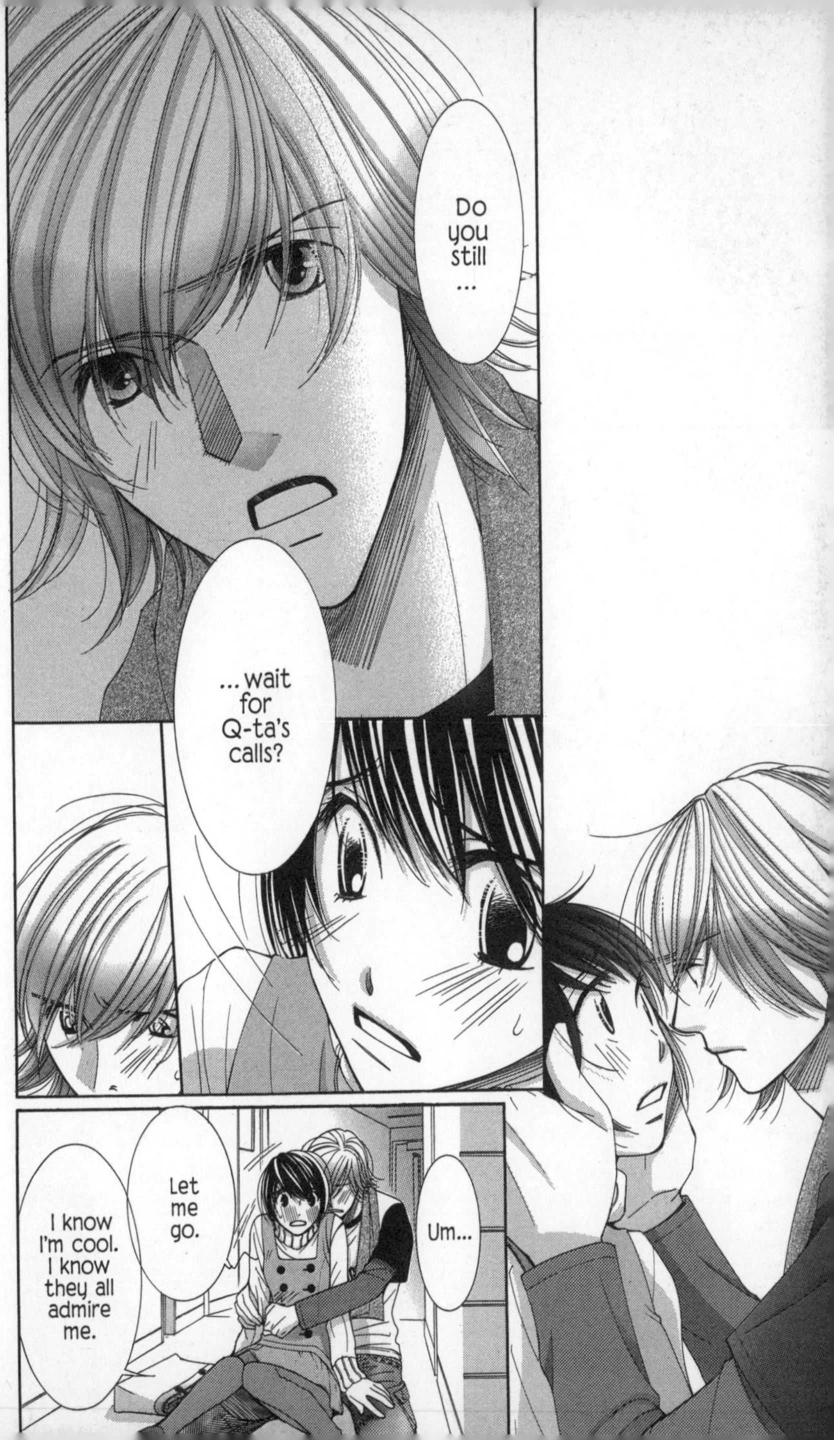
Do you still ...
... wait for Q-ta's calls?
Um...
Let me go.
I know I'm cool. I know they all admire me.

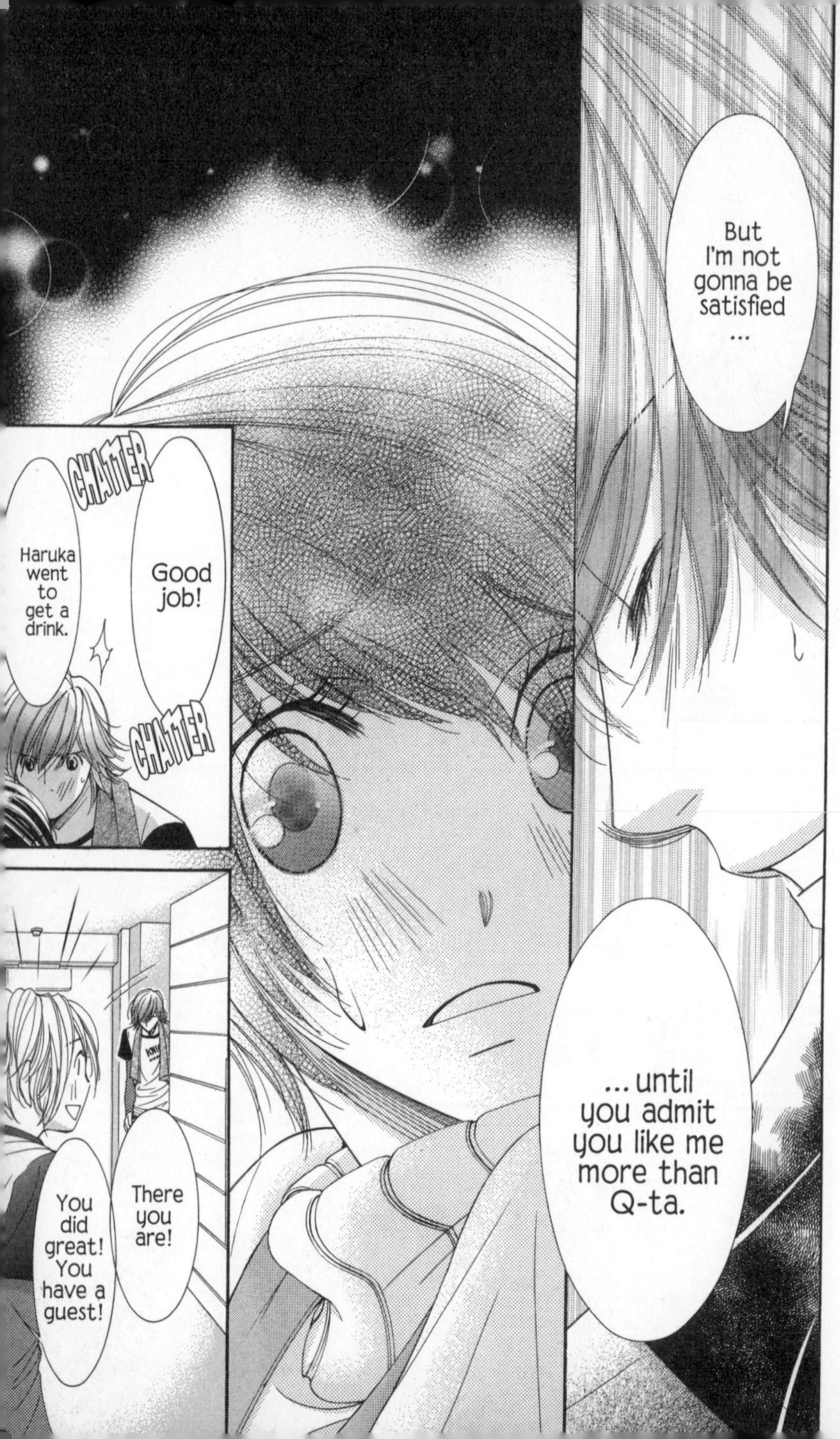
But I'm not gonna be satisfied ...
... until you admit you like me more than Q-ta.
CHATTER
Good job!
Haruka went to get a drink.
CHATTER
There you are!
You did great! You have a guest!

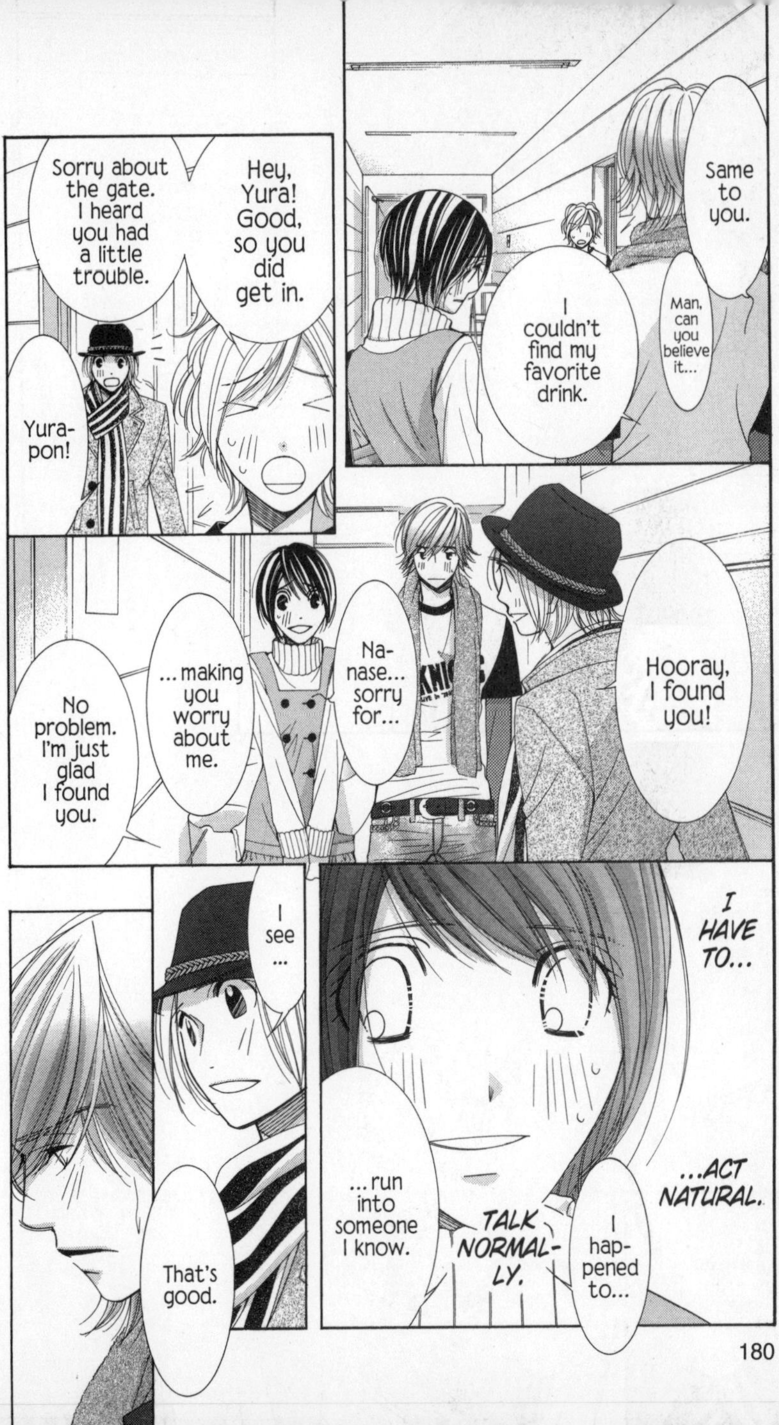
Same to you.
Man, can you believe it...
I couldn't find my favorite drink.
Hey, Yura! Good, so you did get in.
Sorry about the gate. I heard you had a little trouble.
Yura-pon!
Hooray, I found you!
Na-nase... sorry for...
...making you worry about me.
No problem. I'm just glad I found you.
I HAVE TO...
...ACT NATURAL.
TALK NORMAL-LY.
I hap-pened to...
...run into someone I know.
I see...
That's good.

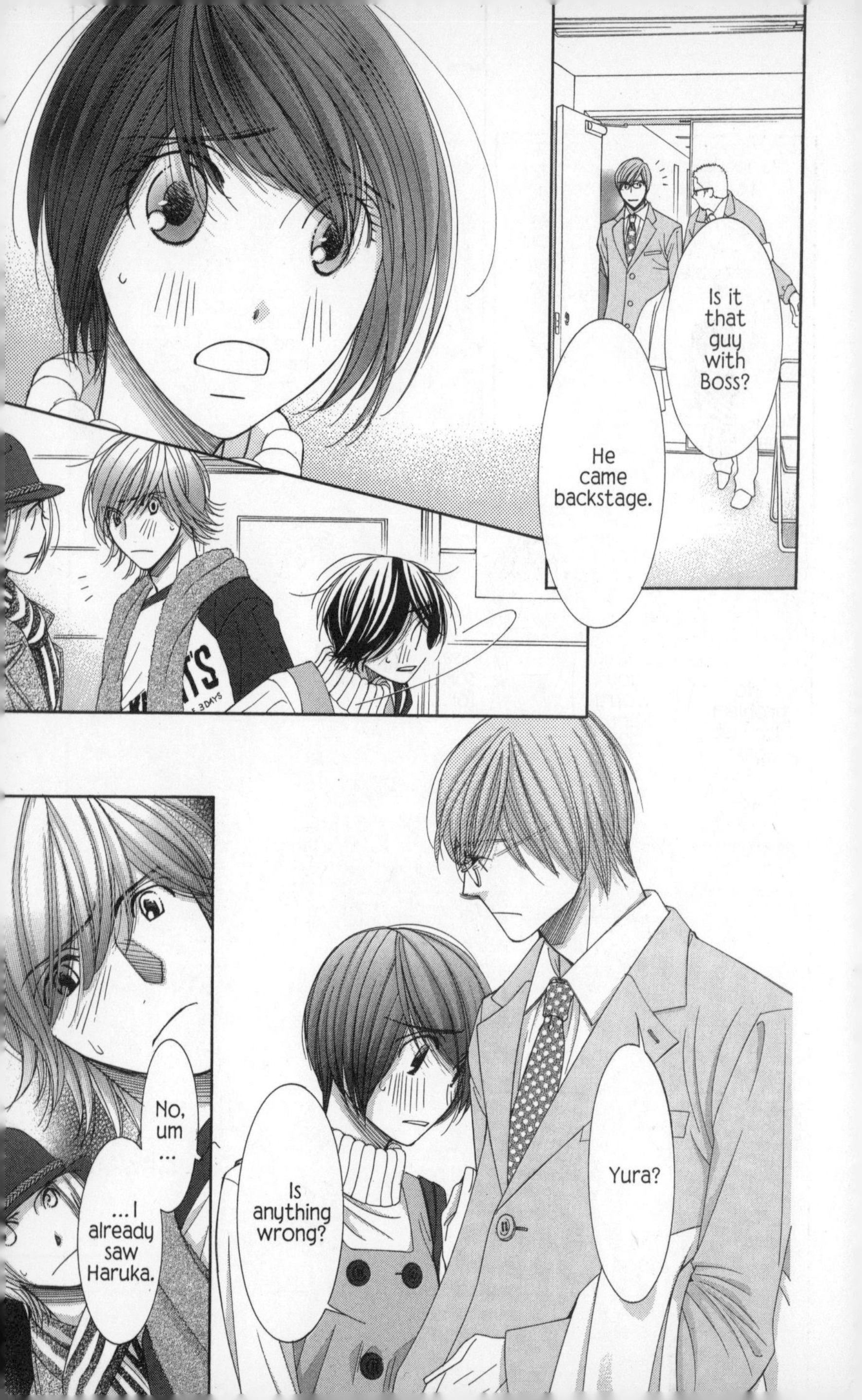
Is it that guy with Boss?
He came backstage.
Yura?
Is anything wrong?
No, um ...
...I already saw Haruka.

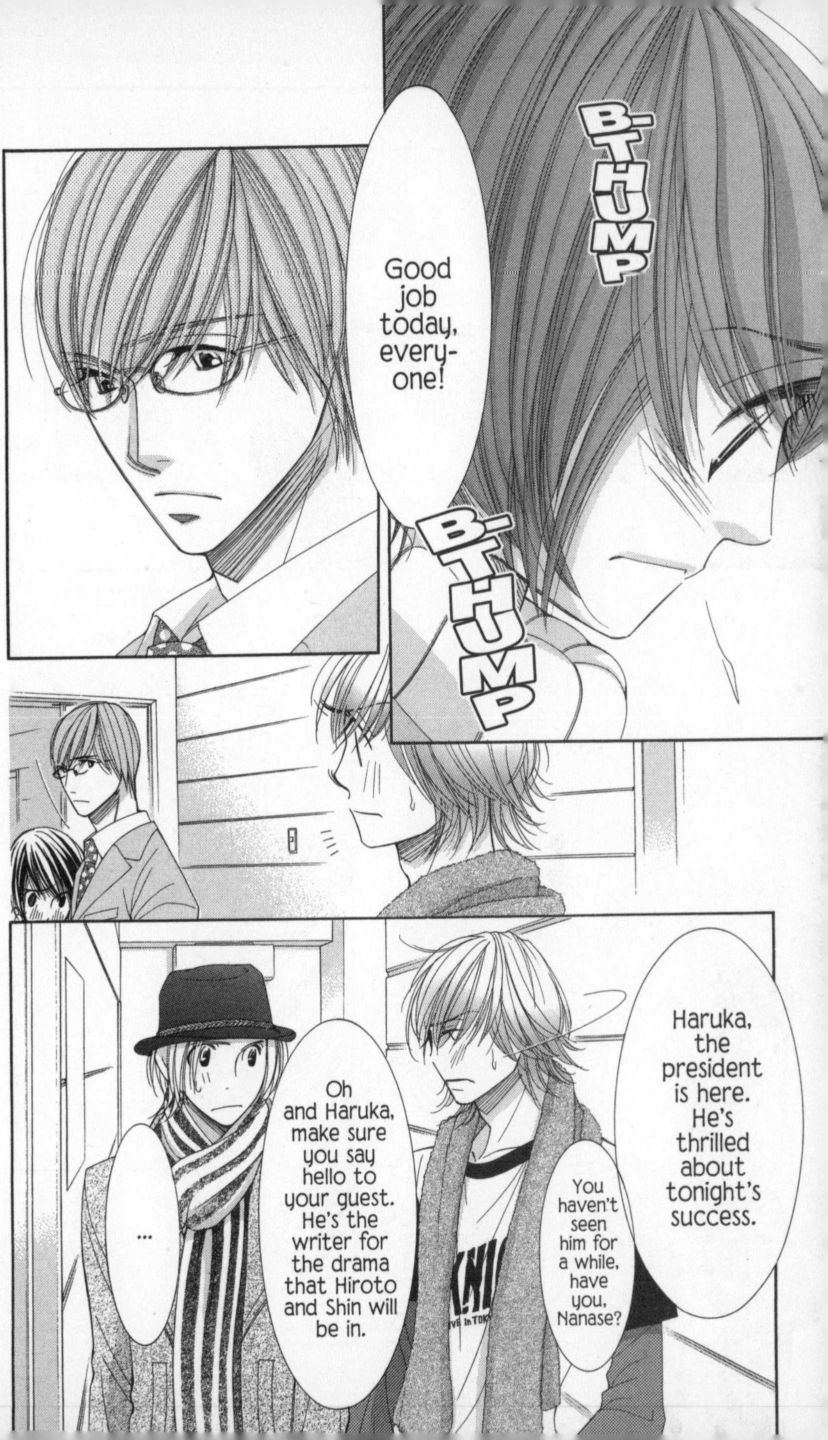
B-THUMP
Good job today, every-one!
B-THUMP
Haruka, the president is here. He's thrilled about tonight's success.
You haven't seen him for a while, have you, Nanase?
Oh and Haruka, make sure you say hello to your guest. He's the writer for the drama that Hiroto and Shin will be in.
...

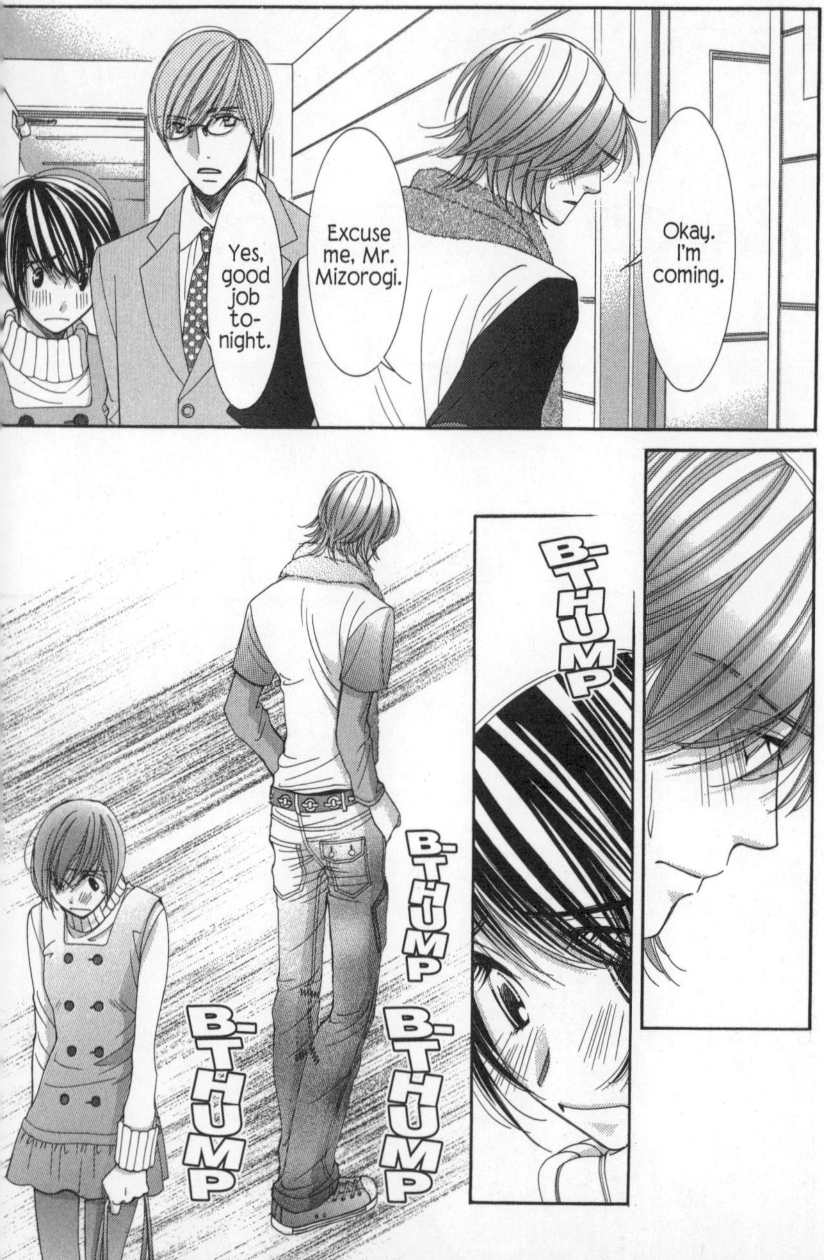
Okay. I'm coming.
Excuse me, Mr. Mizorogi.
Yes, good job to-night.
B-THUMP
B-THUMP
B-THUMP
B-THUMP

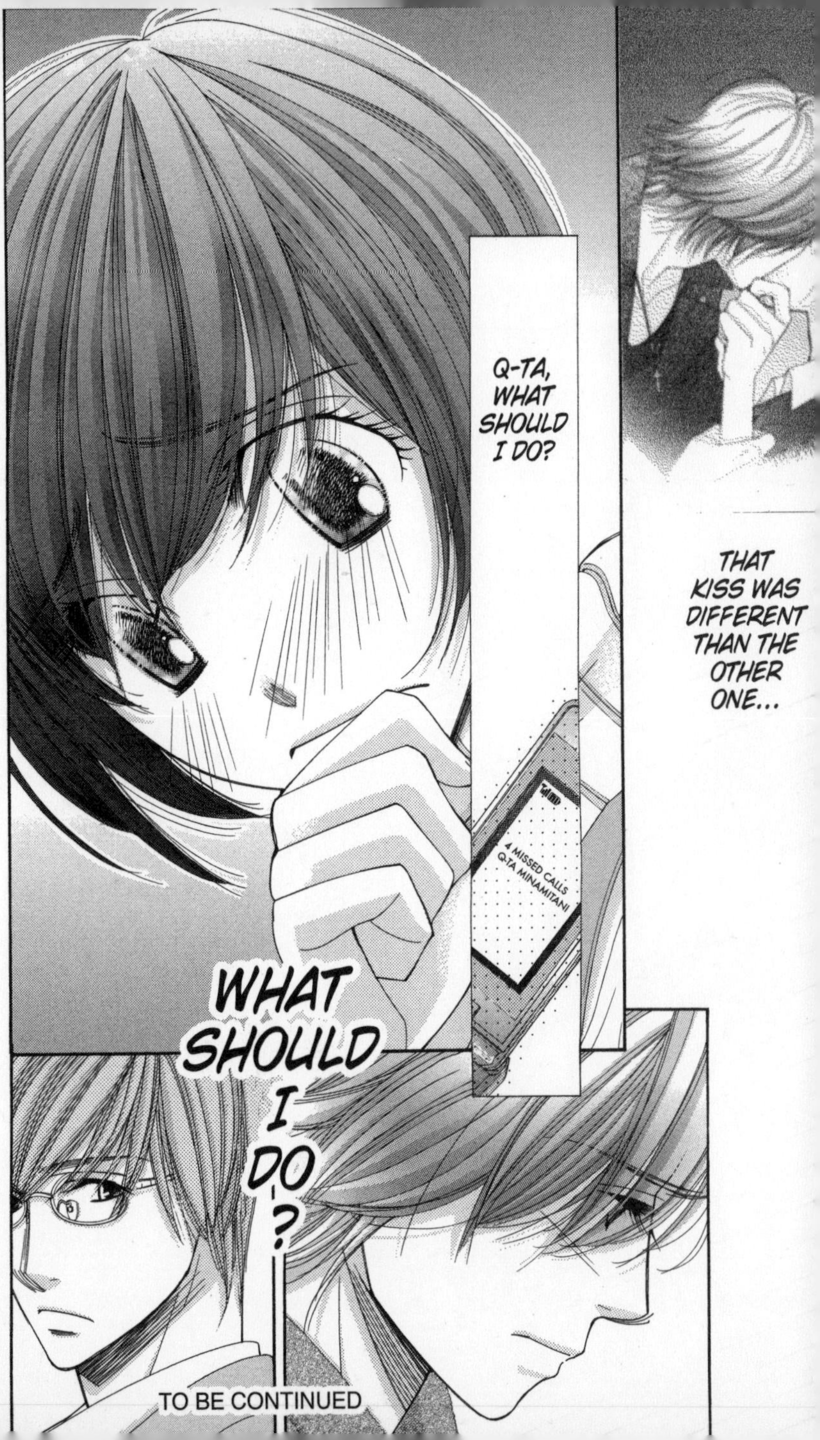
THAT KISS WAS DIFFERENT THAN THE OTHER ONE...
Q-TA, WHAT SHOULD I DO?
4 MISSED CALLS
Q-TA MINAMITANI
WHAT SHOULD I DO?
TO BE CONTINUED

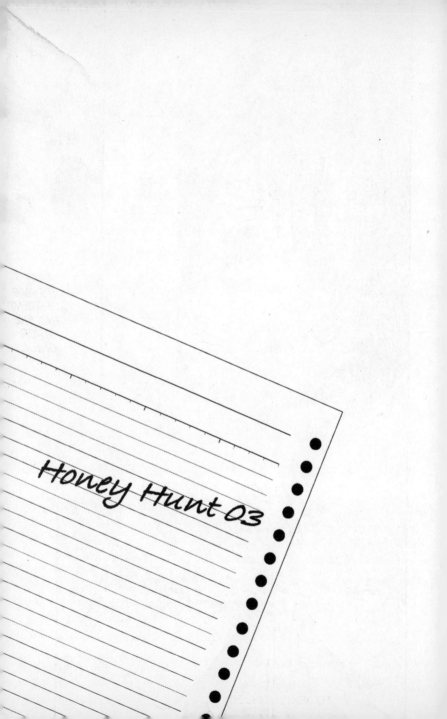

Honey Hunt 03

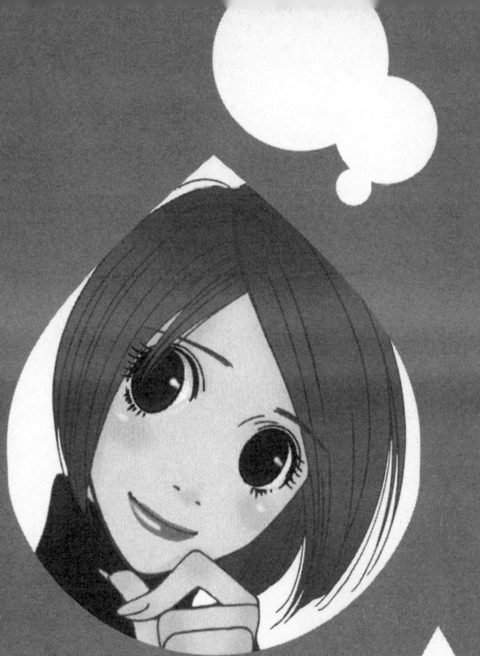

MIKI AIHARA

Here we go with the third volume! This volume is more about KNIGHTS. Although the heroine is plain (heh), it's Yura, so don't let that bother you!

Miki Aihara, from Shizuoka Prefecture, is the creator of the manga series *Hot Gimmick*. She began her career with *Lip Conscious!*, which ran in *Bessatsu Shojo Comic*. Her other work includes *Seiten Taisei* (The Clear, Wide Blue Sky), *So Bad!*, and *Tokyo Boys & Girls*. She's a Gemini whose hobbies include movies and shopping.

Honey Hunt
VOL. 3

The Shojo Beat Manga Edition

This manga volume contains material that was originally published in English in *Shojo Beat* magazine, July 2009 issue. Artwork in the magazine may have been altered slightly from what is presented in this volume.

STORY AND ART BY MIKI AIHARA

English Adaptation/Liz Forbes
Translation/Ari Yasuda, HC Language Solutions, Inc.
Touch-up Art & Lettering/Rina Mapa
Design/Ronnie Casson
Editor/Kit Fox

VP, Production/Alvin Lu
VP, Publishing Licensing/Rika Inouye
VP, Sales & Product Marketing/Gonzalo Ferreyra
VP, Creative/Linda Espinosa
Publisher/Hyoe Narita

Printed in Canada

Published by VIZ Media, LLC
P.O. Box 77010
San Francisco, CA 94107

Shojo Beat Manga Edition
10 9 8 7 6 5 4 3 2 1
First printing, November 2009

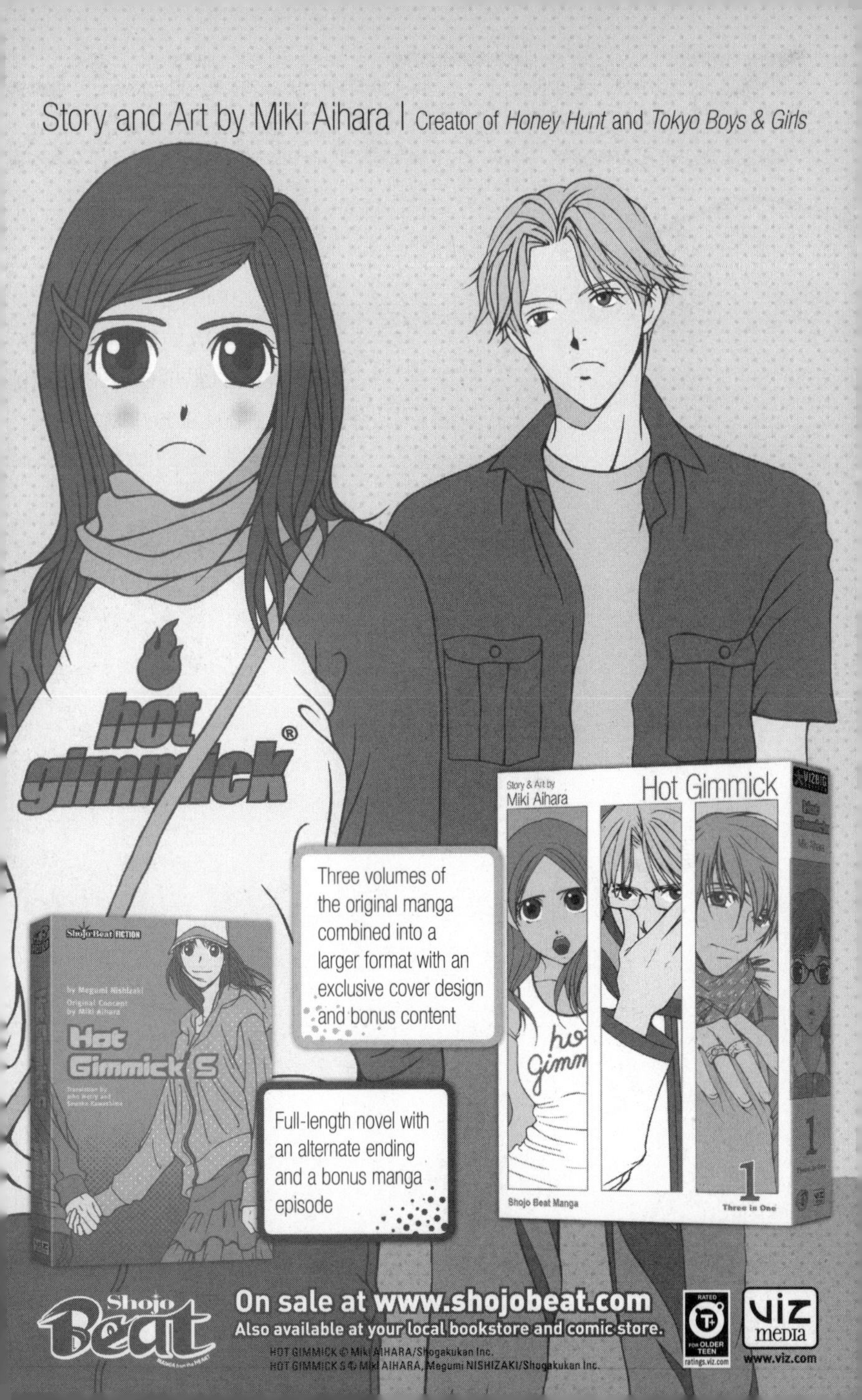

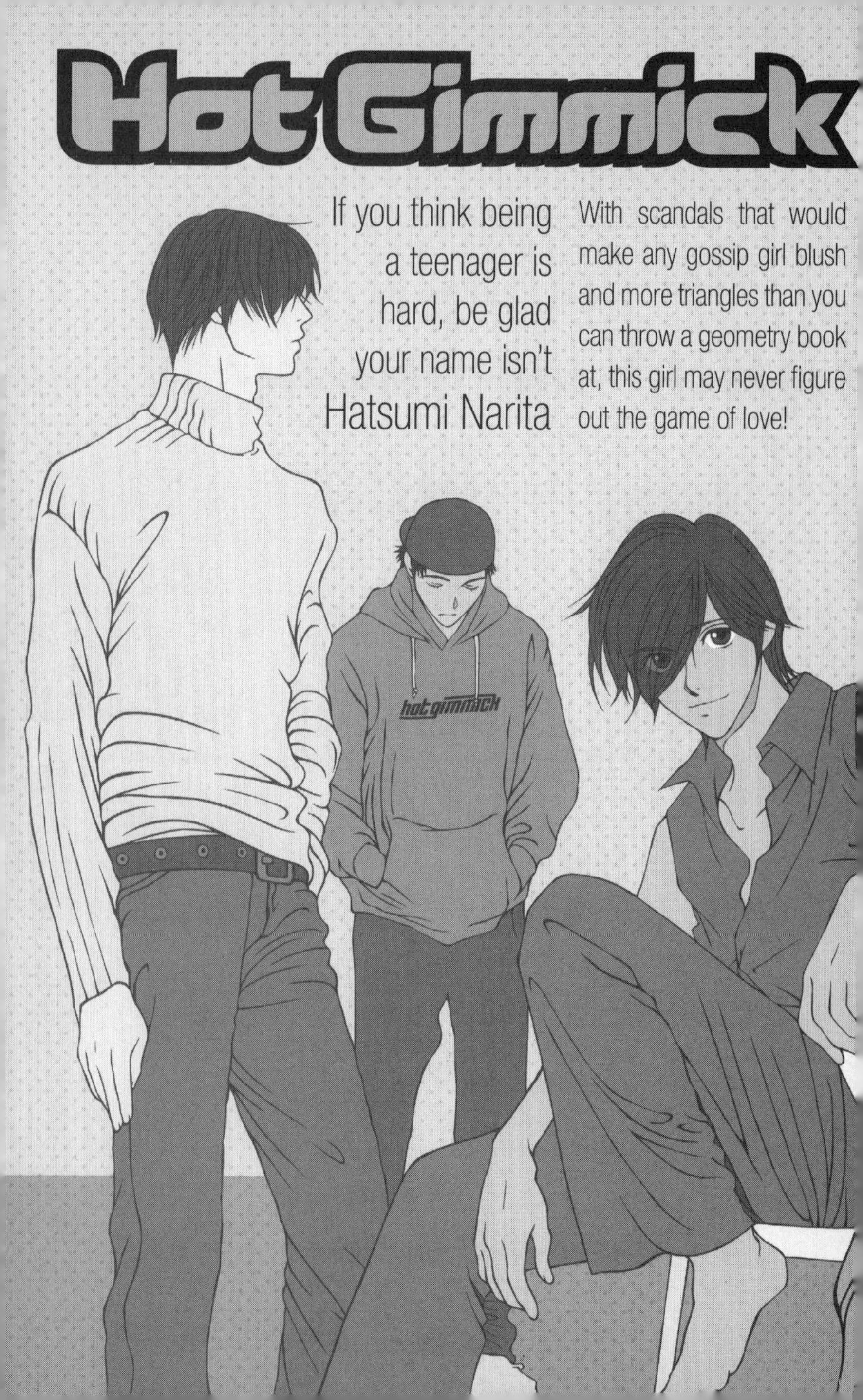
Hot Gimmick
If you think being a teenager is hard, be glad your name isn't Hatsumi Narita
With scandals that would make any gossip girl blush and more triangles than you can throw a geometry book at, this girl may never figure out the game of love!
hotgimmick

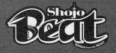

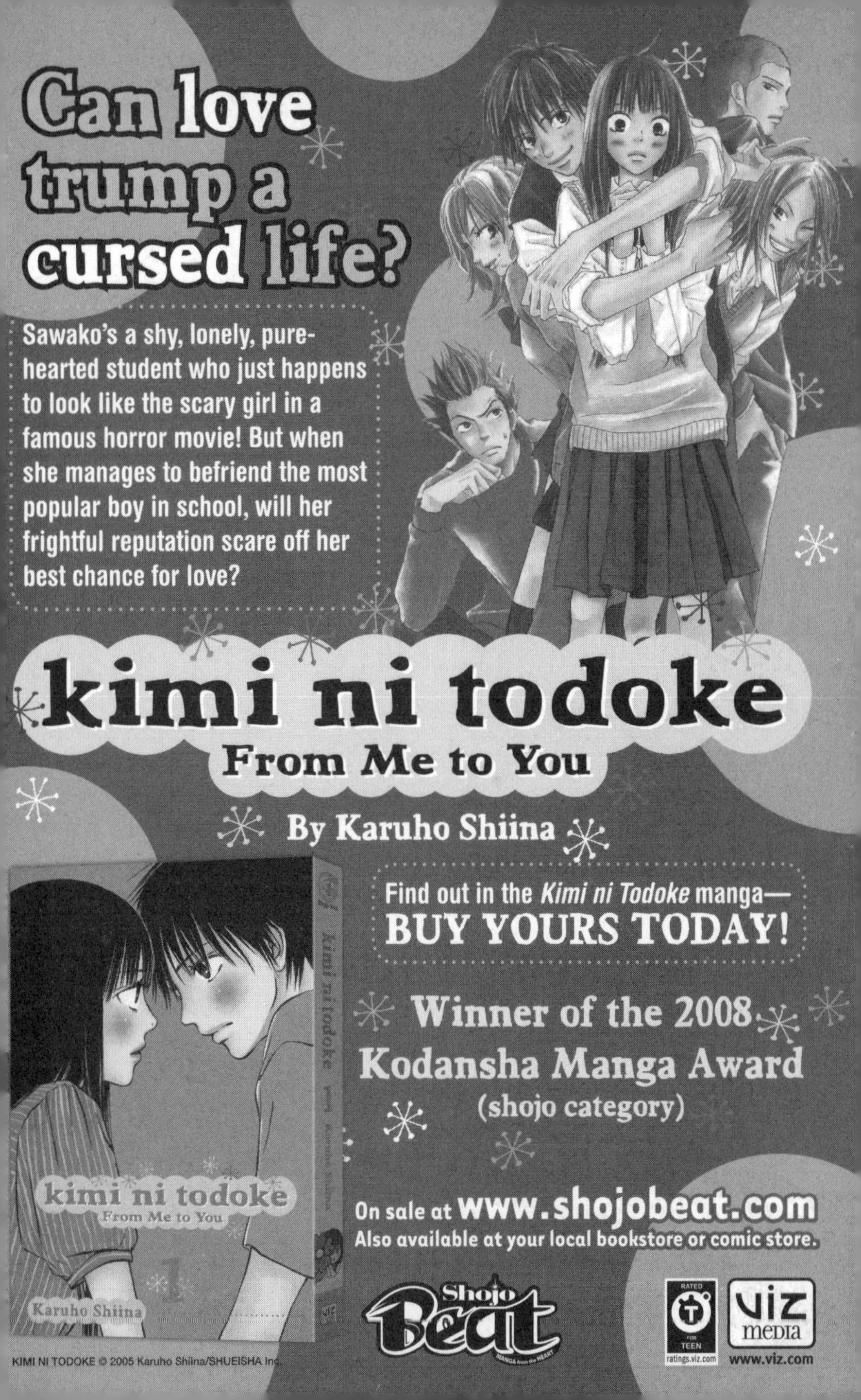

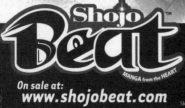

Tell us what you think about Shojo Beat Manga!

Our survey is now available online. Go to:

shojobeat.com/mangasurvey

Help us make our product offerings better!